Milton's *Lycidas*

Milton's *Lycidas*
The Tradition and the Poem

New and Revised Edition

Edited by C. A. Patrides
Foreword by M. H. Abrams

University of Missouri Press
Columbia, 1983

Copyright © 1983 by
The Curators of the University of Missouri
University of Missouri Press, Columbia, Missouri 65211
Library of Congress Catalog Card Number 83–3611
Printed and bound in the United States of America

Library of Congress Cataloging in Publication Data
Main entry under title:

Milton's Lycidas : the tradition and the poem.

    Rev. ed. of: Lycidas. [1961]
    Bibliography: p.
    1. Milton, John, 1608–1674. Lycidas—Addresses,
essays, lectures. I. Patrides, C. A. II. Milton,
John, 1608–1674. Lycidas. 1983.
PR3558.M54 1983   821′.4   83–3611
ISBN 0–8262–0412–0

For copyright acknowledgments, see p. 367.

IN MEMORIAM

CHARLES MONROE COFFIN

Contents

Foreword to the First Edition (1961)

M. H. Abrams

On the basis of a decade of experiment with almost exactly the materials gathered in this book, I can bear witness that this is a very valuable anthology, remarkably versatile in its possibilities. It will be equally useful for courses in the history or theory of literary criticism and for courses in the introduction to literature, or in Milton, or in English poetry. It will be no less valuable for that person to whose formation all our educational endeavors are in theory directed, whose very existence has often been doubted, but who is now proving his reality by buying excellent paperbacks in enormous quantities —the cultivated reader, who turns to poetry not as an academic duty, but for illumination and delight.

The essays collected here manifest dramatically that criticism really matters. They silently refute the widespread opinion that a critic's theory—his stated principles and method of procedure—is merely a philosophical excursus, happily jettisoned when he gets down to his proper job of explicating and evaluating a text. With equal finality they refute the opinion (often but mistakenly deduced from the modern view that a poem is an "autonomous" object, to be discussed "as poetry and not another thing") that a literary work contains within itself everything needed for its interpretation and will yield its full and unequivocal meaning to any reader who will approach it with a lively sensibility, unimpeded by critical pre-

possessions or by historical knowledge of poetic kinds and conventions. For here we have several critics, all of them skilled
and sensitive readers, who address themselves to the one work
and issue with an astonishing diversity of interpretations. The
essays impress upon us that a poem, which looks so fixed and
determinate on the printed page, is in fact a variable, dependent
in a high degree not only on the "taste," but on the rational
premises, categories, and criteria of a given critic, as well as
on his tact, intelligence, and the range of pertinent historical
knowledge he can bring to bear. The student of criticism finds
his investigation of critical theories in the abstract come alive
in this demonstration of the fascinating play of diverse theories
put skillfully to work on a given text. On his side the student
of poetry finds himself shocked into taking a fresh, long look
at the poem and facing up to the hard but necessary questions (which some of these essayists themselves raise) about
how we validate a critical assertion and about the proper role
of the text and of its historical context in determining our
choice between conflicting interpretations. That is why this
mode of working with a classic text as the focus of sharp critical disagreement seems to me the most profitable recent innovation in the teaching of literature.

For such a use, Milton's *Lycidas* is the ideal document. It
is short enough to be managed at a single reading, yet long
and complex enough to raise all the basic issues and great
enough to have attracted a large number of the best critics,
whose essays have independent value as distinguished instances
of the critical art. But hitherto the teacher has been thwarted
by the need for the students to have simultaneous access to
a great many books, some of them learned periodicals possessed
only by large libraries and none of them in a sufficient number
of copies to be practicable for any class larger than a small
seminar. Professor Patrides has done us the service of making
available to each student the equivalent of a sizable shelf of
books, and he has made the collection self-sufficient by adding
well-edited texts of Milton's two pastoral elegies as well as an
annotated guide to everything important that has been written
about *Lycidas*, which may be the greatest, and is at any rate
the most often discussed, of all lyric poems.

Foreword to the Revised Edition

M. H. Abrams

The full-scale critical essays that were included in the first edition were written between 1930 and 1960. This was during the heyday of the New Criticism and of other critical modes which focused attention on the text of the poem itself, and all the essays, whatever the variety of their theoretical premises, exploited the reigning method of a close reading of the verbal and imagistic particulars of the poem. In addition, all except the archetypal essayists (who assimilated the protagonist and structure of the poem to the archetypes of the dying-reviving god and of the seasonal cycle) conceived *Lycidas* to be a free-standing and sufficient whole. The prestige of the New Criticism has waned in the two decades since that edition; the publication of close readings of *Lycidas*, however, has accelerated, in an unbroken flow of essays, chapters, and even books devoted to explicating a text of only 193 lines. *Lycidas*, it is clear, has in our time become the lyric of lyrics, a standing challenge to critics to demonstrate their capacity to make profitable discoveries about a poem which has been scrutinized by scores of earlier analysts.

The number and excellence of prior critiques adds to the challenge set by the poem, the challenge to justify still another explication by saying some things which have not been said about it before. The essays added to the second edition are among those which have met this double challenge without succumbing to the temptation to be innovative at all costs, by imposing readings which violate what we know about Milton's language, or about the poetic forms that were available to him, or about the central and recurrent concepts and beliefs that he manifests in the body of his other writings.

To a considerable extent the added essays have achieved their insights by carrying farther interpretive procedures which had been introduced by their critical precursors. One common way to bring out novel aspects of the poem has been to cast off the theoretical unease of the New Criticism about transgressing the boundaries of the poem itself, by freely bringing to bear on the text such "external" matters as the context and implications of echoes from earlier pastoral elegies and from the Bible, or by exploiting the pertinence of self-referential passages from Milton's other writings in prose and verse, or else by applying to the design of the lyric the exegetical principle of typology, well known to Milton, which identifies in the course of history a sequence of types that prefigure, and are fulfilled by, Christian revelation. Another way has been to explore, more thoroughly than earlier critics, the import of local elements of the poem such as the repeated phrase "once more," or the shifts in the speaker or speakers of various passages, or the alternations between the present and past tense of the verbs in the course of the lyric exposition. A third way of altering our responses to the poem has been to stress more than prior explicators the "violence" that underlies the ritual ceremony and formal decorum of Milton's pastoral elegy. A number of critics, especially in the last decade, use a vigorous vocabulary themselves in order to heighten our awareness of the "brutally direct opening" and the "explosive force" of the phrases "forc'd fingers rude" and "shatter your leaves," or to force on our attention the recurrent "assault on the poem's own assumptions" by harsh realities, as well as by the "incursions," "disjunctions," and "disruptions" of lyric continuity occasioned by abrupt shifts in speakers, narrative procedures, and rhetorical idiom.

It is an index to the strength and complex artistry of *Lycidas* that it has proved its capacity not only to survive the flood of interpretive commentaries, but to yield new aspects, subtleties, and interrelations of significance to highly diverse critical perspectives, insofar as each of these is mediated by the sensibility, tact, and relevant literary knowledge of an expert critic. But the prime measure of the poem's greatness is that the individual reader can return again and again to the familiar text with undiminished excitement and delight to experience yet once more what Rosemond Tuve has called "the most poignant and controlled statement in English poetry of the acceptance of that in the human condition which seems to man unacceptable."

Preface to the First Edition (1961)

"In *Lycidas*," declared Mark Pattison in 1879, "we have reached the high-water mark of English Poesy." If there has been no universal concurrence with this judgment, at least no impartial critic has ever failed to number the poem among the foremost productions of the human mind. Samuel Johnson was persuaded, certainly, that in *Lycidas* "the diction is harsh, the rhymes uncertain, and the numbers unpleasing"; but even then the judgment ran so far counter to the general estimate that William Cowper claimed, as many critics have since, that Dr. Johnson had "no ear for poetical numbers, or that it was stopped by prejudice against the harmony of Milton's."

Yet, as we know only too well, Dr. Johnson was often partly right even where he seems to have been most appallingly mistaken. Thus, while censuring the metaphysical poets, he was still perceptive enough to discern and comment upon the essential peculiarities of their achievement; and, similarly, when he attacked the form of *Lycidas* as "easy, vulgar, and therefore disgusting," he expressed precisely the dissatisfaction still felt by readers who are unfamiliar with the tradition of the pastoral elegy. The present edition, in part at least, hopes to eliminate this fundamental difficulty by making available, together with Milton's two pastoral elegies, Professor Hanford's comprehensive study of the elegiac tradition.

The appreciation of the tradition, however, forms only part of a proper background for the reading of *Lycidas*. Funda-

mentally, far more significant is our method of approach to the
poem as a poem; and here, happily, we may seek the enlightened
advice of a number of modern critics, most of them exponents
of the remarkably varied theories of criticism advanced thus far
in this century, who have concentrated on *Lycidas* as a poem deserving of special consideration. The commentaries made available here are printed in the chronological order of their original
composition.

The Latin text of the *Epitaphium Damonis* is accompanied
by Miss Helen Waddell's translation—decidedly not a literal
translation, but one that captures the emotional intensity of
the original to such an extent that it deserves greater attention
than it has hitherto received. The first edition of the translation
in 1943 was dedicated to "The Memory of George Frederick
Waddell Martin, Major R.E., Served in the defence of Tobruk
1941, Killed March 17, 1942, Aged 23; And of the men, his
brothers-in-arms, who died young."

Changes have been made only in three of the essays reprinted
here. Professor Hanford's study, having appeared for the first
time in 1910, necessitated slight changes in the light of subsequent work by other scholars; the revisions, undertaken with
the author's permission, are indicated by brackets. Two essayists have been generous enough to revise their own work: Professor R. P. Adams, who has condensed his essay out of sympathy with my concern over the limited space at my disposal;
and Professor Josephine Miles, who graciously consented to
write an essay for this edition, a drastic revision of the section
on *Lycidas* in *The Primary Language of Poetry in the 1640's*
(1948). Of this revision Professor Miles writes, "Additional
study of Milton's predecessors and successors makes it possible
to discriminate the terms characteristic not only of the general
mode of *Lycidas* but also of the poem as individual structure.
The description of the language made in 1948 is therefore placed
in the context of this further knowledge."

It is not to be thought that I was unassisted in my editorial
tasks. Indeed, I am deeply obliged to numerous individuals for
their concern with this edition, but particularly to Professor
M. H. Abrams, who has encouraged me from the very beginning and has given generous advice on numerous aspects of this
book; to Professor Wayne Shumaker for his welcomed criticism

of the content and style of my work; to Professors Merritt Y. Hughes of the University of Wisconsin, A. S. P. Woodhouse of the University of Toronto, James H. Hanford of Princeton University, Rosemond Tuve of Connecticut College, Thomas P. Harrison of the University of Texas, Robert M. Durling of Cornell University, Eugene Brunelle of Mills College, and Bertrand H. Bronson, Howard Hugo, Alain Renoir, Robert L. McNulty, and Mrs. Dorothee M. Finkelstein of the University of California at Berkeley, for various suggestions; and to a number of editors of *Lycidas*, notably Miss Helen Darbishire and Professors Hughes, Hanford, Coffin, and Fletcher. Finally, I am deeply grateful to Professor Abrams for permission to publish his essay on *Lycidas* in advance of its appearance in another volume.

This edition is dedicated to the late Charles M. Coffin. Shortly after my arrival from Greece, when good fortune led me to Kenyon College in 1948, the wonders of English literature were revealed to me principally by Professor Coffin. When at length I resolved to devote myself to the study of Milton, the deciding factor was the inspiration I received from Professor Coffin; so that should I in the future write something of value on Milton, it will be only a minor footnote to what he taught me of the Renaissance in general and of Milton in particular. In the meantime, this edition is a very small earthly recompense for his labors, not to be compared with the fairer guerdon he found upon his death on July 20, 1956.

C. A. P.
Berkeley, California
January 1961

Preface to the Revised Edition

It is gratifying to realize that the essays selected twenty-two years ago to represent some of the better critical strategies deployed apropos *Lycidas* are still viable. One essay, Paul Elmer More's "How to Read *Lycidas*," is not made available again, but that loss is more than redressed by the addition of seven essays, one of which predated the first edition of the present volume and the rest of which were written since its initial appearance.

The intervening two decades have witnessed a veritable explosion of essays, articles, and notes on *Lycidas*, as the much expanded bibliography attests. Indeed, there have been two books devoted exclusively to the poem, David S. Berkeley's *Inwrought with Figures Dim: A Reading of Milton's "Lycidas"* (1974) and Clay Hunt's *"Lycidas" and the Italian Critics* (1979), even as J. B. Leishman's *Milton's Minor Poems* (1969) and Joseph A. Wittreich's *Visionary Poetics: Milton's Tradition and his Legacy* (1979) have provided sustained readings of the poem from very different standpoints. It is to be regretted that the very length of these studies prevented me from adequately representing their arguments here. It should all the same be noted, however, that the present collection was not initially envisaged merely as a "case book" on *Lycidas*. From the outset, my primary concern was to expand our understanding of the poem through some of the most notable critical strategies now current, their very variety an indication as much of the multiform nature of criticism as of the continuing relevance of *Lycidas*.

I am deeply grateful to three of the new contributors, Professors Friedman, Lowry, and Tayler, for the readiness with which they revised their essays for incorporation into this volume. I am also obliged to several friends for their indispensable advice, among them Professors Stanley Fish of The Johns Hopkins University, Roland M. Frye of the University of Pennsylvania, John R. Knott, Jr., of the University of Michigan at Ann Arbor, Balachandra Rajan of the University of Western Ontario, John R. Roberts of the University of Missouri at Columbia, Raymond B. Waddington of the University of California at Davis, and Joseph A. Wittreich of the University of Maryland. Yet my primary obligation—the same now as it was in 1961—is to Professor M. H. Abrams, whose generosity of spirit "redoubles still, and multiplies."

C. A. P.
Ann Arbor, Mich.
April 1983

Part I
The Texts

Lycidas

In this Monody the Author bewails a learned Friend, unfortunatly drown'd in his Passage from *Chester* on the *Irish* Seas, 1637. And by occasion foretels the ruine of our corrupted Clergy then in their height.

> Yet once more, O ye Laurels, and once more
> Ye Myrtles brown, with Ivy never-sear,
> I com to pluck your Berries harsh and crude,
> And with forc'd fingers rude,
> Shatter your leaves before the mellowing year.   5
> Bitter constraint, and sad occasion dear,

Lycidas, the "learned Friend," is Edward King (1612–1637), the youngest of six sons of Sir John King, an Irish administrator. A promising youth distinguished by wide learning and a limited poetic faculty, King entertained thoughts of an ecclesiastical career. Soon he attracted the attention even of Charles I: the mandate of his election to a fellowship at Christ's College, Cambridge, states that His Majesty was "well ascertained both of the present sufficiency and future hopes" of young Edward (*DNB*, 11:128). Milton, similarly impressed by King's "great Learning and Parts," contracted "a particular Friendship and Intimacy" with him (Edward Phillips, *The Life of Mr. John Milton*, 1694). King's untimely death occurred in August 1637 while he was on a journey to Ireland to visit members of his family. Milton's tribute was the last in a collection of memorial poems published in 1638, signed "J.M." The present text adheres largely to the version in *Poems of Mr. John Milton*, 1645 (see Appendix, below, 346 ff.).

The headnote was first prefixed to the poem in 1645: it is not in the edition of 1638 (the manuscript of the poem at Trinity College, Cambridge, contains only the first sentence).

[1] Ten lines inclusive of the first are unrhymed.

[1-2] *Laurels, Myrtles, Ivy*: evergreens with which the ancient poets were crowned; hence, traditional symbols of poetry.

[2] *never-sear*: never dry or withered.

[3] *crude*: unripe.

[6] *dear*: heartfelt.

Compels me to disturb your season due:
For *Lycidas* is dead, dead ere his prime
Young *Lycidas,* and hath not left his peer:
Who would not sing for *Lycidas?* he well knew   10
Himself to sing, and build the lofty rhyme.
He must not flote upon his watry bear
Unwept, and welter to the parching wind,
Without the meed of som melodious tear.

   Begin then, Sisters of the sacred well,   15
That from beneath the seat of *Jove* doth spring,
Begin, and somwhat loudly sweep the string.
Hence with denial vain, and coy excuse,
So may som gentle Muse
With lucky words favour my destin'd Urn,   20
And as he passes turn,
And bid fair peace be to my sable shrowd.
For we were nurst upon the self-same hill,
Fed the same flock, by fountain, shade, and rill.

   Together both, ere the high Lawns appear'd   25
Under the opening eye-lids of the morn,
We drove a field, and both together heard
What time the Gray-fly winds her sultry horn,
Batt'ning our flocks with the fresh dews of night,
Oft till the Star that rose, at Ev'ning, bright   30

[10-11] *he well knew / Himself to sing*: King was the author of a modest number of Latin verses. *well*: not in any of the poem's editions; added by Milton himself on two copies of the 1638 memorial volume.

[13] *welter*: toss about.

[14] *meed*: reward.
   melodious tear: "tearful melody," mourning song, elegy in general.

[15-16] *Sisters*: the nine Muses, daughters of Zeus and Mnemosyne; both *the sacred well* (Aganippe) and *the seat of Jove* (the altar of Zeus) were on Mount Helicon. Cf. Hesiod, *Theogony*, 1–4.

[18] *coy*: modest; also disdainful.

[19] *Muse*: i.e., poet.

[20] *lucky*: auspicious; of an unstudied felicity.

[22] *sable*: black.

[25] *high Lawns*: meadows, pastures.

[26] *opening*: "glimmering" (according to the 1638 ed.).

[28] *winds*: blows.

[29] *Batt'ning*: feeding; also enclosing.

[30] *the Star*: Hesperus. In the 1638 ed., the line reads: "Oft till the ev'n-starre bright."

Toward Heav'ns descent had slop'd his westering wheel.
Mean while the Rural ditties were not mute,
Temper'd to th'Oaten Flute,
Rough *Satyrs* danc'd, and *Fauns* with clov'n heel,
From the glad sound would not be absent long, 35
And old *Damœtas* lov'd to hear our song.

But O the heavy change, now thou art gon,
Now thou art gon, and never must return!
Thee Shepherd, thee the Woods, and desert Caves,
With wilde Thyme and the gadding Vine o'regrown, 40
And all their echoes mourn.
The Willows, and the Hazle Copses green,
Shall now no more be seen,
Fanning their joyous Leaves to thy soft layes.
As killing as the Canker to the Rose, 45
Or Taint-worm to the weanling Herds that graze,
Or Frost to Flowers, that their gay wardrop wear,
When first the White thorn blows;
Such, *Lycidas*, thy loss to Shepherds ear.

Where were ye Nymphs when the remorseless deep 50
Clos'd o're the head of your lov'd *Lycidas?*
For neither were ye playing on the steep,
Where your old *Bards*, the famous *Druids* ly,
Nor on the shaggy top of *Mona* high,
Nor yet where *Deva* spreads her wisard stream: 55
Ay me, I fondly dream!

---

[31] *westering*: "burnisht" (according to the 1638 ed.).
[36] *Damœtas*: possibly a tutor at Cambridge (for conjectures concerning his identity, see under Marjorie Nicolson, below, 363.
[40] *gadding*: straying, wandering.
[45] *the Canker*: the cankerworm (cf. Milton's *Arcades,* l. 53: "hurtful worm with canker'd venom bites").
[46] *Taint-worm*: parasitic worm that taints or infects *weanling* (lately weaned, not full-grown) *Herds.*
[48] *the White thorn*: the hawthorn.
[53] *Druids*: members of a religious order in ancient Gaul, Britain, and Ireland.
[54] *Mona*: the isle of Anglesey, off the northern coast of Wales.
[55] *Deva*: the river Dee, which passes through Chester (the port from which Edward King sailed to Ireland) and empties into the Irish Sea; called *wisard* because of its reputed powers of prophecy (cf. *Druids*).
[56] *fondly*: foolishly.

Had ye bin there—for what could that have don?
What could the Muse her self that *Orpheus* bore,
The Muse her self, for her inchanting son
Whom Universal nature did lament,   60
When by the rout that made the hideous roar,
His goary visage down the stream was sent,
Down the swift *Hebrus* to the *Lesbian* shore.
   Alas! What boots it with uncessant care
To tend the homely slighted Shepherds trade,   65
And strictly meditate the thankles Muse,
Were it not better don as others use,
To sport with *Amaryllis* in the shade,
Or with the tangles of *Neæra's* hair?
Fame is the spur that the clear spirit doth raise   70
(That last infirmity of Noble mind)
To scorn delights, and live laborious dayes;
But the fair Guerdon when we hope to find,
And think to burst out into sudden blaze,
Comes the blind *Fury* with th'abhorred shears,   75
And slits the thin spun life. But not the praise,
Phœbus repli'd, and touch'd my trembling ears;

---

⁵⁷⁻⁶³ For Milton's extensive revisions of this passage, see below, 12.

⁵⁸ *the Muse*: Calliope, the mother of Orpheus and chief of the nine muses, who presided over eloquence and heroic poetry.

⁶¹⁻⁶³ Orpheus, traditionally regarded as "the father of song" (Pindar, *Pythian Odes*, 4.176), is said to have withdrawn to the wilds of Rhodope and Haemus after the loss of Eurydice; but some Thracian maenads, infuriated because he paid no attention to them, dismembered him and cast his severed head into the river Hebrus, whence it floated to the island of Lesbos. Cf. Virgil, *Georgics*, 4.517-27, and Ovid, *Metamorphoses*, 11.1-60.

⁶⁴ *boots*: profits, avails.

⁶⁵ *Shepherds trade*: poet's craft.

⁶⁷ *use*: do.

⁶⁹ *Or with*: "Hid in" (according to the 1638 ed.).

⁷⁰⁻⁸⁴ Cf. *Paradise Regained*, 3.47-70.

⁷⁰ *clear*: pure.

⁷³ *Guerdon*: reward.

⁷⁵ *blind Fury*: Atropos, the "inflexible," one of the three Fates of classical mythology, who cut the thread of life spun by Clotho and measured by Lachesis.

⁷⁷ *Phoebus*: Apollo, the god of youth, beauty, poetry, and music. *touch'd my trembling ears*: a gesture of disapproval. Thus Apollo plucked Virgil's ear in an attempt to curtail his excessive ambition (*Eclogue VI*, 3-5). In part at least, the allusion may be to the predicament of Midas, who foolishly refused to acknowledge Apollo as the best musician and was punished with a pair of ass's ears (Ovid, *Metamorphoses*, 11.146-79).

Fame is no plant that grows on mortal soil,
Nor in the glistering foil
Set off to th'world, nor in broad rumour lies,   80
But lives and spreds aloft by those pure eyes,
And perfet witnes of all-judging *Jove;*
As he pronounces lastly on each deed,
Of so much fame in Heav'n expect thy meed.

   O Fountain *Arethuse,* and thou honour'd floud,   85
Smooth-sliding *Mincius,* crown'd with vocall reeds,
That strain I heard was of a higher mood:
But now my Oat proceeds,
And listens to the Herald of the Sea
That came in *Neptune's* plea,   90
He ask'd the Waves, and ask'd the Fellon winds,
What hard mishap hath doom'd this gentle swain?
And question'd every gust of rugged wings
That blows from off each beaked Promontory;
They knew not of his story,   95
And sage *Hippotades* their answer brings,
That not a blast was from his dungeon stray'd,
The Ayr was calm, and on the level brine,
Sleek *Panope* with all her sisters play'd.
It was that fatall and perfidious Bark   100
Built in th'eclipse, and rigg'd with curses dark,
That sunk so low that sacred head of thine.

---

   [79] *foil*: the thin gold leaf placed under a precious stone to augment its brilliance.
   [85] *Arethuse*: a spring in the island of Ortygia at Syracuse near the birthplace of Theocritus; here used as symbolic of Sicilian bucolic poetry (cf. note to l. 132).
   [86] *Mincius*: Mincio, a river in Lombardy near the birthplace of Virgil; here used as symbolic of Latin pastoral poetry.
   [87] *mood*: the mode (*modus*) or scale in which a piece of music was composed.
   [88] *Oat*: oaten or pastoral pipe (cf. l. 33: *Oaten Flute*; also *Comus*, l. 345: "pastoral reed with oaten stops").
   [89] *the Herald of the Sea*: Triton, a sea demigod, son of Poseidon and Amphitrite; the sounding of his trumpet raised or calmed the waves.
   [91] *fellon*: savage, wild.
   [96] *Hippotades*: Aeolus, the god of winds.
   [99] *Panope*: a sea-nymph, one of the fifty daughters of Nereus who attended on Poseidon.
   [101] *in th'eclipse*: i.e., ill-omened, in line with the common association of eclipses with catastrophes.

Next *Camus*, reverend Sire, went footing slow,
His Mantle hairy, and his Bonnet sedge,
Inwrought with figures dim, and on the edge   105
Like to that sanguine flower inscrib'd with woe.
Ah! Who hath reft (quoth he) my dearest pledge?
Last came, and last did go,
The Pilot of the *Galilean* lake,
Two massy Keyes he bore of metals twain,   110
(The Golden opes, the Iron shuts amain)
He shook his Miter'd locks, and stern bespake,
How well could I have spar'd for thee young swain.
Anow of such as for their bellies sake,
Creep and intrude, and climb into the fold?   115
Of other care they little reck'ning make,
Then how to scramble at the shearers feast,
And shove away the worthy bidden guest.
Blind mouthes! that scarce themselves know how to hold
A Sheep-hook, or have learn'd ought els the least   120
That to the faithfull Herdmans art belongs!
What recks it them? What need they? They are sped;

---

[103] *Camus*: the river Cam at Cambridge, symbolizing the university.

[106] *that sanguine flower inscrib'd with woe*: the hyacinth; according to legend, a flower sprung from the blood of Hyacinthus, a beautiful Spartan prince unwittingly slain by his lover Apollo, was marked in such a way as to bear the Greek word "alas" (*AI*). Cf. Apollodorus, *Bibliotheca*, 1.3.3; Lucian, *Dial. deorum*, 14; and Ovid, *Metamorphoses*, 10.162–219.

[107] *pledge*: child.

[109] *the Pilot of the Galilean lake*: St. Peter, keeper of the keys of heaven (Matthew 16:19) and the first bishop of the Church (cf. 112: *Miter'd locks*). But the allusion is by some readers said to be to Christ, and by others to a composite portrait.

[111] *amain*: with force, vehemently.

[114] *Anow*: i.e., enough.

[114ff] There are a number of biblical echoes here, as from John 10:1 ("He that entereth not by the door into the sheepfold, but climbeth up some other way, the same is a thief and a robber") and I Peter 5:2–4 ("Feed the flock of God which is among you, taking the oversight thereof, not by constraint, but willingly; not for filthy lucre, but of a ready mind. . . . And when the chief Shepherd shall appear, ye shall receive a crown of glory that fadeth not away").

[119] *Blind mouthes*: see Ruskin's explanatory comment on this double metaphor, below, 364.

[120] *Sheep-hook*: the bishop's pastoral staff.

[122] *They are sped*: they have prospered.

And when they list, their lean and flashy songs
Grate on their scrannel Pipes of wretched straw,
The hungry Sheep look up, and are not fed,   125
But swoln with wind, and the rank mist they draw,
Rot inwardly, and foul contagion spread:
Besides what the grim Woolf with privy paw
Daily devours apace, and nothing sed,
But that two-handed engine at the door,   130
Stands ready to smite once, and smite no more.
    Return *Alpheus*, the dread voice is past,
That shrunk thy streams; Return *Sicilian* Muse,
And call the Vales, and bid them hither cast
Their Bels, and Flourets of a thousand hues.   135
Ye valleys low where the milde whispers use,
Of shades and wanton winds, and gushing brooks,
On whose fresh lap the swart Star sparely looks,
Throw hither all your quaint enameld eyes,
That on the green terf suck the honied showres,   140
And purple all the ground with vernal flowres.
Bring the rathe Primrose that forsaken dies.
The tufted Crow-toe, and pale Gessamine,
The white Pink, and the Pansie freakt with jeat,
The glowing Violet.   145
The Musk-rose, and the well attir'd Woodbine,

---

[124] *scrannel*: weak, feeble.

[129] *nothing*: "little" (according to the 1638 ed.).

[130-31] For various interpretations of this famous riddle, see below, 356-57

[132] *Alpheus*: a river in Arcady; according to legend, after the river god Alpheus was enamored of the wood nymph Arethusa, she was transformed by Artemis into a subterranean stream which, still pursued by Alpheus, rose again in the *Fountain Arethuse* (l. 85) on the island of Ortygia at Syracuse. Cf. Pausanias, *Description of Greece*, 5.2.2, and Ovid, *Metamorphoses*, 5.865–978.

[133] *Sicilian Muse*: i.e., of Theocritus and the Greek bucolic poets in general.

[136] *use*: are wont to reside.

[138] *the swart Star*: Sirius, the Dog Star, under whose malign influence vegetation withers.

sparely: seldom.

[142-50] For Milton's extensive revisions of this passage, see below, 13.

[142] *rathe*: early.

[143] *Crow-toe*: the wild hyacinth.

Gessamine: jasmine.

[144] *freakt*: freckled, spotted; also adorned.

jeat: attesting mourning.

With Cowslips wan that hang the pensive hed,
And every flower that sad embroidery wears:
Bid *Amaranthus* all his beauty shed,
And Daffadillies fill their cups with tears,   150
To strew the Laureat Herse where *Lycid* lies.
For so to interpose a little ease,
Let our frail thoughts dally with false surmise.
Ay me! Whilst thee the shores, and sounding Seas
Wash far away, where ere thy bones are hurld,   155
Whether beyond the stormy *Hebrides*,
Where thou perhaps under the whelming tide
Visit'st the bottom of the monstrous world;
Or whether thou to our moist vows deny'd,
Sleep'st by the fable of *Bellerus* old,   160
Where the great vision of the guarded Mount
Looks toward *Namancos* and *Bayona's* hold;
Look homeward Angel now, and melt with ruth,
And, O ye *Dolphins*, waft the haples youth.

Weep no more, woful Shepherds weep no more,   165
For *Lycidas* your sorrow is not dead,
Sunk though he be beneath the watry floar,
So sinks the day-star in the Ocean bed,
And yet anon repairs his drooping head,

---

[147] *wan*: pale.

[149] *Amaranthus*: literally, "the unfading flower"—an imaginary flower reputed never to fade (cf. *Paradise Lost*, 3.353: "Immortal Amarant").

[156] *Hebrides*: islands off the west coast of Scotland.

[157] *whelming*: "humming" (according to the 1638 ed.).

[158] *the monstrous world*: the world of sea monsters.

[159] *moist vows*: tearful prayers.

[160] *Bellerus*: a mythical giant, here connected with Bellerium, the Roman name for Land's End in the extreme southeast of Cornwall.

[161] *the guarded Mount*: Mount St. Michael in Cornwall, guarded by the archangel; *the great vision* refers to the *fable* (l. 60) that Michael is often seen at the mountain's summit.

[162] *Namancos and Bayona's* [*strong*] *hold*: districts in Spain; thus, *the great vision* is conceived as looking southward.

[163] *Angel*: i.e., Michael, *the great vision*, to whom the speaker is now addressing his plea for mercy (*melt with ruth*).

[164] Dolphins are said to have carried to safety the Greek poet and musician Arion. They are also said to have borne the dead bodies of Melicertes, who became the sea-god Palaemon (the Roman god of harbors, Portunus); of another poet, Hesiod; and of Apollo's son, Icadius.

[168] *the day-star*: the sun.

[169] *repairs*: renovates.

And tricks his beams, and with new spangled Ore,   170
Flames in the forehead of the morning sky:
So *Lycidas* sunk low, but mounted high,
Through the dear might of him that walk'd the waves;
Where other groves, and other streams along,
With *Nectar* pure his oozy Lock's he laves,   175
And hears the unexpressive nuptiall Song,
In the blest Kingdoms meek of joy and love.
There entertain him all the Saints above,
In solemn troops, and sweet Societies
That sing, and singing in their glory move,   180
And wipe the tears for ever from his eyes.
Now *Lycidas* the Shepherds weep no more;
Henceforth thou art the Genius of the shore,
In thy large recompense, and shalt be good
To all that wander in that perilous flood.   185

    Thus sang the uncouth Swain to th'Okes and rills,
While the still morn went out with Sandals gray,
He touch'd the tender stops of various Quills,
With eager thought warbling his *Dorick* lay:
And now the Sun had stretch'd out all the hills,   190
And now was dropt into the Western bay;
At last he rose, and twitch'd his Mantle blew:
To morrow to fresh Woods, and Pastures new.

---

170 *tricks*: adorns, decks.

173 *him that walk'd the waves*: Christ, whom "the disciples saw . . . walking on the sea" (Matthew 14:26).

176 *unexpressive*: inexpressible; or, possibly, inapprehensible. In using the marriage metaphor here, Milton is invoking a tradition extending from the Mosaic era through the great prophets—notably Hosea and Jeremiah—to the New Testament, particularly the Book of Revelation (cf. 19:9: "Blessed are they which are called unto the marriage supper of the Lamb").

177 The line was not in the 1638 ed.

181 As before (ll. 114 ff.), biblical allusions abound in this section too—such as Revelation 7:17 and 21:4 ("God shall wipe away all tears from their eyes").

183 *Genius*: guardian spirit (cf. the "genius of the wood" in both *Arcades*, l. 26, and *Il Penseroso*, l. 154).

184 *recompense*: reward (cf. 14: *meed*, and 73: *Guerdon*).

186 *the uncouth Swain*: the unknown or rustic poet—the anonymous singer of the pastoral elegy, here concluding the *melodious tear* (l. 14) in the tradition-bound, orderly form of the *ottava rima* (186–93).

189 *Dorick*: the dialect of the Greek bucolic poets; hence, "pastoral."

192 *twitch'd*: pulled up; the word also suggests the movement of fingers across the strings of a musical instrument.

blew: blue is the traditional symbol of hope.

Corrigenda

Textual notes are listed below, 346 ff. Here, for the convenience of
the reader, are indicated the most significant corrections made by Milton in
the course of his composition of *Lycidas*. The corrections are reproduced
from the manuscript of the poem presently at Trinity College, Cambridge.

Lines

4-5	~~before the mellowing yeare~~ and wth forc't fingers rude
	~~and crop yor young~~ shatter yor leaves before ye mellowing yeare
8	for ~~young~~ Lycidas
10	he well knew
22	and ~~to~~ bid
26	~~glimmering;~~ *in margin:* opening
30	oft till the ~~ev'n~~ starre ~~bright~~ that rose in Evning bright
31	~~burnisht;~~ *in margin:* westring
47	~~buttons weare beare;~~ *in margin:* wardrope weare
51	~~youn~~ lov'd Lycidas
57-63	~~had yee~~ bin there, ~~for~~ what could that have don?

        ~~what could the golden hayrd Calliope~~

        for her inchaunting son

        ~~when shee beheld (the gods farre sighted bee)~~

        ~~his goarie scalpe rowle downe the Thracian lee~~

                        *whome universal nature

                          might lament

                        ~~and heaven and hel deplore~~

                        ~~when his divine head downe~~

                        the streame was sent

                        downe the swift Hebrus to

                        the Lesbian shore.

    Re-written thus:

    what could the muse her selfe that Orpheus bore

    the muse her selfe for her inchaunting son.

    ~~for her inchanting son~~

                   did

    whome universal nature ~~might~~ lament

    when by the rout that made the hideous roare

               gorie

*goarie his ~~divine~~ ∧ visage downe the streame was sent

downe the swift Hebrus to ye Lesbian shoare.

69 ~~hid in;~~ *in margin:* or with

85 ~~smooth;~~ *in margin:* fam'd; *then corrected to* honour'd

86 ~~soft;~~ *in margin:* smooth

105 scraul'd ore, *not crossed out; but margin has:* inwraught

129 ~~nothing;~~ *in margin:* little; *but* nothing *restored*

138 ~~sparely;~~ *in margin:* faintly; *but* sparely *restored*

139 ~~bring;~~ *in margin:* throw

142-150 Bring the rathe primrose that unwedded dies

~~collu~~ colouring the pale cheeke of uninjoyd love

and that sad floure that strove

to write his owne woes on the vermeil graine

next adde Narcissus y^t still weeps in vaine

the woodbine and ye pancie freak't wth jet

the glowing violet

the cowslip wan that hangs his pensive head

and every bud that sorrows liverie weares

let Daffadillies fill thire cups ∧^(with) teares

bid Amaranthus all his beautie shed

to strew the laureat herse &c.

Above passage cancelled; then re-written thus:

Bring the rathe primrose that forsaken dies

the tufted crowtoe and pale Gessamin

the white pinke, and ∧^(y^e) pansie freakt wth jet

the glowing violet the well-attir'd woodbine

the muske rose and ~~the garish columbine~~

wth cowslips wan that hang the pensive head

and every flower that sad escutcheon ∧^(× weare) ~~beares~~ imbroidrie ^(× weares) ~~beares~~

2 ∧^(&) ~~let~~ daffadillies fill thire cups wth teares

1 bid Amaranthus all his beauties shed

to strew &c.

153 ~~sad;~~ *in margin:* fraile

154 ~~floods;~~ *in margin:* shoars

157 the humming tide

160 ~~Corineus;~~ *in margin:* Bellerus

176 ~~listening;~~ *in margin:* & heares

Epitaphium Damonis
Edited by H. W. Garrod

ARGUMENTUM

Thyrsis & Damon ejusdem vinciniæ Pastores, eadem studia
sequuti a pueritiâ amici erant, ut qui plurimùm. Thyrsis animi
causâ profectus peregrè de obitu Damonis nuncium accepit.
Domum postea reversus, & rem ita esse comperto, se, suamque
solitudinem hoc carmine deplorat. Damonis autem sub personâ
hîc intelligitur Carolus Deodatus ex urbe Hetruriæ Luca paterno
genere oriundus, cætera Anglus ; ingenio, doctrina, clarissimisque
cæteris virtutibus, dum viveret, juvenis egregius.

Himerides nymphæ (nam vos & Daphnin & Hylan,
Et plorata diu meministis fata Bionis)
Dicite Sicelicum Thamesina per oppida carmen :
Quas miser effudit voces, quæ murmura Thyrsis,
Et quibus assiduis exercuit antra querelis,   5
Fluminaque, fontesque vagos, nemorumque recessus,
Dum sibi præreptum queritur Damona, neque altam
Luctibus exemit noctem loca sola pererrans.
Et jam bis viridi surgebat culmus arista,
Et totidem flavas numerabant horrea messes,   10
Ex quo summa dies tulerat Damona sub umbras,
Nec dum aderat Thyrsis, pastorem scilicet illum
Dulcis amor Musæ Thusca retinebat in urbe.

Ast ubi mens expleta domum, pecorisque relicti
Cura vocat, simul assuetâ sedítque sub ulmo,   15
Tum vero amissum tum denique sentit amicum,
Cœpit & immensum sic exonerare dolorem.
   Ite domum impasti, domino jam non vacat, agni.
Hei mihi! quæ terris, quæ dicam numina cœlo,
Postquam te immiti rapuerunt funere, Damon?   20
Siccine nos linquis, tua sic sine nomine virtus
Ibit, & obscuris numero fociabitur umbris?
At non ille, animas virgâ qui dividit aureâ,
Ista velit, dignumque tui te ducat in agmen,
Ignavumque procul pecus arceat omne silentum.   25
   Ite domum impasti, domino jam non vacat, agni.
Quicquid erit, certè nisi me lupus antè videbit,
Indeplorato non comminuere sepulcro,
Constabitque tuus tibi honos, longúmque vigebit
Inter pastores, illi tibi vota secundo   30
Solvere post Daphnin, post Daphnin dicere laudes
Gaudebunt, dum rura Pales, dum Faunus amabit:
Si quid id est, priscamque fidem coluisse, piúmque,
Palladiásque artes, sociúmque habuisse canorum.
   Ite domum impasti, domino jam non vacat, agni.   35
Hæc tibi certa manent, tibi erunt hæc præmia, Damon,
At mihi quid tandem fiet modò? quis mihi fidus
Hærebit lateri comes, ut tu sæpe solebas
Frigoribus duris, & per loca fœta pruinis,
Aut rapido sub sole, siti morientibus herbis?   40
Sive opus in magnos fuit eminùs ire leones
Aut avidos terrere lupos præsepibus altis;
Quis fando sopire diem, cantuque solebit?
   Ite domum impasti, domino jam non vacat, agni.
Pectora cui credam? quis me lenire docebit   45
Mordaces curas, quis longam fallere noctem
Dulcibus alloquiis, grato cùm sibilat igni
Molle pyrum, & nucibus strepitat focus, at malus auster
Miscet cuncta foris, & desuper intonat ulmo.
   Ite domum impasti, domino jam non vacat, agni.   50
Aut æstate, dies medio dum virtitur axe,
Cum Pan æsculeâ somnum capit abditus umbrâ,
Et repetunt sub aquis sibi nota sedilia nymphæ,

Pastoresque latent,'stertit sub sepe colonus,
Quis mihi blanditiásque tuas, quis tum mihi risus,   55
Cecropiosque sales referet, cultosque lepores?
    Ite domum impasti, domino jam non vacat, agni.
At jam solus agros, jam pascua solus oberro,
Sicubi ramosæ densantur vallibus umbræ,
Hic serum expecto, supra caput imber & Eurus   60
Triste sonant, fractæque agitata crepuscula silvæ.
    Ite domum impasti, domino jam non vacat, agni.
Heu quàm culta mihi priùs arva procacibus herbis
Involvuntur, & ipsa situ seges alta fatiscit!
Innuba neglecto marcescit & uva racemo,   65
Nec myrteta juvant; ovium quoque tædet, at illæ
Mœrent, inque suum convertunt ora magistrum.
    Ite domum impasti, domino jam non vacat, agni.
Tityrus ad corylos vocat, Alphesibœus ad ornos,
Ad salices Aegon, ad flumina pulcher Amyntas,   70
Hîc gelidi fontes, hîc illita gramina musco,
Hîc Zephyri, hîc placidas interstrepit arbutus undas;
Ista canunt surdo, frutices ego nactus abibam.
    Ite domum impasti, domino jam non vacat, agni.
Mopsus ad hæc, nam me redeuntem forte notârat   75
(Et callebat avium linguas, & sydera Mopsus)
Thyrsi quid hoc? dixit, quæ te coquit improba bilis?
Aut te perdit amor, aut te malè fascinat astrum,
Saturni grave sæpe fuit pastoribus astrum,
Intimaque obliquo figit præcordia plumbo.   80
    Ite domum impasti, domino jam non vacat, agni.
Mirantur nymphæ, & quid <de> te, Thyrsi, futurum est?
Quid tibi vis? ajunt, non hæc solet esse juventæ
Nubila frons, oculique truces, vultusque severi,
Illa choros, lususque leves, & semper amorem   85
Jure petit, bis ille miser qui serus amavit.
    Ite domum impasti, domino jam non vacat, agni.
Venit Hyas, Dryopéque, & filia Baucidis Aegle
Docta modos, citharæque sciens, sed perdita fastu,
Venit Idumanii Chloris vicina fluenti;   90
Nil me blanditiæ, nil me solantia verba,
Nil me, si quid adest, movet, aut spes ulla futuri.
    Ite domum impasti, domino jam non vacat, agni.

Hei mihi quam similes ludunt per prata juvenci,
Omnes unanimi secum sibi lege sodales, 95
Nec magis hunc alio quisquam secernit amicum
De grege, sic densi veniunt ad pabula thoes,
Inque vicem hirsuti paribus junguntur onagri;
Lex eadem pelagi, deserto in littore Proteus
Agmina Phocarum numerat, vilisque volucrum 100
Passer habet semper quicum sit, & omnia circum
Farra libens volitet, serò sua tecta revisens,
Quem si fors letho objecit, seu milvus adunco
Fata tulit rostro, seu stravit arundine fossor,
Protinus ille alium socio petit inde volatu. 105
Nos durum genus, & diris exercita fatis
Gens homines aliena animis, & pectore discors,
Vix sibi quisque parem de millibus invenit unum,
Aut si sors dederit tandem non aspera votis,
Illum inopina dies quâ non speraveris horâ 110
Surripit, æternum linquens in sæcula damnum.
    Ite domum impasti, domino jam non vacat, agni.
Heu quis me ignotas traxit vagus error in oras
Ire per aëreas rupes, Alpemque nivosam!
Ecquid erat tanti Romam vidisse sepultam, 115
Quamvis illa foret, qualem dum viseret olim,
Tityrus ipse suas & oves & rura reliquit,
Ut te tam dulci possem caruisse sodale,
Possem tot maria alta, tot interponere montes,
Tot sylvas, tot saxa tibi, fluviosque sonantes? 120
Ah certè extremùm licuisset tangere dextram,
Et bene compositos placidè morientis ocellos,
Et dixisse vale, nostri memor ibis ad astra.
    Ite domum impasti, domino jam non vacat, agni.
Quamquam etiam vestri nunquam meminisse pigebit, 125
Pastores Thusci, Musis operata juventus,
Hic Charis, atque Lepos; & Thuscus tu quoque Damon,
Antiquâ genus unde petis Lucumonis ab urbe.
O ego quantus eram, gelidi cum stratus ad Arni
Murmura, populeumque nemus quà mollior herba, 130
Carpere nunc violas, nunc summas carpere myrtos,
Et potui Lycidæ certantem audire Menalcam.
Ipse etiam tentare ausus sum, nec puto multùm

Displicui, nam sunt & apud me munera vestra
Fiscellæ, calathique & cerea vincla cicutæ,   135
Quin & nostra suas docuerunt nomina fagos
Et Datus, & Francinus, erant & vocibus ambo
Et studiis noti, Lydorum sanguinis ambo.
  Ite domum impasti, domino jam non vacat, agni.
Hæc mihi tum læto dictabat roscida luna,   140
Dum solus teneros claudebam cratibus hœdos.
Ah quoties dixi, cùm te cinis ater habebat,
Nunc canit, aut lepori nunc tendit retia Damon,
Vimina nunc texit, varios sibi quod sit in usus;
Et quæ tum facili sperabam mente futura   145
Arripui voto levis, & præsentia finxi,
Heus bone numquid agis? nisi te quid forte retardat,
Imus? & argutâ paulùm recubamus in umbra,
Aut ad aquas Colni, aut ubi jugera Cassibelauni?
Tu mihi percurres medicos, tua gramina, succos,   150
Helleborûmque, humilésque crocos, foliûmque hyacinthi,
Quasque habet ista palus herbas, artesque medentûm.
Ah pereant herbæ, pereant artesque medentûm,
Gramina postquam ipsi nil profecere magistro.
Ipse etiam, nam nescio quid mihi grande sonabat   155
Fistula, ab undecimâ jam lux est altera nocte,
Et tum forte novis admôram labra cicutis,
Dissiluere tamen rupta compage, nec ultra
Ferre graves potuere sonos, dubito quoque ne sim
Turgidulus, tamen & referam, vos cedite silvæ.   160
  Ite domum impasti, domino jam non vacat, agni.
Ipse ego Dardanias Rutupina per æquora puppes
Dicam, & Pandrasidos regnum vetus Inogeniæ,
Brennúmque Arviragúmque duces, priscúmque Belinum,
Et tandem Armoricos Britonum sub lege colonos;   165
Tum gravidam Arturo fatali fraude Jögernen,
Mendaces vultus, assumptáque Gorlöis arma,
Merlini dolus. O mihi tum si vita supersit,
Tu procul annosa pendebis fistula pinu
Multùm oblita mihi, aut patriis mutata camœnis   170
Brittonicum strides, quid enim? omnia non licet uni
Non sperasse uni licet omnia, mi satis ampla
Merces, & mihi grande decus (sim ignotus in ævum

Tum licet, externo penitúsque inglorius orbi)
Si me flava comas legat Usa, & potor Alauni,   175
Vorticibúsque frequens Abra, & nemus omne Treantæ,
Et Thamesis meus ante omnes, & fusca metallis
Tamara, & extremis me discant Orcades undis.
　Ite domum impasti, domino jam non vacat, agni.
Hæc tibi servabam lentâ sub cortice lauri,   180
Hæc, & plura simul, tum quæ mihi pocula Mansus,
Mansus Chalcidicæ non ultima gloria ripæ
Bina dedit, mirum artis opus, mirandus & ipse,
Et circùm gemino cælaverat argumento:
In medio rubri maris unda, & odoriferum ver,   185
Littora longa Arabum, & sudantes balsama silvæ,
Has inter Phœnix divina avis, unica terris
Cæruleùm fulgens diversicoloribus alis
Auroram vitreis surgentem respicit undis.
Parte alia polus omnipatens, & magnus Olympus,   190
Quis putet? hic quoque Amor, pictæque in nube pharetræ,
Arma corusca faces, & spicula tincta pyropo;
Nec tenues animas, pectúsque ignobile vulgi
Hinc ferit, at circùm flammantia lumina torquens
Semper in erectum spargit sua tela per orbes   195
Impiger, & pronos nunquam collimat ad ictus,
Hinc mentes ardere sacræ, formæque deorum.
　Tu quoque in his, nec me fallit spes lubrica, Damon,
Tu quoque in his certè es, nam quò tua dulcis abiret
Sanctáque simplicitas, nam quò tua candida virtus?   200
Nec te Lethæo fas quæsivisse sub orco,
Nec tibi conveniunt lacrymæ, nec flebimus ultrà,
Ite procul lacrymæ, purum colit æthera Damon,
Æthera purus habet, pluvium pede reppulit arcum;
Heroúmque animas inter, divósque perennes,   205
Æthereos haurit latices & gaudia potat
Ore Sacro. Quin tu cœli post jura recepta
Dexter ades, placidúsque fave quicúnque vocaris,
Seu tu noster eris Damon, sive æquior audis
Diodotus, quo te divino nomine cuncti   210
Cœlicolæ norint, sylvísque vocabere Damon.
Quòd tibi purpureus pudor, & sine labe juventus
Grata fuit, quòd nulla tori libata voluptas,

En etiam tibi virginei servantur honores;
Ipse caput nitidum cinctus rutilante corona,   215
Letáque frondentis gestans umbracula palmæ
Æternùm perages immortales hymenæos;
Cantus ubi, choreisque furit lyra mista beatis,
Festa Sionæo bacchantur & Orgia Thyrso.

Lament for Damon
Translated by Helen Waddell

ARGUMENT

Thyrsis and Damon, shepherds of the same neighborhood, from childhood had pursued the same interests and were most affectionate friends. While studying abroad, Thyrsis received the report of Damon's death. When, later, he returned home and found that it was so, he bewailed himself and his loneliness in this song. Now Damon represents Charles Diodati, who through his father was descended from the Tuscan city of Lucca, but in all else was an Englishman—a youth who, while he lived, was outstanding for genius, learning, and every other splendid virtue.

O nymphs that haunt the old Sicilian stream,
Himera's stream, you that do still remember
Daphnis and Hylas, and the death of Bion
Lamented these long years,
Sing dirge beside these English river towns,   5
Sing by the Thames, as once in Sicily,
The low lament, the ceaseless bitter weeping
That broke the quiet of the caves,
River and forest ride and fleeting water,
Where Thyrsis went, bewailing his lost Damon,   10
Walking at dead of night in the silent places
Uncomforted, alone.

It is the second year.
Twice has the green corn come to ear,
And twice the barns are filled with golden grain,   15
Since the ending day that took him to the shadows,
And I not there. I was in Tuscany,
Making my verses.
But now, my mind assuaged and the old task calling,
Now that I am come home,   20
Sitting again beneath the familiar elm,
Now, now, I know him gone,
And know how vast my grief.

Away, my lambs, unfed : your shepherd heeds you not.

O grief! what gods are there in heaven or earth   25
That I can cry to, since they've taken thee
In unrelenting death? O Damon, so to leave us,
And all thy valour pass, and no man name thee
In that dim fellowship of shades? Ah no!
Sure He whose golden bough divides men's souls   30
Shall lead thee to thy chosen company
And keep at bay the sluggish silent herd.

Away, my lambs, unfed : your shepherd heeds you not.

What e'er befall—unless the wolf first spy me—
Thou shalt not moulder in an unwept grave.   35
Thy honour shall abide, and have long life
Among the shepherds : thou wilt be remembered
When they remember Daphnis, after Daphnis
They'll fall to praising you, whilst the kind gods
Of field and fold still haunt the countryside :   40
If it be aught to have kept the ancient faith,
And loved the arts, and had a poet friend.

Away, my lambs, unfed : your shepherd heeds you not.

These things are yours, O Damon, they are yours,
And yours for ever :   45
But Damon, Damon, what's to become of me?
Who'll walk with me forever by my side,

As you did, through the frost and through the mire,
In the fierce sun, the thirsting dying grass?
Or face the lion but a spear's cast off,   50
Or scare the hungry wolves from the high folds?
Or talking, singing, lull the day to sleep?

Away, my lambs, unfed : your shepherd heeds you not.

To whom can I speak my heart? To whom shall I go
To learn to master the dark thoughts that tear me,   55
And cheat the night with talking, while the pears
Are hissing on the fire and all the hearth
Crackling with chestnuts, and the wind from the South
Is wrecking all without, and overhead
The elm tree cries and groans?   60

Away, my lambs, unfed : your shepherd heeds you not.

Summer and noon, Pan sleeping under the oak,
The nymphs all fled to their cool haunt under the waters,
The shepherds gone to the shade and the swineherd snoring—
But who will bring me back that smiling enchantment,   65
The Greek salt of your wit, and all your ways?

Away, my lambs, unfed : your shepherd heeds you not.

Alone through the plough lands I go, alone through the pas-
    ture,
Down where the branching trees grow thick in the valley,
There do I wait the night : above my head   70
Sadly the west wind sighs and the falling rain,
And sighs the shivering twilight of the trees.

Away, my lambs, unfed : your shepherd heeds you not.

The fields that once I ploughed are tangled with weeds,
Couch grass and bindweed : and the standing corn   75
Bows and rots where it grew : the virgin grape
Is shrivelling where it hangs on the unkempt vine.
I am sick of my sheep and the pitiful creatures bleat,
Crowding reproachful faces around their master.

Away, my lambs, unfed : your shepherd heeds you not.   80

One lad shouts from the hazels, and one from the rowans,
One is among the willows, and one by the river.
"Here's a spring well, and grass that is silky with moss,
A warm west wind and water lapping the branches"—
They cry to a deaf man. There's sanctuary in the forest.　85

Away, my lambs, unfed : your shepherd heeds you not. . . .

O God, if one were a bullock!
All of them moving together roaming the field,
Any steer of the herd as good a friend as another.
The jackals crowd at their feasting, and the wild ass　90
Will rub his shaggy head against his neighbour
Indifferent of choice.
This too is the law of the sea : out on the desolate sands
Proteus calls, and the seals come to him in shoals.
Aye, even the lowly sparrow　95
Has never far to seek for company,
Cheerfully pecking his grain, flickering here and there,
Homing again at dusk to the familiar eaves :
Yet should Fate strike down his comrade,
Spitted on beak of hawk, or limed in a ditch,　100
Straight is he off again, the sociable creature,
To find another mate.
But what of men?
Men, the hard stock, schooled by grim destiny,
Alien, aloof in soul,　105
Discordant in their hearts?
Hardly in thousands may a man find one
That is his fellow.
And if at last Fate hath not proved unkind,
Hath given the heart's desire,　110
Comes stealthily the day you had not looked for,
The hour undreaded,
And snatches him, and leaves loss infinite,
For ever and for ever.

Away, my lambs, unfed : your shepherd heeds you not.　115

O grief! what craze for wandering captured me,
Drew me to unknown shores,

Climbing the sky-flung rocks, the Alps in snow?
Was it so great a thing to look on Rome,
Low in her grave—   120
Even had she been as when the Virgilian shepherd
Left his own flocks and herds to gaze on her—
When for her I must lack thy company
And set between us deep estranging seas,
Mountains and woods and rocks and sounding rivers?   125
O had it but been given me at the last
To touch thy hand in the still hour of dying,
And close those eyes beneath the carven brows,
And say "Farewell : go forth on thy high journey :
And still remember me."   130

Away, my lambs, unfed : your shepherd heeds you not.

God knows I do not grudge the memory
Of you, the men I found in Tuscany,
Poets and shepherds : Grace and Wit are there—
And Damon, Damon was himself a Tuscan,   135
His father's house from Lucca of the kings,
Etruscan kings and priests.
How high my heart was, stretched beside the Arno
Cool-fleeting past me, or in shadow of the poplars,
Where the grass is deeper, and violets to gather,   140
Myrtle to reach high for, listening to my poets
Arguing and versing : and sometimes, greatly daring,
I too made verses, that did not much displease.
Dati, Francini, I still have the gifts you gave me,
Fruit baskets, wine bowls, wax for my shepherd's flute.   145
Still I remember the song you made about us,
Singing under the beeches : lyric poets and scholars,
Both of you famous, both of Etruscan blood.

Away, my lambs, unfed : your shepherd heeds you not.

How I would dream there, at moonrise and dewfall,   150
Solitary, closing in the little tender goats,
How often said—and the earth dark above thee!—
"Damon will be singing now, or out to trap a hare,
Weaving his osiers for all his little contraptions !"

And so light-hearted, so sure was I of to-morrow,   155
I held it in my hand, the time to come.
Here! are you busy? If there is nothing you must do,
Shall we go and lie in the glancing quivering shade
Down by the Colne, or the fields above St. Albans,
And you can recite me all your herbs and simples,   160
Hellebore and iris and the saffron-crocus,
And the herbs in the marshland and all the arts of healing.
—O perish all the herbs, and all the arts of healing,
Perish all the simples that could not save their master!
And I—more than a se'nnight gone—so grand, so grave
    a note   165
Rang from my pipe—I scarce had put my lips to it,
The reeds were new—and yet they leapt asunder,
Broke at the join, and that deep resonance
Could bear no more.
I fear I am too bold : yet let me speak,   170
Speak to the silent woods.

Away, my lambs, unfed : your shepherd heeds you not.

I shall sing of the Trojan prows
Cleaving the seas beneath the cliffs of Kent,
And the old Kingdom that was Imogen's,   175
And Arvirach, was son to Cymbeline,
And Bren and Belin, ancient British captains,
And the Breton coast brought under Britain's law,
And Igraine great with child that shall be Arthur,
And the false face of Uther that begat him,   180
Masking her husband's likeness and his armour,
Through Merlin's guile. O, if I live, yet live,
Thou shalt hang, my shepherd's pipe, on some ancient pine,
Remote, all but forgotten—
Unless thou change thy note   185
From the classic cadence to the harsher speech
Of the English tongue.
And then? What then?
It is not given to one man to have all things,
Or even to hope for all things.   190
Enough, enough for me, and grand the honour—

Although I be unknown in time to come,
Yea, be inglorious in the outer world—
If my own folk will chant me in the meadows
Beside the cowslip Ouse and the springs of Allen   195
And the swirling tides of the Severn, and wooded Trent,
And Thames—above all, my Thames—and Tamar tawny
   with ore,
And the far Orkneys in the furthest seas.

Away, my lambs, unfed : your shepherd heeds you not.

These songs I was keeping for thee, in the bark of the   200
   laurel :
These, and how many more!—and the goblets I was given
By Manso, glory of the Campanian shore,
Two chalices of marvellous workmanship
—Yet the old man no less marvellous than they—
Carved and inlaid with two-fold argument :   205
Here, the Red Sea, the long Arabian coast,
And fragrant-breathing spring and the woods of spice,
And in the midst the Phoenix, the divine,
Sole in the earth, blazing with azure wings
Diversely bright, her eyes upon the dawn   210
That breaks above the green crystalline sea.
Obverse, the vast over-arching of the sky,
Height of Olympus,
And Love, aye, Love himself, against the clouds,
The dazzling bow, the torch, the arrows of fire.   215
No puny soul, no sordid breast his target.
Those burning eyes go seeking through the worlds
For the high heart, the proud undaunted spirit.
These, not the sprawling, are his arrows' mark,
The noblest minds, beauty as of the gods,   220
He kindles, and they burn.

And thou art with them, Damon, thou art there,
This is no cheating hope.
Thou too art there : where else should be
That holy sweet simplicity,   225
That radiant valiancy?

We did thee wrong to seek thee in the mirk
Of Lethe's waters.
No tears, no tears for thee, and no more wailing.
I'll weep no more. He hath his dwelling place   230
In that pure heaven,
He hath the power of the air, himself as pure.
His foot hath spurned the rainbow.
Among the souls of the heroes, the gods everlasting,
He drinks deep draughts of joy.   235

Thou hast the freedom of heaven : be with me now.
Canst hear me, Damon, come unto thy peace?
Art thou our Damon still,
Or do they call thee by thine other name,
The given of God, the name they knew in heaven,   240
But Damon in the woods.
Thine was untarnished youth, the flush of honour
Untouched by wantonness : and now to thee
The glories kept for virgin souls are given.
Upon thy radiant head a glittering crown,   245
And in thy hand the joyous green of the palm,
Thou goest deathless to the immortal feast,
Where the sound of the lyre and the voice of singing
Kindle and quicken the dancing feet,
Where the Bridegroom's feast is toward,   250
And the mystic wine is poured,
The madness and the ecstasy of Heaven.

Part II
The Commentaries

1. On the Tradition

The Pastoral Elegy and Milton's *Lycidas*

James H. Hanford

I

To most modern readers the pastoral setting of Milton's *Lycidas* is far from being an element of beauty. It is doubtful whether anyone, approaching *Lycidas* for the first time, fails to experience a feeling of strangeness, which must be overcome before the poem can be fully appreciated; and not infrequently the pastoral imagery continues to be felt as a defect, attracting attention to its own absurdities and thereby seriously interfering with the reader's enjoyment of the piece itself. The reason for this attitude lies in the fact that we have today all but forgotten the pastoral tradition and quite lost sympathy with the pastoral mood. The mass of writing to which this artificial yet strangely persistent literary fashion gave rise seems unendurably barren and insipid; to return and traverse the waste, with its dreary repetitions of conventional sentiments and tawdry imagery, is a veritable penance. Yet this, if we are to judge fairly of *Lycidas*, or if we are to remove the hindrances to our full enjoyment of it

From *Publications of the Modern Language Association* 25 (1910), 403–447; revised by the editor with the author's approval.

as poetry, is what in a measure we must do. For in Milton's eyes
the pastoral element in *Lycidas* was neither alien nor artificial.
Familiar as he was with poetry of this kind in English, Latin,
Italian, and Greek, Milton recognized the pastoral as one of the
natural modes of literary expression, sanctioned by classic practice, and recommended by not inconsiderable advantages of its
own. The setting of *Lycidas* was to him not merely an ornament,
but an essential element in the artistic composition of the poem.
It tended to idealize and dignify the expression of his sorrow,
and to exalt this tribute to the memory of his friend, by ranging
it with a long and not inglorious line of elegiac utterances, from
Theocritus and Virgil to Edmund Spenser.

To consider this tradition with reference to *Lycidas* is the
object of the present essay. I do not propose to write a history
of the pastoral elegy, but simply to indicate the origin of those
elements of the elegiac tradition which appear in *Lycidas*, and to
show in detail Milton's indebtedness to each of the greater examples of the type. Many of the borrowings are noted in the
various editions of Milton's works; some of the identifications
are new. The material has never, so far as I know, been collected
and used for the present purpose.[1]

II

The trifling and artificial spirit of the pastoral would seem
at first thought to render the form utterly inappropriate for
serious laments; according to the accepted view the pastoral
was in its very origin a sort of toy, a literature of make-believe.
The poetry which grew up in the happy school of Greek bards
who masqueraded as countrymen on the "pleasant sward" of
Cos, and whiled away the hours learning to be poets by imitating
the song contests of the Sicilian shepherds, could hardly have
been anything but pretty and artificial. We might have supposed
that it would be as transitory as the conditions which gave it
birth. That this *jeu d'esprit* became a permanent literary form
and a mode of expression for serious as well as lighter themes,
was due to the superior genius of Theocritus, whose dramatic
imagination, aided by his knowledge of the sober realities of
Sicilian shepherd life, carried him beyond the imitation of mere

---

[1] [For other studies of the elegiac tradition, most of them written after
the appearance of the present essay, see *infra,* pp. 352 ff.—Ed.]

externals and led him really to identify himself with the characters which he portrayed. All the charm of rustic manners, all
the fresh beauties of Sicilian scenery were preserved in the idyls
of Theocritus; but these served only as a setting for human
passions.

That the change in point of view, the shift of attention from
the machinery of the pastoral to its essence, did not come to
Theocritus all at once, may be inferred from the idyls themselves.
In ·the Polyphemus idyls, for example, where the monster Cyclops is represented in the grotesque role of a sentimental lover,
we seem to see the poet barely touching the serious note. The
sixth idyl gets little farther than burlesque; in the eleventh, on
the other hand, the author makes us feel not only the absurdity
of Polyphemus in love, but also, by flashes, the pathos of it:

> Come forth, Galatea, [he cries] and forget as thou comest, even
> as I that sit here have forgotten, the homeward way. . . .
> There is no one that wrongs me but that mother of mine, and her
> do I blame. Never, nay, never once has she spoken a kind word
> for me to thee, and that though day by day she sees me wasting.
> I will tell her that my head and both my feet are throbbing, that
> she may also suffer somewhat, since I too am suffering. O
> Cyclops, Cyclops, whither are thy wits wandering? Ah that
> thou wouldst go, and weave thy wicker-work and gather broken
> boughs to carry to thy lambs; in faith, if thou didst this, far
> wiser wouldst thou be.[2]

The author is still trifling, but his imagination has carried him
into the situation; he seems to be holding two points of view,
that of the Cyclops and that of the unsympathetic world which
is laughing at him. In another lover's lament extravagant sentimentality takes the place of incongruity as an element of humor.
The song is addressed to cruel Amaryllis by her disappointed
lover, who, when he finds himself rejected in spite of presents,
prayers, and harmless threats, gives way to despair. "My head
aches, but thou carest not. I will sing no more, but dead will I
lie where I fall, and here may the wolves devour me." [3] In this
passage the contemplation of death as the result of the thwart-
ing of the shepherd's passion brings us a step nearer to the
elegy. The spirit of the piece is, to be sure, not too serious; this

[2] xi, 63 ff.; trans. Andrew Lang.
[3] iii, 53 ff.

lover's "complaint" is the very stuff of which the later sentimental or burlesque pastoral was made. Still there are serious
and even tragic possibilities in the theme; characters and passions originally designed as burlesques may spring into life under
the creative touch of genius, and refuse to remain within the
narrow bounds of parody.

It is in the first and second idyls that Theocritus becomes
fully possessed by his theme. Here the spirit of banter and make-
believe is cast aside for a serious artistic purpose. The subject
of the poems is still disappointed love, but the laments are no
longer mere lovers' rhetoric. They claim and receive our sympathy. The second idyl is not pastoral and does not concern us
here, except as it serves to show the trend of Theocritus's poetic
and dramatic genius. It is the monologue of a ruined and deserted girl, who is trying the forlorn hope of magic to bring
back her faithless lover. She tells the story of her passion with
poignant pathos, murmuring an incantation to the moon the
while, and directing a servant in the magic rites. In Virgil's
imitation of this poem (Eclogue VIII) the incantations prove
successful; in Theocritus no lover comes, and the ending is consistent with the hopeless tone of the whole piece. "But do thou
farewell, and turn thy steeds to Ocean, Lady, and my pain I will
bear, even as till now I have endured it." Virgil is primarily interested in the magic machinery and in the sonorous poetry;
Theocritus, in the truth of the character and the tragic pathos
of the situation.

The greatest of the idyls and by far the most important for
the present discussion is the first. For not only is it in many respects the archetype of the pastoral elegy, but it bears a direct
and particularly significant relation to *Lycidas*. The poem opens
with a pretty scene in which Thyrsis, the sweet singer of the vale,
is urged by a goatherd to make pleasant the noontide hour by
singing the "Affliction of Daphnis." A wondrous ivy bowl, and
the privilege of thrice milking a goat that is mother of twins,
shall be his reward. Thyrsis consents and begins the beautiful
lament. The theme is how Daphnis, the ideal hero of pastoral
song, was subdued by a new love, after his marriage to the fairest
of the nymphs, and chose rather to die than to yield. The singer
first rebukes the nymphs for failing to save their Daphnis, and
tells of the universal lament of nature for his loss; he then de-

scribes the visits of Hermes, Priapus, and Cypris to the afflicted shepherd, the first two with words of consolation, the last with a cruel taunt. To her alone does Daphnis reply, reproaching her and bidding her begone to boast of her success; he bids farewell to his native woods and rivers; bequeaths his pipe to his successor, and dies lamenting his own sad fate. The shepherd-singer concludes and claims the gifts, which the goatherd gladly grants, with praise for his companion's song.

The extent to which this poem moulded the tradition of the pastoral elegy will be clear from our discussion of the later examples of the form. That Milton was familiar with it at first hand and consciously adopted it as one of the classical models for *Lycidas* seems practically certain, notwithstanding the wide divergence of the two poems in setting, spirit, and subject matter. For the general plan of making various beings come one after another to add their part to the lament, Milton had a precedent also in the tenth eclogue of Virgil. It is impossible to say that he was influenced more by the one poet than by the other. It is noteworthy, however, that in the *Epitaphium Damonis*, where Milton uses the same motive, he is clearly following Theocritus I. The poem is twice explicitly referred to, and the name of the mourner in both laments is Thyrsis. In the *Epitaphium* the shepherds and nymphs come, not to mourn for the dead as in *Lycidas*, but, in their mistaken way, to bring comfort to the mourner; the contrast between the affliction of the shepherd and the shallow consolations of his friends serves, as with Theocritus and Virgil, to heighten the effect.

A more detailed borrowing is to be found in the passage in *Lycidas* beginning "Where were ye Nymphs." The lament of Thyrsis opens thus:

> Begin, ye Muses dear, begin the pastoral song.
> Thyrsis of Etna am I, and this is the voice of Thyrsis. Where,
> ah! where were ye when Daphnis was languishing; ye nymphs
> where were ye? By Peneus beautiful or by the dells of Pindus?
> for surely ye dwelt not by the great stream of the river Anapus,
> nor on the watchtower of Etna, nor by the sacred water of Acis.
> Begin, ye Muses dear, begin the pastoral song.

The familiar lines from *Lycidas* are substantially the same, but they bear the touch of a mightier hand:

> Where were ye Nymphs when the remorseless deep
> Clos'd o're the head of your lov'd *Lycidas?*
> For neither were ye playing on the steep,
> Where your old *Bards,* the famous *Druids* ly,
> Nor on the shaggy top of *Mona* high.[4]

For the use of this motive too Milton had the double precedent
of Theocritus and Virgil [5]; that the lines are directly reminiscent of the Greek rather than the Latin poet is clear from the
fact that whereas Milton, like Theocritus, mentions places near
the region where his shepherd met his fate, Virgil declares that
the nymphs were absent, not from Arcady where the scene of
his eclogue is laid, but from their accustomed haunts in Sicily.

At the close of the lament in Theocritus I there is a passage
which bears a still more essential relation to *Lycidas.* "Nay,
spun was all the thread that the fates assigned," the shepherd
sings, "and Daphnis went down the stream. The whirling wave
closed over (literally 'the eddy washed away') the man whom
the muses loved, the man not hated of the nymphs." In view of
the circumstances of the death of Edward King, these lines are
particularly interesting. That Milton noticed their special ap-
plicability to his own subject is clear from the passage already
quoted:

> Where were ye Nymphs when the remorseless deep
> Clos'd o're the head of your lov'd *Lycidas?*

May it not be that these lines from Theocritus first suggested
to Milton the idea of giving his elegy on the death of his friend
a pastoral form? It is quite possible that this passage occurred
to Milton when he first learned that King was drowned, thus
drawing his attention to Theocritus I and to the pastoral elegy
in general as an instrument for the expression of idealized grief.
The external circumstances of Daphnis's death would at least
lead Milton in a manner to identify his own dead shepherd with
this legendary hero of pastoral song, and to regard Theocritus's
exquisite lament as the prototype of his own elegy.

The influence of Theocritus on *Lycidas* is by no means
limited to the Daphnis idyl. The elegiac pastoral tradition is
only a part of the pastoral tradition in general, and the whole

---

[4] *Lycidas,* 50 ff.
[5] Cf. Eclogue x, 9 ff.

body of the poetry of Theocritus, as the ultimate source of this general tradition, must be regarded as contributory to the pastoral elegy. Theocritus was the great storehouse of pastoral material; he was plundered again and again, and his plunderers were plundered in their turn, until the incidents, expressions, and motives used by him became common property among pastoral writers. Of this material a due proportion appears in *Lycidas*, whether borrowed directly from Theocritus or descended from him through many hands.[6]

Of the later bucolic writers of the Alexandrine age, but two are known to us by name: Moschus and the somewhat younger Bion, both of whom flourished in the latter half of the third century B.C. Bion's most famous idyl, the *Lament for Adonis*, is, strictly speaking, not a pastoral at all; Adonis was a hunter, not a shepherd. The poem is associated with the pastoral, however, because of its form and because it is the work of a pastoral poet. Its erotic tone serves also to ally it with pastoral poetry. It is not surprising, therefore, that we find the poem influencing the pastoral elegy. The sober and classic genius of Milton seems to have rejected this decadent elegy; for neither *Lycidas* nor the *Epitaphium Damonis* shows any direct trace of its influence. Other pastoral writers, however, have made liberal use of the poem, and it must rank as one of the great classical models of the pastoral elegy.[7] The poem, moreover, derives a special importance in the development of the tradition from its connection with the *Lament for Bion*.

The latter piece, which is commonly attributed to Moschus but probably belongs to a somewhat younger Italian contemporary, is of the greatest significance in the history of the pastoral elegy. It marks, as we shall see, the full development of the pastoral lament as an independent type, and, notwithstanding its sentimentality and absurd exaggeration of the pathetic fallacy, it was adopted as a model by numerous later writers.[8] The origi-

---

[6] The passages in Milton which are directly and certainly traceable to other idyls of Theocritus are very few. Cf., however, *Idyl* VII, 35, with *Lyc.*, 25–27; *Idyl* I, 16–17, with *Ep. Dam.*, 51–52; and *Idyl* I, 27 ff., with *Ep. Dam.*, 181 ff.

[7] For an extensive account of the influence of this poem in the Renaissance and later, see W. P. Mustard, "Later Echoes of the Greek Bucolic Poets," *American Journal of Philology*, XXX (1909), 275 ff. Shelley's *Adonais* is formally modeled on the *Lament for Adonis*.

[8] *Ibid.*, pp. 279 ff.

nals of the *Lament for Bion* were clearly Bion's own *Lament for
Adonis* and Theocritus's first idyl; but the poem differs con-
spicuously from its predecessors in being a lament for the death
of an actual person conceived as a shepherd. Adopting the lyric
form of the *Lament for Adonis* and the pastoral setting and
many of the motives of Theocritus I, the writer has substituted
for the legendary character, whether shepherd or hunter, the
person of his own friend. Bion was a writer of pastorals; therefore for poetical purposes Bion was a shepherd. By thus applying the imagery of the pastoral to a real person, the author of
the *Lament* had transformed what was previously a *genre* of
erotic verse into the more serviceable type of the personal elegy
in pastoral form.

The pastoral fiction, once employed in lamenting a pastoral
poet, was easily extended to poets who did not touch on pastoral
themes, and then to men who were not poets at all. The time was
soon to come when as unpastoral a figure as Julius Cæsar could
be dubbed Daphnis and made the subject of a shepherd's lament.
Poor poet as he was, the author of the *Lament for Bion* has the
credit of having established a permanent literary form.

The influence of the *Lament for Bion* extended farther than
merely to establish the use of pastoral imagery in elegies on the
death of real persons; many of the particular motives and ideas
which characterize the later tradition may be traced to this
first example of the form. The favorite application of the pastoral treatment continued to be to poets. Thus in later times
Sir Philip Sidney, John Keats, Arthur Hugh Clough, and Matthew Arnold have been mourned in pastoral song. Even when the
person lamented is not primarily a poet, the writer is prone to
adopt the old convention and refer to him as one of the sweet
singers of the vale. Edward King was not a poet; but Milton
did not forget that he wrote verse:

> Who would not sing for *Lycidas?* he knew
> Himself to sing, and build the lofty rhyme.

This character of the shepherd as a poet gives rise to another
common motive: namely, the fiction that the writer of the elegy
is himself the poetical successor of the dead shepherd. In the
first idyl of Theocritus, Thyrsis, who sings the lament, was, as

Daphnis had been before him, the most famous of the rustic poets. The writer of the *Lament for Bion* professes to be heir to his master's song.[9] This sense of personal relation as a poet to the subject of his song justifies the writer in allowing himself digressions concerning his own poetic achievements and aspirations. In *Lycidas* this tendency appears in the passage about fame (ll. 64 ff.), beginning:

> Alas! What boots it with uncessant care
> To tend the homely slighted Shepherds trade,
> And strictly meditate the thankles Muse.

In the *Epitaphium Damonis* the digression is still more personal and explicit (ll. 161 ff.).

Closely connected with the supposed superiority of the shepherd as a rustic poet is the fiction that he is the particular darling of all the creatures of the vale and that they all lament his death. The first suggestion of this motive was undoubtedly found in Theocritus. Not only were the boys and maidens stricken with grief at the loss of Daphnis, but jackals, lions, bulls, and calves bewailed his death. In the *Lament for Bion* everything worth mentioning in nature adds after its fashion to the universal moan. Indeed, the first third of the poem is wholly given over to the agonies of created things. In *Lycidas* we have the motive employed in a passage which may be a direct echo of the *Lament for Bion*:

> Thee Shepherd, thee the Woods, and desert Caves,
> With wilde Thyme and the gadding Vine o'regrown,
> And all their echoes mourn.
> The Willows, and the Hazle Copses green,
> Shall now no more be seen,
> Fanning their joyous Leaves to thy soft layes.

From this conventional use of the "pathetic fallacy" Milton, it will be observed, gets a very different effect from that of his Greek originals. For he does not dwell on the fiction that the natural objects express grief; he is taken up with the beauty of the things themselves. It is the description that we remember, not the conceit.

[9] "To others didst thou leave thy wealth, to me thy minstrelsy" (l. 97).

That Milton regarded the *Lament for Bion*, together with
the first idyl of Theocritus, as a great classical original of the
pastoral elegy is clear from the invocation in the *Epitaphium
Damonis:*

> *Himerides nymphæ (nam vos & Daphnin & Hylan,*
> *Et plorata diu meministis fata Bionis)*
> *Dicite Sicelicum Thamesina per oppida carmen.*

Traces of direct imitation, on the other hand, are very slight.
In addition to the lines quoted above, the flower passage in
Lycidas has been cited as echoing the opening lines in the *Lament.*[10] The resemblance is a shade closer than to the similar
passages in Virgil.

With the *Lament for Bion*, the pastoral elegiac tradition in
Greek, at least as far as we can trace it, comes to an end. The
pastoral form was on its way toward complete decadence; it
seemed on the point of total dissolution when it was revived in
a new spirit by Virgil.

III

The ampler strain in which Virgil bids the Muses sing his
prophecy of the approaching millenium [11] is the keynote of a
change in the style and spirit of the pastoral which is of the
greatest importance in the history of the pastoral elegy. The
tone of the Virgilian eclogue is determined not by the lightness
and delicate urbanity of Theocritus, nor by the decadent beauty
of his successors, but by the essentially dignified and noble genius
of Virgil himself. With all his literary indebtedness to the Alex-
andrians, Virgil was thoroughly Roman; he was by nature an
epic poet, and even in the bucolics he strikes the epic note. Corresponding to this change in expression, and intimately related
to it, there came with Virgil a change in the nature of the tradition. The Roman poet, unlike his master, had never known a
shepherd life like that which Theocritus describes; the peculiar
conditions of simplicity and happiness which had existed in Sicily
two centuries before could hardly have been found among the
peasants of northern Italy at the close of the civil wars. Hence
if Virgil was to write pastorals at all, he must either change the

[10] Mustard, *op. cit.,* pp. 281–282.
[11] Ecl. IV, 1 ff.: *"Sicilides Musae, paulo maiora canamus!"* etc.

setting so as to bring it into accord with the rural life he knew, or he must accept the pastoral setting of his master as a literary convention. But the fiction of a shepherd contest was the very essence of the 'pastoral as a literary form. Accordingly, Virgil took the latter course, thereby completing the process of which we have seen the beginning in the *Lament for Bion*. From Virgil's time forth, conventionality in setting, adherence to an established literary tradition, is a marked characteristic of the pastoral.

That Virgil should have been willing to accept his pastoral setting ready made is partly explained by the fact that he was not particularly interested in this setting for its own sake. His purpose was first of all stylistic. There is in Virgil no such insight into character and dramatic situation as in the first and second idyls of Theocritus; there is no such variety of pastoral ideas and images. In compensation, the Roman poet has taken infinite pains to secure artistic finish. Each eclogue is a carefully constructed whole, usually beginning with something corresponding to an invocation and progressing to a definite artistic close. The verse is polished almost to a point of overrefinement. But style and form are not by any means Virgil's only interest in the eclogues. The methods of personal reference suggested by the practice of Theocritus and the author of the *Lament for Bion* are extensively employed by Virgil and turned to panegyric purposes. The pastoral was, with Virgil, to a large degree personal and allegorical; indeed, if we take the realistic idyls of Theocritus as the type, the eclogues can hardly be considered as pastorals at all.

This change in the spirit and intention of the pastoral in Virgil's hands was, as I have already remarked, of the greatest importance in the history of the pastoral form. It is not only that Virgil reinstated the pastoral and exemplified it in a language which was to be the literary medium for centuries; he also transformed it into an easy and serviceable instrument for a variety of literary purposes. It was no longer necessary to know anything about country life in order to write good pastorals; it was only necessary to know the pastoral formulas—to be able to manipulate the pastoral machinery. Moreover, the pastoral was henceforth to be a garment that would fit all figures. It was a thin and graceful disguise for personal allusion, and especially for panegyric.

What, then, was Virgil's influence on the pastoral elegy? The
form already had, as we have seen, a certain grace and pathos to
recommend it; it suffered, at least in its later examples, from
pettiness, from exaggeration, from erotic sentimentality. In
Virgil's hands it was ennobled and made an instrument really
worthy of the highest themes. True it is that there were few
who could follow Virgil in raising the pastoral by exalted expression; but for those who could, Virgil had shown the way. Of
all his successors in the higher pastoral vein, none had more
clearly the spirit of the master than John Milton. He echoes the
Roman's very lines in bidding his muse rise to the dignity of a
loftier theme:

> Begin then, Sisters of the sacred well,
> That from beneath the seat of *Jove* doth spring
> Begin, and somwhat loudly sweep the string.[12]

If Virgil had never written his eclogues, Milton might yet have
sung of the death of King in an epic strain; for such expression
was as native to Milton's genius as to Virgil's own; but it is not
so likely that he would have chosen the pastoral as the form in
which to cast his lament. With this elevation of the tone of the
pastoral elegy there comes also an enlargement of its scope. The
character of the subjects treated by Virgil, which are in many
cases serious and far beyond the narrow range of strictly pastoral interests, brought the pastoral nearer to the elegy proper,
in which we naturally expect an element of contemplation and
didacticism. It also established a precedent for the introduction
into the pastoral elegy of a great variety of miscellaneous material, a practice of which the invective against the clergy in
Lycidas is a striking example.

Two of the eclogues of Virgil, the fifth and tenth, are deserving of especial consideration. Eclogue x is a love lament in imitation of Theocritus i; but here the shepherd is no mythical
Daphnis but the flesh and blood poet, Cornelius Gallus, whose disappointment in love is presumably an actual fact. The poem is
conventional in imagery, but sincere in feeling and elevated in
tone. It begins with an invocation of Arethusa. There follows a
passage lamenting the absence of the nymphs from their accustomed haunts; then comes the inevitable lament for nature. The

¹² *Lycidas*, 15–17; cf. note 14.

shepherds, Apollo and Pan, come to offer their consolation. At length, as in Theocritus I, Gallus himself bewails his misfortune, struggles for a time against fate, then yields. The poem concludes with eight lines in the regular style of the Virgilian close.

In general outline this poem resembles *Lycidas* much more closely than any other of the poems of Virgil or Theocritus. In both we have an invocation at the beginning but no mention of the shepherd singer until the end; in both the motive of a procession of mourners is employed; both poems close with eight lines, very similar in spirit, referring to the end of day and the departure of the shepherd. In addition to these general resemblances there are a few detailed borrowings.[13]

Virgil's fifth eclogue marks a step in advance in the development of pastoral elegy; for here we have for the first time a lament for a great man who was not a poet and who appears, not in his own person, but disguised under a pastoral name. The Daphnis of the fifth eclogue is in all likelihood Julius Cæsar. Reference is apparently made to his reputed descent from Venus, to his introduction into Rome of the Bacchic rites, and lastly to his apotheosis. The setting is the familiar dialogue of Theocritus I. Two shepherds, Menalcas and Mopsus, meet and sing together the death of Daphnis. Mopsus tells of the sorrows of nature for the shepherd's fate: the nymphs wept; lions, mountains, and forests are said to have uttered groans. Pales and Apollo have left the fields; darnel and oats grow instead of barley, thistles instead of violets. Then the shepherds are invited to scatter flowers over Daphnis's grave and build his tomb, and Menalcas concludes, addressing Daphnis as a god:

> *Candidus insuetum miratur limen Olympi*
> *Sub pedibusque videt nubes et sidera Daphnis.*

The note of joy, thus introduced by Virgil with reference to the deification of the first Cæsar, is henceforth seldom or never absent from the pastoral elegy. In general, the resemblance between this passage and the end of *Lycidas* is not specific. Christianity has lent a new coloring to the consolation in the later poem. With the last three lines, however, where Lycidas is invoked as

---

[13] Cf. Ecl. x, 2–3, 4–5, and 24, with *Lyc.*, 81, 19 ff., and 103–104, respectively. There are several echoes of Eclogue x in the *Ep. Dam.*; cf. Ecl. x, 8, 42, 55–68, 63, with *Ep. Dam.*, 73, 71, 35–43, and 160, respectively.

the "Genius of the shore," the case is different. The conception
contained in them is more pagan than Christian, and it is hard
to believe that they would have appeared in *Lycidas* had not
the idea held an important place in this eclogue of Virgil.

The influence of the bucolics on *Lycidas* is by no means confined to the fifth and tenth eclogues. No edition of *Lycidas* has
ever given anything like an exhaustive list of the passages in
Virgil which Milton either borrowed or imitated. One can never
feel sure that one has got them all; for they extend to the merest
minutiæ, such as the borrowing of a single word. The beautiful
passage in *Lycidas* beginning "Bring the rathe Primrose" bears
only a general resemblance to the similar flower groupings in
the bucolics [14]; Milton is far more imaginative in his description
than Virgil. The Roman poet speaks of "pallid violets," "waxen
prunes," and "quinces with their tender bloom"; the English, of
"Cowslips wan that hang the pensive hed." The reference to
myrtles and laurels at the beginning of *Lycidas*, however, is
clearly reminiscent of line 54 in Eclogue II. In Eclogue III, ll.
26–27, there is a touch of satire which reminds us of *Lycidas*,
l. 124. The moving of natural objects to the song of a shepherd
is twice mentioned in Virgil [15]; so, too, Milton's "smooth-sliding
Mincius, crown'd with vocall reeds," is an echo of Virgil's "*hic
viridis tenera prætexit harundine ripas Mincius.*" [16] The phrase,
"touch'd my trembling ears," used of the admonition of Phœbus,
is borrowed from Eclogue VI. The beginning of the passage on
fame, "Were it not better don as others use, To sport with
Amaryllis in the shade," is evidently modeled on Virgil II, 14–15:
"*Nonne fuit satius tristis Amaryllidis iras Atque superba pati
fastidia.*" [17]

In trying to appraise the relative influence of Theocritus (including the *Lament for Bion*) and Virgil on Milton's pastoral
style, it is necessary to take into account the fact that the Greek
muse, as the first inspirer of pastoral verse, was naturally regarded as the more original and the more authentic. In *Lycidas*
both the Greek and Roman pastoralists are invoked together:

[14] Cf. Ecl. IV, 19 ff.; Ecl. V, 35–60; *Aeneid,* VI, 883–884.
[15] Ecl. VI, 27–38 (directly imitated in *Lyc.,* 33–35); and Ecl. VIII, 4.
[16] Ecl. VII, 12–13, and *Lyc.,* 86.
[17] Two further parallels might be given: cf. Ecl. I, 2 and 84, with *Lyc.,* 66
and 190, respectively.

O Fountain *Arethuse,* and thou honour'd floud,
Smooth-sliding *Mincius,* crown'd with vocall reeds.

But *Lycidas* is called a "*Dorick* lay," and after the church digression, Milton bids the "Sicilian Muse" return. So, too, in the
Epitaphium Damonis it is the "*Himerides nymphæ*" who are invoked. On the other hand, as we have seen, the direct reminiscences of Theocritus in *Lycidas,* are few, while those of Virgil
are many. The latter passages, too, have been more completely
assimilated; the Virgilian phrases are part and parcel of the
style. It seems probable, therefore, that though Milton honored
the Sicilian as his original and consciously incorporated some
of his motives, he turned to Virgil with greater familiarity. It
was the Virgilian rather than the Theocritean phrase which
sprang first to his mind when he would express himself in pastoral terms. We may, perhaps, refer the gentler and sweeter
passages in *Lycidas* to the flexible and sunny Greek of the author
of Daphnis; we must certainly attribute the "higher strain,"
which is most characteristic of the poem, to the influence of
Virgil. It is perhaps significant that Milton, in changing from
the harsh tones of invective to strains of pathos and beauty,
invokes the presence of the Greek pastoral alone:

Return *Alpheus,* the dread voice is past,
That shrunk thy streams; Return *Sicilian* Muse.

IV

The paramount importance of the classical examples of the
pastoral elegy, not only as establishing the type for future ages
but also as furnishing Milton with his most important models,
has led me to dwell on the subject at considerable length. But
these poems are not alone sufficient to account for the form of
Lycidas, nor are they the only elegies to which Milton is indebted for motives, phrases, and minute turns of style. The pastoral elegy was greatly enlarged in scope by the freer treatment
of the Middle Ages and Renaissance; it was to a certain degree
changed in essence by its contact with Christianity. It remains,
therefore, to examine the chief later modifications of the elegiac
tradition, and to consider in particular those poems with which
Milton seems to show familiarity.

The later Roman pastoral writers, Calpurnius and Nemesian, had but little influence on the pastoral tradition. Their eclogues reveal the tendency inherent in the pastoral as interpreted by Virgil, to become more and more personal and allegorical. The pastoral writers are no longer content to suggest a personal application of the eclogue as a whole; but, following what they believe to have been the practice of their master, they attempt to give a meaning to each detail, to make each character in the dialogue represent a definite person. The pastorals of Calpurnius contain no elegy; Nemesian I, entitled "Epiphunus Melibœi," is a lament after the style of Virgil v, but containing possible reminiscences of Theocritus. The aged Melibœus is probably a real person, but there is no evidence for his identification. It is interesting to observe that the pastoral consolation does not appear in this elegy. Melibœus is said to be worthy of the councils of the gods, but not to have been made one of their number. In the ordinary pagan eclogue such a passage could find no place. Its occurrence in the fifth eclogue of Virgil was due to a special fact connected with the subject of the lament. With the introduction of Christianity into the elegy, the consolation became essential.

The slender stream of pastoral writing which connects the classical eclogues with the bucolic poetry of the Renaissance need detain us but a moment. The renewed tradition owes little if anything to the Middle Ages, but derives its source directly from the classical originals as interpreted by the allegorical method which had been applied to the works of Virgil almost from the start. The pastoral poetry of the Carolingian Renaissance has, however, an interest of its own, and one elegy belonging to this period deserves consideration here as illustrating the trend of the form in Christian hands, and as anticipating, if it did not suggest, certain important later developments. The poem is a lament for Adalhard, Abbot of old and new Corbeil, and was written by Paschasius Radbertus. Two maidens, Galatea and Fillis, who prove to be personifications of the two monasteries, mourn for their abbot in alternate strains; as usual in the Carolingian eclogue, the writer is interested rather in the content than in the form. The pastoral idea had in it little to attract the writers of the circle of Charles, but fortified as they were with the allegorical interpretation of Virgil, they saw in the

eclogue a convenient form for the expression of a wide variety
of nonpastoral ideas. The pastoral setting tends constantly to
fall away from the skeleton of the dialogue. Radbertus, in the
poem under discussion, has not gone so far as to desert entirely
the Virgilian model, but he has dealt freely with the form, and
by introducing into his poem several new features has taken a
further step in the progressive widening of the scope of the pastoral elegy. Chief among these features are the following: (1)
extended praise of the subject of the lament; (2) abundant
references to his life and work; (3) an invective against death;
(4) a description of the joys of Paradise. The allusions in the
poem to the immortality of the deceased were pretty clearly suggested by Virgil v, but they contain a note of joy and rapture
which is new to the pastoral elegy and reminds us forcibly of
Lycidas. Of particular importance in the history of the pastoral
elegy is the confusion, or rather the direct combination of the
classical pastoral imagery with the Christian figure of the pastor
and his flock, which inevitably took place when the pastoral
came to be treated by religious writers. In a Latin eclogue of
the fourth century by Severus Sanctus, Christ is introduced as
averting a plague from the cattle of a shepherd who worshipped
him. In the poem just discussed, the identification of the two
kinds of "pastor" and the two kinds of "flock" is clearly made.
The connection thus established between the classical pastoral
and the Christian religion served greatly to extend the utility
and scope of the pastoral form. It opened the way, in the eclogue,
for the treatment of matters ecclesiastical, and rendered the
pastoral elegy as appropriate to the death of a member of the
clergy as it was to that of a poet. The significance of these remarks will be clear when we recall the ecclesiastical satire in
Lycidas and remember that Edward King had intended to enter
the church.

It is not to an obscure elegy of the Carolingian Renaissance,
however, that we must trace the direct impulse toward the introduction into the pastoral of ecclesiastical material, which was
so strong in later times, but to the first users of the form in
modern times, Boccaccio and Petrarch. Adopting the allegorical
practices of the Middle Ages and following closely in the supposed footsteps of Virgil, these poets used the pastoral solely
as a means of expressing their political, religious, and moral

ideas. In Eclogues VI and VII of Petrarch an elaborate allegorical
satire against the corruptions of the church is introduced. In
Eclogue VI Pamphilus, Saint Peter in pastoral guise, rebukes
Mitio, Clement V, who was leading a corrupt life at Avignon,
for the ill-keeping of his flocks; in Eclogue VII Epy or France
conspires with Mitio, whom she has corrupted. In the introduction of ecclesiastical satire into the pastoral, Petrarch led
the way for Mantuan and Marot, who were followed in turn by
Spenser. It is the latter poet to whom we naturally look as the
predecessor in this respect of Milton. Yet the presence of Saint
Peter in the satires of both Milton and Petrarch suggests a
connection between the two works, and it is quite possible that
Milton had read the Latin eclogues.

The freedom with which Petrarch and Boccaccio treated the
pastoral form in general is observable in their handling of the
pastoral elegy, in so far as they entered that field at all. In the
two or three poems of Petrarch's which can be called elegies
(Eclogues II, X, XI), the formal lament is subordinate to an
elaborate allegorical setting. The classical motives appear, but
not in great abundance. Boccaccio's interesting fourteenth eclogue, though it is rather a vision than a lament, is allied to the
pastoral elegy by the elaborate description which Olympia, the
spirit of Boccaccio's dead daughter, gives of Paradise and her
happiness there. I am unable to find traces in any of these poems
of direct influence on Milton's *Lycidas*.

The practice of making the eclogue a vehicle for didacticism
and personal allegory, thus inaugurated by Petrarch and Boccaccio, characterizes in a varying degree the work of their successors in the pastoral literature of the Renaissance. The typical
representative of this didactic tradition is Giovanni Battista,
called Mantuan, whose ten eclogues, connected in a kind of series,
and entitled *Adulescentia*, were in the sixteenth century regarded
not only as an ideal example of pastoral composition but as a
goodly moral work, more worthy of being put into the hands of
boys than the eclogues of Virgil. They furnished the models for
a host of later didactic dialogues, including the crude English
pastorals of Barclay, and, in a degree, *The Shepheardes Calender*
of Spenser. The influence of this conception of the eclogue on
the pastoral elegy was to open the way still further for the introduction of alien materials, personal, philosophic, and didactic.
The long personal digressions in the *Epitaphium Damonis* and

Lycidas, while they are hardly to be paralleled in any preceding elegy, are easily explicable when we consider that the pastoral eclogue had been used again and again since Petrarch as a means of expressing in a modest disguise the personal aspirations of its author.[18]

But while poets like Mantuan were handling the classical eclogue in what may be called the medieval spirit, the Renaissance had seized upon the pastoral for purposes of its own. Elaborating the original pastoral motive of simplicity into the fully developed conception of the golden age, the pastoral writers of the Renaissance soon found a wider field for their activity. The new wine of Arcadianism could by no means be contained in the old bottles of the classical eclogue form; and the pastoral idea invaded the realms of the drama and the prose romance. These developments were, to be sure, reserved for the vernacular; but the renewed interest in the pastoral setting for its own sake had its influence, too, on the more conservative Latin eclogue, bringing about a more consistent employment of the pastoral machinery and a closer adherence to the original form. Especially important was the effect of the rediscovery of Theocritus, whose idyls, unlike the bucolics of Virgil, furnished models in which the interest was purely pastoral. It was no longer felt as essential, though it was still common, to conceal an elaborate idea beneath the "cortex" of the eclogue.

From this renewed tendency to seek classical models, the pastoral elegy was not entirely exempt; the laments of the later humanistic writers are generally characterized by excessive conventionality and the absence of real grief. The *Lament for Bion* furnished an abundance of new motives, which were repeated *ad nauseam*. The interest of the pastoral poet was apt to be fully as much in the spectacle of the woeful shepherd and in the propriety of his pastoral language as in the substance of his lament. Nevertheless, the form remained of necessity personal, and might at any time in the hands of an individual poet be expanded to include new elements growing out of special circumstances connected with the subject of the elegy or his personal relation to the writer.

Among the few Latin elegies which are, like the *Epitaphium*

---

[18] Numerous examples of the Latin elegy may be found in the *Carmina Illustrium Poetarum Italorum* (Florence, 1719). [See also the edition by T. P. Harrison, cited *infra*, p. 353.]

Damonis and *Lycidas*, the expression of personal feeling, restrained through artistic combination with the conventional elements of the form, is Castiglione's *Alcon*. The poem is especially
interesting for the present discussion because of its emphasis
in pastoral terms of the friendship existing between the dead
shepherd and the singer of the lament. "We lived together from
tender years," the shepherd sings; "we bore together heat and
cold, nights and days; we fed our kine together. These flocks
of mine were thine also." The resemblance between these lines
and the passage in *Lycidas* beginning, "For we were nurst
upon the self-same hill," is less striking when we consider how
narrow the range of pastoral equivalents for friendship must
necessarily be. The possibility of a connection between the poems
is strengthened, however, by still another resemblance. Castiglione's shepherd regrets the fact that he was absent when Alcon
died; and says he will build an empty tomb, "nostri solatia
luctus." So the singer in *Lycidas*, "to interpose a little ease,"
fancies that he is decking the tomb of Lycidas. There follows
in *Alcon* a flower passage like that in *Lycidas*.

The only other Latin elegy of the Renaissance which has, as
far as I know, been suggested as having furnished material for
Lycidas, is Sannazaro's first piscatory eclogue, a lament for the
drowned shepherdess Phyllis, put into the mouth of a shepherd
named Lycidas. Unlike the majority of the Renaissance elegies
this poem is, apparently, pure fiction. It was characteristic of
Sannazaro, who wrote the most famous of all the pastoral romances, and made his Latin eclogues an interesting innovation
on the old tradition by shifting the scene from the plains of
Arcady to the shores of the Bay of Naples, to be interested even
when writing an elegy in the pastoral fiction for its own sake.
We must look, then, in the poem, not so much for personal feeling as for a beautiful and appropriate handling of the old material. What must have attracted Milton to this poem, if he did
indeed know it, is its felicity of style, and the circumstance that
the lament is for one who had met death by drowning. The
closest parallel to *Lycidas* is to be found in the passage in the
Latin work in which the shepherd hails the departed spirit wherever it may be and bids it look towards its former home:

> *At tu, sive altum felix colis æthera, seu iam*
> *Elysios inter manes cœtusque verendos*

Lethæos, sequeris per stagna liquentia pisces;
Seu legis æternos formosa pollice flores,

. . . .

Aspice nos, mitisque veni. Tu numen aquarum
Semper eris; semper lætum piscantibus omen.[19]

In *Lycidas*, it will be remembered, the shepherd after speculating where the body of his friend may be, bids his spirit "look homeward." Later he invokes Lycidas not merely as a protecting spirit, as in Virgil's fifth eclogue, but specifically as the "genius of the shore," and that in words almost identical with those used by Sannazaro:

> Henceforth thou art the Genius of the shore,
> In thy large recompense, and shalt be good
> To all that wander in that perilous flood.

The lines in *Lycidas* following that quoted above,

> Where thou perhaps under the whelming tide
> Visit'st the bottom of the monstrous world,

may perhaps have been suggested by an earlier passage in Sannazaro's poem, in which the shepherd declares that he will wander through and over the sea, amidst its monsters. It is interesting to note, too, that Sannazaro as well as Milton mentions the name of the not very familiar nymph, Panope. These resemblances are too striking to be the result of accident. Sannazaro's eclogues were among the best known of the Latin pastorals of the Renaissance, and it is natural that Milton should have read them.[20]

From the new vernacular developments of the pastoral, the pastoral elegy in the stricter sense remained apart. Lovers' laments exist in the Arcadian literature of the Renaissance in abundance; laments for the death of imaginary shepherds may occasionally be found; but the renewed interest in the pastoral idea for its own sake, which is predominant in the romances of Sannazaro, Montemayor, and Sidney, excluded the lament for a real person. Such belong to the didactic and classical tradition of the eclogue, and when serious elegies came to be written in the vernacular they adhered more closely to the original forms.

[19] *Pisc. Eclogue* I, 91 ff.
[20] The influence of Sannazaro may be traced in England in Phineas Fletcher's *Piscatorie Eclogues,* which were published only four years before *Lycidas.*

Even in the case of the fictitious elegy, the influence of the classical conventions remained strong. Eclogue xi in Sannazaro's *Arcadia*, for example, is an almost slavish imitation of the *Lament for Bion*, with the addition of the inevitable consolation. Eclogue v in the same work is, to be sure, composed in an elaborate lyric stanza rather than in the terza rima, which was the common measure for the didactic eclogue in Italian; but even in this poem there is hardly a motive which is not derived from the *Lament for Bion* or from the fifth eclogue of Virgil.

Of the vernacular elegies which preceded *Lycidas*, other than those in English, very little need be said. In general they conform to the type established by the Latin works and depend in large measure on the classics for their pastoral and elegiac motives. The process of transplanting and naturalizing the elegy was not, however, entirely without its effect. Conformably to the spirit and genius of the Renaissance, and to its freer conception of the pastoral, the elegies of the vernacular are somewhat richer in coloring, somewhat more prone to the use of fanciful ornament, than are the classical representatives of the form. The adoption of rhyme and in some cases of a less regular measure made possible a more effective handling of the music of the dirge with its changing keys. The tendency of the didactic Latin pastoral to make the rustic setting merely perfunctory, as in the case of Mantuan, was somewhat checked; the vernacular elegies have rather more of the pastoral atmosphere and of the original grace of the pastoral imagery. On the other hand, the vernacular elegy was even freer than the Latin in its admission of personal references and digression. Ronsard's elegy on the death of Henry II, though sung by a fictitious shepherd in the the course of an elaborate pastoral contest, contains references to Henry's deeds under the slightest veil of pastoral imagery:

> *La sera ton Janot, qui chantera tes faits,*
> *Tes guerres, tes combats, tes ennemis desfaits,*
> *Et tout ce que ta main d'invincible puissance*
> *Osa pour redresser la houlette de France.*

Deserving of particular mention among the French elegies, as the original of Spenser's November eclogue, is Marot's lament for Louise de Savoy. The poem resembles *Lycidas* in having no one of the great classical elegies as its particular model, but

employing motives from them all and handling these motives
with unusual freedom. Notwithstanding the fact that Marot
takes care in general to preserve the genuine pastoral mood, the
poem is filled with personal allusions. We are told, for example,
how "Bergère Loyse" used to lecture her shepherdesses (the
maids of honor?) on the sin of indolence; and how they would
straightway betake themselves, one to her needle, another to
planting her garden, another to feeding doves. After a description of the happy state of the blessed spirit, which may have
influenced Milton through Spenser, we have a flower passage,
interesting as showing how this classical motive was inevitably
elaborated and colored in the vernacular. One stanza may be
quoted.

> *Passeveloux de pourpre colorez,*
> *Lavande franche, œilletz de coleur vive,*
> *Aubepins blanc, aubepins azurez,*
> *Et toutes fleurs de grand beauté nayfve.*

The influence of the Renaissance pastoral in Italian and
French may in a general way be traced in *Lycidas;* but it is im-
probable that Milton owes a special debt to any one of the
Continental writers. He must of course have read the great
dramas of Tasso and Guarini and the romance of Sannazaro;
he probably knew many of the elegies. It is not surprising, however, if few of the latter impressed themselves upon his memory.
Samuel Johnson, in his criticism of *Lycidas,* remarks that Milton owed the peculiar metrical structure of his poem to the
Italians. This seems entirely probable.[21] The irregular introduction of short lines and the use of an irregular rhyme scheme
are characteristic of the choruses of the *Aminta* and the *Pastor
Fido,* and they occur but rarely, if at all, in English poetry
before *Lycidas.* But what Milton owes to the specifically Renaissance developments of the pastoral he derived not so much from
the Italian and French direct as through the pastoral tradition
of his native land.

V

First among the English pastorals in importance, and practically first in time, stands *The Shepheardes Calender* of Spenser,

---

[21] [See the subsequent work by F. T. Prince, *infra,* pp. 157 ff.]

published anonymously in 1579. The earlier attempts of Barclay and Googe were by that time forgotten, and Spenser regarded himself as a pioneer, setting out deliberately, as "E. K." tells us, "to furnish our tongue with this kind wherein it faulteth." From the publication of this work the stream of pastoral writing in English flows on without interruption until the date of the publication of *Lycidas*.[22] Spenser's poem exhibited a striking divergence from the familiar pastoral tradition, and improvement on it. First of all, it combined in an unusual way the two main tendencies of the Renaissance pastoral, that represented by the Latin eclogue and that represented by the various classes of pastoral writing in the vernacular. Spenser drew without discrimination from the works of Mantuan, Sannazaro (both in his Latin eclogues and in his Italian romance), from the French eclogues of Marot, and from the classics. He added, moreover, to the didactic elements of the eclogue and to the pretty sentiment of the Arcadian pastoral, a freshness of interest in rustic life and a lyric quality which are peculiarly Elizabethan and English. The eclogues of Spenser have little of the epic sweep of Virgil; they have rather the qualities of gentleness, grace, and rustic charm which are characteristic of Theocritus and are more congenial to the true pastoral.

The most important of Spenser's innovations in the pastoral was his introduction of artistic unity into a series of eclogues. Three of the eclogues (January, June, and December) deal with progressive stages in Colin's love, and the moods of the poems change with the changing year. Now the story thus narrated is melancholy, even tragic, and the prevailing tone of the series, notwithstanding the fact that single eclogues are lighthearted or even humorous, is one of gloom. The poems in which Colin gives expression to his grief and despair are particularly mournful; they produce essentially the same effect as the first and second idyls of Theocritus, and are thus closely allied with the pastoral elegy. The series contains, moreover, one formal elegy, a lament "for some maiden of great blood, whom he, the author, calleth Dido." The poem, which is modeled closely on Marot's lament for Louise de Savoy, forms a striking contrast in spirit and style with *Lycidas*. The dominant characteristics of the earlier

[22] [But see the subsequent studies by W. B. Austin, H. M. Hall, T. P. Harrison, *et al.*, cited *infra*, pp. 352 ff.]

poet's pastoral style were such as tended to emphasize the very qualities which pastoralism lends to the elegy, a grace and charm which relieve the sad theme and make grief more tolerable by surrounding it with images of beauty. The elaborate lyric stanza in which the poem is written gives an effect far different from the irregular versification of *Lycidas*, which is hardly lyric at all. The fact that Spenser adopts the form of his eclogue with little modification from Marot minimizes the personal element in the elegy.

Less conventional and richer in personal allusion but equally in contrast with *Lycidas* in tone is Spenser's *Astrophel*, one of the numerous pastoral elegies on the death of Sir Philip Sidney. The prevailing note of gentleness is struck in the opening stanza of lament:

> A gentle shepherd borne in Arcady,
> Of gentlest race that ever shepherd bore,
> About the grassie bancks of Hæmony
> Did keep his sheep, his little stock and store.
> Full carefully he kept them day and night,
> In fairest fields; and Astrophel he hight.

The spirit of the closing lines of *Lycidas* has, to be sure, much in common with the above-quoted passage; but in general the later poem strikes a higher note than any heard in Spenser's pastorals. For a parallel in the pastoral to the loftiness of Milton's style we must go not to *The Shepheardes Calender* nor to any English poem, but to the eclogues of Virgil.

Yet Spenser too had his share in supplying the pastoral material of *Lycidas*. Three poems in *The Shepheardes Calender*, the May, July, and September eclogues, contain ecclesiastical satire; and one passage in the first of these bears a marked resemblance to the invective in *Lycidas*.[23] That Milton found in

[23] May, 38 ff:

> Those faytours little regarden their charge,
> While they, letting their sheepe runne at large,
> Passen their time, that should be sparely spent,
> In lustihede and wanton merryment . . .
> But they been hyred for little pay
> Of other, that caren as little as they
> What falleth the flocke, so they han the fleece . . .
> I muse what account both these will make . . .
> When great Pan account of shepherdes shall aske.

Cf. *Lycidas*, 113 ff.

Spenser the best and nearest precedent for the introduction of
such material into the elegy can hardly be doubted. He may also
have found there a precedent for bringing in allusions to his
own poetic aspirations. The October eclogue sets forth "the perfect patern of a poet, which, finding no maintenance of his state
and studies, complaineth of the contempt of poetry, and the
causes thereof." Cuddie, the disheartened bard, laments thus to
his friend Piers:

> The dapper ditties that I wont devise,
> To feede youthes fancie, and the flocking fry,
> Delighten much: what I the bett forthy?
> They han the pleasure, I a sclender prise:
> I beate the bush, the byrdes to them do flye:
> What good thereof to Cuddie can arise?

And Piers replies:

> Cuddie, the prayse is better than the price,
> The glory eke much greater than the gain.[24]

The familiar passage in *Lycidas* about fame is prompted by the
same feeling of the uselessness of poetic endeavor, and it contains a very similar turn of thought:

> But not the praise,
> *Phœbus* repli'ed, and touch'd my trembling ears.

The consolation in *Lycidas* resembles the close of the November eclogue to a marked degree; the parallels are, to be sure,
little closer than in some of the other Christian elegies; but it
is natural to refer the passage particularly to Spenser, from
whom, aside from the classics, Milton would have been most
likely to derive his conception. It seems probable also that the
flower passage in *Lycidas* owes something to the April eclogue,
the lines (136 ff.) beginning:

> Bring hether the pincke and purple cullambine,
>   With gelliflowers;
> Bring coronations, and sops in wine,
>   Worne of paramoures.

For Milton, like Spenser, adds to the conventional enumeration
a considerable amount of fanciful description:

[24] October, 13 ff.

> Bring the rathe Primrose that forsaken dies.
> The tufted Crow-toe, and pale Gessamine,
> The white Pink, and the Pansie freakt with jeat . . .

The above-mentioned parallels, together with a few detailed reminiscences,[25] are, I believe, sufficient to place Spenser among Milton's direct sources for the pastoral tradition, second only in importance to Virgil.

The vast and multifarious pastoral literature which was written in England between the publication of *The Shepheardes Calender* in 1579 and that of *Lycidas* in 1638, did little or nothing to modify the types established by the classics and by the Arcadian and didactic traditions of the Renaissance. In the eclogues and lyrics, the influence of Spenser continued strong, imparting to the English pastoral a healthier and more genuinely rustic tone than that of the sentimental Italian models which were dominant in the drama and romance. Throughout this literature there was the usual proportion of pastoral elegies on the death of real individuals. A great impulse to this kind of composition was given by the death of Sir Philip Sidney in 1586, an inevitable subject for the pastoral lament. Most important of the tributes to Sidney was the series entitled *Astrophel*, containing the Spenserian elegy already referred to, the *Doleful Lay of Clorinda*, written probably by the Countess of Pembroke, two poems by Lodowick Bryskett, and three nonpastoral laments. The volume contained also a long elegy by Spenser, the *Daphnaïda*, which, though pastoral in imagery and tone, has little relation to the formal elegy, being modeled on Chaucer's *Book of the Duchess*. Among the later elegies, William Browne's poem on the death of Mr. Thomas Manwood, the fourth eclogue in the collection entitled *The Shepheard's Pipe*, published in 1614, is frequently referred to as the source or inspiration of *Lycidas*. It is doubtful, however, if a single undoubted borrowing on Milton's part can be established. The poem, like a dozen others, belongs to the general type of *Lycidas;* it differs from the latter elegy, however, in having the narrative introduction, and in being without digressions. The passages which have been

---

[25] Cf. November, 37–38, with *Lyc.*, 9–10. For a similar repetition, see *Astrophel*, 6–8. The phrase "scorn of homely shepheard's quill" (June, 67) seems to be echoed in Milton's "homely slighted shepherd's trade" (*Lyc.*, 65).

quoted in evidence of a connection between the two poems are of little weight in view of the extreme conventionality of the form.

It is not likely that Milton was much impressed by any of the English elegies beside those of Spenser. Adhering in general to the established tradition, and offering little that was individual in thought or expression, they would, while carrying on the didactic and elegiac tradition to the very date of *Lycidas* and making the eclogue a contemporary type of literature,[26] simply range themselves in his mind with the three or four great examples of the form. Pastoral poetry had a remarkable faculty of holding to the commonplace. It was easy to write pleasingly in the pastoral style; to write in that style a poem that was really great demanded a genius which could triumph over the restrictions imposed upon it by the fact that it must accept much of its poetry ready made. In all the long history of the pastoral before *Lycidas* there are three or four great names. For later writers their works sum up the pastoral tradition. It is to them that the poet will look for direct inspiration. Theocritus, Virgil, and his own Spenser—with these Milton felt a kinship of genius; from them, when he chose to write at all in the most conventional of literary forms, he drew both the conventions themselves and the secret of finding his way beyond them into the realms of lofty and original poetry.

Yet *Lycidas* is to a remarkable degree the result of growth; "it gathers within its compass," says W. W. Greg, "as it were, whole centuries of pastoral tradition." The vast assimilative power of Milton had here its greatest opportunity; for the merit of a pastoral consisted not so much in its originality as in its faithful reproduction of the type. In one important respect Milton does indeed depart from, or rather greatly extend, the traditional practice: in no previous poem of the kind had the author introduced so many allusions to his own poetic career. The opening passage in *Lycidas*, the digression on fame, and the concluding line, are purely personal; in the *Epitaphium Damonis*, fifteen lines are devoted to a description of Milton's Italian journey and over twenty-five to an account of his poetic projects. The introduction of ecclesiastical satire is also new to the pastoral lament. The other characteristics of *Lycidas*

---

[26] *The Shepherd's Oracle* by Francis Quarles, written a few years before *Lycidas* but not published till 1646, contains an abundance of religious satire.

were without exception predetermined by the literary tradition of the pastoral elegy, and even for these Milton had, as we have seen, ample precedent in the pastoral at large.

What, then, shall we say of *Lycidas* as a work of art? Is it the less a perfect whole because it is composite? Does the fact that it is conventional make it any the less original in the highest sense? If we know *Lycidas* well and read it in a fitting mood, we find ourselves forgetting that its pastoral imagery is inherently absurd. The conventions which at first seem so incongruous with the subject, gradually become a matter of course. And when once we have ceased to regard these conventions as anything more than symbols, we find them no longer detracting from the beauty of the poem, but forming an essential element of its classic charm. For the supreme beauty of *Lycidas* lies partly in the very fact of its conventionality. Its grief is not of the kind that cries aloud; it soothes and rests us like calm music. For a moment, indeed, we are aroused by an outburst of terrible indignation, but the dread voice is soon past and we sink back again into the tranquil enjoyment which comes from the contemplation of pure beauty, unmarred by any newness of idea, unclouded by overmastering emotion.

2. On the Poem

from *The Life of Milton*

Samuel Johnson

One of the poems on which much praise has been bestowed is *Lycidas*, of which the diction is harsh, the rhymes uncertain, and the numbers unpleasing. What beauty there is we must therefore seek in the sentiments and images. It is not to be considered as the effusion of real passion; for passion runs not after remote allusions and obscure opinions. Passion plucks no berries from the myrtle and ivy, nor calls upon Arethuse and Mincius, nor tells of rough *satyrs* and *fauns with cloven heel*. Where there is leisure for fiction there is little grief.

In this poem there is no nature, for there is no truth; there is no art, for there is nothing new. Its form is that of a pastoral, easy, vulgar, and therefore disgusting; whatever images it can supply are long ago exhausted, and its inherent improbability always forces dissatisfaction on the mind. When Cowley tells of Hervey, that they studied together, it is easy to suppose how much he must miss the companion of his labours, and the partner of his discoveries; but what image of tenderness can be excited by these lines?—

> We drove a field, and both together heard
> What time the grey fly winds her sultry horn,
> Battening our flocks with the fresh dews of night.

From *The Lives of the Most Eminent English Poets* (London, 1783), I, 218–220. First published in *The Works of the Most Eminent English Poets* (London, 1779), Vol. II.

We know that they never drove a field, and that they had no flocks to batten; and though it be allowed that the representation may be allegorical, the true meaning is so uncertain and remote that it is never sought because it cannot be known when it is found.

Among the flocks, and copses, and flowers, appear the heathen deities—Jove and Phœbus, Neptune and Æolus, with a long train of mythological imagery, such as a college easily supplies. Nothing can less display knowledge, or less exercise invention, than to tell how a shepherd has lost his companion, and must now feed his flocks alone, without any judge of his skill in piping; and how one god asks another god what is become of Lycidas, and how neither god can tell. He who thus grieves will excite no sympathy; he who thus praises will confer no honour.

This poem has yet a grosser fault. With these trifling fictions are mingled the most awful and sacred truths, such as ought never to be polluted with such irreverend combinations. The shepherd likewise is now a feeder of sheep, and afterwards an ecclesiastical pastor, a superintendent of a Christian flock. Such equivocations are always unskilful; but here they are indecent, and at least approach to impiety, of which, however, I believe the writer not to have been conscious.

Such is the power of reputation justly acquired, that its blaze drives away the eye from nice examination. Surely no man could have fancied that he read *Lycidas* with pleasure had he not known its author.

from *Milton*

E. M. W. Tillyard

About two months before *Lycidas*, in September 1637, Milton wrote two letters to Diodati. In the first he mentions how exacting and unintermitted his studies have been: the idea that his excursions to London were much relaxation cannot be allowed. He writes:

> Your method of study is such as to admit of frequent interruptions, in which you visit your friends, write letters, or go abroad; but it is my way to suffer no impediment, no love of ease, no avocation whatever, to chill the ardour, to break the continuity, or divert the completion of my literary pursuits.

The second letter gives other and more definite information. First, and this is important as showing the state of mind out of which *Lycidas* grew, he is struck by the longing for immortality. He writes:

> You ask what I am meditating? By the help of Heaven, an immortality of fame. But what am I doing? πτεροφυῶ, I am letting my wings grow and preparing to fly; but my Pegasus has not yet feathers enough to soar aloft in the fields of air.

Of the restlessness or rather mental anguish which *Lycidas* proves to have resulted at times from this longing he indeed states nothing; but he admits that he is tired of Horton and is thinking of a move to London.

From *Milton* (London, 1930), 79–85.

> I will now tell you seriously what I design: to take chambers
> in one of the inns of court, where I may have the benefit of a
> pleasant and shady walk; and where with a few associates I may
> enjoy more comfort when I choose to stay at home, and have
> more elegant society when I choose to go abroad. In my present
> situation you know in what obscurity I am buried, and to what
> inconveniences I am exposed.

A cause for restlessness, particularly in the mind of one who had
nearly finished a long period of preparation for some great work,
was that in 1636 and 1637 the plague had been bad in England.
In the latter year it spread to Horton, and a number of people
there died of it. This is a fact to be remembered in reading
Lycidas.

Lycidas is the last and greatest English poem of Milton's
youth. Though shorter, it is greater than *Comus*, written with
newly won but complete mastery and expressing a mental experience both valuable and profound.

Most criticism of *Lycidas* is off the mark, because it fails to
distinguish between the nominal and the real subject, what the
poem professes to be about and what it is about. It assumes that
Edward King is the real, whereas he is but the nominal subject.
Fundamentally *Lycidas* concerns Milton himself; King is but
the excuse for one of Milton's most personal poems. This cannot
be proved: it can only be deduced from the impression the poem
leaves. Most readers agree that Milton was not deeply grieved
at King's death, as they agree that the poem is great. If it is
great, it must contain deep feeling of some sort. What then is
this deep feeling all about?

From the circumstances in which *Lycidas* was written and
from the two obviously personal passages the question can be
answered. When Milton wrote *Lycidas* in 1637 he was twenty-nine
years of age, and early in the next year he set out for Italy with
perhaps the intention of going on to Greece. Whether the last
line of the poem,

> To morrow to fresh Woods, and Pastures new.

refers to this intended journey is doubtful; it may well do so.
Anyhow at the time of writing *Lycidas* Milton must have had the
Italian and possibly the Greek journey in his mind. When he
heard of King's death, and still more when by consenting to

write the elegy he had to make his mind dwell on it, he cannot
but have felt the analogy between King and himself. Milton and
King had been at the same college in the same university. Their
careers and interests had been similar there. Milton was a poet,
King had written verse too. King had made a voyage on the sea,
Milton was about to make voyages. How could Milton have
missed the idea that *he* might make the analogy complete by getting drowned, like King, also? At a time when, through plagues
and what not, life was less secure than in modern times of peace,
Milton, having sacrificed so much to his great ambition, must
anyhow, as the time of preparation drew to an end, have dwelt
on the thought that it might be all for nothing. Not that he was
a coward: but the fear that his ambitions might be ruined at
the last moment must have been at times difficult to endure.
Those who had experience of the late war must have known the
miserable anxiety suffered immediately before going on leave.
It was not that people feared to die more then than at other
times, but the thought of being baulked by death of their desire
for home was peculiarly harrowing. Milton's state of mind must
at times have been somewhat similar, and in considering King's
fate his fears must have come crowding on him. That he was at
least partly thinking of his own possible fate is made clear by
the reference in the first paragraph to his own destined urn and
sable shroud. As a reason for his singing of Lycidas he writes:

> So may som gentle Muse
> With lucky words favour my destin'd Urn,
> And as he passes turn,
> And bid fair peace be to my sable shrowd,
> For we were nurst upon the self-same hill,
> Fed the same flock, by fountain, shade, and rill.

In other words, "If I die, some one will requite me with a requiem,
for in other ways the analogy between us was complete." And
much more agonizingly does the thought of premature death
start in his mind when he writes of poetic fame and "the blind
Fury with th' abhorred shears." Why should he have submitted
himself to rigorous self-denial, if to no end?

But his fears of premature death, though part of the subject,
are not the whole. The real subject is the resolving of those fears

(and of his bitter scorn of the clergy) into an exalted state of mental calm. The apotheosis of Lycidas in the penultimate paragraph has a deeper meaning: it symbolizes Milton's own balanced state of mind to which he won after the torments he had been through. This is the secret of the strength of *Lycidas* and the reason why it is a greater poem than *Comus:* in the one calm after struggle, in the other calm of a kind but without the preliminary struggle. To prove that the deepest and most satisfying calm is that which follows on mental struggle one has only to point to the greatest tragedies.

If the above idea is accepted, it is possible to see in *Lycidas* a unity of purpose which cannot be seen in it if the death of King is taken as the real subject of the poem. In particular the outburst against the clergy, usually regarded as a glorious excrescence, will be found perfectly in keeping with the profounder and less elegiac significance of the whole. Let me try to explain this harmony by describing how the purpose of the poem develops.

Milton begins with characteristic egotism. His first lines do not concern King but his own reluctance to write a poem before he is mature. But he must write, for Lycidas died prematurely —"*Young* Lycidas"—and for a premature death he must be willing to risk premature poetry. Moreover, if he writes an elegy for Lycidas, some other poet may reward him when he dies with an elegy too. The introduction, lines 1 to 24, thus ends on Milton's possible death.

The first section, beginning "Together both, ere the high Lawns appear'd," consists of lines 25 to 84. It contains a lament for the death of Lycidas, regret that the Muse could not protect her son, and leads up to the first great cause of pain in Milton's own mind: the risk of death before his great work is completed. What has been the use of all his laborious preparation, his careful chastity (for doubtless he means this by his references to Amaryllis and Neaera), if fame, for whose sake he has denied himself, is to escape him, anticipated by death? Earthly fame, he replies to himself in the person of Phoebus, has nothing to do with heavenly fame: it depends on deeds, not on what those deeds effect. So he argues, but one does not get the impression of emotional conviction yet: the final impression of the first section is that it would be a cruel shame and a wicked waste, if he were

to die. It should be noted with what consummate skill Milton
in this section works the subject from King to its climax in himself.

In the second section, lines 85 to 131, beginning "O Fountain
Arethuse," he does exactly the same thing. In the elegiac tradition various persons come to visit the body. It is perfectly
natural that St. Peter should come to visit a priest, and equally
natural that he should proceed from lamenting the death of a
good priest to denouncing the bad. But this denunciation reveals
the second great cause of mental pain in Milton: his quarrel
with contemporary Englind, typified by the rottenness of the
clergy. Thus St. Peter's outburst is not an excrescence but
strictly parallel with Milton's earlier outburst about the blind
Fury. One can even see a close connection of ideas between the
two grievances. One grievance is that "the hungry Sheep look
up and are not fed": England has bad or useless teachers;
the other is that he, Milton, whose ambition was to teach by
writing a great epic, to feed the hungry sheep of England, may
easily be cut off before it can be realized. It should be noted
that the second grievance, like the first, is answered at the end
of the second movement. Punishment is waiting; the two-handed
engine stands ready to smite. But even less than at the end of the
first section has mental calm been attained. The end of the second section marks the climax of the poem. Milton has stated
his quarrel with life: we await the conclusion.

Of the third section, lines 132 to 164, beginning "Return
Alpheus," it is more difficult to describe the function. Some
quieter interlude is clearly necessary between St. Peter's bitter
outburst and the heavenly triumph of the final movement. But
it is more than an interlude, it has value as a transition too. The
sudden change from the terror of the two-handed engine to the
incredible beauty of the description of the flowers contains an
implication that somehow the "Dorique delicacy," of which the
description of the flowers is the highest example in Milton, is
not irreconcilable with the sterner mood, and hence is able to
insinuate some comfort. So too from the dallying with a false
surmise, the escape into a region of pure romance

> Where the great vision of the guarded Mount
> Looks toward *Namancos* and *Bayona's* hold,

some comfort is allowed. But these sources of comfort are but
minor, leading up to the greater solution.

The fourth section purports to describe the resurrection of
Lycidas and his entry into heaven. More truly it solves the
whole poem by describing the resurrection into a new kind of
life of Milton's hopes, should they be ruined by premature death
or by the moral collapse of his country. The loss or possible
loss of human fame is made good by fame in heaven, the corrupt
clergy are balanced by

> all the Saints above
> In solemn troops and sweet Societies,

and the harsh forebodings of Peter, the pilot of the Galilean
lake, are **forgotten**

> Through the dear might of him who walk'd the waves.

But above all the fourth section describes the renunciation of
earthly fame, the abnegation of self by the great egotist, and the
spiritual purgation of gaining one's life after losing it.

Some people might call *Lycidas* a religious poem, for Milton
appears to found his comfort on his hopes of heaven: others
might object that his grounds of comfort are extraordinarily
flimsy and that the pessimism of *Paradise Lost* is truer to the
facts of life than the optimism of *Lycidas*. But the question of
beliefs is unimportant; what matters and what makes *Lycidas*
one of the greatest poems in English is that it expresses with
success a state of mind whose high value can hardly be limited
to a particular religious creed. Milton, by ridding himself of
his inhibiting fears, by subordinating the disturbing ambition
to have done a thing to the serene intention of doing it as well
as possible, had proved his mettle and issued from the ordeal a
great man. *Lycidas* expresses a mind of the keenest sensibility
and most powerful grasp acutely aware of a number of most
moving sensations, but controlling these sensations so that they
do not conflict but rather by contrast reinforce one another: a
mind calm after struggle but keyed up to perform heroic deeds,
should they need to be done.

A Poem Nearly Anonymous

John Crowe Ransom

It was published in 1638, in the darkness preceding our incomparable modernity. Its origins were about as unlikely as they could be, for it was only one of the exhibits in a memorial garland, a common academic sort of volume. It appeared there without a title and signed only by a pair of initials, though now we know it both by a name and by an author. Often we choose to think of it as the work of a famous poet, which it was not; done by an apprentice of nearly thirty, who was still purifying his taste upon an astonishingly arduous diet of literary exercises; the fame which was to shine backwards upon this poem, and to be not very different from the fame which he steadily intended, being as distant as it was great. Unfortunately it is one of the poems which we think we know best. Upon it is imposed the weight of many perfect glosses, respecting its occasion, literary sources, classical and contemporary allusions, exhausting us certainly and exhausting, for a good many persons, the poem. But I am bound to consider that any triteness which comes to mind with mention of the poem is a property of our own registration, and does not affect its freshness, which is perennial. The poem is young, brilliant, insubordinate. In it is an artist who wrestles with an almost insuperable problem, and is kinsman to some tortured modern artists. It has something in common

From *The World's Body* (New York, 1938), pp. 1–28; first published in the *American Review*, IV (1933).

with, for example, *The Waste Land*. In short, the poem is *Lyc-idas*.

A symbol is a great convenience in discussion, and therefore I will find one in the half-way anonymity of the poem; symbolic of the poet's admirable understanding of his art, and symbolic of the tradition that governed the art on the whole in one of its flourishing periods. Anonymity, of some real if not literal sort, is a condition of poetry. A good poem, even if it is signed with a full and well-known name, intends as a work of art to lose the identity of the author; that is, it means to represent him not actualized, like an eyewitness testifying in court and held strictly by zealous counsel to the point at issue, but freed from his juridical or prose self and taking an ideal or fictitious personality; otherwise his evidence amounts the less to poetry. Poets may go to universities and, if they take to education, increase greatly the stock of ideal selves into which they may pass for the purpose of being poetical. If on the other hand they insist too narrowly on their own identity and their own story, inspired by a simple but mistaken theory of art, they find their little poetic fountains drying up within them. Milton set out to write a poem mourning a friend and poet who had died; in order to do it he became a Greek shepherd, mourning another one. It was not that authority attached particularly to the discourse of a Greek shepherd; the Greek shepherd in his own person would have been hopeless; but Milton as a Greek shepherd was delivered from being Milton the scrivener's son, the Master of Arts from Cambridge, the handsome and finicky young man, and that was the point. In proceeding to his Master's degree he had made studies which gave him dramatic insight into many parts foreign to his own personal experience; which was precisely the technical resource he had required the moment he determined to be a poet. Such a training was almost the regular and unremarked procedure with the poets of his time. Today young men and women, as noble as Milton, those in university circles as much as those out of them, try to become poets on another plan, and with rather less success. They write their autobiographies, following perhaps the example of Wordsworth, which on the whole may have been unfortunate for the prosperity of the art; or they write some of their intenser experiences, their loves, pities, griefs, and religious ecstasies; but too literally, faithfully, piously, ingenuously. They seem to want to do without wit and playfulness, dramatic sense, detachment, and it cuts them off from the practice of an art.

Briefly, it was Milton's intention to be always anonymous as a poet, rarely as a writer of prose. The poet must suppress the man, or the man would suppress the poet. What he wanted to say for himself, or for his principles, became eligible for poetry only when it became what the poet, the dramatis persona so to speak, might want to say for himself. The poet could not be directed to express faithfully and pointedly the man; nor was it for the sake of "expression" that the man abdicated in favor of the poet.

Strictly speaking, this may be a half-truth. But if we regard with a reformer's eye the decay, in our time, of poetry, it becomes almost the whole truth we are called to utter. I do not mind putting it flatly; nor drawing the conclusion that poetry appeared to the apprentice Milton, before it could appear anything else, and before it could come into proper existence at all, as a sort of exercise, very difficult, and at first sight rather beside the point. It was of course an exercise in pure linguistic technique, or metrics; it was also an exercise in the technique of what our critics of fiction refer to as "point of view." And probably we shall never find a better locus than *Lycidas* for exhibiting at once the poet and the man, the technique and the personal interest, bound up tightly and contending all but equally; the strain of contraries, the not quite resolvable dualism, that is art.

For we must begin with a remark quite unsuitable for those moderns to whom "expression" seems the essential quality of poetry. *Lycidas* is a literary exercise; and so is almost any other poem earlier than the eighteenth century; the craftsmanship, the formal quality which is written on it, is meant to have high visibility. Take elegy, for example. According to the gentle and extremely masculine tradition which once governed these matters, performance is not rated by the rending of garments, heartbreak, verisimilitude of desolation. After all, an artist is standing before the public, and bears the character of a qualified spokesman, and a male. Let him somewhat loudly sweep the strings, even the tender human ones, but not without being almost military and superficial in his restraint; like the pomp at the funeral of the king, whom everybody mourns publicly and nobody privately. Milton made a great point of observing the proprieties of verse. He had told Diodati, as plainly as Latin elegiacs allowed, that "expression" was not one of the satisfactions which they permitted to the poet: "You want to know in verse how much I love and cherish you; believe me that you will scarcely discover this in verse, for love like ours is not contained within cold measures, it does not come to hobbled feet." As for memorial verse, he had already written, in English or Latin, for the University beadle, the University carrier, the Vice-Chancellor, his niece the Fair Infant Dying of a Cough, the Marchioness of Winchester, the Bishop of Winchester, the Bishop of Ely; he was yet to write for his Diodati, and for Mrs. Katharine Thomason. All these poems are exercises, and some are very playful indeed. There is no great raw grief apparent ever, and sometimes, very likely, no great grief. For Lycidas he mourns with a very technical piety.

Let us go directly to the poem's metre—though this feature may seem a bristling technicality, and the sort of thing the tender reader may think he ought to be spared. I do not wish to be brutal, but I am afraid that metre is fundamental in the problem posed to the artist as poet. During the long apprenticeship Milton was the experimentalist, trying nearly everything. He does not ordinarily, in the Minor Poems, repeat himself metrically; another poem means another metre, and the new metre will scarcely satisfy him any better than the last one did. Evidently Milton never found the metre in which as a highly individual poet he could feel easy, and to which he was prepared to entrust his serious work, until he had taken the ragged blank verse of contemporary drama and had done something to it; tightening it up into a medium which was hard enough to exhibit form, and plastic enough to give him freedom. In other words, it defined the poet as somebody with a clipped, sonorous, figurative manner of speaking; but it also gave a possible if indirect utterance to the natural man. Here let us ask the question always in order against a Milton poem: What was the historic metrical pattern already before him, and what are the liberties he takes with it? For he does not cut patterns out of the whole cloth, but always takes an existing pattern; stretches it dangerously close to the limits that the pattern will permit without ceasing to be a pattern; and never brings himself to the point of defying that restraint which patterns inflict upon him, and composing something

altogether unpatterned. That is to say, he tends habitually towards the formlessness which is modern, without quite caring to
arrive at that destination. It is the principle we are interested
in, not the literal answer to the question, which I will try to get
over briefly.

The answer given by the Milton scholars, those who know
their Italian, might well be that in this poem he made a very
free adaptation of the canzone. This was a stanza of indeterminate length, running it might be to twenty lines or so, marked
by some intricate rhyming scheme, and by a small number of
six-syllable lines inserted among the ten-syllable lines which constituted the staple. The poet was free to make up his own stanza
but, once that was given, had to keep it uniform throughout
the poem. Milton employs it with almost destructive freedom, as
we shall see. Yet, on the other hand, the correct stanza materials
are there, and we can at least say that any one of the stanzas
or paragraphs might make a passable canzone. And lest his ir-
regularities be imputed to incompetence, we must observe the
loving exactitude of his line-structure, that fundamental unit
of any prosody, within the stanzas. He counts his syllables, he
takes no liberties there: consisting with our rather fixed impression that he scarcely knew how in all his poetry to admit an imperfect line.

The Milton scholars know their Italian and have me at a dis-
advantage. Milton knew his Italian. But he also knew his Spenser,
and knowing that, it seems unnecessary to inquire whether he
knew his Italian too; for he had only to adapt a famous Spenserian stanza, and his acquaintance with the canzone becomes really
immaterial. I imagine this point has a slight importance. It
would have something to do with the problem of the English
poet who wants to employ an English technique in addressing
himself to an English public which can be expected to know its
English formal tradition. Spenser anticipated Milton by employing the canzone effectively in at least two considerable poems;
they were not elegies, but at least they were marriage hymns. In
1596 he published his *Prothalamion*, upon the occasion of a
noble alliance; the stanzas are exactly uniform, and they compose an admirable exercise in Italian canzoni. But he had published in 1595 his *Epithalamion*, upon the occasion of his own
wedding, which is much more to Milton's purpose, and ours.

Here are ten eighteen-line stanzas, but here are also twelve nine-
teen-line stanzas, and one of seventeen lines; and one of the
eighteen-line stanzas does not agree in pattern with the others.
If these details escape the modern reader, it is not at all certain
that they were missed by Spenser's public. I should like to think
that the poetical consciousness of the aristocratic literati of
that age was a state of mind having metrical form in its foreground, and Spenser intended frankly to make use of the situation. Perhaps he calculated that if they would go to the trouble
to analyze a poem composed of intricate but regular canzoni,
they might go to still greater pains to analyze a poem whose
canzoni were subtly irregular. I suppose this was something of
a miscalculation, like other of his plans. But if it were a just
calculation: then the advantage to be reaped by their going to
such pains—it was their advantage as much as his—was the
sort of addition to total effect which a labor of love can furnish.
A public like Spenser's, if we are to construe it at its best, participates in the poem as does the author, and it is unfortunate if
there lives today some modern Spenser who does not hope for
such a reward to his efforts. But probably the sad truth is that
a subtle art is unlikely in the first place, whose artist does not
reckon upon the background of a severe technical tradition, and
the prospect of a substantial public body of appreciation.

The enterprising Spenser prepared the way for the daring
Milton, who remarks the liberties which his celebrated exemplar
has taken and carries his own liberties further, to a point just
this side of anarchy. The eleven stanzas of *Lycidas* occupy 193
lines, but are grossly unequal and unlike. Such stanzas are not
in strictness stanzas at all; Milton has all but scrapped the
stanza in its proper sense as a formal and binding element. But
there is perhaps an even more startling lapse. Within the poem
are ten lines which do not rhyme at all, and which technically
do not belong therefore in any stanza, nor in the poem.

Now we may well imagine that the unrhymed lines did not
escape Milton's notice, and also that he did not mean nor hope
that they should escape ours. The opening line of the poem is
unrhymed, which is fair warning. The ten unrhymed lines should
be conspicuous among the 183 rhymed ones, like so many bache-
lors at a picnic of fast-mated families. Let us ask what readers
of *Lycidas* have detected them, and we shall see what readers

are equipped with the right sensibility for an effect in form. And if the effect in this case is an effect of prose formlessness, and if nevertheless it is deliberate, we had better ask ourselves what Milton wanted with it.

It is tempting to the imperious individualism of the modern reader, especially if he has heard somewhere about the enormous egoism of John Milton, to say that the "expression" in these lines must have seemed to their author "inevitable," and superior to any obligation to the law of the form. Just as we find them, they had leapt out of the tense creative fury of the poet, notable, possibly prophetic; and what higher considerations were there anywhere requiring him in cold blood to alter them? But that does not make sense as an account of the poetic processes of a Milton. The ten lines, as it happens, look at them hard as we like, do not seem more important than ten others, and are not the lines by which he could have set special store. As a matter of fact, he might have altered them easily, tinkering with them as long as necessary in order to bring them within the metre, and they would scarcely have been, by whatever standard, any the worse. So great is the suggestibility of the poet's mind, the associability of ideas, the margin in the meaning of words. It is the inexperienced artist who attributes sanctity to some detail of his inspiration. You may ask him to write a poem which will make sense and make metre at the same time, but in the performance he will sacrifice one or the other; the consequence will be good sense and lame metre, or good metre and nonsense; if he is a man of interests and convictions, the former. But the competent artist is as sure of his second thoughts as of his first ones. In fact, surer, if anything; second thoughts tend to be the richer, for in order to get them he has to break up the obvious trains of association and explore more widely. Milton was not enamored of the ten lines, and they stand out from their context by no peculiar quality of their own but only because they do not belong to it metrically. Therefore I would say that they constitute the gesture of his rebellion against the formalism of his art, but not the rebellion itself. They are defiances, showing the man unwilling to give way to the poet; they are not based upon a special issue but upon surliness, and general principles. It is a fateful moment. At this critical stage in the poet's career, when he has come to the end of the period of Minor Poems, and is turn-

ing over in his head the grand subjects out of which he will produce great poems, he is uneasy, sceptical, about the whole foun-
dation of poetry as an art. He has a lordly contempt for its
tedious formalities, and is determined to show what he can do
with only half trying to attend to them. Or he thinks they are
definitely bad, and proposes to see if it is not better to shove
them aside.

In this uncertainty he is a modern poet. In the irregular stanzas and the rhymeless lines is registered the ravage of his modernity; it has bit into him as it never did into Spenser. And we
imagine him thinking to himself, precisely like some modern poets
we know, that he could no longer endure the look of perfect
regimentation which sat upon the poor ideas objectified before
him upon the page of poetry, as if that carried with it a reflection
upon their sincerity. I will go further. It is not merely easy for
a technician to write in smooth metres; it is perhaps easier than
to write in rough ones, after he has once started; but when he
has written smoothly, and contemplates his work, he is capable
actually, if he is a modern poet, of going over it laboriously and
roughening it. I venture to think that just such a practice, speaking very broadly, obtained in the composition of *Lycidas;* that
it was written smooth and rewritten rough; which was treason.

I will make a summary statement which is true to the best of
my knowledge. There did not at the time anywhere exist in English, among the poems done by competent technical poets, another poem so wilful and illegal in form as this one.

An art never possesses the "sincerity" that consists in speaking one's mind, that is, in expressing one's first impression before
it has time to grow cold. This sincerity is spontaneity, the most
characteristic quality in modern poetry. Art is long, and time
is fleeting, and we have grown too impatient to relish more than
the first motions towards poetic effect. The English and American Imagists exploited and consolidated this temper, which was
no longer hospitable to a finished art. In their defence it may be
said with justice that the writing of formal poetry, which they
interrupted, was becoming a tedious parlor performance in which
the poet made much ado about saying nothing of importance,
while the man behind him quite escaped acquaintance through
sheer lack of force. The verslibrists were determined to be bright,
and fresh, and innocent of deep and ulterior designs; but their

prose art was an anomaly. It wore out, and strict artistic economy has had a certain recovery; nothing like a complete one,
for they left their mark upon our poetry, and I shall certainly
not be so dogmatic as to say it has been entirely unfortunate.

It depends ultimately on taste whether we prefer prose to
poetry, or prefer even a mixture of prose and poetry. Let us
suppose two gentlemen talking a little wildly over their cups,
until Mr. *A* insults Mr. *B*. Now if *B* is a modern man, he immediately strikes *A* down, with his knife if it happens to be in
in his hand, or his stick, or his fist. He has acted spontaneously,
with a right and quick instinct, and he is admired for it. (I do
not mean to raise any moral issues with my analogy.) But if
the time is about a century or two earlier, *B* steps back and says
drily: "My seconds will wait upon you, Sir." The next dawn *A*
and *B* repair to the grove, attended by their respective partisans,
draw their rapiers, and with great ceremony set in to kill each
other. Or apparently they do; but if they are not really prepared to be hurt, nor to hurt each other, but are only passing
the time until they are informed that their honors are satisfied,
it is a bogus and ineffective action and the serious spectators
feel cheated; that represents the sort of art against which the
free versifiers revolted. If they fight till *A* puts his steel through
the vitals of *B*, or vice versa, the spectators are well rewarded,
and the ceremonial has justified itself, though it took time; that
stands for the true art. But if they lose their tempers on the
field and begin to curse, and kick, and throw stones and clods
at each other, they are behaving too spontaneously for a formal
occasion. Why were they not spontaneous yesterday if that was
their intention? They will have to be recalled to the occasion and
come to a conclusion under the terms nominated; and here we
have the mixed affair of poetry and prose, a problem in taste;
here, I am afraid, we have *Lycidas*.

At any rate Milton thought something of the kind. For he
never repeated his bold experiment; and he felt at the time that
it was not an altogether successful experiment. The last stanzas
become much more patterned, and in the postscript Milton refers
to the whole monody as the song of an "uncouth Swain," who
has been "with eager thought warbling his *Dorick* lay." That is
descriptive and deprecatory.

There is another possibility. Milton had much of the modern

poet's awareness of his public; in this case the awareness of a public not quite capable of his own sustained artistic detachment. What sort of poem would it like? Too perfect an art might look cold and dead; and though an elegy had to be about the dead, it did not want itself to look dead, but to display incessant energy. So he read the formal poem he had written, and deformed it; or he had read other formal poems, like the *Epithalamion*, and remarked that the public, an increasingly mixed lot, thought them a little dull, and he now, as he composed his own poem, remembered to write into it plenty of formlessness. "The formalism," he was thinking, "if unrelieved, will dull the perceptions of my reader, and unprepare him for my surprises, and my tireless fertility. Therefore let him sense an exciting combat between the artist and the man, and let the man interrupt with his prose (comparative prose) the pretty passages of the artist." In that case the artist was only pretending to give way to the man, calculating with the cunning of a psychologist, perhaps of a dramatist, and violating the law of his art entirely for its public effect; a Jesuit of an artist. But the Jesuit, according to the Protestant tradition which reaches me, and which I will trust to the extent of this argument, has an excessive respect for the depravity of the humanity he ministers to, and he needs beyond other priests to be firmly grounded in his principles, lest from fighting the devil with fire he change his own element insensibly, become himself a fallen angel, and bear the reputation of one. The best thing to say for Milton is that his principles were strong, and he did not again so flagrantly betray them.

But if the poem is a literary exercise, it does not consist only in a game of metrical hide-and-seek, played between the long lines and short lines, the rhymed and unrhymed. It is also a poem in a certain literary "type," with conventions of subject-matter and style. Milton set out to make it a pastoral elegy, and felt honor-bound to use the conventions which had developed in the pastoral elegies of the Greeks, of Virgil, of the Italians, of Spenser; possibly of the French. The course of the poem in outline therefore is not highly "creative," but rather commonplace and in order, when the dead shepherd is remembered and his virtues published; when nature is made to lament him, and the streams to dry up in sympathy; when the guardian nymphs are asked why they have not saved him; when the untimeliness of his doom is moralized; when the corrupt church is reproached; when the flowers are gathered for the hearse; and finally when it appears to the mourners that they must cease, since he is not dead, but translated into a higher region, where he lives in bliss of a not definitive sort. In the pastoral elegy at large one of my friends distinguishes eleven different topics of discourse, and points out that Milton, for doubtless the first time in this literature, manages to "drag them all into one poem"; a distinction for him, though perhaps a doubtful one. But in doing so he simply fills up the poem; there are no other topics in it. And where is Milton the individualist, whose metrical departures would seem to have advertised a performance which in some to-be-unfolded manner will be revolutionary?

When we attempt to define the poetic "quality" of this poet's performances, we are forced to confess that it consists largely in pure eclecticism; here is a poet who can simply lay more of his predecessors under tribute than another. This is not to deny that he does a good job of it. He assimilates what he receives, and adapts it infallibly to the business in hand, where scraps fuse into integer, and the awkward articulations cannot be detected. His second-hand effects are not as good as new but better; the features of pastoral elegy are not as pretty in *Lycidas* as they were in Moschus, or Virgil, or Spenser, but prettier; though generically, and even in considerable detail, the same features. We remember after all that Milton intended his effects; and among others, this one of indebtedness to models. He expected that the reader should observe his eclecticism, he was scarcely alarmed lest it be mistaken for plagiarism. It is because of something mean in our modernism, or at least in that of our critics, that we, if we had composed the poem, would have found such an expectancy tainted with such an alarm. Like all the artists of the Renaissance, Milton hankered honestly after "Fame"; but he was not infected with our gross modern concept of "originality." The æsthetic of this point is perfectly rational. If a whole series of artists in turn develop the same subject, it is to the last one's advantage that he may absorb the others, in addition to being in whatever pointed or subtle manner his own specific self. His work becomes the climax of a tradition, and is better than the work of an earlier artist in the series. Unfortunately, there will come perhaps the day when there is no artist prepared to carry on the tradition; or, more simply, when the tradition has gone far enough and is not worth carrying further; that is, when it is worn out as a "heuristic" principle, and confines more than it frees the spirit. (Very few pastoral elegies can have been written since *Lycidas* in our language; very few critics can have deplored this.) On that day the art will need its revolutionist, to start another tradition. It is a bold step for the artist to take, and Milton did not think it needful to take it here. The revolutionist who does not succeed must descend to the rating, for history, of rebel; the fool of a wrong political intuition.

But revolutions, for all that, little and private ones if not big and general ones, come frequently into a healthy literary history, in which variety is a matter of course. The poet may do better with a make-believe of his own than with a time-honored one. There is no theoretical limit upon the variety of literary types, and each good type permits of many explorers, but tends at last to be exhausted. The point of view of Greek shepherds, as romantic innocents and rustics, is excellent, and offers a wide range of poetic discourse concerning friendship, love, nature, and even, a startling innovation of the Italian pastoralists, the "ruin of the clergy." The point of view of the amorous cavalier presenting his compliments and reproaches to his lady is also a good one; it ran through many hundreds of lyrics in the sixteenth and seventeenth centuries, and is still better than no point of view at all, which we find in some very young poet speaking in his own person to his own love. The studied "conceit" of the seventeenth century offered another field of discourse in which poetic exercises took place; logical and academic, but having rich possibilities, and eligible even for religious experiences. The sonnet is primarily a metrical form, but behind it there is an ideal and rather formidable speaker, far from actual, who must get what he has to say into a very small space and, according to the rules, into a very concise style of utterance. The ballad offers a point of view quite alien to the ordinary cultivated poet, because speaking in that form he must divest himself of the impedimenta of learning and go primitive. All these forms lend themselves to individual variations and innovations; call for them, in fact, in the course of time, when the poet can find no fresh experience within the usual thing. It is entirely according to the æsthetic of this art if a poet wants to enter the book of literature with a series of Choctaw incantations, provided he is steeped in Choctaw experience and able to make a substantial exhibit; or with a set of poems from the character of a mere Shropshire lad; or from that of a dry New England countryman. It is important mostly that the poet know his part and speak it fluently.

Of Milton's "style," in the sense of beauty of sound, imagery, syntax and dystax, idiom, I am quite unprepared to be very analytic. It is a grand style; which is to say, I suppose, that it is *the* grand style, or as much a grand style as English poets have known: the style produced out of the poet's remembrance of his classical models, chiefly Virgil. Milton has not been the only English poet to learn from Virgil, but he is doubtless the one who learned the most. Until the nineteenth century Virgil was perhaps the greatest external influence upon English literature. Dryden venerated but could not translate him:

> . . . must confess to my shame, that I have not been able to Translate any part of him so well, as to make him appear wholly like himself. For where the Original is close, no Version can reach it in the same compass. Hannibal Caro's, in the Italian, is the nearest, the most Poetical, and the most Sonorous of any Translation of the Æneid's; yet, though he takes the advantage of blank Verse, he commonly allows two lines for one of Virgil, and does not always hit his sence. . . . Virgil, therefore, being so very sparing of his words, and leaving so much to be imagined by the Reader, can never be translated as he ought, in any modern Tongue. To make him Copious, is to alter his Character; and to translate him Line for Line is impossible; because the Latin is naturally a more succinct Language than either the Italian, Spanish, French, or even than the English (which, by reason of its Monosyllables, is far the most compendious of them). Virgil is much the closest of any Roman Poet, and the Latin Hexameter has more Feet than the English Heroick.

But in spite of the unfitness of an uninflected language like English, poets have occasionally managed a Virgilian style in it. We think at once of Marlowe. Naturally, it was not entirely beyond Shakespeare's powers; but Shakespeare at his highest pitch likes to rely on fury and hyperbole rather than the "smoothness" and "majesty" which Dryden commends in Virgil. Shakespeare writes:

> Rumble thy bellyful! Spit, fire! Spout, rain!

and

> You sulphurous and thought-executing fires,
> Vaunt-couriers of oak-cleaving thunderbolts,
> Singe my white head!

which is in a sublime style but not, if we care to be precise, the grand style. But Milton very nearly commanded this style. And with reason; for he had written Minor Poems in Latin as well as Minor Poems in English, and they were perhaps the more important item in his apprenticeship. This is one of the consequences:

> But now my Oate proceeds,
> And listens to the Herald of the Sea,
> That came in *Neptune's* plea,
> He ask'd the Waves, and ask'd the Fellon winds,
> What hard mishap hath doom'd this gentle swain?
> And question'd every gust of rugged wings
> That blows from off each beaked Promontory,
> They knew not of his story,
> And sage *Hippotades* their answer brings,
> That not a blast was from his dungeon stray'd,
> The Ayr was calm, and on the level brine,
> Sleek *Panope* with all her sisters play'd.
> It was that fatall and perfidious Bark
> Built in th' eclipse, and rigg'd with curses dark,
> That sunk so low that sacred head of thine.

It is probable that no other English poet has this mastery of the Virgilian effect; it is much more Virgilian, too, than the later effect which Milton has in the lines of the *Paradise Lost*, where the great departure from the epical substance of the Virgil makes it needful to depart from the poetic tone. But Milton proves here that he had fairly mastered it. He had simply learned to know it in the Latin—learning by the long way of performance as well as by the short one of observation—and then transferred it to his native English; where it becomes a heightened effect, because this language is not accustomed at once to ease and condensation like this, and there is little competition. The great repute of the Miltonic style—or styles, variants of a style—in our literature is a consequence of the scarcity of Miltons; that is, of poets who have mastered the technique of Latin poetry before they have turned to their own.

But the author of *Lycidas*, attended into his project by so much of the baggage of tradition, cannot, by a universal way of thinking, have felt, exactly, free. I shall risk saying that he was not free. Little chance there for him to express the interests, the causes, which he personally and powerfully was developing; the poem too occasional and too formal for that. Of course the occasion was a fundamental one, it was no less than Death; and there is nobody so aggressive and self-assured but he must come to terms with that occasion. But a philosophy of death seems mostly to nullify, with its irony, the philosophy of life. Milton was yet very much alive, and in fact he regarded himself as having scarcely begun to live. The poem is almost wasted if we are seeking to determine to what extent it permitted Milton to unburden his heart.

But not quite. The passage on mortality is tense; Professor Tillyard finds the man in it. It goes into a passage on the immortality of the just man's Fame, which gives Milton's Platonic version of the ends of Puritanism. More important perhaps is the kind of expressiveness which appears in the speech of Peter. The freedom with which Milton abuses the false shepherds surpasses anything which his predecessors in this vein had indulged. He drops his Latinity for plain speech, where he can express a Milton who is angry, violent, and perhaps a little bit vulgar. It is the first time in his career that we have seen in him a taste for writing at this level. With modern readers it may be greatly to his credit as a natural man that he can feel strongly and hit hard. Later, in the period of his controversial prose, we get more of it, until we have had quite enough of this natural man. In the *Paradise Lost* we will get some "strong" passages again, but they are not Milton's response to his own immediate situation, they are dramatically appropriate, and the persons and scenes of the drama are probably remote enough to bring the passages under the precise head of artistic effect. This may be thought to hold for *Lycidas*, since it is Peter speaking in a pastoral part, and Peter still represents his villains as shepherds; but I feel that Peter sounds like another Puritan zealot, and less than apostolic.

Before I offer some generalizations about the poet and his art, I wish to refer, finally, to a feature of *Lycidas* which critics have rarely mentioned, and which most readers of my acquaintance, I believe, have never noticed, but which is technically astonishing all the same, and ought to initiate an important speculation upon the intentions of this poet. Pastoral elegies are dramatic monologues, giving the words of a single shepherd upon a single occasion; or they are dialogues giving, like so much printed drama, the speeches of several shepherds in a single scene. They may have prologues, perhaps so denominated in the text, and printed in italics, or in a body separate from the elegy proper; and likewise epilogues; the prologues and epilogues being the author's envelope of narrative within which is inserted the elegy. The composition is straightforward and explicitly logical.

Milton's elegy is otherwise. It begins without preamble as a monologue, and continues so through the former and bitterer half of the passage on Fame:

> But the fair Guerdon when we hope to find,
> And think to burst out into sudden blaze,
> Comes the blind *Fury* with th'abhorred shears,
> And slits the thin spun life. . . .

At this point comes an incredible interpolation:

> . . . But not the praise,
> *Phœbus* repli'd, and touch'd my trembling ears . . .

And Phœbus concludes the stanza; after which the shepherd apologizes to his pastoral Muses for the interruption and proceeds with his monologue. But dramatic monologue has turned for a moment into narrative. The narrative breaks the monologue several times more, presenting action sometimes in the present tense, sometimes in the past. And the final stanza gives a pure narrative conclusion in the past, without the typographical separateness of an epilogue; it is the one which contains Milton's apology for the "Dorick" quality of his performance, and promises that the author will yet appear in a serious and mature light as he has scarcely done on this occasion.

Such a breach in the logic of composition would denote, in another work, an amateurism below the level of publication. I do not know whether our failure to notice it is because we have

been intoxicated by the wine of the poetry, or dulled by the drum-
fire of the scholars' glosses, or intimidated by the sense that the
poem is Milton's. Certainly it is Milton's; therefore it was intended; and what could have been in his mind? I have a suggestion. A feature that obeys the canon of logic is only the mere
instance of a universal convention, while the one that violates the
canon is an indestructibly private thing. The poor "instance"
would like so much to attain to the dignity of a particular. If
Milton had respected the rule of composition, he must have appeared as any other author of pastoral elegy, whereas in his
disrespect of it he can be the person, the John Milton who is
different, and dangerous, and very likely to become famous. (It
is ironical that the lapse in question celebrates Fame.) The logical difficulties in the work of an artist capable of perfect logic
may be the insignia of an individuality which would otherwise
have to be left to the goodness of the imagination; and that is
a calculation which lies, I think, under much modern art. There
are living poets, and writers of fiction, and critics at the service
of both, who have a perfect understanding of the principle. The
incoherence or "difficulty" in the work is not necessarily to be
attributed to the unresourcefulness of the artist, as if he could
not have straightened everything out if he had desired, but sometimes to his choice. Under this head comes that licentious typog-
raphy in which we may find one of the really magnificent mani-
festations of our modernity. The author is like some gentleman
in the world of fashion who is thoroughly initiated, yet takes
great pains to break the rule somewhere in order that nobody
will make the mistake of not remarking his personality. If there
is any force in this way of reasoning, we may believe that Milton's bold play with the forms of discourse constitutes simply
one more item in his general insubordinacy. He does not propose
to be buried beneath his own elegy. Now he had done a thing
somewhat on the order of the present breach in his *L'Allegro* and
Il Penseroso. There is a comparative simplicity to these pieces
amounting almost to obviousness, but they are saved in several
ways. For one thing, they are twin poems, and the parallelism or
contrast is very intricate. More to our point, there is a certain
lack of definition in the substantive detail: long sentences with
difficult grammatical references, and uncertainty as to whether
the invocation has passed into the action and as to just where

we are in the action. That trick was like the present one, indicating that the man is getting ahead of the poet, who is not being allowed to assimilate the matter into his formal style.

More accurately, of course, *they would like to indicate it;* the poet being really a party to the illusion. Therefore he lays himself open to the charge of being too cunning, and of overreaching himself; the effect is not heroic but mock-heroic. The excited Milton, breathless, and breaking through the logic of composition, is charming at first; but as soon as we are forced to reflect that he counterfeited the excitement, we are pained and let down. The whole poem is properly an illusion, but a deliberate and honest one, to which we consent, and through which we follow the poet because it enables him to do things not possible if he were presenting actuality. At some moments we may grow excited and tempted to forget that it is illusion, as the untrained spectator may forget and hiss the villain at the theatre. But we are quickly reminded of our proper attitude. If the author tends to forget, all the more if he pretends to forget, we would recall him to the situation too. Such license we do not accord to poets and dramatists, but only to novelists, whose art is young. And even these, or the best of these, seem now determined, for the sake of their artistic integrity, to surrender it.

So *Lycidas,* for the most part a work of great art, is sometimes artful and tricky. We are disturbingly conscious of a man behind the artist. But the critic will always find too many and too perfect beauties in it ever to deal with it very harshly.

The Primary Language
of *Lycidas*

Josephine Miles

A study of the primary language of *Lycidas* tells us some-thing of the poem's character. By "primary language," I mean the words of reference, the nouns, adjectives, and verbs most repeated throughout the poem; by "character" I mean relation of elements, both internal and external, both in entity and in context.

Repetition is at the heart of poetry; poetry's beats, its meas-ures, its assonances and alliterations, its rhymes and refrains, its repeated structures, all by their recurrence provide its mean-ingful pattern. Different poems repeat in different ways. In *Lyc-idas*, just the reference, in addition to sound and structure, takes at least three forms of repetition. It echoes for emphasis, *For Lycidas is dead, dead ere his prime.* It parallels for guid-ance to main points of view, as in the addresses, *Begin then, Sisters . . . , Where were ye Nymphs . . . , O Fountain Are-thuse . . . , Return Alpheus.* It recurs in less emphatic posi-tions, in new contexts, to establish the variation on the themes: *For Lycidas is dead . . . For Lycidas your sorrow is not dead.* Or, *. . . sunk so low that sacred head of thine . . . , Sunk*

From *The Primary Language of Poetry in the 1640s,* University of California Publications in English, XIX (1948), 86–90; revised for this book by the author.

*though he be beneath the watry floor . . . , So Lycidas sunk
low, but mounted high.* A look at some of these more subtle re-
currences will tell us not only of primary substance and shaping
structure but of the poem's place in the continuity of poetry.

Most of the repeated terms in *Lycidas* are of common importance for the poets of Milton's day, especially for that certain group which wrote in the line of the "Aureate" poets and
Spenser. Such are the terms like *gentle, old, high, sad, come, go,
lie, sing, hear, shepherd, flower, muse, power,* in the pastoral
tradition, and *eye, tear, dead, weep,* in the elegiac tradition.

Some, on the other hand, were brought into strong use first
by Milton, and these particularly help define the singularities
of *Lycidas: fresh, new, pure, sacred, green, watry, flood, leaf,
morn, hill, shade, shore, stream, star, wind, fame, ask, touch.*
What are the particular qualities of these words as a group?
They refer primarily to the natural world, in more specific and
sensory terms than were usual before Milton's time. They include an unusually large proportion of adjectives, and the adjectives name qualities of intensive value. The verbs are less
essential. The nouns establish a physical world of earth and
water freshly seen, and emphasized in contrast to star and sun
in the more spiritual world of the heavens. Like Satan in *Paradise Lost,* the physical bodily force of earth and water dominates
the inventive substance, then to be subdued by the triumph of
significant structure, the rising from low to high, from sea and
land to heaven, in the sun's motion of renewal. Like Adam and
Eve in *Paradise Lost,* the shepherd in *Lycidas* finally takes up
life on earth again in the light of his vision of heaven, in the
light of hope beyond earth, tomorrow, fresh, and new.

Let us see how this essential motion from low to high, paralleled by that from past to future, takes place through the primary characteristic words of the poem. The opening words *Yet
once more I come* become the completing *At last he rose.* The
plucked brown leaves of mourning become the twitched blue mantle of hope. The meed of some melodious tear becomes the nectar
pure of the blest kingdoms. The singing of Lycidas' own lofty
rhymes moves through the lofty meed of **fame granted by Jove,
to the singing of the nuptial song by the solemn troops and**
sweet societies of the blest kingdoms in their glory. The mem-

ories both pastoral and mythological, of old Damoetas, old
Bards, Bellerus old, become the reviews of Camus and St. Peter,
of false pastors and even of false pastures—valleys low, shades
and wanton winds, sad embroideries—as our frail thoughts
"dally with false surmise," until at last, presaged by "those pure
eyes and perfet witnes of all-judging *Jove*," the angel looks
homeward from the whelming tide, and Lycidas, sunk though
he be, rises like the day-star, "through the dear might of Him
that walk'd the waves," to preside from above as the good genius
of the shore. Even the shepherd, bound to the pastoral earth,
looks up and forward, to sun and hills, to the pastures of
tomorrow. *Fresh, high, new, pure, sacred*, are the especial terms
of value; *pure* and *sacred* both classical and Christian, *pure*
marking the two key passages of height, the classical and Christian heavens. The poem tries twice for what it achieves; first
in the words of Phoebus and Jove, that fame is no mortal plant;
then after a deeper pitch into despair of waters and of earth,
more triumphantly in the natural analogy of the sun and the
Christian terms of grace.

Two passages in the poem participate less than the rest in
the process of cumulative repetition. One is the procession of
guardians, Hippotades, Camus, and the Pilot of the Galilean
lake, with their special details of reference, especially those for
the false shepherd: lean and flashy songs, scrannel Pipes of
wretched straw, foul contagion, grim Wolf with privy paw, two-
handed engine. The other immediately follows, in ostensible contrast, the details of flowers, "so to interpose a little ease": honied
showers, rathe Primrose, pale Jessamine, Pansy freak'd with jet.
These two passages come between the climactic vision of fame in
the first mourning section and the final vision of recompense and
redemption in the last section. They make up the central portion, less closely patterned than the rest because, as an antis-
trophe, like a fourth act in a drama, they explore the counter-
forms of what the poem has been concerned with, the implications of the pastoral tradition in a world of spirit. Neither false
pastors nor surmised flowers redeem the physical pastoral world
of the human spirit; only as it looks higher is it redeemed and
reconciled.

These amplifying passages lead us to see another strong characteristic of Milton's language, its richness in adjectival quality. All the way through we have noted repeated nouns, adjectives, and verbs, but where there is least repetition and most variation the inventive variation in the adjectives is especially perceptible. If we try to define actual proportions, in order to corroborate this impression, we find that the poem uses about twelve adjectives, sixteen nouns, and nine verbs per ten lines; in other words, more adjectives than verbs, while most poetry in English uses more verbs than adjectives and proportionately more nouns. The quantitative power of adjectives in *Lycidas* supports the qualitative powers we have noted; namely, the use of recurring adjectives to emphasize structure and theme, the focus on a few key adjectives to carry the *fresh high pure* values of the poem, and the use of strong variety in a few passages of amplification.

When we suggest that Milton's use of repetition, especially his strong repetition of the adjective form, is characteristic not only because of its integral function in the poem itself but also because of its unusualness in English poetry, we move into the realm of comparison. As a unit, *Lycidas* is unique, incomparable, as is any individual work of art. But in its selection and arrangement of materials it may follow choices like or unlike those in other poems, and thus provide some basis for comparison, of elements and patterns if not of wholes. Indeed, comparison by contrast may heighten our perception of the individuality of the poem.

By mid-seventeenth century, few poems were so individual in their use of dominant and repeated language as *Lycidas*. Only one poet, Phineas Fletcher, out of some forty or fifty preceding Milton, had emphasized adjectives as Milton did. Of major terms, those most repeated, only about half in *Lycidas* were strongly traditional for poetry: the *dead, dear, old, eye, head, shepherd, power, heaven, flower,* and most of the verbs. Of the rest, a few had been stressed before by a special and limited group: *sad, gentle,* and *new* by Spenser and one or two followers; *sacred* and *muse,* by Sidney, Chapman, and a few other; a few echoes from the "aureate" fifteenth century. This emotional language was poetic language not in the more active traditions of Chaucer, Jonson, and Donne but in the more artful and æsthetic tradition of Spenser and Sidney, the poets most fond of pastoral. A few

lines from Spenser's *Astrophel*, the earlier pastoral elegy, will
suggest Milton's relation to the tradition.

> A gentle shepherd borne in Arcady,
> Of gentlest race that ever shepherd bore:
> About the grassie bancks of Haemony,
> Did keepe his sheep, his little stock and store.
> Full carefully he kept them day and night,
> In fairest fields, and Astrophel he hight.

The repetitions, of words, of line-lengths, of rhyme-sounds, of
alliterations, of phrasal constructions, are tighter than in *Lycidas*, but less related to meaning. The second characteristic
term *gentle* has no particular bearing on the first, for example;
and the *borne . . . bore* echo is simple word-play; the adjective
grassie tells us much; but *fair*, little. Note also the later stanza
on Astrophel's soul in paradise: like Milton's it relates flowers
to immortality, but much more pictorially, less profoundly. Milton's flowers keep their reality and their relative subordination
in fancy and on earth, while Spenser's cheerfully bloom in
heaven:

> Ah no: it is not dead, ne can it die,
> But lives for aie, in blissful Paradise:
> Where like a new-borne babe it soft doth lie
> In bed of lillies wrapt in tender wise.
> > And compast all about with roses sweet,
> > And daintie violets from head to feet.

What Milton makes of these two concepts, physical and spiritual, by the widening of the physical and the heightening of the
spiritual, is central to the difference between the two poets who
in their love of æsthetic sense belong to the same school. Spenser's
main repeated terms in *Astrophel* are more frequent, more abundant, and more usual: *dear, fair, gentle, great, good, day, flower,
heart, love, shepherd, verse, make, see, hear, sing.* These are
specializations within the main line of English poetic vocabulary,
upon the sensuous, emotional, and artful. Milton shared more
deeply in these specializations than in any other, but took them
further, into individual emphasis and interpretation.

One reason that his individual emphases do not sound idio-
syncratic to us today is that the language of *Lycidas* has had a

powerful effect on English, especially American, poetry. The poem drew on the concrete references, the verbal harmonies, the interwoven and cumulative structures of classical sources, especially Virgil, and turned them to the intense purposes of Protestantism with its sense of the natural scope and magnificence of the universe as God's creation, encompassing the depth of hell and sea, the height of heaven and sky. Thus the special vocabulary of *fresh, high, pure, sacred, new, fountain, hill, leaf, morning, shade, stream, shore, star, wind*, while extremely rare as dominant vocabulary before *Lycidas*, becomes dominant in the mid-eighteenth century, with poets like James Thompson, Collins, Dyer, Blake, and Wordsworth. Especially in America, from Dwight and Trumbull on, the liberal and natural Protestant spirit continued its poetizing in these terms of scope and sacred feeling, one of the most characteristic American poetic adjectives being the *pure* of *Lycidas*. To us today, the integration of sense-imagery with sound-pattern and emotional harmonic structure is natural to poetry. The imagists and symbolists have called for such integration, and we find it in Keats, in Dylan Thomas, in Hart Crane; these are poets in the tradition of *Lycidas*.

To come back, then, from history and tradition to the poem itself: one good way to read it is in its own terms of emphasis, and one of these is its repetition, with variation, of the primary language. Its thematic terms carry the poem's sense of renewal from old past to new future, from deep waters and sad flowers to high heavens, from Jove's fame to Christ's redemption, from westering to rising star. For *Lycidas*, for Milton, for English poetry, this was a fresh beginning.

from *A Study of Literature*

David Daiches

It was not until his former fellow-student at Christ's was drowned in the Irish Sea in August 1637 that Milton was moved to write another English poem. This, too, was wrung from him before he felt himself ready, not this time by the request of an aristocratic family but by "bitter constraint, and sad occasion deare." Edward King does not appear to have been a very intimate friend of Milton's, but he had been a learned and virtuous young man dedicated to a career in the Church, and there must have been some sympathy and fellow feeling between them even though King, unlike Milton, was appointed to a college fellowship by royal mandate and was not "Church-outed by the Prelats." The shock to Milton of seeing a promising and dedicated contemporary cut off in his youth must have been great. Here he was, taking his time in preparing himself to become a poet who would "leave something so written to after-times, as they should not willingly let die," and suddenly the prospect of sudden and premature death was violently brought before him. If he were to die as King had died, what would have been the use, then, of all his laborious self-preparation? The very slowness and deliberation of Milton's progress towards his goal must have increased the shock enormously. He might well have said, as Marvell was to say in another context,

From *A Study of Literature* (Ithaca, N.Y., 1948), 170–195, as revised in *Milton* (London, 1957), 73–92.

> Had we but World enough, and Time,
> This coyness Lady were no crime.

He had been acting on the assumption that he had world enough and time; and perhaps, after all, he had not. This is not to say that the elegy which Milton wrote for King was not about King but about himself, but it does indicate one of the major streams of feeling that flowed into the poem.

Lycidas, Milton's elegy on King, appeared in a memorial volume which came out in two parts in 1638, the first and larger part containing Latin and Greek poems and the second containing poems in English. *Lycidas* concludes the second part; it is signed "J. M." All but two of the other eleven English elegies are signed with the author's name. It is strange to look at *Lycidas* as it first appeared, tucked away at the end of a collection of poems most of which are uninspired and conventional laments. Henry King's poem begins:

> No Death! I'le not examine Gods decree,
> Nor question providence, in chiding thee:
> Discreet Religion binds us to admire
> The wayes of providence, and not enquire.

Joseph Beaumont's piece began:

> When first this news, rough as the sea
> From whence it came, began to be
> Sigh'd out by fame, and generall tears
> Drown'd him again, my stupid fears
> Would not awake; . . .

Cleveland's opens:

> I like not tears in tune; nor will I prise
> His artificiall grief, that scannes his eyes:
> Mine weep down pious beads: but why should I
> Confine them to the Muses Rosarie?
> I am not Poet here; my pen's the spout
> Where the rain-water of my eyes run out
> In pitie of that name, whose fate we see
> Thus copied out in griefs Hydrographie.

Among this company, Milton's poem stands out at once for its gravity of utterance, its artfully modulated verse, and its formal use of the conventions of the pastoral elegy, as developed in Greek, Latin, and Italian poetry.

The verse of *Lycidas* owes much to Milton's study of Italian poetry. While Milton does not employ the *canzone* (which consists of a complex rhymed verse-paragraph repeated in the same form several times before the concluding *commiato*, which is a shorter stanza), nevertheless his handling of the verse-paragraphs and of varying line-lengths clearly derives from the *canzone*, and the concluding passage of eight lines is his own adaptation of the *commiato*. Mr. F. T. Prince has traced in detail the influence on *Lycidas* of sixteenth-century Italian pastoral poetry, and he has shown how the structure of the *canzone*, as originally explained by Dante in the *De Vulgari Eloquentia*, with its stanza divided into two sections linked by a *chiave*, illuminates the sustained technical discipline shown by Milton in his handling of rhyme-pattern, pauses and transitions in their relation to the movement of thought and emotion.

Lycidas begins with a statement of the occasion which prompted it:

> Yet once more, O ye laurels, and once more,
> Ye myrtles brown, with ivy never-sere,
> I come to pluck your berries harsh and crude,
> And with forc'd fingers rude
> Shatter your leaves before the mellowing yeare.
> Bitter constraint, and sad occasion deare
> Compells me to disturb your season due:
> For Lycidas is dead, dead ere his prime,
> (Young Lycidas!) and hath not left his peere.
> Who would not sing for Lycidas? he knew
> Himself to sing, and build the lofty rhyme.
> He must not flote upon his watery biere
> Unwept, and welter to the parching wind
> Without the meed of some melodious tear.

The very first line introduces Milton in his capacity of young and ambitious poet: he is young because he has to pluck the berries of his art before they are ripe; he has already begun his career as a poet because this is not the first time he has plucked the unripe berries; and he thinks of himself (potentially at least) as a poet in the great classical tradition, as is made clear by his use of such images as laurel, myrtle, and ivy with their tradi-

tional associations with triumphant art. The berries may be unripe, but they are the true berries of art. He has to interrupt
his period of apprenticeship to attempt a mature poem, because
the fate of a fellow-poet compels him.

The note of compulsion is urgent. "Yet once more"—in these
three opening words, three equally stressed monosyllables which
take the reader into the poem suddenly and passionately yet
which in themselves are very "ordinary" words with no obvious
poetic qualities, we have the first hint of that strongly felt personal concern with himself and his own fate which is to be fully
developed later in the poem. Yet that concern is not with his
fate simply as man: it is with that aspect of himself which links
him with the dead Lycidas and in the light of which Lycidas is
himself an impressive subject—they are both poets (or poet-
priests: we have seen how the two concepts were linked for Milton).

> Who would not sing for Lycidas? he knew
> Himself to sing, and build the lofty rhyme.

If the subject of the poem is not simply Edward King as man,
neither is it (as Tillyard would have it) simply Milton himself.
It is man in his creative capacity, as Christian humanist poet-
priest. Lycidas has been drowned before he could fulfill his potentialities as poet-priest: man is always liable to be cut off before making his contribution; hence the lament, hence the problem, hence the poem. In *Lycidas* Milton circles round the problem, and with each circling he moves nearer the centre (he is
spiralling rather than circling), and he reaches the centre only
when he has found a solution, or at least an attitude in terms of
which the problem can be faced with equanimity.

Of the many points worthy of detailed attention in these opening lines, only a few can be selected for brief comment. The
image of the unripe berries and such phrases as "season due"
and "mellowing yeare" introduce thus early in the poem the
richly suggestive notion of the changing seasons with all the
emotional implications of seedtime and harvest, of the death of
the year being inevitably followed by its rebirth in the spring.
These implications (which, it might almost be said, convey a
suggestion of comfort even while introducing the cause for lament) are not overstressed, but delicately handled by the rhymes

and the rhythms. The first sentence of the poem moves up to a climactic autumn image:

> Shatter your leaves before the mellowing yeare.

"Yeare" rhymes with "sere" (dry) at the end of the second line, and the two rhyme words echoing together form a contrast between the withered and the ripe, between death and hope. Thus not only is the theme fully presented in these opening lines; there is also an anticipation of the way in which it is going to be worked out. In the very run of this fifth and just-quoted line there is an implication both of action and of hope, the sharp gesture of "shatter" giving way to the image of "mellowing yeare" as the line slows down, so that the "forced" and "rude" fingers plucking the unripe berries almost become, for a brief moment, harvesting images of active labourers gathering ripe fruit.

The young poet faces the premature death of the unfulfilled fellow-poet. His first reaction is to sing a lament for him:

> He must not flote upon his watery biere
> Unwept, and welter to the parching wind
> Without the meed of some melodious tear.

These three lines bring the first verse-paragraph to an end, on a note which combines resignation with resolve. This quiet close of the introduction not only provides a perfect balance for this opening paragraph, which rests, as it were, on these three lines; it also holds a note of anticipation, and so draws the reader further into the poem.

It is with deliberate awareness of the classical pastoral tradition that Milton begins the actual elegy in the second verse-paragraph:

> Begin then, Sisters of the sacred well . . .

He is invoking the muses with an almost ironic deliberation, the second word of the line, "then," almost suggesting that this is the thing to do, the proper routine. There is an echo of Theocritus' first Idyll in the line, and this adds to the suggestion of routine, of Milton doing his duty. But this is more than a conventional elegy, and its subject is more than Lycidas—or rather, its subject is Lycidas rather than Edward King, for when he

has given his dead friend a classical name, he has elevated him
to the status of fellow-poet and from there the expansion to
creative man can proceed. He does not stay long with these traditional sentiments, but, with a significantly short line, turns the
subject to himself as poet:

> So may some gentle Muse
> With lucky words favour my destin'd urn,
> And as he passes, turn
> And bid fair peace be to my sable shroud.

He will do this for Lycidas so that it will be done in turn for
him; it is what is due to a poet. The death of Lycidas is now
linked to the inevitable death of all men, however talented, however great their promise or achievements; even the present cele-
brator will in his turn become the celebrated. There is a restrained note of self-pity here, conveyed not so much by the
actual words used as by the suggestion given to the words by
rhyme and metre. The short lines in which he breaks off to draw
the parallel with himself are echoed by a later short line which
is pure action or gesture—a striking image of Milton's elegist
turning to invoke peace on *his* remains:

> And as he passes, turn
> And bid fair peace be to my sable shroud.

Nothing could better illustrate the importance of metrical and
semantic context in poetic expression than the first of these two
lines. In itself, it is a wholly "neutral" line, containing no ar-
resting word or phrase, no striking image. But in its context
the very simplicity of the expression, the shortness of the line
(echoing in length the other short line two lines before, but rhyming with the immediately preceding long line), and its effect
purely as sound (three light monosyllables followed by a leaning on the first syllable of "passes" and then on "turn") combine with the purely intellectual meaning to flash forth a significant and moving gesture. Milton has now substituted himself
for Lycidas in the poem, but not before both men have been
identified with a larger and more general conception of man.
Having made the substitution, he again points out why he has
done it:

> For we were nurst upon the self-same hill,
> Fed the same flock, by fountain, shade, and rill; . . .

This is a restatement of the earlier

> Who would not sing for Lycidas? he knew
> Himself to sing, and build the lofty rhyme.

But whereas the first time it was an explanation of why he should
sing for Lycidas, the second time it is an explanation of why
both Lycidas and himself merit the same consideration. They
are both poets: the reason is the same in each case. The description, in the following verse-paragraph, is not so much an
account in pastoral imagery of their life together as students
in Cambridge; it is an account of their joint self-dedication as
poets, and the pastoral imagery is employed in order to link
their function as poets with the tradition of Western literature.
This continuous linking of the theme with classical mythology is
not decorative but functional: it keeps the poem rooted in an
elevated conception on the nature, scope, and historical significance of the poet's art.

One notes in this third paragraph a genuine emotion about
Nature, which blends effectively with the purely conventional
characteristics of the pastoral imagery and which reminds the
reader of such earlier images as "mellowing yeare":

> Together both, ere the high lawns appear'd
> Under the glimmering eye-lids of the morn,[1]
> We drove a-field, and both together heard
> What time the gray-fly winds her sultry horn,
> Batt'ning our flocks with the fresh dews of night,
> Oft till the ev'n-starre bright [2]
> Toward heav'ns descent had slop'd his burnisht [3] wheel.
> Meanwhile the rural ditties were not mute
> Temper'd to th'oaten flute:
> Rough Satyres danc'd, and Fauns with cloven heel
> From the glad sound would not be absent long,
> And old Dametas lov'd to heare our song.

[1] This is the reading of the 1638 ed. Milton later changed "glimmering" to
"opening."
[2] So 1638. Milton altered the line to "Oft till the Star that rose, at Ev'ning,
bright."
[3] So 1638. Later, "westering."

In the first part of this paragraph we get a sense of community
in an elemental activity. Such a phrase as "the opening [*earlier*,
"glimmering"] eye-lids of the morn" (a literal rendering of a
Hebrew phrase used in the third chapter of Job, though also
common in Elizabethan poetry) or the revised line "Oft till the
Star that rose, at Ev'ning, bright" introduces that favourite
attitude to Nature regarded with a sense of the passing of time
already hinted at in the fifth line of the poem and to be used at
the end of the poem in a single great phrase suggesting the dawn
of a new day unobtrusively yet with immense promise:

> To morrow to fresh woods and pastures new.

The two poets are thus described pursuing their activities together against a background of changing nature, which culminates with the rising of the evening star. And so our gaze is
shifted from earth to heaven ("Toward heav'ns descent had
slop'd his burnisht wheel"), and so a whole sense of cosmic implication, before the images suggesting poetry ("rural ditties",
"oaten flute") are introduced. There is almost a suggestion of
dance rhythms about the two lines ending "mute" and "flute",
the second, short line rhyming with the immediately preceeding
longer one. We do not need to speculate on the identity of "old
Dametas" (later spelt "Damætas") in order to see in him a symbol of the approval of the properly constituted judges of poetry
or at least of poetic ambition.

> And old Dametas lov'd to heare our song

ends the paragraph on a note of self-satisfaction: they were
both recognized as promising young poets. They pleased both
those who judge merely by instinct (the rough satyrs and the
fauns with cloven heel) and the cultivated critic. They were, in
fact, both on their way to literary fame.

No sooner has he suggested this than Milton realizes afresh
that one of them is no longer there, that poetic promise is not
enough to guarantee immortality:

> But oh the heavy change, now thou art gone,
> Now thou art gone, and never must return!

The images of Nature which have previously suggested growth
and maturity (i.e., change implying progress and hope) are replaced by images of Nature suggesting decay and death:

> Thee shepherd, thee the woods, and desert caves
> With wild thyme and the gadding vine oregrown,
> And all their echoes mourn.
> The willows and the hasil-copses green
> Shall now no more be seen
> Fanning their joyous leaves to thy soft layes.
> As killing as the canker to the rose,
> Or taint-worm to the weanling herds that graze,
> Or frost to flowers that their gay wardrobe wear,
> When first the white-thorn blowes;
> Such, Lycidas, thy losse to shepherds eare.

One does not need to emphasize the emotional effect of such repetitions as "now thou art gone, and never must return" or "thee shepherd, thee the woods . . ." or the sharpening of the meaning by the inversion in the latter of these. And here again it is Lycidas as poet who is mourned: it is the loss of his song, his loss to shepherd's *ear*, that matters. Even the songster cannot be saved—even the Muses cannot protect their own, as the succeeding verse-paragraph immediately points out:

> Where were ye Nimphs when the remorselesse deep
> Clos'd ore the head of your lov'd Lycidas?

This is the second reference in the poem to the fact that Lycidas had met his death by drowning, and it is introduced here in order that Milton may avail himself of appropriate mythological references. The water nymphs could not save him, nor could the tutelary spirits of that region near which the ship went down:

> For neither were ye playing on the steep,
> Where the old Bards the famous Druids lie,
> Nor on the shaggie top of Mona high,
> Nor yet where Deva spreads her wisard stream:
> Ah me, I fondly dream!
> Had ye been there—for what could that have done?
> What could the Muse her self that Orpheus bore,
> The Muse her self, for her inchanting sonne?
> Whom universall nature did lament,
> When by the rout that made the hideous rore
> His goary visage down the stream was sent,
> Down the swift Hebrus to the Lesbian shore.

King had been drowned off the north coast of Wales, a fact which allows Milton to exploit the old Celtic traditions of Eng-

land (in which he had always been interested) and enrich the
classical pastoral conception of the poet with references to the
ancient Druids (who were poet-priests), associated especially
with the island of Mona or Anglesey, and to the whole Celtic
conception of the bard with its implications. "Deva" is the River
Dee, which forms part of the boundary between England and
Wales, and is rich in Celtic folk traditions (hence "wisard
stream"). Milton has here deftly widened his conception of the
poet to include both the classical and the Celtic; and to clinch
this paragraph he returns to a classical image, picturing the
frightful death of Orpheus, himself the son of Calliope, one of
the Muses, and the very embodiment of poetic genius. Orpheus,
the founder and symbol of poetry and a son of the Muse, could
not be saved from a more frightful death than that which befell
Lycidas; and Milton briefly but effectively touches on the grue-
some story (told both by Virgil and Ovid) of his being torn to
pieces by the frenzied Thracian women, his head being cast into
the River Hebrus and carried out to the island of Lesbos. The
emotion reaches its height with that final, terrible image:

> His goary visage down the stream was sent,
> Down the swift Hebrus to the Lesbian shore.

This passage is much worked over in the Trinity manuscript,
and the sustained power of the final version is the result of several careful revisions. Milton always found the death of Orpheus
a peculiarly moving and somehow a very personal story: in the
opening of the seventh book of *Paradise Lost* he asks his divine
muse to drive far off the royalist revellers whom the restoration
of Charles II had brought back to London and compares them
to the bacchanalian mob that murdered Orpheus:

> But drive farr off the barbarous dissonance
> Of *Bacchus* and his Revellers, the Race
> Of that wilde Rout that tore the *Thracian* Bard
> In *Rhodope,* where Woods and Rocks had Eares
> To capture, till the savage clamor dround
> Both Harp and Voice; nor could the Muse defend
> Her Son.

"Nor could the Muse defend her Son." "What could the Muse
her self that Orpheus bore / The Muse her self, for her inchant-

ing sonne? . . ." To be a poet was no guarantee against sudden death.

The concept of the poet has by now been completely universalized; it is no longer Milton and his friend but the poet in both his classical and Celtic aspects: yet this is the fate he may expect. Why, then, he asks in the paragraph that follows, should one bother to dedicate oneself to a life of preparation for great poetry?

> Alas! what boots it with uncessant care
> To tend the homely slighted shepherds trade,
> And strictly meditate the thanklesse Muse?

Is it worth trying to be a poet? One pursues fame, but before one has won it one is liable to be cut off. This is the theme of this well-known passage in which Milton effectively contrasts images of self-dedication with images of self-indulgence. Can man as Christian humanist achieve anything more than man as mere sensualist? This is one of the main questions posed by the poem and its answer emerges implicitly only at the poem's end. For the moment, the poet finds a tentative answer, but it clearly does not satisfy him any more than it provides a satisfactory conclusion to the poem.

> Fame is no plant that growes on mortall soil,
> Nor in the glistring foil
> Set off to th'world, nor in broad rumour lies;
> But lives, and spreads aloft by those pure eyes
> And perfect witnesse of all-judging Jove:
> As he pronounces lastly on each deed,
> Of so much fame in heav'n expect thy meed.

This reply, given to the poet by Phoebus (Apollo, the god of song and music), is not convincing even in purely formal terms. An explicit reply of this kind would have to be given by a more inclusive representative of poetry than Apollo, for the poem includes nonclassical (e.g., Celtic and Christian) concepts of the poet as well. And the pat aphoristic nature of that final couplet—

> As he pronounces lastly on each deed,
> Of so much fame in heav'n expect thy meed . . .

—could not possibly be a solution to such a complex poem as
Lycidas. There is almost a note of irony in the copy-book lesson.
It is a deliberately false climax, and Milton returns to his pas-
toral imagery to contemplate his theme again.

In the next verse-paragraph Milton develops his earlier question—What were the responsible authorities doing to allow such
a disaster to befall Lycidas?—in traditional pastoral terms.
This fact is in itself sufficient indication that he is not satisfied
with the solution he has just brought forward. The god of the
sea, the god of the winds, and the Nereids are each interrogated
or considered, and each is acquitted of having caused Lycidas'
death. The poet has here given up for the moment any attempt
at a larger solution to the whole problem posed by his friend's
death and is trying to find out only who is immediately responsible. But he can find no answer to the question, except the
baffling one that it was destiny:

> It was the fatall and perfidious bark,
> Built in th' eclipse, and rigg'd with curses dark,
> That sunk so low that sacred head of thine.

The section thus ends on a note of frustration and even despair.
Dark images of superstition and fatalism provide the only response to Milton's questions. This seventh verse-paragraph,
which moves from cheerful pastoral imagery to the suggestion
of man's helplessness against fate, is worth careful consideration: in structure, movement, and balance it shows a remarkable craftmanship. Note, for example, the sense of muttering
frustration to which the poet is reduced at the end:

> That sunk so low that sacred head of thine.

But with the adjective "sacred" a new thought emerges: Lycidas, like Milton, had been a dedicated man (Edward King
had, in fact, been destined for the Church). His university could
ill spare such a student and the Church could ill spare such a
recruit. The hero as poet is now enlarged to encompass the hero
as Christian champion, and as such his loss is deplored both by
Cambridge (represented by Camus, the River Cam) and St.
Peter. (It is worth noting that Milton uses biographical facts
about King only when they help him to expand his meaning at

the proper point in the poem; otherwise he ignores or even dis-
torts them.)

The point now becomes not the loss suffered by the poet himself by dying young and being unable to fulfil his potentialities,
but the loss to society when the poet (who is now spiritual leader
as well as singer) dies before he can serve it. And so we have the
famous statement of St. Peter:

> Last came, and last did go,
> The Pilot of the Galilean lake,
> Two massie keyes he bore of metalls twain,
> (The golden opes, the iron shuts amain).
> He shook his mitred locks, and stern bespake,
> How well could I have spar'd for thee, young swain,
> Enough of such as for their bellies sake
> Creep and intrude and climb into the fold?
> Of other care they little reckoning make,
> Then how to scramble at the shearers feast,
> And shove away the worthy bidden guest.
> Blind mouthes! that scarce themselves know how to hold
> A sheephook, or have learn'd ought else the least
> That to the faithfull herdmans art belongs!
> What recks it them? what need they? they are sped;
> And when they list their lean and flashie songs
> Grate on their scrannel pipes of wretched straw,
> The hungry sheep look up, and are not fed,
> But swoln with wind, and the rank mist they draw,
> Rot inwardly, and foul contagion spread:
> Besides what the grimme wolf with privy paw
> Daily devoures apace, and little said.
> But that two-handed engine at the doore,
> Stands ready to smite once, and smite no more.

This passage is, of course, an attack on the Anglican clergy,
but it is not the digression that critics have generally assumed
it to be. Milton has been developing the theme that the good are
destroyed while the bad remain—a theme which in turn emerges
from his earlier point that there is no sense in choosing a life of
self-dedication to great art if the dedicated man is given no pref-
erential treatment by fate over that accorded to mere sensual-
ists and opportunists. Not only is the potential poet-priest no
more likely to survive and fulfil his promise, he seems actually

less likely to survive than the evil men who do harm to society where the poet-priest would have done good. Granted that the poet must take his chance of survival along with everybody else, is it fair to *society* to cut him off and let the drones and the parasites remain? The theme of *Lycidas* is the fate of the poet-priest in all his aspects, both as individual and as social figure.

Even this bitter passage retains the pastoral imagery. The shepherd as the symbol of the spiritual leader is of course an old Christian usage, and goes right back to the Bible. But in the classical tradition the shepherd also sings and pipes. So by combining Christian and classical pastoral traditions Milton can use the shepherd as a symbol for the combination of priest and poet which was such an important concept to him. (With reference to the Biblical element in the imagery of this passage, it is worth noting that the first verse of the twenty-third psalm in the English Psalter of 1530 reads: "The lorde is my pastore and feader: wherfore I shal not wante.") The association of classical and Biblical imagery in the passage is further emphasized in the lines

> Of other care they little reckoning make,
> Then how to scramble at the shearers feast,
> And shove away the worthy bidden guest,

with the reference to the parable in the twenty-second chapter of Matthew.

The technical devices employed in this passage to indicate the poet's contempt for those he is attacking have often been noted and scarcely need elaboration here. Once again we have the gesture, the clearly seen movement, presented in terms which associate it with an attitude of contempt:

> Creep and intrude and climb into the fold.

This is a very precise line, with three verbs each possessing an exact, different but complementary meaning. One might note also the effect in their contexts of such phrases as "shove away", "scramble" and "swoln with wind". And one need hardly catalogue the effective qualities of such lines as:

> What recks it them? what need they? they are sped;
> And when they list their lean and flashie songs
> Grate on their scrannel pipes of wretched straw.

Mr. Prince sees in these lines an echo of "rustic raillery" found in the Italian pastorals of Sannazaro, where, in humorous passages with double rhyme, he presents exchanges of abuse between two rival shepherds. But, though Milton might have learned something technically from this sort of Italian verse, the tone here is his own and far from humorous.

The conclusion of St. Peter's outburst suggests, with deliberate and effective vagueness, that something will be done about those who abuse society's trust:

> But that two-handed engine at the doore,
> Stands ready to smite once, and smite no more.

There is no need to follow generations of editors in their speculations on what Milton really meant by the "two-handed engine": all that is really necessary for an understanding of the poem is to note that retribution is certain through a device which suggests purposive activity on the part of society. The implication of "two-handed" is that men will use it with their own two hands, and this suggestion of purposive activity anticipates and prepares the way for the final resolution of the problem posed by the poem—which is that man as poet and moralist should, so long as he remains alive, keep on working and striving, continuing to proceed from task to task until he is no longer able. Thus, though the poem opens on a note of regret that the poet is forced once again to write before his talent is mature, it ends by his turning with renewed zeal to fresh poetic activity:

> To morrow to fresh woods and pastures new.

Having suggested the lines on which the resolution of the poem is to be achieved, Milton returns to the dead Lycidas, aware of the fact that the only answer to the problem posed by his premature death is for those who survive to carry on more zealously than ever. Such an answer implies an abandonment of sorrow and a leaving behind of thoughts of the dead potential poet, and before he can bring himself to do this he must try to transmute the dead Lycidas into something beautiful and fragrant. And so, as a sort of apology to Lycidas before leaving him for ever, he turns passionately to his dead body and attempts to smother it with flowers:

> Bring the rathe primrose that forsaken dies,
> The tufted crow-toe, and pale gessamine,
> The white pink, and the pansie freakt with jeat,
> The glowing violet, . . .
> To strew the laureat herse where Lycid lies.

Milton apparently added this passage later; the Trinity manuscript shows it as an insertion, in two versions, the first longer
and more elaborate than the one finally worked out. Perhaps the
idea of making some sort of amends to Lycidas, as it were, for
having to forsake him at the last, occurred to Milton on reading
over a first draft of the poem, and he therefore inserted the
passage as a transition from the attack on the clergy to the
picture of Lycidas' body washed out to sea. Yet he is still reluctant to leave him:

> Ay me! whil'st thee the shores and sounding seas
> Wash farre away, where ere thy bones are hurl'd,
> Whether beyond the stormy Hebrides,
> Where thou perhaps under the humming tide [4]
> Visit'st the bottom of the monstrous world;
> Or whether thou to our moist vowes deni'd,
> Sleep'st by the fable of Bellerus old,
> Where the great vision of the guarded mount
> Looks toward Namancos and Bayona's hold;
> Look homeward Angel now, and melt with ruth,
> And, O ye dolphins, waft the haplesse youth.

The body of the dead Lycidas refuses to be smothered with
flowers, refuses to allow the poet to "interpose a little ease" and
"dally with false surmise." He is indeed drowned—but no sooner
has Milton accepted this fact anew than, with a deliberate echo
of the references to Mona and Deva in the fifth verse-paragraph,
he exploits geography with tremendous effect. Lycidas lies
drowned off the coast of Wales. Perhaps his body has been
washed northwards up to the romantic Hebrides; perhaps he is
exploring the monstrous depths of the ocean; perhaps—and here
the emotion rises—he has made his peace with the great Celtic
guardians of pre-Anglo-Saxon Britain (Celtic Britain always
had an immense fascination for Milton) and sleeps with "the
fable of Bellerus old," i.e., with the fabled Cornish giant from
whose name the Roman name for Land's End, Bellerium, was

[4] So 1638. Later changed by Milton to "whelming tide."

supposed to have been derived. Milton here suddenly projects an image of the southwest corner of England (Wales and Cornwall, with their associations with the Celtic heritage of Britain) and infuses into this projection a passionate sense of English history and English patriotism. "The guarded mount" is St. Michael's Mount, near Penzance. Following the imagined drifting of Lycidas' body, Milton is led to associate it with that part of England, so rich in history and folklore, which projects into the sea and looks towards Spain (Nemancos and Bayona's hold, i.e., stronghold, were districts in northern Spain, so marked in several seventeenth-century maps; Nemancos was misspelled "Namancos" in Ojea's map of Galicia and in subsequent maps, including Mercator's atlas). England looking towards Spain suggests the whole challenge of Anglo-Spanish relations of the late sixteenth century, culminating in the defeat of the Spanish Armada in 1588. Catholic Spain remained the enemy for the very Protestant Milton, and this passage has its links with the earlier reference to the "grimme wolf with privy paw," which refers to the proselytizing Roman Catholic Church. To see Lycidas in this context is to see him in conjunction with English history and with the guardian angel of England, St. Michael, who looks out over the sea towards the long-since-defeated Spanish enemy. He has thus at last managed to associate Lycidas with a sense of triumph, and he can now afford to leave the dead for a moment and interpose a great cry for his country:

> Look homeward Angel now, and melt with ruth,
> And, O ye dolphins, waft the haplesse youth.

He seems to be saying here: "Look no more out towards Spain, but look instead homeward towards Lycidas." But surely there is a strong implication here of a plea that England's guardian angel should cease to look away from home but look homeward at the state of the country, ministered to by a clergy whose corruption and inefficiency he has already so vividly described. "Look homeward Angel now" rings out like a passionate cry for his country and for himself. The dolphins can take care of the dead man; England and England's potential great poet John Milton require your present aid.

Lycidas can now be disposed of conventionally. The problem has moved beyond him, so Milton can let himself picture his reception in Heaven with all the triumphant resources of Christian imagery. And that is the function of the penultimate verseparagraph beginning:

> Weep no more, wofull shepherds, weep no more.

There is a content here, a restrained passion, a controlled happiness. Milton has prepared the way for the emergence of the attitude in the light of which the question posed by the poem can be answered—What shall the Christian humanist do in the face of imminent death, what shall man the creator do in the prospect of extinction?—and having done so he can at last accept the conventional Christian answer to the question of Lycidas' own fate. The note of acquiescence emerges clearly here, as it did not in the answer provided earlier by Phoebus. Yet the picture of Lycidas' triumph in Heaven is not altogether conventionally Christian. Lycidas hears "the unexpressive nuptiall song," and this is another echo of Milton's passionate belief in the special reward waiting in Heaven for those who kept themselves chaste on earth. We have seen how that belief combines Pythagorean, Platonic, and Christian elements and is related both to his view of the music of the spheres and his interpretation of the first five verses of the fourteenth chapter of Revelation. He is more explicit and detailed about the mystic joys of heavenly nuptials reserved for those who were chaste on earth in the conclusion of another elegy, the Latin *Epitaphium Damonis* he was to write two years later for his friend Diodati.

But this cannot be the end of the poem, as it should have been if Milton were writing a conventional Christian elegy. He has to return to himself, to man as poet and creator, and give his final statement on the question posed by the poem. What shall the creator do when he knows he may die at any time? The answer, already prepared for in several passages, emerges at the end firmly and with conviction. We return to Milton, to the poet who has been mourning his dead friend. And as we return to him, a new day dawns, and he sets out on new tasks. The answer is not dissimilar to that given in the sonnets on his twenty-third birthday and on his blindness: man can only do what in him lies as best he can.

> Thus sang the uncouth swain to th' oaks and rills,
> While the still morn went out with sandals gray;
> He touch'd the tender stops of various quills,
> With eager thought warbling his Dorick lay:
> And now the sunne had stretch'd out all the hills,
> And now was dropt into the western bay;
> At last he rose, and twitch'd his mantle blew,
> To morrow to fresh woods and pastures new.

He returns at the end to those pastoral images most suggestive of the poet. He pays his respects to the Greek pastoral poets ("Dorick lay") and to the Latin (the fifth line is Virgil's *Majoresque cadunt altis de montibus umbrae*) and thus associates himself firmly with the Western literary tradition. And the last line suggests a determination to proceed to yet greater poetic achievements. Lycidas is forgotten: the world remains in the hands of the living and is shaped by their purposes. Keats, in his sonnet "When I have fears that I may cease to be," faced the same problem Milton faced in *Lycidas*. Suppose he died "before my pen has gleaned my teeming brain"? Keats' answer was to lose himself in a mood of sad-sweet contemplation:

> then on the shore
> Of the wide world I stand alone, and think
> Till love and fame to nothingness do sink.

Milton's answer is very different. His poem ends by his stepping out of himself, as it were, instead of losing himself in introspection. He sees himself humbly, as an "uncouth swain" singing as a new dawn comes up and brings new work to do.

The Archetypal Pattern of
Death and Rebirth in *Lycidas*

Richard P. Adams

It has been made increasingly evident by critics in recent
years that the drowning of Edward King was the occasion,
rather than the subject, of *Lycidas*. Milton's concern was generally with the life, death, and resurrection of the dedicated
poet, and specifically with his own situation at the time. From
this premise it follows that there are no digressions in the poem
and that the form and traditions of pastoral elegy are entirely
appropriate to its intentions.

Every serious poet must at some time come to an emotional
realization of the length of art and the shortness of life. He,
more than most men, desires immortality, which he tries to
achieve in his works, to leave, as Milton said, "something so
written to aftertimes, as they should not willingly let it die." It
is an appalling thought that he may die himself before his work is
done, and this thought may be most sharply imposed upon him
by the death of a friend or acquaintance who is also a poet of
some worth or promise. Such an event is likely to be felt as an
impelling occasion to find some way of reconciling the desire
for immortality with the certainty of death. Many poets, from

From *Publications of the Modern Language Association*, LXIV (1949), 183–
188; condensed for this book by the author.

Moschus (or whoever wrote the *Lament for Bion*) to Matthew
Arnold, have used for this purpose the conventions of pastoral
elegy as established by Theocritus in his *Lament for Daphnis*.
They have made additions and modifications, but the continuity
of the traditional form remains unbroken. Milton chose it because he considered it an appropriate vehicle for the expression
of his feelings. The result renders any apology absurd.

The conventions of pastoral elegy were appropriate because
they had been hammered out over the centuries by poets concerned, as Milton was, with the problem and the mystery of
death. In the cultural medium of their origin, the Hellenistic
world of the third century B.C., the most popular solutions of
the problem of death were expressed in the rituals of various
fertility cults. It is therefore not surprising to find that Adonis
appeared in the Fifteenth and Thirtieth Idylls of Theocritus
and that Bion's pastoral elegy was a *Lament for Adonis*. Similarly, in the *Lament for Bion*, a long list of mourners was capped
by the statement that "Cypris loves thee far more than the kiss
wherewith she kissed the dying Adonis." Analogies between the
conventions of fertility ritual and those of pastoral elegy are
numerous and obvious, and some of them at least were clearly
seen by Milton, who used them to reinforce the imagery of
Lycidas.[1] He also used appropriate Christian materials and
some references to mediæval history and legend where they
matched his pattern.

The result is a remarkably tight amalgam of death-and-
rebirth imagery, drawn from a more than catholic variety of
sources. It is far from being merely eclectic, however. Each individual image and reference has its immediate purpose and its
relevancy to the form of the whole.

The emotional pattern of the poem consists of a twofold
movement. First it goes from the announcement of the friend's
death downward through various expressions of sorrow to de-

---

[1] Milton's general familiarity with the fertility cults is attested by his
references to Ashtaroth, Thammuz, Isis, and Osiris in the *Nativity Ode* (200–
213) and to Adonis and "th' Assyrian *Queen*" in *Comus* (998–1001). His
immediate source for all these might have been John Selden's *De Diis Syriis*
(London, 1617), *Syn.* II, *Cap.* X, but Lucian's *De Dea Syrea* and Plutarch's
Of Osiris would have been good collateral sources. The material was also
scattered plentifully through Hesiod's *Theogony*, the *Praeparatio Evangelica*
of Eusebius, and the other early church fathers and the classical historians
whose works Milton studied during the Horton period.

spair; then comfort is offered, and the sequence reverses itself
until the conclusion is reached in heavenly joy. It is the conventional pattern of pastoral elegy, at least from the time of
Virgil, and it is at the same time the pattern of Milton's feeling
about death at the time he wrote *Lycidas*. There is no mystery
or contradiction in the facts that *Lycidas* is one of the most
richly traditional and conventional of all pastoral elegies, and
that it is at the same time one of the most intensely personal in
its expression of the poet's emotion. The two things do not conflict; they work together and reinforce each other. This effect
can be demonstrated by an examination of individual images in
relation to the over-all pattern.

The opening invocation exposes a vein of death-and-rebirth
imagery concerned with various forms of vegetation. The laurel,
the myrtle, and the ivy are evergreens. Besides being emblems
of poetry they are symbols of immortality generally, in contrast to deciduous plants. All of them have been held sacred to
fertility gods and demigods. Adonis, in one version of the myth,
was born out of a myrtle tree.[2] The laurel was supposed to have
been a sweetheart of Apollo transformed into a tree to escape
his pursuit. The ivy was sacred to Dionysus.

The transformation by some deity of a mortal into a plant
or flower was a favorite symbol of immortality in the classical
myths. It is recalled in Milton's reference to "that sanguine
flower inscrib'd with woe" (l. 106) ; that is, the hyacinth, which
sprang from the blood of a young prince of Amyclae beloved and
accidentally killed by Apollo, just as the rose (l. 45) was said
to have sprung from the blood of Adonis and the violet (l. 145)
from that of Attis, the fertility demigod of Phrygia.[3] The
amaranth (*Amaranthus*, l. 149) was also a symbol of immortality; its Greek root, coined for the purpose, meant "unfading."

These specific references are of course in addition to the general applications of the annual cycle of blighted and reviving
vegetation. The ritual observances in the fertility cults were
designed partly to assist in the completion of the cycle, the
revival of the demigod being accompanied by a sympathetic revival of fertility in plants and animals. In this connection the

---

[2] Ovid, *Metamorphoses*, X, 512.
[3] J. G. Frazer, *The Golden Bough: Adonis Attis Osiris* (London, 1922), I,
313.

pathetic fallacy, one of the most persistent of the conventions of pastoral elegy, is no fallacy at all but a perfectly logical aspect of the ritual. In pastoral elegy, however, the application is often reversed, as it is in *Lycidas*, so that flowers, and vegetation generally, symbolize the promise of rebirth for the poet's friend as well as the mourning for his death.

The fact that King died by drowning perhaps fortuitously but nonetheless effectively opened up to Milton a much larger range of death-and-rebirth imagery, which he exploited with his usual thoroughness. Several references involving water are specifically to themes of death and rebirth, one of the most definite being the legend of Alpheus and Arethusa (ll. 132–133), to which Milton had referred in *Arcades:*

> Divine *Alpheus,* who by secret sluse,
> Stole under Seas to meet his *Arethuse.* . . . [30–31]

The nymph herself, transformed into a fountain, is a symbol of immortality in much the same sense as the rose, the violet, and the hyacinth. Milton's personification of Cambridge University as the River Cam (*Camus,* l. 103) is in harmony, and St. Peter as "The Pilot of the *Galilean* lake" (l. 109) is nearly related.

Milton goes to some length to show that water, the principle of life, is not responsible for the death of Lycidas. Triton ("the Herald of the Sea," l. 96) testifies that the winds were at home and that the Nereids ("Sleek *Panope* with all her sisters," l. 99) were attending to their duty as protectresses of ships and sailors. The blame is put finally on the man-made ship which, in defiance of the powers of nature, had been "Built in th' eclipse, and rigg'd with curses dark" (l. 101).

The descent into and re-emergence from water is specifically related by Milton to the setting and rising of the sun as a symbol of death and rebirth (ll. 165–173). Besides respecifying and reinforcing the reference to St. Peter's adventure (l. 109) this passage coordinates two accounts of the sun's journey from rising to setting. The first of these represents in parallel the life of the two friends at Cambridge (ll. 25–31), and the second represents the life of the surviving poet (ll. 186–193). These passages render in a very striking way the pattern of life, death, and rebirth with which the poem as a whole is concerned.

Milton was expressing his own feelings in *Lycidas,* and not any abstract or general or public sorrow. The personal note established in the first five lines is maintained throughout. It is struck again in the passage where he puts himself in the dead man's place (ll. 19–22), hoping that "some gentle Muse" will turn aside to confer on him the immortality which he is giving King. He deliberately takes to himself here the emotional experience of death and, at least by implication, of rebirth.

The nadir of the movement from life through death to resurrection follows logically by way of the reference to Orpheus, in which death is presented as final. The reference expands in at least three directions, two of which are exploited. Orpheus's descent into the underworld and not-quite-successful effort to rescue Eurydice is the most obvious, and perhaps for that reason the one that Milton neglects. The death of Orpheus at the hands of the Bacchanals, his dismemberment, and the journey of his head to Lesbos are the things that occupy Milton's attention first. The parallels between this event and the deaths of Adonis, Attis, Osiris, and other fertility demigods have been pointed out by modern scholars.[4] The facts that he was a singer, i.e., a poet, that he died a violent death, that his head was thrown into the water, and that his mother Calliope, the muse of epic poetry, mourned his death made him sufficiently adaptable to the general pattern of pastoral elegy and to Milton's treatment. The third direction gives Milton, in the "digression" on fame, most scope for the expression of his personal feelings, both of despair and of hope. Identifying himself with Orpheus as before with King, he asks what is the use of casting his pearls before the swine by whom the god is killed, to whom he had paid his respects in *Comus* and whom he is about to attack in the passage on the corrupt clergy. Then Phoebus, the patron of Orpheus, representing Milton's patron Christ, promises him his final reward in Heaven.

Such are the means by which Milton in *Lycidas* interrelated elements from the fertility cults, the tradition of pastoral elegy, the Christian religion, and his own past with the purpose and

---

[4] *Ibid.,* II, 99. Milton was undoubtedly familiar with the custom of throwing a vase woven of papyrus, with letters inside, into the sea at Alexandria, whence it floated to Byblos. There the women, who had been mourning the death of Adonis, received it with rejoicing as the reborn demigod. This ritual is described by Lucian and cited from him by Selden, who particularly emphasizes the fact that the vase was called "a papyrus head."

most richly the effect of rendering his present emotion. Such, by the same token, is the meaning of the phrase "With eager thought," and such again is the promise of "fresh Woods, and Pastures new."

The Orpheus Image in *Lycidas*

Caroline W. Mayerson

Our understanding of *Lycidas* may be enriched by a study of the interrelationships between its imagery and its other constituents, since the most commonly accepted interpretations of the poem have focused attention perhaps too narrowly on the relationship of theme to biographical data or on pastoral and occasional features. This essay will be particularly concerned with testing the hypothesis that the allusion to Orpheus (ll. 56–63) is an important functional image closely linked by connotation to other elements of the poem. A brief review of Renaissance concepts of Orpheus, reconstructed from references in Milton's literary background and in his own works, will clarify the symbolic implications of the image.

Seventeenth-century ideas of Orpheus were the result of an accruing tradition whose historical beginnings lay in the sixth century B.C. and to which many writers contributed. *Lycidas* directs attention to four aspects of this tradition: (1) the attributes of Orpheus, conceived of as a person; (2) the legend of his death; (3) his long association with the pastoral elegy; and (4) the synthesis of the myth with Christian and moral ideas by medieval and Renaissance allegorists.

Orpheus's association with Greek religion was only vaguely known to Christian Europe. Nevertheless, the tradition persisted that Orpheus had been a *theologos*; his nature had been supreme-

From *Publications of the Modern Language Association* 64 (1949), 189–207; condensed for this book by the author.

ly gentle, his music had calmed and attracted all, and he had contributed to civilization by suppressing cannibalism and fostering agriculture and writing.

Though Milton of course knew all three of the stories comprising the Orpheus myth, he refers specifically in *Lycidas* to the circumstances surrounding Orpheus's death. Details of this story emphasized by both classical and Renaissance writers are Orpheus's retreat from society in Rhodope, his power over universal nature, his destruction and dismemberment by the Bacchides, his mourning by nature, and the disposition of the remains, the head and harp, which drifted to Lesbos, where they were preserved by Apollo and honored by the Lesbians, whom Apollo rewarded with the gift of song.

For centuries Orpheus was associated with the pastoral elegy. The classic pastorals contain many allusions to his musical skill and power over nature. The elegiac writers of the Italian Renaissance followed the convention of comparing the youth they eulogized to Orpheus, and the myth had extensive circulation in Poliziano's *La Favola d'Orpheo*. Orpheus appears in well-known English elegies by Spenser (1591) and Drayton (1593). Thus, by 1637 an allusion to Orpheus in an elegy as frankly derivative as *Lycidas* would not be remarkable. What is remarkable is Milton's use of the death story, a phase of the myth which suggests a ritual sacrificial death and thus implies rebirth. The Greek elegy, ancestor of the pastoral lament, originated as a ritual dirge, and Orpheus was early and naturally associated with the youths conventionally memorialized in these dirges. Like Orpheus, the youths were musical, met untimely deaths, and were mourned by universal nature. Milton's allusion seems highly appropriate in light of the death-rebirth pattern implicit in both the myth and the elegy and the possibility that a common origin accounts for this pattern. We shall find that Milton's literary environment contained clues to the symbolism which informed the myth and that the allusion in *Lycidas*, far from being an example of superficial eclecticism, helps to illuminate the central meaning of the poem.

The integration of the Orpheus myth with Christian ideas and symbols in *Lycidas* directs our attention to euhemeristic and allegorical interpretations existing in Milton's literary milieu. Euhemeristic interpretation had two results: Orpheus was ad-

mired as a teacher of civil arts, an ancient prophet of the true
God, a man wise before his time—an attitude documented by
numerous allusions; and he was metaphorically identified with
Christ. This identification was primarily the result of similar
attributes: gentleness and power to subdue and reconcile hostile
and mutually antagonistic forces. While contemporary instances
are rare, they suggest acceptance of the subtle but demonstrable
association found in *Lycidas*.

The works of the mythographers offer the most conclusive
evidence that during the Renaissance Orpheus was understood
as a civilizing force. Because they demonstrate that interest in
moral allegory extended into Milton's lifetime, the interpretations of the myth in Bacon's *De Sapientia Veterum* (1609) and
in George Sandys's commentary on Ovid's *Metamorphoses*
(1632) are important to readers of *Lycidas*. Both mythographers see the story of Orpheus's final days and death as
symbolic representation of the cyclic development of cultures.
Bacon conventionally emphasizes Orpheus's gentleness and
magnetism; his asceticism is interpreted as a manifestation of
professional ambition—a desire to achieve self-perpetuation
through fame rather than through offspring. His power over
nature is a symbol of civil philosophy, which teaches self-
control and love of virtue, equity, and peace. The result of its
application is social organization; for example, woods and stones
following Orpheus symbolize development of agriculture and
cities. Similarly, Sandys interprets Orpheus's magnetism as the
force of his teachings, which brought men to civil arts and to
God, and of his music, which induced harmony among all. To
both mythographers the death represents a cycle terminated by
war. Laws are silenced, habitations are left desolate, and letters
and philosophy are fragmented as men return to barbarism.
But the relics of the culture (the head and the harp) are trans-
posed to where they can thrive; thus, according to Sandys, the
Lesbians "succeeded Orpheus in the fame of Lyricall Poesy."
Using a different version of the aftermath (Helicon, in grief
and indignation, sank underground), Bacon also interprets the
phenomenon as a symbol of rebirth: the waters will surface again,
but "among other nations, and not in the places where they were
before."

Among Renaissance poets, Milton alone seems to have made

poetic use of Orpheus's death. However, Orpheus was used as a symbol of civilization and order in at least four poems, three of which Milton certainly knew, and all of which indicate that the idea was familiar to his contemporaries. In one of several parallels between "October" (*The Shepheardes Calendar*) and *Lycidas*, Spenser metaphorically comments on his shepherd poets' social functions in terms of Orpheus's power to establish and maintain order (ll.19–30), an attribute similarly alluded to in *The Faerie Queene* (4.2.1). George Chapman's concern with the chaotic state of contemporary affairs and his several references to Orpheus as a civilizing agent might well have made *Hymnus in Noctem* of special interest to Milton. The most striking analogues are found in Michael Drayton's *Poly-Olbion*, for many allusions in *Lycidas* point to Milton's acquaintance with this poem. Milton localizes the classical pastoral background in British place-names which Drayton associates with the Druids, whom he praises as England's first poet-prophets, teachers of monotheism and morality, musicians of peace; he regards Orpheus as their Greek prototype. Drayton recounts legends of St. Michael's Mount and describes Land's End looking toward Spain. Furthermore, he refers to Orpheus as civilizer in two passages containing an idea which Milton also incorporates in *Lycidas*—the neglect of true poets by a trivial-minded society. In the first of these passages, the speaker is the River Cam, who of course is also personified in *Lycidas*.

These examples of the ideas associated with Orpheus in Milton's literary environment indicate that the seventeenth-century reader of *Lycidas* would have found the Orpheus passage richly connotative. Milton's own conception of Orpheus may be hypothesized from many allusions; while only a close study of *Lycidas* itself will reveal the special significance of the image in the poem, references in other works help to clarify the meanings the myth held for Milton. He mentions Orpheus as author of the hymns and *Argonautica* in writings from various periods and makes many conventional references to Orpheus's musical skill and consequent power over nature. The most important passages for our purposes, however, are those which show Milton identifying himself with Orpheus and making use of the allegorization of the myth.

He makes an analogy between his own career and Orpheus's

in the *Sixth Elegy* and in *Ad Patrem*, both of which reflect youthful hopes of becoming a poet-prophet. In the elegy, presenting his view of the asceticism and purity required of epic poets, he names Tiresias, Linus, Calchas, Orpheus, and Homer and recalls their traditional office: "For the bard is sacred to the gods, he is priest of the gods." In *Ad Patrem*, again expressing his aspirations and his concept of the poet's sacred role, he uses Orpheus to distinguish between the value of music and song (poetry). He extols the divine powers of song in Orphean metaphor: it can arouse Tartarus, bind the gods, and restrain the Manes. Mere music is

> . . . empty of words and their meanings. . . . Such strains befit the woodland choirs, not Orpheus, who by his songs held fast the streams, and added ears to the oaks by his songs, not by his lyre, and by his singing compelled to tears the shades.

Though the older Milton in *Paradise Lost* repudiated the Orphean lyre in favor of the higher inspiration of Urania, the apprentice poet demonstrates in these passages that he revered Orpheus as one of the models on whose traditional careers he was shaping his own. Thus, to find him making further identification with Orpheus in *Lycidas* soon after writing the *Sixth Elegy* and *Ad Patrem* is not surprising.

The *Seventh Prolusion*, which, E. M. W. Tillyard argues, contains "the essence of *Lycidas*," also contains references to Orpheus which recall the mythographers' interpretation of him as a symbol of human reason and art. Men lived as beasts, says Milton, until "the Arts and Sciences breathed their divine breath into the savage breasts . . . and instilling . . . [self]-knowledge . . . gently drew them to dwell together within . . . cities." This passage is linked to a subsequent allusion: even beasts were lifted above their base level by social organization; even stocks, stones, and forests uprooted themselves and "hurried to hear . . . Orpheus."

Milton twice makes poetic adaptation of the death of Orpheus: in *Lycidas* and in *Paradise Lost* (7.30–39). The later passage is an important gloss for *Lycidas*, for Milton again identifies with Orpheus at the moment of his destruction. Here Milton is "on evil dayes . . . fall'n," and he fears that he again will be silenced prematurely. This passage shows Milton's continued awareness that the poet's office provides no sanctuary; the youthful courage that *Lycidas* displays has been reduced by time and circumstance. The older man passionately implores Urania to defend him from the "barbarous dissonance" and savagery of his contemporaneous "Wilde Rout" until his appointed task is accomplished.

Sufficient evidence emerges from this selective history of the Orpheus myth to enable us to reconstruct with some certainty the primary associations which ll. 56–63 of *Lycidas* had for their author and contemporary reader. The name *Orpheus* meant a revered musician-poet-prophet-teacher who had sung of God and creation, whose songs had affected man and beast, stock and stone, even the inhabitants of Hades. His music and teachings had helped to establish a harmonious and civilized society. His musical skill, his power over nature, and his premature death kept alive his historic association with the pastoral elegy. To the Christian world, his personality and accomplishments invited comparison with those of other venerated prophets, both heathen (the Druids, among others) and sacred (Christ). Finally, for a society traditionally inclined to allegorical exegesis, Orpheus became a symbol of human wisdom directed to social ends, the civilizing force which renews itself despite periodic annihilation. In Orpheus thus interpreted we recognize another expression of the faith incarnated in the tragic hero, a faith in the inextinguishable spiritual power of humanity. Death, rebirth, and the corollary affirmation of good that exists even in limited actuality is the traditional theme of tragedy. I suggest that it is also the theme of *Lycidas* and that Milton found in Orpheus an appropriate symbol to express and develop it.

II

Explanation of the role of the Orpheus allusion of course depends upon understanding the complex interplay between the occasional, personal, and pastoral elements of the poem. These elements require no further historical elaboration here, but their associative relationships may be usefully recalled. Though we cannot definitively reconstruct the creative process, we can see in *Lycidas* that Milton associated King's drowning with the problem of evil which shadowed his professional ambitions and his nation's welfare. Allusions to the circumstances of the death not only would seem appropriate to King's friends, but could be adapted, with some help from the widely known Orpheus myth, to a symbolic treatment of Milton's struggle with the temptation to fear and doubt. Milton gained several advantages by consolidating the conventions of various pastoral modes. He directly criticizes contemporary society but also escapes to Arcadia, both in the recollection of the beatitude of college life and in the flower passage. Precedents invited artistic unification of the subjectively related but disparate topics which concerned him. The multiple connotations of *shepherd* made Lycidas a potentially complex symbol: he could be an humble poet and priest and the personification of a society whose welfare depended upon his; and he could become, as he does at the end of the poem, the spirit entrusted with guarding his master's flocks forever. From the beginning, the poet suggests through his imagery that King's death is only the occasion for treatment of more universal concerns. With the Orpheus image Milton reinforces the pastoral machinery and gives it special direction, implying that the elegiac and tragic theme of death and rebirth will be realized through a conflict between order and chaos, which we may expect him to attempt to reconcile in a more comprehensive order that takes both into account. The Christian connotations of pastoral suggest that the reconciliation may be made through the use of Christ as a symbol of universal order in which all human conflicts are reflected and resolved. In an analysis of the development of the poem we will see how this synthesis is achieved and how the Orpheus image functions in the process.

The Orpheus passage and the preceding divisions are mutually illuminating. Lines 1–24 introduce an abnormal, disordered situation. The speaker is mournful and insecure. He feels unready yet compelled to follow poetic tradition by memorializing the death of his friend and fellow worker, a young shepherd-poet lost at sea. The idea that a poet's death engenders more poetry gives insufficient solace. We anticipate his search for an explanation of the death, because he may be enabled through understanding its meaning to regain security and compensate for the loss.

As recollections of shared experience stimulate thoughts of his own future, the speaker investigates the circumstances affecting a poet's ability to plan his career with assurance (ll. 25–63).

His waning confidence as he examines the evidence leads to the expression of despair which follows. This section begins with a nostalgic review of the beautifully ordered world the youths had helped create by fulfilling pastoral duties and by attracting and charming all with their songs. But this idyllic harmony ended with Lycidas's death, which has devastated his fellows and is mourned by all nature. The reader realizes that the youth so mourned is not merely a dead theological student; King's identity, imaginatively fused with Lycidas's, has been extended and idealized. He was the harmonizing influence in a world which depended upon him for its well-being.

In lines 50–55, the connotative values of the region in which King drowned are fully exploited. One effect of the allusions is a fuller clarification of the meaning of Lycidas. By associating him with the Druids and, soon after, with Orpheus, Milton suggests that the pastoral poet-shepherd of the opening passages is, more specifically, the poet-prophet, the civilizer. But while the allusions augment the implications of Lycidas's role, they simultaneously narrow its scope. Classical mythology is domesticated in English place-names and merged with English tradition. Belief in a world governed by order is being tested with particular reference to English poets and to England.

The allusion to Orpheus follows. The speaker realizes that his reprimand to the local nymphs, presumably guardians of English poet-prophets, was futile. Even Calliope had been impotent under similar circumstances. The mournful tone and violent note which contrast with the surface serenity of much of the poem are especially apparent in the description of Orpheus's death. This passage is an important structural unit. Antecedent material both prepares us for it and is, in turn, clarified by it; and it advances the central thought by implications that are extended and amplified in the remainder of the poem. Identification with Orpheus more firmly establishes Lycidas as poet-prophet. Furthermore, it introduces the suggestion that he is a symbol of rationality directed to social ends. The world so profoundly shaken by his death is part of "universal nature" that lamented Orpheus. We remember that Lycidas's body, like the head of Orpheus, floats upon his watery bier and welters to the parching wind. We remember, too, that the speaker seeks recompense for this situation and that the continuity of poets (now poet-priests) was an initial premise. In this passage Orpheus's head is carried only "to the Lesbian shore," but the possibility of eventual solace for Lycidas is suggested by recollection of the end of the myth, a possibility reinforced, of course, by the traditional resolution of the pastoral elegy. At this point, however, the resolution is only dimly foreshadowed. More clearly, the passage marks the climax of an analysis of the individual's indeterminate security in an order which he shapes and which depends upon his survival. The image suggests that the force of civilization is vulnerable to attacks by the destructive and anarchistic nature of man himself ("the rout that made the hideous roar") ; the semidivine attributes of the civilizer afford insufficient protection.

There follows (ll.64–84) the speaker's questioning of the value of his calling, its compensation weighed against its costs. He had undertaken his arduous training under the belief that a good and gifted man, by teaching and delighting, could bring harmony to his world and thereby win fame. But what use "to scorn delights and live laborious days" in view of the "thin spun life" of the greatest poet-prophets and the tenuous stability of their world? Phoebus's ready answer is that true justice will be meted out in heaven. By proceeding further, the poet rejects it as inadequate. The security and effectiveness of the gifted individual still seem important and still seem to depend upon the caprice of blind destiny; he is not ready to accept the ideas of so unintelligible a universe. The investigation must continue (ll.85–103).

The poet calls witnesses—if Lycidas's death was part of a larger plan, confidence in order may be restored. But Triton can explain nothing; the death was sheer accident. (While the Orpheus-Lycidas analogy is not a feature of this passage, Milton recalls it by using the synecdoche "sacred head" [l.102]).

Leading the procession of mourners is Camus, symbol of man trained to understand and control his world through reason, but he is as mournfully confused as the speaker. With St. Peter's arrival the earlier reference to Lycidas and his companions as shepherds is suffused with biblical connotations. Lycidas, in his little circle, had faithfully performed his pastoral duties, thus creating well-being and harmony. But any residual confidence in the prevalence of order is demolished by this exposure of clerical corruption. "The rout that made the hideous roar" which drowned out Orpheus's voice and lyre are still abroad. They now play "lean and flashy songs" on "scrannel pipes of wretched straw." And they kill spiritually as well as physically; their flocks rot and are left defenseless against their enemies. Furthermore, St. Peter's solution to the problem of evil is ultimately as unsatisfactory as was Phoebus's. Harsh invective followed by threats of violent retribution shows, to be sure, that heaven is mindful of the situation, but this vengeful spirit is clearly at odds, not only with the tranquillity that characterized the pastoral world, but with the doctrine and practice of Christ, the Good Shepherd, and of Orpheus. What place has the gentle poet-prophet in an order maintained by violence, different in intent but so little different in kind from the violence resulting from man's bestiality? These unanswered questions are only implicit in the poem, but the abrupt shift to the next movement indicates that, despite the immediate relief his vision of retribution has provided, the poet has not gained the assurance he seeks.

The passage that follows is more than a decorative set piece; its imagery may also be related to other images in the poem. The lush description recalls the pastoral world disrupted by Lycidas's death (ll.25–36) ; the baneful Dog Star recalls the evening star under whose generative aegis the flocks had battened. Moreover, the shift in content and tone between th opening lines of the poem and lines 25–36 is here paralleled and intensified by the juxtaposition of the flower passage and the description of Lycidas's body afloat in the ocean (ll.154–164). These contrasts suggest that the land-ocean imagery of the poem symbolically reinforces the cosmos-chaos antithesis which constitutes its central conflict. The pastoral landscape represents the serene world of the poet's desire; the turbulent ocean is a symbol of the disorder which circumstance has revealed. Later imagery, in particular the synthesis achieved through Christ (l.173), supports this interpretation. Lines 151–153 are ambiguous: possibly the "false surmise" is only that Lycidas's body has been recovered. But the context suggests that the poet is seeking "a little ease" through a more soothing fantasy—that cosmos (the old ordered world) remains inviolate, that Lycidas has died as he had lived, in a flower-filled valley protected from evil. At any rate, the whole passage seems to be a retreat from the dark forces which now appear to govern destiny, from the world view of the barbarian whose fate depends upon such phenomena as eclipses and the light of the "swart Star," a view which has been forced upon the speaker by actuality.

The escape motif, however, is only momentary. The poet returns to reality and envisions the chaos which has engulfed his world (ll.154–164). The cumulative violence and mournfulness characteristic of passages throughout the poem rise to a peak of tragic grandeur in the music and imagery of these lines. His body hurled about in the vast reaches of the "whelming tide," Lycidas is lost to mere human solace.

At the end of this passage, so powerfully expressive of the insignificance of the human being, comes the beginning of the answer which resolves the conflict. With tremendous evocative effect, Milton synthesizes (ll.161–185) minor myths and major symbols through which man has affirmed his abiding faith in the power of God and in his own spiritual worth and indestructibility. The symbols are consistent with those noted earlier in the poem. The fate of Orpheus's head is recalled by the sun's "drooping head" which sinks but rises again and by Lycidas's "oozy Lock's" bathed in nectar. But the most significant image, that which embodies the resolving insight of the poem, is Christ who "walk'd the waves." Lycidas has sunk beneath the "watry floar," the symbol of chaos. But for Christ and his faithful disciples the water was indeed a floor; Christ alone can transform chaos into cosmos, make the sea firm land.

The apotheosis of Lycidas goes beyond conventional doctrinal consolation. The pastoral beauty and music of heaven are in many respects a glorification of the earthly paradise previously described. In *Lycidas* reward and punishment are unimportant to one who understands God's grace, who hears the great song sung before the throne. Though man is limited by his human comprehension, his confidence in himself and his world is restored by his ability to envision the divine order of which he is a part, an order in which both good and evil exist, but in which good must inevitably triumph.

Lines 182–185 contain a unique adaptation of the Orpheus myth, closely related to the land-ocean imagery of the poem.

Here is revealed the place of the patriotic poet-prophet in the universal scheme. We recall the mythographers' allegorization of the disposal of Orpheus's remains; cycles of civilization and barbarism succeed one another, but not in the same place—another nation inherits the tradition. But in *Lycidas* the angel looks homeward, and the dolphins respond to the speaker's prayer. Lycidas's recompense is to be his brother's keeper, the Genius of the shore, line of demarcation between order and chaos. To all that wander in the perilous flood of doubt or through the chaos of national corruption, he stands as guide to security founded on faith and as testament that the gentle and harmonizing forces of poetry and learning and divine revelation have been and will again be capable of establishing at least limited order in England.

Lycidas ends on a note of quiet assurance. The mourning song, like Orpheus's, sung to the oaks and rills, is finished. The poet is ready to carry on the work of the poet-prophets before him, creating harmony and order in fresh woods and new pastures. The task is more arduous than he had supposed, and the problems with which he has wrestled perhaps elude final and definitive solution. But new insight has armed him with courage to face what he must, and he feels that if he, like Lycidas, should perish on the way, what he stands for will nevertheless endure.

This analysis is predicated on the view that idea and image are so reconciled in *Lycidas* that its structure may be described as a chain of images linked by connotations, the full implications of which depend upon historical data as well as upon aesthetic sensibility. Reconstruction of the meaning of the Orpheus image explains the potential symbolic significance of the allusion. Examination of the poem has shown it to be permeated by ideas associated with Orpheus, which coverge in lines 56–63. Orpheus is identified with Lycidas, and through this identification, Lycidas's importance as the poet-prophet who is the ordering factor in his world is emphasized. Mythographers' interpretations of the myth imbue Lycidas's death and rebirth by water with symbolic value. Finally, the personality and powers of Orpheus associate him with Christ, whose cosmic omnipotence is the means of resolving the poem's conflict. Milton's adaptation of the Orpheus myth in *Lycidas* unquestionably goes beyond the uses made of it by others. But our knowledge of the tradition helps us understand the extent to which Milton wove the meanings of the myth into the texture of his poem and, in so doing, made them his own.

Flowerets and Sounding Seas: A Study in the Affective Structure of *Lycidas*

Wayne Shumaker

More insistently, perhaps, than any other poem in English, *Lycidas* raises the purely æsthetic problem of how the emotions may be stirred by lines which at first are much less than perspicuous to the intellect and even after many readings remain obscure at two or three points. Johnson's attack to one side, *Lycidas* has received all but universal praise, couched often in language so high-pitched that it absorbs easily adjectives like "exquisite," "thrilling," "tremendous," and "supreme." Why is the emotional impact so powerful? A reply must be sought (I think) in the affective connotations of words, phrases, and images in formal combination; and it is worth finding because if in one of its aspects literature is history, in another, and not unimportant, aspect it is immediate experience.

In the present paper I shall attempt to make only a small contribution to the complete explanation. I propose, specifically, to extract two of a large number of formal strands and discuss them as musical themes which blend into a total emotional harmony both massive enough and piercing enough to be overpowering.

From *Publications of the Modern Language Association*, LXVI (1951), 485–494.

I must begin by discussing the place of the two strands in the large structure. Three movements are enclosed within a pastoral introduction and conclusion, each movement in turn depending to some extent on pastoral machinery for its organization. I cannot improve on a summary given by Arthur Barker.

> The first movement laments Lycidas the poet-shepherd; its problem, the possible frustration of disciplined poetic ambition by early death, is resolved by the assurance, "Of so much fame in heaven expect thy meed." The second laments Lycidas as priest-shepherd; its problem, the frustration of a sincere shepherd in a corrupt church, is resolved by St. Peter's reference to the "two-handed engine" of divine retribution. The third concludes with the apotheosis, a convention introduced by Virgil in *Eclogue* V but significantly handled by Milton. He sees the poet-priest-shepherd worshipping the Lamb with those saints "in solemn troops" who sing the "unexpressive nuptial song" of the fourteenth chapter of Revelation. The apotheosis thus not only provides the final reassurance but unites the themes of the preceding movements in the ultimate reward of the true poet-priest.

Barker is almost certainly right in assigning a large part of the poem's impressiveness to the "three successive and perfectly controlled crescendos," culminating in a second triumphal resolution of tensions already half-released in their appropriate sections. The two strands with which I am presently concerned— thematic strands, as will appear shortly—help prepare in the first and second movements for the final resolution in the third.

The third movement begins with the celebrated catalogue of flowers. One function of this passage is to modulate between St. Peter's angry speech about the corruption of the English Church and the exultant description of Edward King's reception into Paradise. The catalogue interposes a little ease, as Milton himself says, which is to lead ultimately into the fuller and less deceptive comfort accessible through the realization that in its largest implications the drowning has not been tragic. It cannot have been tragic, for earthly life is continuous with eternal, in which temporal misfortunes are recompensed. But the image of flowers banking a drowned man's hearse cannot develop immediately into ecstatic and thrilling joy. The notion is too pretty-pretty, too conventionally poetic to carry a heavy emotional weight. Moreover, in this context the thought of floral offerings is consciously and deliberately delusive. Accordingly the next mood is one of profound spiritual depression; and this, by a natural emotional rhythm, illustrated on the abnormal level by the familiar manic-depressive pattern, passes into the final rapture. The three parts of the final movement are thus organically related, the first being emotionally causal to the second, and the second, and through it the first, emotionally causal to the third. The structure is not logically but emotionally inductive. Much of the value of the first two of the three parts lies in their power to entail the third. The first two parts, however, in their turn have been implied by everything that has gone before. The catalogue of flowers that "sad embroidery" wear picks up and utilizes many preceding references to a blight that has been placed on vegetative nature by King's death, and the description of the sounding seas which hurl his body to and fro is the poetically inevitable culmination of many earlier references to water.

I do not know how many readers have noticed the remarkable consistency with which Milton has made every mention of vegetation in the first 132 lines of the elegy suggest a sympathetic frustration in nature to balance the human frustrations about which the poem is built. The technique goes far beyond the use of simple pathetic fallacies. It extends to descriptions of objects which seem not to be conscious of any involvement in the death of the poet-priest-shepherd.

The theme appears at the very beginning and is resumed several times, usually quite briefly and often glancingly, before the climactic enumeration of mournful flowers. The laurels and myrtles invoked in lines 1–5 have berries which are *harsh* and *crude*. The leaves of both laurels and myrtles are to be *shattered* by Milton's singing before they have an opportunity to reach mature exuberance ("before the mellowing year"). The emphasis now shifts to other matters; but when in the fourth verse-paragraph vegetation again comes momentarily into focus, the connotations are similarly depressing. The woods and caves that lament the accident are overgrown with *wild* thyme and *gadding* vines, the adjectives implying, perhaps not quite rationally, a desperate and uncontrolled abandon to grief. The willows and hazel copses have ceased to react with joyous activity to pastoral songs; their leaves, having left off their "fanning," presumably droop in dejection. The rose is subject to canker;

early flowers (Lycidas was a young man) succumb to frost. The tree-covered island of Mona mentioned a few lines later is not verdant but *shaggy*. The sixth paragraph offers a slight touch of relief: the *shade* in which the poet contemplates sporting with Amaryllis is thought of as a cool retreat. But Camus, when he appears, is described as wearing a bonnet of inelegant sedge variegated along the borders by figures which resemble "that sanguine flower inscrib'd with woe," and no further relief is offered. The regularity with which natural growth is made to carry lugubrious associations in the introduction and first two movements is remarkable. So pervasive is the blight that as early as line 78, when Phoebus wishes to praise true fame, he is able to do so effectively by simply dissociating it from plants that grow on mortal soil.

All this would seem easily accountable if it were not for the fact that paragraph three recalls the happier times before King's death. Here one might expect attention to be diverted from gloom sufficiently to permit an avowal that for man's gayer hours (as Bryant said) nature has a voice of gladness and a smile and eloquence of beauty. The avowal is there, but it is phrased in terms of sunlight, the sounds of insects, stars, and other nonbotanical phenomena. The only exception is in the mention of "high Lawns" in the first line of the description. For the rest, there is a studious avoidance of precisely those faces of nature which one would imagine to be most important to a shepherd. The comparative lightness of the paragraph depends not at all on images of energetic or brilliant growth. The opening eyelids of the morn carry the suggestion of an awakening, a stirring in preparation for the day's chores; the winding of the grayfly's sultry horn is associated with a genially warm air; the brightness of the evening star implies fine weather; the dancing of the satyrs and fauns is indicative of high spirits. The green of the pasturage, however, is hinted only by the single word "lawns," and nothing whatever is said at this point about shade trees or flowers. The flocks, which anywhere else would eat grass, in this setting batten themselves on "the fresh dews of night." The association of plants with depression of the spirit is not compromised.

Against this background the catalogue of flowers takes on strong emotional meanings. It resumes and develops an established theme, which, however, is now partly inverted. Although the emotional connotations set up earlier are not exactly denied, they are subdued to provide a poignant contrast to the ease the poet has announced himself to be seeking. The primrose, we are reminded, dies forsaken; the cowslips hang their pensive heads; the daffodils fill their cups with tears. The floral offerings are in fact meant to include "every flower that sad embroidery wears." On the other hand, the coloring is no longer somber. The myrtles addressed in line 2 were *brown*, and throughout the first two of the three movements the visual imagery has been prevailingly dull. The whiteness of the thorn which blows in early spring and the redness of the sanguine flower have only deepened the general murkiness by contrast. Now, suddenly, we are asked to imagine bells and flowerets *of a thousand hues*. Certain colors are specified—the *purple* of enameled eyes, the *green* of the turf, the *paleness* of the jasmine, the *whiteness* of the pink, the *jet* of the pansy, the glowing *violet*—and others are evoked by the names of flowers like the daffodil, which can hardly be visualized in more than one way. The result is that the grief, while remaining grief, is lifted and brightened. For the moment it is made tolerable by association with beautiful objects. At the same time the reader feels relief of another kind. Up to the present he has been under a constraint to imagine nature in only one of its moods; he has been forced, as it were, to consent to a perversion of what he knows to be the full truth. His conscious mind, which is aware of Milton's elegiac purpose, has assented to the fiction that a human death has lessened the objective beauty of woods and fields. But there is a part of his mind which is not controlled by his will, and this part has perhaps been, hardly perceptibly, uncomfortable, like the part of a father's mind which feels guilty about the answers he has given to his child's questions about the wind and the moon. The injustice is now partly rectified. In the catalogue of flowers Milton says not only, "There is brilliance as well as dullness in nature," but also, more indirectly, "The flowers named here are those poetically associated with sadness. I have made a selection to suit my elegiac theme." He is not, then, unhinged by his grief. He does not really distort. The largeness of his mind permits him to acknowledge a partiality in his descriptions; and his reward is the conquest of a tiny but not wholly insignificant scruple.

The second theme is somewhat less peripheral than the first, though it also lies to one side of the poem's exact center. The description of King's body as it is washed far away by the sounding seas, whether northward, toward or beyond the Hebrides, or southward, toward Cornwall, has been even more elaborately prepared for in advance. The first visual image of the dead poet-priest-shepherd is that of a corpse rocked to and fro on ocean swells swept by a dry wind. From the beginning, accordingly, the sea is in the background of the reader's consciousness. Images of water have considerably greater prominence than images of trees and plants and have frequently been noticed by critics. Sometimes the water moves forward into clear focus; again it flashes rapidly across the margin of attention, half-unnoticed and significant chiefly because the glimpses sustain a theme that must not be allowed to lose continuity.

Some of the references to water carry only a very indirect reminder of the sea, and, with it, the manner of King's death. For example, the invocation in the second paragraph calls up the image of a well: "Begin then, Sisters of the sacred well, / That from beneath the seat of *Jove* doth spring." The well is not, however, quiescent; the word "spring" suggests movement, and the movement of water, though now on a small scale, both carries on the visual motif and, by reducing the image's physical and emotional dimensions, modulates into the calmer passage which follows. A somewhat analogous technique is used at five other points: in the mention of Deva's wizard stream, in the apostrophe to the Fountain Arethuse and smooth-sliding Mincius, in the personification of the River Cam, in the description of St. Peter as pilot of the Galilean lake, and in the reassurance addressed to the River Alpheus. Each of these glancing evocations of water helps keep the theme alive by giving the reader's memory of it a little fillip. In a similar way the fountain, the three rivers, and the Sea of Galilee, by faintly echoing the water motif, prevent the reader from ever quite losing sight of the fact that King died by drowning.

I should like to dwell for a moment on a representative passage, that which contains—and surrounds—the laments of the University and the Church. At the beginning of the paragraph the University is represented, appropriately enough, by the personified figure of the leisurely, rush-lined Cam. I should not like to pretend that every reader has a momentary glimpse of a river sliding among reeds when he comes to these lines; never-theless the complete dissociation of the river from the figure would be difficult. St. Peter next appears as the "Pilot of the *Galilean* lake," the description providing an ironic contrast to the reader's knowledge that King was *not* rescued from the sea. After this introduction comes a thunderous attack on the state of the English Church; but the attack has no sooner ended in the climactic prediction of the two-handed engine than the water theme is again stated: "Return *Alpheus*, the dread voice is past, / That shrunk thy streams." The transition could hardly be more apt. The hint of timidity in the stream lowers the key from indignation at the same time the words "dread voice" carry the last reverberations of anger. Moreover, the ideas of water and fright have been associated before and will be as-sociated again. The relationship in the present passage is curi-ous, however, for now it is the water that is frightened by the man. The effect is somewhat like that of an inverted musical phrase, which remains recognizable despite the fact that it has been turned upside down.

The address to the Fountain Arethuse and smooth-sliding Mincius performs a somewhat analogous function a little ear-lier. It too uses water imagery to reassert the pastoral medium just when the need for a reassertion is felt. The mention of Deva's wizard stream is incidental to the fixing of a geographi-cal location, but the motor quality of the verb "spread" adds vividness by making the movement seem the result of an act of will. The Dee spreads its waters as a housewife might spread a tablecloth or a bird its wings.

We have seen, then, that there are six muted statements of the water theme besides the more resonant ones to be noted pres-ently. The sacred well, the River Cam, the Galilean lake, the River Alpheus, the Fountain Arethuse and smooth-sliding Min-cius (I count them as one because they occur in such close juxtaposition), and the River Dee prevent the Irish Sea from ever quite slipping out of the reader's consciousness. Milton's awareness of the manner in which King died is not wholly sup-pressed even in parts of the elegy in which he is mainly occupied in talking about something else. Formally, the six passages contribute to a massive harmony without themselves being very distinctly heard. It will be approximately accurate to say that

their structural function is similar to that of the middle notes
of triads struck on the piano. Only the analytic listener pays
careful heed to them, but anyone would feel a slight decrease of
tonal richness if they were omitted.

The more resonant statements of the theme begin in the description of Lycidas on his watery bier and continue at lines
50, 62, 89, and 154. At each of these points the drowning is
specifically mentioned or water is in some other way made to
appear menacing. There are also two later passages, at lines
167 and 183, which perform for the water theme the function
performed for the flower theme by the catalogue.

The first statement, already once referred to, has evoked the
image of a body rocking helplessly on ocean swells. The second
is less grisly but in a way even more distressing, for it recreates
briefly the exact instant at which a human life succumbed to
an indifferent natural force: "Where were ye Nymphs when the
remorseless deep / Clos'd o'er the head of your lov'd *Lycidas?*"
The visual image is that of a face sinking for the last time beneath water, the motor image that of a rejoining of fluid edges;
and there is perhaps induced also a slight muscular strain, as
of an effort to fight one's way upward toward air. To describe
small things by large, the effect is now rather that of fright than
of nausea. (I hope the reader will understand that the only way
in which I can make some of my points at all is by overstating
them.)

The third statement picks up the nausea and drops the fright
—for I should suppose no one to feel personal danger in the sight
of a severed and bleeding head being tumbled down a precipitous
river bed by the current. The head is that of Orpheus, who, like
Lycidas, was a singer.

> by the rout that made the hideous roar,
> His goary visage down the stream was sent,
> Down the swift *Hebrus* to the *Lesbian* shore.

The cold passivity of the second image has been replaced by
the movement of the first; but there are in addition angry sound
and the blood that is so frequently an accompaniment of violence. The association of water and death, however, has remained constant.

The same association is present in the fourth statement, which

recurs to the passivity of the second image and develops it in
considerable detail. The herald of the sea

> ask'd the Waves, and ask'd the Fellon winds,
> What hard mishap hath doom'd this gentle swain? . . .
> And sage *Hippotades* their answer brings,
> That not a blast was from his dungeon stray'd,
> The Ayr was calm, and on the level brine,
> Sleek *Panope* with all her sisters play'd.

The drowning and its circumstances are again set in contrast;
death is described as having occurred in a peaceful setting. On
the other hand, the feeling appropriate to this statement is
neither fright nor nausea but perplexity. Within limits, variations in the emotional demands made on the reader increase
the affective pull by activating dormant parts of the psyche.
At the same time continuity is provided by the maintenance of
the association of water and death.

Up to this point the Irish Sea has been described once as weltering and twice—if I do not misread the connotations of lines
50–51—as tranquil. The tranquillity has been insisted on at
greater length than the movement and is probably more vividly
present in the reader's imagination. Yet the possibility of movement in the Sea has been strongly asserted by the verb "welter"
and implied by the swift motion of the Hebrus. In the longest,
and climactic, development of the water theme the vastness of
the Sea is brought together with the swiftness of the river to
produce an impression of great violence.

> Ay me! Whilst thee the shores, and sounding Seas
> Wash far away, where ere thy bones are hurld,
> Whether beyond the stormy *Hebrides,*
> Where thou perhaps under the whelming tide
> Visit'st the bottom of the monstrous world . . .

The Irish Sea has become a resistless, unsympathetic force
which deals with the body of the poet-priest-shepherd exactly
as the Hebrus has dealt with the severed head of Orpheus, tossing it about with the indifference with which it would toss a
plank broken from the hull of the wrecked ship. The effect is
overwhelming (the word is suggested by the passage), and more
than one critic has testified that for him this is the most powerful part of the elegy.

Relief, however, is at hand, for the depressing thought of a tossed and ruined body generates immediately, by contrast, that of a redeemed and joyous soul. The flower and water themes, in direct juxtaposition, thus lead directly into the apotheosis, in which all the tensions are finally resolved. Little more needs to be done with the flower theme. It has served its purpose and will appear only once more, disguised almost beyond recognition, in the last line of all: "To morrow to fresh Woods, and Pastures new." The water theme, on the other hand, has carried a much heavier emotional weight and cannot be so easily dropped. Moreover, growing nature has already been adequately purged of blight, whereas the sea continues to hold a menace. It too must be purified. The mourners must be reconciled to the physical world as well as to the turnings of human destiny.

Accordingly the transition from despair to hope is made by images drawn from the very water that we have just been led to believe coldly and impersonally fearful:

> So sinks the day-star in the Ocean bed,
> And yet anon repairs his drooping head,
> And tricks his beams, and with new spangled Ore,
> Flames in the forehead of the morning sky:
> So *Lycidas* sunk low, but mounted high,
> Through the dear might of him that walk'd the waves . . .

The sun is not harmed by the sea. Christ walked on its waves. Indeed, the very man who was killed by water on earth can seek out its Heavenly equivalent as a comfort: "other groves, and other streams along, / With *Nectar* pure his oozy Lock's he laves." Even this is not all. The element *water* has been purified, but the Irish Sea must be especially cleared of threat. Hence we are told that travelers on the Sea will gain composure by recalling the "large recompense" which we now realize to have followed the brief torment of drowning.

> Now *Lycidas* the Shepherds weep no more;
> Hence forth thou art the Genius of the shore,
> In thy large recompense, and shalt be good
> To all that wander in that perilous flood.

For myself—I do not pretend to speak for others—there is a slight dissatisfaction in the reading of these lines. If the source of composure is to be an understanding of the total meaning of King's death, the word *all* provokes resistance. Calmness of mind will be accessible only to voyagers who, having known King, have been led by reflections on his fate to an acceptance of death similar to that expressed in the poem. If, on the other hand, we are to imagine King's spirit as extending physical protection to voyagers on the Sea, the implication that death is to be avoided as significantly bad contradicts the whole drift and meaning of the elegy. The structural function of the passage, however, is clear. A *formal* means of escape from the last tension has been provided. Not only is the poet-priest-shepherd living after all; the mourners can again face nature courageously and take delight in its external beauty. Everything is as it should be, and daily activities can be taken up at the point where they were dropped.

The two minor themes, then, come into prominence at various places in the first and second movements and at other places are hinted in ways that have been described. In the third movement they are developed side by side in preparation for the apotheosis, in which sorrow is finally transcended and the mind restored to peace. There is a difference, however, both in their intrinsic importance and in their usefulness in preparing for the resolution. The flower theme shows a temporary effect of profound grief, the water theme is intimately related to the cause. The distortion of vision must wear off before adjustment to the irremedial cause becomes possible; hence it is altogether proper that the former of the two themes should be resolved a little in advance of the latter. Yet each has its function, and the emotional impact would be weakened if either were omitted from the third movement. The first paragraph of the final movement, unaccounted for by Barker's explanation of the structure, is thus only less necessary than the apotheosis. It fits not only into a design but also into an emotional pattern; not only into a form but also into a response.

Essays in Analysis: *Lycidas*

Cleanth Brooks and John Edward Hardy

With *Lycidas,* as so often elsewhere with Milton, Dr. Samuel Johnson's comments form an excellent point of departure. When Dr. Johnson castigates *Lycidas* for the mingling of pagan with Christian references, he puts his finger firmly on the matter of first importance for a reading of the poem, even though it is a finger of the left hand and the gesture is deprecatory. Here again Johnson in failing to appreciate the poem has given us a valuable clue for our own understanding.

The problem of the pagan-Christian conflict has to be faced: the mingling either is turned to account in a rich synthesis, or it is not, and it disfigures the poem as a clumsy confusion. It will not do to write off the discrepancies as due to an improper attention to what Milton meant only as "conventional ornament." We had better side with Johnson in taking the poem seriously, in reading narrowly and precisely, in assuming that the pattern of statement is important, than try to save the poem by ignoring the implications of the pattern. If the poem cannot survive a serious and close reading, we can be sure that Milton least of all would have wished it to survive.

It can, of course, survive the most rigorous reading. It can be closely read, for it has been closely written. We shall certainly need to take certain conventions into account as we read,

From *Poems of Mr. John Milton* (New York, 1951), pp. 169–186.

but it will become clear that the poem does not lean unduly upon them: rather it reinvigorates and justifies them. The first lines will illustrate Milton's characteristic treatment of the conventions and the general tightness of the structure he employs. Milton's praise for Edward King is that "he knew / Himself to sing, and build the lofty rhyme." Milton's own poem in King's memory is *built* in every sense of the word, and, if we are to explore the poem, we must be prepared to become acquainted with its architecture, and an intricate and subtle architecture at that.

The laurel is a symbol of poetic fame. The poet comes to pluck the berries before they are ripe; that is, the poet apologizes for the fact that his own art is immature. The meaning of the conventional symbolism is plain. But Milton is not content to make a conventional *use* of the convention.

> I com to pluck your Berries harsh and crude,
> And with forc'd fingers rude,
> Shatter your leaves before the mellowing year.

Not only are the fingers which pluck the berries "forc'd"; the unripe berries are themselves "forc'd" from the stem. We have here a rich and meaningful ambiguity. And so with the whole passage: the fingers are "rude" not only in their brutal compulsion, but also in their unmannerliness and clumsiness. The poet is unripe, but Lycidas, "dead ere his prime"; Lycidas for whom the berries are to be plucked, was also unripe, untimely dead; and there is therefore a kind of ironic justification in the poet's being compelled to sing thus prematurely.

We can see in the manner in which this idea is expressed yet another kind of unconventionality. The passage looks forward to the development of the pastoral mode in the poem—the plucking of the berries is "appropriate" to the shepherd—but the poet has taken care that it be sufficiently realistic. We have not, in the figure of the shepherd here, merely the often shadowy character of the conventional pastoral. It is, after all, Milton, the self-conscious young poet, speaking. Evidently this is not the first time he has come forward with an immature performance:

> Yet once more, O ye Laurels, and once more
> Ye Myrtles brown, with Ivy never-sear,
> I com . . .

He should know better; but even so,

> Bitter constraint, and sad occasion dear,[1]
> Compels me . . .

The point we are making here is not that the passage is difficult and cannot be understood but that it is rich; that the words are carefully chosen; that the network of connotations is important; that the "poetry" resides in the total structure of meanings. The opening lines, then, give us warning, if we care to heed it, that the various smaller items in the poem are mortised together most cunningly; and they offer the hint that we shall do well to expect, and look forward to, the same kind of careful articulation of the larger elements.

The shepherd imagery, simply as such, hardly calls for any special comment. It is pervasive, and it is important, particularly in helping to provide a basis for the fusion of the Christian-pagan elements: the "pastor" as pagan shepherd and as Christian "pastor." Further consideration of the pastoral machinery may await a discussion of some of the elements that are not ordinarily part of the pastoral convention—elements that we should not be able to predict merely from the assumption that this is a pastoral poem.

One of the most important of these elements—and one of the most startling, once it is seen—is the water imagery. Milton does not forget that King met his death by drowning. He makes much of the sea in this poem, and he makes much of water in general—the tear, the stream, the Galilean lake, etc.

The first instance of the water imagery occurs in the twelfth line:

> He must not flote upon his watry bear
> Unwept, and welter to the parching wind,
> Without the meed of som melodious tear.

The funeral couch is the tossing sea itself. *Welter* means "to roll" or "to toss"—but there was another *welter* in this period, a word which meant "to wither" or "to wilt"; and Milton's phrase, "welter to the parching wind," would seem to indicate that this latter meaning is present too.

---

[1] The word "dear" here means, of course, *heartfelt, profoundly affecting.* But it can also mean *dire* (see *N.E.D.*). The effect of the ambiguity is to emphasize the inescapable, fatal character of the poet's obligation to Lycidas.

Actually, one can make out a case for the double meaning in terms of the context—and thereby give some point to the otherwise rather pointless statement that Lycidas must not toss upon the waves without one more drop of moisture, the "melodious tear," which must be added to the ocean in which the drowned body is already immersed. The submerged metaphor at which the double meaning of "welter" hints is something like that of a shipwrecked man tossing on his raft, surrounded by water, and yet parching.

The contrast between the salt water of the immensity of the sea and the salt water of the melodious tear may not seem to be of much importance; but as the poem develops it comes to mean a great deal. The "melodious tear" promises to overwhelm the "sounding Seas." Even at this point one can see something of the complexity of the symbol; and a little attention to it here will be very helpful in the important task of defining the theme of the poem.

It has been pointed out that Milton did not necessarily have any close friendship with King and that he therefore took the young man's death as a convenient peg on which to hang his elegy. The expression of grief is thus, we are inclined to say, conventional, and the elegy itself a *conventional* poem. But the term should not imply that Milton's feelings are not seriously engaged: the question is rather, what is the real subject? What theme does engage the poet's feelings? The answer can be found in the poem itself: Milton is at his most conventional in describing his personal association with King ("We drove a field, and both together heard . . .") ; and he can afford to be conventional here, for what counts in the poem is not Edward King as an individual but rather what King stands for, the young poet and pastor. But if Milton is not deeply concerned with King as a person, he is deeply concerned, and as a young poet personally involved, with a theme—which is that of the place and meaning of poetry in a world which seems at many points inimical to it. In the dramatic development of this theme the "conventional" figure of King has, of course, the leading role. It is this theme that dominates the poem, and a variant of it—the relation of the poet to the forces of nature—which shapes the first paragraphs.

Immediately after the reference to the "melodious tear" the

speaker invokes the "Sisters of the sacred well." Is the tear wept
by the sorrowing speaker? Or since it is "melodious," is it drawn
from the well of the Muses? Or is it wept by the Muses themselves? The ambiguity is not a meaningless one: the primary
matter is the relation of the poet to the Muses; or, to put the
question in other terms, whether the personal lament of the
speaker can transcend the *merely* personal. The equivocation is
meaningful and intended, for the speaker carries it further in
the next lines. It is *he* in the first verse paragraph who apologizes for daring to write at this time; but it is the *Muses* to whom
he says in line 18,

> Hence with denial vain, [2] and coy excuse . . .

And in the next line he makes it plain that the "gentle Muse"
who he hopes will sing an elegy at his death is masculine—a
poet like himself.

The relation of the poet to the Muse—even the question
whether the Muse has any existence apart from the poet himself
—is thus crucial for the theme of the poem, though Milton
might be considered merely gracefully conventional in beginning his elegy by invoking the Muses and paying the usual
tribute to the sacredness of the well with which they are associated. On this level the "sisters" are the nine Muses of Greek
mythology, but Milton is careful to relate them to the island of
Britain, and more intimately still to the scene of the disaster, to
the Welsh coast itself. It is true that the beings whom he reproaches (l. 50) for failing to protect Lycidas are the
"Nymphs." But as the phrase "your old *Bards*" suggests, these
nymphs are not merely deities of field and stream; they have
the poets under their care and are thus associated with the
Muses. (If there is any doubt on this point, it is resolved by the
very excuse which the speaker supplies for the nymphs: they
are not to be blamed for failing to protect Lycidas since "the
Muse her self that *Orpheus* bore" could not protect her son.)

There is a sense, of course, in which the nymphs are conventional nymphs. They might have been expected to be playing
"on the steep / Where . . . the famous *Druids* ly" or on the

---

[2] "Vain" means "useless"; "Bitter constraint" forces the tribute. But it also
means "desirous of admiration": the denial is an effect of vanity which asks
for further urging.

"top of *Mona* high" or by the stream of the Deva. They *are* the deities of hill and stream. However, since in this poem poethood is first identified with the pastoral, it is only proper that this should be so. The description of Lycidas's career as a poet has prepared for just this kind of association, for in his and the poet's earlier life together

> . . . the Rural Ditties were not mute,
> Temper'd to th'Oaten Flute,
> Rough *Satyrs* danc'd, and *Fauns* with clov'n heel.

The pastoral is a poetry of wild innocence, close to nature, a part of the music of nature, and the nymphs are its natural muses and guardians. On the day of Lycidas's death the nymphs were not playing where one would have expected them to play. The speaker knows this—because, had they been there, they would surely have tried to save Lycidas. Calliope is mentioned simply to emphasize the deeper pessimism into which the elegist falls at this point—not only were the nymphs absent; even had they been present they would have been ineffectual, as the Muse herself (of a higher order, yet of the same kind) was powerless to save her son.

The point is that *all* the divine guardians of the classical tradition—from the highest and most remote, the Muse herself, to the lowest and most intimate, the nymphs—appear to be ineffectual. And one can see an implication of yet deeper despair. The exclamation, "Ay me, I fondly dream!," placed as it is *after* the statement that the nymphs were not present and *before* the statement that they would have been useless in any case, could mean either that the existence of the nymphs or their effectuality is a "fond dream." But the two propositions come to the same thing; to say nymphs are ineffectual is tantamount to denying their existence. The poet enjoys no special status. The old intimate relation between the poet and the forces of nature has lapsed—if it *ever* existed, save as a fable of some early and lost golden age.

To sum up: by hinting that the Muse cannot save her votaries, the poet has called in question the efficacy of the melodious tear, for which the poet has turned to the well of the Muses. Is the tear, after all, other than the waste salt water which it resembles and on the waves of which the body of the dead poet

now welters? Is the sacred well really sacred? Does one not do
better to turn to the flesh-and-blood Amaryllis than to this
"thankles" shadowy being, who seems powerless and who perhaps does not even exist? The poem at this point has moved
dangerously close to a naturalism which divests nature of any
special sanctity and the poet of any supernatural function.

The last statement may seem to read too much into the
passage in question; and yet this is the general meaning up to
which the whole of verse paragraph four leads. In lines 37–49,
nature is represented as mourning. And, with regard solely to
Lycidas himself, one might take the statement that the trees
"Shall now no more be seen, / Fanning their joyous Leaves to
thy soft layes" to mean simply that the sympathetic emotion of
nature has *changed*—from joy to sorrow. But for the elegist it
would seem to be not merely a change, but a *loss* of the sense of
nature's sympathy. Milton has been careful in this stanza *not*
to give us personifications of nature: "Woods . . . desert Caves
. . . And all their echoes mourn." The dancing satyrs and fauns
of the preceding stanza are not represented here as weeping;
neither they nor the nymphs are mentioned at all. When the
nymphs are mentioned in the next stanza, they are referred to
as absent. In this stanza, then, we are presented with an emptied
nature, a nature which allows us to personify it only in the sense
that its sounds seem mournful; and, finally, the interpretation
that they *seem* mournful is justified by the concluding lines of
the stanza:

> Such, *Lycidas,* thy loss to Shepherds ear.

It is the *ear* of the shepherd speaker that has been affected.
He is not saying merely that he can no longer hear the song of
Lycidas. The music of nature which accompanied that song, and
(it is implied) which prompted the song, has also been stilled.
But the voice of nature is not silenced by her own grief. The
change which the death of Lycidas has brought is not actually a
change in nature itself; the death is not a loss to nature, but a
numbing of the poet's sensitivity to nature. What has happened
to the ear is particularized quite explicitly: it is the same sort
of thing that happens to the sheep when the taint-worm attacks
them or that happens to early flowers cut off by a late frost. It
is as though the shepherd in his grief, though he still calls him-

self "Shepherd," sees himself reduced to the level of his charges, the sheep themselves, in his relation to the forces of nature. In the elegist's compliment, Lycidas is made a kind of shepherd to him, without whom now he is abandoned and helpless. Nature is no more sympathetic with him in his sorrow than it would be with the sheep if their keeper should die and leave them to fend for themselves. Nature has no apparent respect for the memory of Lycidas. And it is questionable whether she had any for him alive. For Lycidas too, beyond the terms of the present compliment, is just such a shepherd as the speaker himself—as much as he, one of the helpless sheep.

The entire passage *can* be read simply as a compliment to the music of Lycidas; and the next stanza, with its implied comparison of Lycidas to Orpheus, whom "Universal nature" also lamented, carries the compliment further. But the passage, including again its reference to the fate of Orpheus, also reads as a dark commentary on any hopeful view of the relation of the poet to nature. The poet enjoys no special status. To judge by the fate of either Lycidas or Orpheus, the poet's name is literally written in water.

The poet is shrewd enough not to appeal to the justification of fame. That, too, is an effect of pride, "That last infirmity of Noble mind." Men live laboriously and stringently in the hope of fame; they endure a life of hardship, only to have that life extinguished by the "Blind *Fury*"—"blind" in the sense that she cannot see they are about to burst into a blaze of light, and could not see the blaze even if it had already flared forth. Better to eschew the light altogether, therefore, and "sport with *Amaryllis* in the shade."

It is here that the pastoral tone is first broken by a "strain . . . of a higher mood," by the voice of Apollo himself, who, touching the poet's deadened ears, points out that true fame transcends this world. (True fame here is distinguished from "broad rumour" or "report," the sense in which the term is first used in the passage. The fame of which Phœbus speaks has taken on something of the meaning of "praise"—"But not the praise, / Phœbus repli'd"— a word retaining from its Latin root a much stronger sense of evaluation and judgment than *fame* usually carries. The effect of *pronounce* may also be noted— "*Jove* . . . pronounces lastly on each deed"—with its sense of an authoritative judgment behind the "speaking" which, again, *fame* does not ordinarily have.) True fame is immortal, and does not grow on mortal soil.

This passage makes a distinction between the pagan deities of wood and field and stream—the genii of the place—and the higher deities—the gods of "heaven"—and therefore seems an anticipation of the specifically Christian doctrine with which the poem is to end. But we should be careful to remember that Apollo and Jove, even so, are *pagan* deities. The shock of transition from pagan to Christian is being cushioned by the poet's having one of the classic gods proclaim in effect that his "Kingdom is not of this world." But "cushioned" really overstates the case. Milton obviously wants us to feel some kind of clash in all three places: between the high utterance of Apollo here and the pastoral world of the poem; between St. Peter's words and that same pastoral mood; and between, in the largest terms, Christian and pagan, at the moment of St. Peter's entrance.

By addressing the "fountain *Arethuse*" and the river Mincius (ll. 85–86) he calls attention to the interruption of the pastoral, before proceeding again in that mode:

> But now my Oate proceeds
> And listens to the Herald of the Sea . . .

The transition is not one to a more hopeful mood. Nature cannot protect the poet, as the section reproaching the nymphs has indicated. But the sea is a part of nature too, and as the next section shows, if nature does not protect man, it is at least neutral: there is no culprit to be found among the sea deities. The disaster must be attributed to something outside nature, something supernatural, as is hinted by the dark reference to—

> . . . that fatall and perfidious Bark
> Built in th' eclipse, and rigg'd with curses dark.

But, again, if the sea deities are not actively hostile to man, the sea over which they preside is consistently presented in the poem as unfriendly and alien. It covers the "monstrous world." Its waters are presented several times as something which is sterile and meaningless: the first picture of the drowned man "welter[ing] to the parching wind"; the second, of the "sound-

ing Seas" which "hurl" the drowned man's bones; the third,
of "that perilous flood."

In this poem, for obvious reasons, the sea is associated with
death—the death of King, and also with the death of Orpheus.
But, in relation to the theme of fate as announced in the earlier
sections of the poem, it is associated with a kind of aimless confusion, type of nameless oblivion in which the known and familiar human world is swallowed up. The streams and fountains
which run throughout the poem flow with life-giving water:
they are "crown'd with vocall reeds," or flowers. They flow
to some purpose—they go somewhere—whereas the seas flow
chaotically without pattern—mere tumbling water. (It is ironical, of course, that the streams all have for their destination
the sea, and seem to lose themselves in its purposeless waste:
but this is the very point of the analogy: the lives of men, too,
with their purposes and meanings, spill themselves finally into
the sea of oblivion.)

But whatever the precise meaning of the sea symbol, it can
hardly be an accident that all the "resurrection images" have to
do with a circumvention of the sea, or a rising out of the sea:
Alpheus, in his love for Arethusa, flowing under the sea to come
up again in Sicily and mingle his waters, still fresh and life-
giving, with hers; the day-star rising from the sea; "the dear
might of him that walk'd the waves." On the purely naturalistic
level, all life eventually ends in the sea, and thus far in the poem
we have had a naturalistic account of the state of affairs. Devotion to nature—devotion to the muses, in Milton's deliberate
confusion of these figures with the nymphs—cannot save the
poet. Nature is neutral: it is not positively malignant, but
neither is it beneficent. The only answer that can suffice to
justify "the homely slighted Shepherds trade" is an answer that
does not fall properly to the rural deities at all. It has had to
come from the lips of Apollo, and it has had to consist of an
affirmation of value that transcends this world.[3]

[3] Even Phœbus's words, to speak very strictly, do not really "suffice." This
is perfectly apparent from the mere fact that the elegy continues from this
point. And one insufficiency of the pronouncement is immediately clear, that
which is remedied by St. Peter. But something still more complex is involved in the allusion to the traditional conflict of Apollo and Pan implied
in the words, "and touched my trembling ears." (Pan with his flute and Apollo

The pastoral mode, restored so briefly, is, of course, soon broken again—this time, more decisively, by a voice that transcends not only those of the deities of stream and field, but those of the whole classic order. But Milton attempts to bring St. Peter on the scene in accordance with the forms of the occasion. The "Oate proceeds," as it must, since the conventions required by the pastoral form of the poem cannot yet be abandoned. Neptune has called up Æolus to make his report. Next comes Camus, attired as a river god, "His Mantle hairy, and his Bonnet sedge." (Whether he comes also in answer to "Neptune's plea" is left ambiguous. Presumably he does not, but he is presented as a river god just as St. Peter is introduced as the "Pilot of the *Galilean* lake.")

Yet, though Milton has thus accommodated the Christian figure to the classical procession, he does not attempt to conceal his Christian character. St. Peter's locks are "mitred"; he carries his keys. Moreover, if the University under the guise of Camus utters a plaint which can easily be called a conventional pastoral lament, St. Peter emphatically does not. He is talking about "pastors," it is true, but not the *pastores* of Virgil.

By Dr. Johnson's time, the two meanings of *pastor* had, for a serious mind, become so far divorced that Johnson must have thought Milton was taking advantage of a connection as frivolous as that which joins the discrepant meanings in a pun. But we must try to avoid prejudging what Milton is doing. Milton's age felt, and Milton himself felt, that the classic ages and Chris-

---

with his lyre were fabled to have engaged in a musical contest in which Apollo was the victor. But Midas dissented from the decision, preferring the music of Pan, and Apollo turned his ears into ass's ears as a sign of his inferior taste.) In the passage of *The Shepheardes Calender* (June, ll. 65 ff.) in which Spenser makes a similar allusion the influence of the Muses is dissociated entirely from the pastoral. The Muses are allied with Apollo in *disdaining* the inferior mode of the pastoral. It is important to note that Milton does *not* so dissociate them. In *Lycidas* the pastoral is true poetry, and its guardians, effectual or ineffectual, are ultimately the same as those of the higher modes of the classical tradition. It is precisely the failure of Apollo here that he speaks from his conventional attitude of *disdain* for the "earth" of the pastoral, its earthly values and earthly concerns. Something different, therefore, is required to satisfy the elegist, an affirmation which transcends but does not disdain the natural world—such consolation in short as that presented in the figure of Christ Himself, heroic and yet pastoral, the divine shepherd. We may see Milton, in his resolution of this problem, exploring again that favorite theme—the relation of heroic and pastoral ideals, and the paradox of the pastoral-heroic—and finding, as usual, the solution of the difficulties of the pagan tradition in the truth of Christian revelation.

tianity could be united—that classic thought foreshadowed what Christianity had revealed, and that the men of the Renaissance were the heirs of both traditions, as indeed they were.

Actually, we beg the question if we assume that St. Peter can a priori have nothing to do with the pastoral tradition. He qualifies it, to be sure, by his very presence. And Milton, as lines 132–33 indicate, expects us to feel a shock. (Milton is simply more keenly aware of the implications—for both the conflict and the larger synthesis—of what he is doing than were his pastoral predecessors who introduced references to the corrupted clergy. The evidence, again of lines 132–33 especially, is that he is one step ahead of Johnson in awareness of the "pun.") But what St. Peter does is to bring in a note not so much completely alien as realistic. The shepherd's life, he reminds us, is not merely one of singing and meditating the muse, though he mentions singing. After all, there are the sheep to be fed and protected. It is a life of some difficulties and dangers: it requires knowledge and diligence. There are worthless shepherds who have their pipes too, oaten pipes like those on which Lycidas played and on which the protagonist now plays, but in St. Peter's angry description they are called "scrannel Pipes of wretched straw."

The worthless shepherds are "blind mouthes"; and the boldness of Milton's metaphor has caused some comment. How can a mouth be blind! Everything that is not specifically an eye is blind, and this is so obvious that some critics have wondered why Milton felt it necessary to imply the eye at all. Yet, even on the literal level, the yawning mouth resembles an eye, a monstrous sightless eye. And when we remember the shepherd's function (much more when we remember the Christian shepherd's function), the shepherds whose watchfulness has become simply a gluttonous and selfish desire are rightly "blind mouthes." Incidentally, the figure is balanced by an equally bold one which occurs a few lines below, but which has not excited critical comment. The poet asks the valleys to throw hither "all your quaint enameld eyes, / That on the green terf suck the honied showres." The "blind mouthes" are thus balanced by "sucking eyes." We shall not claim that Milton has consciously worked out the contrast: such a claim would be difficult to prove. But the patterning, whether it has been arrived at consciously or unconsciously, by design or by chance, confronts us in the poem. And the reader does not have to dismiss either passage as a mere strained conceit. The poet seems to be saying that even the flowers, nature's nurslings, which one expects to do nothing more than "suck the honied showres," by contrast with the worthless shepherds who have failed in the responsibilities of their high office, have the kind of spiritual life and awareness we attribute to a seeing eye.

But to argue this is to anticipate, and we must say a final word on St. Peter's speech before taking up the function of the flower passage. St. Peter, as we have said, brings in a grim and realistic note. Lycidas was a good shepherd in a world in which there are too many bad shepherds. But though the speech as a whole praises Lycidas, in terms of the larger theme it makes his death even more meaningless. The good shepherd has been taken; the wicked remain. And even the warning to the wicked shepherds hardly helps Lycidas's case or that of those who mourn for him. Thus, if St. Peter's speech, like Apollo's, transcends the pastoral mode, it carries us away from the hope that Apollo's words had suggested. For the speech, taken literally, indicates that Lycidas was needed and should have lived: many others could better have been taken. The theme has moved simply from Apollo's hint of individual reward to that of general retribution.

The poet recognizes the disruption the speech has brought. He tries once more to establish the pastoral mode. Just as he invokes the "Fountain *Arethuse*" after the Apollo speech, in line 132, he here invokes the river Alpheus.

> Return *Alpheus,* the dread voice is past,
> That shrunk thy streams . . .

The dread voice has been endowed with something of the effect of blazing light—a hot sun inimical to the cool shadows of mythology and the flowers of pastoral poetry. The voice has shrunk the pastoral stream. In trying to re-establish the conventional mode, the poet attempts to conjure up a cool scene of secluded beauty—

> Of shades and wanton winds, and gushing brooks,
> On whose fresh lap the swart Star sparely looks.

He lavishes upon it all the resources of floral decoration. It is almost as if the poet had said: Very well. I admit that with the intrusion of St. Peter, I have deserted the pastoral. But I'll try to make it up. I'll pick up all your scattered flowers—even the pathetic fallacies.

The flower passage is beautiful, granted. But we mistake its function in the poem if we think that it is merely to add a touch of decorative beauty. Actually, its function in the full context of the poem is ironic. The poet improvises beautifully as he attempts to recapture the pastoral spirit, but the "*Sicilian* Muse" will not return—does not return. Indeed, the poet himself gives over the attempt with lines 152–153:

> For so to interpose a little ease,
> Let our frail thoughts dally with false surmise.

With these words he cuts the ground from under the whole elaborate and beautiful structure. The flowers are not really wearing "sad embroidery" for Lycidas; the cups of the daffadillies are not filled with tears for him. Nature is neutral: it does not participate in grief for the dead man. And since it is a "false surmise" to assume that it does, the surmise can give no real comfort. There is, perhaps, some source of comfort yet remaining—St. Peter's speech has no more finally resolved the problem than has Apollo's—but it is not to be found in this wishful return to the conventional pastoral.

It is entirely proper, therefore, that the flower passage should be followed immediately by a realistic picture of the dead body:

> Ay me! Whilst thee the shores, and sounding Seas
> Wash far away . . .

On the literal level, of course, the very physically real absence of Lycidas, of his body, makes the "surmise" of comfort in the funeral ceremony, the strewing of flowers [4] on the bier, a "false" surmise—the "hearse" is empty. And though the absence and the falseness of comfort are, as we have seen, of a significance far larger than the merely physical and accidental, yet this literal "realism" of the passage gives it much of its strength. This is a realistic passage even in its geography—always a point to which Milton gave careful attention. Since King was

[4] And poems—the "posies" of the convention.

drowned in the Irish Sea, his bones may have been washed out
through the northern passage into the Atlantic beyond "the
stormy *Hebrides*," or perhaps through the southern channel out
beyond Land's End. The poet appeals to the dolphins to "waft
the haples youth" as one of them once in Greek fable carried
the body of the drowned Palæmon to the shore.[5] The poet does
not ask the angel Michael to lift the drowned body from the
sea: his petition goes no further than to ask him to feel pity
for Lycidas and his sorrowing friends:

> Look homeward Angel now, and melt with ruth.

We would seem to be at this point at the nadir of despair.
Even if we can, by looking ahead in the poem, read "homeward"
as "heavenward" and see the gaze of the angel as guiding
Lycidas thither, an unyielding irony remains in the very char-
acter of the spirit to whom the appeal for "ruth" is addressed—
Michael, the warrior prince.

The recovery begins with the next lines. With the command,

> Weep no more, woful Shepherds weep no more

the poet makes the first direct appeal to the Christian supernatural. With all false comforts rejected, the true hope may at
last be entertained. Lycidas is not dead. The sun too sinks into
the sea, only to rise again, and

> Flames in the forehead of the morning sky,

and this flaming is not the "sudden blaze" to be ended igno-
miniously by the "blind *Fury* with th' abhorred shears." Other
symbols of the poem find a restatement here too. The day-star
that flames in the forehead of the morning sky is after all the
same sun which in the season of the "swart *star*" shrinks the
pastoral stream. It is the full blaze of truth in which the poetic
fancies seem to shrivel. In this final passage however it is not a
sultry and parching light, but cool and brilliant as the morning.
And even the sea participates in the resurrection image—is

[5] The reference, as T. O. Mabbott has shown [see *infra*, p. 362], is to Palæmon, not to Arion as most editors have interpreted it. When the poet Arion
was cast overboard by the sailors, the dolphins, who loved his music, brought
him safe to shore. But Lycidas, like Palæmon, is dead: there is no question
of his being saved from the sea.

the "bed" in which the sun repairs its strength for the new day's journey.

Indeed, Lycidas moves through a pastoral scene as the elegy closes, a scene where there are

> . . . other groves, and other streams along

which Lycidas walks, surrounded by the flock of his fellows,

> In solemn troops, and sweet Societies.

The shepherds, under the Good Shepherd, have become the sheep. And since much has been made in the poem of the shepherd as poet and of the shepherd's song, the final passage is pastoral too in that the "sweet Societies"

> . . . sing, and singing in their glory move.

To sum up: the scene is pastoral in that the world of competition and distraction is done away with. It is "simple" in that it is quiet, peaceful, undisturbed, harmonious. But there is the suggestion—if we have attended the earlier sections of the poem —that only here can the true pastoral life exist; only here do the sheep feed perpetually by the still waters in an ideal and beautiful shepherd's world. This is the world which the ancient, pagan pastorals faintly adumbrate. The synthesis which is finally accomplished in *Lycidas* is a typically baroque mingling of Christian and pagan materials: the latter are not made completely false—they remain true insofar as they suggest the final truth of Christian revelation.

But Milton is unwilling to end the poem on just this note. And there follows, consequently, the curious last paragraph of eight lines. There is no third-person section at the beginning of the poem in which the "uncouth Swain" is introduced, and to which this last section recurs. The poem begins with the uncouth swain speaking. It is something of a surprise, therefore, to have this asymmetrical bit at the end.

The anomalous ending has been pointed out before, but we do not believe that its function has ever been adequately commented upon. Actually, it has a most important function: its effect is to throw the whole poem back into perspective. After all, the poem is the utterance of an "uncouth Swain," an unknown poet, and perhaps an awkward and unpolished one. His thought is "eager"—ambitious, ardent, even enthusiastic, it is suggested—but the instrument is rustic, and the mode is the countrified and old-fashioned Doric, the limitations of which the poet has been defining throughout the performance. If the "uncouth Swain" who speaks up to this point is carried away by his own utterance, Milton is not. He has not submerged his total personality as a poet in the character of the "Swain."

The last bit of natural description participates in the general qualification. Only a few lines earlier, the day-star, rising out of the sea, tricking "his beams . . . with new spangled Ore," had become the sign of Lycidas's own resurrection. But now, as the swain prepares to leave, it has

> . . . dropt into the Western bay

and is, along with the bones of the drowned poet,

> Sunk . . . beneath the watry floar.

The effect is not to deny the radiant vision of promise with which the elegy concludes, but only to place it definitely in that perspective which must be an essential part of its truth. Actually it is a perspective of realism, as we have already seen if we have read carefully, but here it is defined precisely and finally. We are simply *reminded* that the vision is one of hope, not yet fulfilled, that the elegy has been composed and delivered in a real world in which suns rise and set, day follows day, the flood remains perilous to all those whom Lycidas has left behind, and the young shepherd has to bethink himself of the duties of the new day. It is realism, but not a narrowing realism—"To morrow to fresh Woods, and Pastures new."

The Italian Element in *Lycidas*

F. T. Prince

Lycidas is the most impressive of Milton's minor poems and one of the chief glories of English lyrical verse. Dr. Johnson's severity towards the pastoral convention of the poem has had little effect upon its reputation and its appeal, and has been sufficiently answered by criticism from the early nineteenth century to our own time. His denial of beauty to the verse may be felt to be equally a revelation of the sharp limits of his sensibility; but it is somewhat more difficult to rebut, since the structure of the verse is indeed peculiar. We are not likely to find that "the diction is harsh, the rhymes uncertain, and the numbers unpleasing." Yet the fact that the principles of structure of *Lycidas* have never been applied by later poets suggests that they have never been completely understood, however much the poem has been admired.

This, the last poem of Milton's youth, and the most perfect, in fact shows him as more conscious than ever before of the possibilities of moulding English verse by Italian methods. *Lycidas* cannot be dissected without a knowledge of the Italian poetry of the sixteenth century. But it must be said that there is no exact parallel in Italian literature to the pattern of Milton's poem; there is no single model to which we can point. The poem results from Milton's appreciation of several different

From *The Italian Element in Milton's Verse* (Oxford, 1954), pp. 71–88.

kinds of Italian verse, and his application of certain first principles to form a new combination of familiar elements. And,
indeed, how could it be otherwise, if the poem was to be what
it is, a unique utterance wrung from the poet by the event and
the circumstances? Much of the power of *Lycidas* flows from
the impression it gives of being thus shaped by a particular
occasion: Milton's personal participation in the poem gives it
its greatest strength. This impression is one with the form of
the poem—a development of the disciplined improvisation of
the lines *On Time* and *At a Solemn Musick*. Such a method of
writing verse must necessarily produce poems which have a
unique shape and movement.

It is possible nevertheless to detect the discipline which guides
such poems, and in *Lycidas* it is the discipline of the *canzone*,
as it was modified and adapted in lyrics and eclogues of the
Cinquecento.

Some aspects of this relationship are obvious enough. W. P.
Ker pointed out that "you cannot fully understand . . .
Lycidas without going back to Italy and the theory and practice of the *canzone*," and insisted that the whole tradition of
solemn odes in English, from Spenser's *Epithalamion* to the
nineteenth century, rested upon Dante's description of the *canzone* in the *De Vulgari Eloquentia*, and in particular on his
consecration of the harmony between hendecasyllables and hep-
tasyllables. The combination of ten-syllable and six-syllable
lines in *Lycidas* of course represents that Italian harmony, but
the connexion with the tradition of the *canzona* goes farther
than that.

The wide deviations from the strict form of the *canzone* are,
however, the first thing to be noticed. A *canzone* consisted of a
complex, fully rhymed stanza of some length, repeated several
times and followed by a shorter concluding stanza, the *commiato*. *Lycidas* consists of eleven "verse-paragraphs" of lengths
varying from ten to thirty-three lines, closely but irregularly
rhymed, and including ten lines, scattered throughout, which
do not rhyme at all; the last verse-paragraph is of eight lines,
rhymed like an *ottava rima*, and undoubtedly corresponds in
its own way to a *commiato*. The six-syllable lines are disposed
as irregularly as the rhymes, but are governed nevertheless by
certain limitations: they are used somewhat sparingly, and they

always rhyme, and always with a ten-syllable line which has gone before.

II

Milton must have been well acquainted with the liberation of some Italian lyric verse from stanzaic form which took place in the latter half of the sixteenth century and which had produced a great flow of facile writing by his own time. There is no need to undertake the difficult task of tracing how this liberation came about, for there can be little doubt that Milton's first and clearest impression of it would have come from two works, Tasso's *Aminta* and Guarini's *Il Pastor Fido*. Tasso's famous pastoral drama must have established the use, for certain purposes, of such irregularly rhymed passages, though it seems that his father Bernardo had experimented with such forms in eclogues and some other elaborate poems. Guarini developed this feature of *Aminta* with great success; among his choruses are to be found, together with the normal use of regular *canzone* form, several examples of a sustained improvised pattern of rhymes. From this type of irregular lyric, and from the partially rhymed semi-lyrical passages of dialogue found both in *Aminta* and *Il Pastor Fido*, Milton would have seen the possibilities of this liberation of the *canzone* for dramatic and lyrical verse. These pastoral dramas were among the most brilliant and most admired works of Italian poetry in the late sixteenth and early seventeenth centuries. Their artistic authority would certainly have been acknowledged even by a poet of so different a temper as Milton.

Nevertheless, the technical innovations of *Aminta* and *Il Pastor Fido* do not in themselves account for the structure of *Lycidas*, though they may help to explain how Milton arrived at his own methods. For with *Aminta* the Italian pastoral began to move away from its dependence on Virgil's example, and entered a new world of its own, preoccupied with the affairs of the Amaryllis and the Neaera who are allotted two lines in Milton's poem. As Italian pastoral poetry became less learned and more facile, it became less evocative of any associations other than erotic. *Lycidas*, with its repeated invocations of the "Sicilian Muse," intends to remain within reach and touch of Theocritus and Virgil; and this intention it shares with the

Italian eclogues of the earlier sixteenth century rather than
with those of the later. The seriousness of the poem, however
personal its intensity may be, is a quality it shares with the
even earlier Latin pastoral tradition; in Italy, as the sixteenth
century ran its course, such allusions as those of Milton to the
Church became impossible.

Lycidas therefore takes advantage of the technical freedom
of the later *Cinquecento;* but it uses that freedom in ways which
recall also the Italian eclogues of the High Renaissance, when
vernacular poetry was absorbed in its imitation of Greek and
Latin.

III

The Italian eclogues of Sannazaro (1458–1530) and Berardino Rota (1509–1575) illustrate some of the technical developments by which it was sought to recreate Greek and Roman
pastoral verse in traditional Tuscan forms. The chief distinction between the methods of these two poets is that by Rota's
time the diction of Italian verse had learned how to reproduce
the movement of Latin syntax, and this made possible a freer
handling of verse-forms.

Sannazaro's eclogues in Italian are interspersed throughout
his pastoral romance, the *Arcadia;* the more lyrical of them
preserve the fixed forms of the *canzone* (including the *sestina*),
but for the purposes of dialogue Sannazaro uses *terza rima*, the
form which was always favoured for colloquial or familiar verse.
The mixture of metres in individual eclogues, and the use of
various elaborate lyric forms, show the problems facing Italian
poets when they set out consciously to rival classical pastorals.
There was no single vernacular metre which could be made
the equivalent of the Virgilian hexameter, moving from dialogue
to song without any change of structure.

Sannazaro does not attempt any profound modification of
the movement of the *canzone* in the elegy which forms his Fifth
Eclogue; he is content to infuse into the diction as much as he
can of the elegiac fluidity and fullness already introduced by
Petrarch in echo of Latin verse:

> *Altri monti, altri piani,*
> *Altri boschetti, e rivi*

> *Vedi nel cielo, e più novelli fiori;*
> *Altri Fauni, e Silvani*
> *Per luoghi dolci estivi*
> *Seguir le Ninfe in più felici amori,*[1]

sings Ergasto to the shade of Androgeo. And a passage which points forward to *Lycidas* describes the grief of Nature:

> *Pianser le sante Dive*
>   *La tua spietata morte;*
>   *I fiumi il sanno, e le spelunche, e i faggi:*
> *Pianser le verdi rive,*
>   *L'erbe pallide e smorte;*
>   *E 'l Sol più giorni non mostrò suoi raggi:*
> *Nè gli animai selvaggi*
>   *Usciro in alcun prato;*
>   *Nè greggi andar' per monti,*
> *Nè gustaro erbe, o fonti:*
>   *Tanto dolse a ciascun l'acerbo fato;*
>   *"Androgèo, Androgèo" sonava il bosco.*[2]

The diction and the placing of the words here are no more complex than in Petrarch; but they are more consciously used, as they are used also by Milton, to reproduce specific Latin effects.

The same modulation of the flow of the sentences is to be seen in some of Sannazaro's *terzetti:*

> *Talor mentre fra me piango, e ragionomi*
>   *Sento la lira dir con voci querule:*
>   *"Di lauro, o Meliseo, più non coronomi."*
> *Talor veggio venir frisoni, e merule*
>   *Ad un mio roscigniuol, che stride, e vocita:*
>   *"Voi meco, o mirti, e voi piangete, o ferule."*
> *Talor d'un alta rupe il corbo crocita:*
>   *"Absorbere a tal duol il mar devrebbesi,*
>   *Ischia, Capri, Ateneo, Miseno, e Procita."* . . .[3]

---

[1] "Other mountains, other plains, other thickets and banks, thou view'st in Heaven, and yet fresher flowers: other Fauns and other Silvans throughout sweet summer places follow the Nymphs in happier loves."

[2] "The holy Goddesses wept for thy despiteful death; the rivers know it, and the caves and beeches: the green banks wept, their grasses pale and withered; and the sun for many days concealed his rays: nor did the wild beasts come forth in the meadows, nor the flocks go to the mountains, nor tasted they grass nor fountain: so greatly each was grieved by thy bitter fate; 'Androgeo, Androgeo' the wood resounded."

[3] "Sometimes while to myself I weep and talk, I hear the lyre that says

The double rhymes of these lines are characteristic of Sannazaro's *terza rima:* their effect is to give the dialogue a sustained
cleverness and a monotony of rhythm, which are both somewhat irritating. Such verse has a certain charm, and a flavour of
common speech; but it is more suited to humorous writing than
to serious, and Sannazaro on the whole uses it for such lighter
passages as this exchange of abuse between rival shepherds:

OFELIA.   *Dimmi, caprar novello, e non t'irascere,*
           Questa tua greggia, ch'è cotanto strania,
           Chi te la diè sì follemente a pascere?
ELENCO.   *Dimmi, bifolco antico, e quale insania*
           Ti risospinse a spezzar l'arco a Clonico,
           Ponendo fra' pastor tanta zizzania?
OFELIA.   *Forse fu allor, ch'io vidi malinconico*
           Selvaggio andar per la sampogna, e i naccari,
           Che gl'involasti tu, perverso erronico.[4]

This jocular intricacy of surface betrays an inner emptiness.
But Milton had a leaning toward this verbal type of humour.
His sardonic sonnets on the reception of his divorce tracts and
on the Long Parliament have roots in this kind of satire in
Italian. There is surely an echo of this manner of rustic raillery
in the description of the singing of the bad shepherds in *Lycidas:*

> And when they list, their lean and flashy songs
> Grate on their scrannel Pipes of wretched straw.

The eclogues of the *Arcadia* display a balance between traditional Tuscan forms and the sustained imitation of Virgil's
diction and manner. This balance is upset in the Italian eclogues
of Berardino Rota, written some forty years later. The form
and diction of these *Egloghe Pescatorie* show what progress
Bembo and his disciples had made towards a close imitation of

---

with querulous tones: 'O Meliseo, I crown me no more with laurel.' Sometimes I see finches and blackbirds come to a nightingale of mine, that cried
and calls out: 'O myrtles, weep with me, and weep, ye fennels.' Sometimes
from a high rock the raven croaks: 'At such a sorrow the sea should swallow
Ischia, Capri, Ateneo, Miseno, and Procita.' "
    [4] OFELIA. "Tell me, new goatherd, and be not angry: this flock of thine,
        that is so odd, who gave it thee so foolishly to graze?"
    ELENCO. "Tell me, old ox-driver, and what madness impelled thee to break
        the bow with Clonico, so setting such discord among shepherds?"
    OFELIA. "Perhaps it was then when I saw Selvaggio go sadly lacking his
        pipe and castanets, which thou robbedst him of, thou wicked stray."

Latin verse in the vernacular. Rota was a younger contemporary of Della Casa, and the latinization of the style in his eclogues recalls Della Casa's infusion of Horatian and Virgilian gravity into the sonnet, and probably owes something to Della Casa's methods.

Neither in Rota's sonnets nor in his eclogues do we find any vivid or concentrated poetic power; but the very conventionality of his matter deflects attention to the small innovations of manner and method which give his eclogues their distinction. Himself a Neapolitan, he imitates and develops in the vernacular the Latin Piscatory Eclogues of Sannazaro. As Virgil invokes the Sicilian Muses, Rota invokes the Nymphs of Mergellina; he derives as much from Sannazaro as from Theocritus and Virgil.

His chief effort is directed towards making a new adjustment between Italian verse-forms and Latinate diction; the result is that the still surviving predominance of the rhymed patterns found in Sánnazaro is here replaced by the predominance of diction as an element of structure. Intricate word-order, carefully sustained repetitions, and lengthy periods tend to relegate rhyme to a secondary position. Such writing is relevant, in however minor a degree, not only to *Lycidas*, but to Milton's blank verse.

In most of the lyrical parts of his eclogues Rota continues to use stanzaic forms; but for dramatic and descriptive dialogue, and for some lyrics, he devises a new formula. His hendecasyllables are built on a submerged pattern of six-line stanzas: a b c a b c e f g e f g, and so on. The use of *terza rima* in pastoral verse is perhaps reflected in the ternary structure of this pattern; but Rota succeeds in eliminating the strongly stanzaic movement of *terza rima* by spacing his rhymes as widely as he does. Moreover, the sense and the diction so habitually disregard the limits of the lines and the "stanza," they profess to observe but really transgress the rhyme-scheme with such consistency, that there is little difference in the effect when, as in the Second Eclogue, submerged rhyme is abandoned for blank verse.

The only satisfactory way to read Rota's rhymed hendecasyllables is indeed as if they were *versi sciolti;* the diction is elaborated in such a way as to impose its own movement on the metre. The following passage from the Eleventh Eclogue will illustrate this effect; Triton sings of various fables of the sea, *a guisa del Sileno di Virgilio:*

A questo aggiunge poi perchè nell' acque	a
Ino col suo figliuol già si sommerse;	b
Come le fu cangiato, il viso, il nome	c
Dal Re del mar: che così a Vener piacque,	a
E in questo e quel Dio poi li converse;	b
E quanto pianta fu la Nimpha, e come	c
Giunone irata le compagne sue	d
Augelli e sassi fece. E di te disse	e
O Scilla ancor, qual fur dannose e vane	f
Le prighiere di Glauco; e quanto fue	d
Circe crudele, e'n quanto duol poi visse	e
L'amante, quando in mar rabbioso cane	f
Latrar t'intese a torto, e poichè scoglio	h
Ti vide, quanto pianse e quanto ancora	i
Ogni nocchier ti fugga, e perchè festi,	j
Rimembrando di Circe il fiero orgoglio,	h
Senza compagni Ulisse. E come fora	i
O Vener bella tu dal mar sorgesti	j
Nata di spume: onde 'l bel nome hai preso.[5]	k

Yet, for all its careful modulations, there is something mechanical about such verse. Rota has fluency, but little energy, and this is perhaps why he clings to a regular scheme of rhyme, when blank verse would seem to be the logical development of his style. His formula is a compromise, and the opposition between the repeated pattern of rhymes and the irregular current of the diction is too constant to be satisfying: it leaves a faint impression of artistic dishonesty or cowardice. Rota's methods point the way to Tasso's *Aminta*, in so far as his eclogues suggest that blank verse on the one hand, or a greater freedom of rhyme on the other, would open up new possibilities; Tasso's "eclogue" combines these more logical methods.

[5] "To this he adds then why Ino with her son was dipped in the waters; how she had her face and name changed by the King of the sea, for so it pleased Venus, and into this and that God then he changed them; and how much bewept was the Nymph, and how angry Juno made her companions stones and birds. And of thee he said, O Scilla, again, how harmful and vain were the prayers of Glaucus; and how cruel Circe was, and in what pain then lived thy lover, when he heard thee bark in the sea as a raging dog, and when he saw thee as a rock, how much he wept and how yet every sailor flees thee; and why thou deprivedst Ulysses of his comrades, remembering the fierce pride of Circe. And how it was that thou, O lovely Venus, rose from the sea, born of foam, whence thy fair name is taken."

A knowledge of Sannazaro's and of Rota's eclogues enables one to distinguish the main factors in the development of Italian pastoral poetry in the sixteenth century. Taken together with *Aminta* and *Il Pastor Fido*, they point to the underlying compulsions of Milton's "monody," why it seeks, and how it achieves, a reconciliation between rhyme and fluent elegiac diction. *Lycidas* is more powerful than any of these elegant literary amusements; but without the technical discoveries they represent Milton would have been unable to give his pastoral its combination of freedom and discipline.

IV

Two technical experiments—the attempt to evolve a poetic diction equivalent to that of Virgil, and the attempt to combine the tradition of the *canzone* with that of the classical eclogue—marked Italian pastoral verse in the sixteenth century. In England both these experiments bore fruit in *Lycidas*. But before considering Milton's poem more closely, it is worth looking at the degree to which these Italian experiments are traceable in earlier English pastoral poetry. The only previous English poet worth considering in this connexion is Spenser, the only poet to show, in *The Shepheardes Calender*, that he believed the pastoral to be capable of "high seriousness." The general Elizabethan and Jacobean notions of pastoral, however delightfully they might enrich plays and lyrics, or narrative and topographical verse, were too popular and superficial to affect Milton's poem.

Spenser's methods in *The Shepheardes Calender* are akin to those of the earlier type of Italian eclogue written by Sannazaro rather than to those tried out by Rota. Roughly speaking, we may say that he is not interested in the problem of metrical unity of effect that began to interest Rota and was solved by Tasso. Writing in stanzas (except in the three "Chaucerian" eclogues), Spenser either preserves the same stanza throughout or introduces songs or "layes" in different measures. The only reflection of *canzone* form in *The Shepheardes Calender* is in the dirge in November, and this, though of some interest in relation to Milton, has no prosodic affinity with *Lycidas*.

It seems clear that Spenser's technique in pastoral verse was formed without reference to the particular Italian technical advances summarized above. This is confirmed by the form of his later pastorals, *Colin Clout's Come Home Againe*, *Daphnaïda*, and *Astrophel*. *Colin Clout* indeed uses a metre not found in *The Shepheardes Calender*, continuous "heroic" quatrains; and the way in which Spenser handles these, so that the limits of the quatrains have little correspondence with the flow of the verse, is faintly suggestive of Rota's device of submerged rhyme. But the analogy is slight because, for one thing, Spenser's quatrains are a shorter and more emphatic pattern than Rota's pattern of six lines and are more difficult to submerge; and for another, Spenser seems to make no effort to submerge them. He does not attempt, by means of a complex word-order or of strong pauses within the lines, to disguise the rhyme-scheme, but rather proceeds with his usual mellifluous facility and produces an effect of his own. There is, moreover, an English parallel to the verse of *Colin Clout*, and that is the verse of Raleigh's surviving fragment of *The Book of the Ocean to Cynthia*. Since the two poets were closely associated at about this time, and Spenser alludes to Raleigh's poetry in *Colin Clout*, it is possible that the quatrains of this poem were suggested by Raleigh's lost poem *Cynthia*, which may have been in the same metre as the later fragment.

Daphnaïda and *Astrophel* were the finest pastoral elegies written in English before *Lycidas*, and must be reckoned important features of Milton's poetic background. Yet in these later and more lengthy poems Spenser does but apply the verse technique he had devised more than a decade before: here, as in the bulk of his poetry, the characteristic rhetoric and music are due to his genius for writing in stanzas. Milton had not attempted to write in stanzas of Spenserian type since he relinquished his poem on *The Passion;* what else *Daphnaïda* had to give him—an example of flowing melody—he must have appropriated long before composing *Lycidas*. The chief interest of a comparison between Spenser's pastoral elegies and Milton's would consist in their divergences: Spenser's regularly woven patterns and leisurely embroidery make an instructive contrast to Milton's more compressed and more passionate variety of movement.

V

It remains to show what specific means Milton employed "to build the lofty rhyme." The final clue to the structure of *Lycidas* is to be found in principles derived from the architecture of the *canzone*.

The structure of the *canzone* was fully explained by Dante in the *De Vulgari Eloquentia;* Tasso also discusses it in his dialogue *La Cavalletta*, and claims to discover some discrepancy between Dante's theory and his practice. But the principle of structure which is relevant to *Lycidas* is never in dispute: it is that the stanza of a *canzone* is most commonly built of two sections, which are linked by a key line or *chiave*. Such a stanza was also called a *stanza divisa*. One or the other of the two parts of such a stanza might also be divided, but not usually both. If the first part was undivided it was called the *fronte* or brow; if it was divided the sub-divisions were called *piedi* or feet. If the second part of the stanza were undivided it was called the *sirima* or *coda;* if divided, the subdivisions were called *versi*. The first part of a *stanza divisa* must be linked to the second by a line rhyming with the last line of the first; this line was the *chiave* or key. The two *versi*, where these existed, might also be linked by a *chiave*.

It is the sense of movement, and the habits of rhetoric, deriving from these divisions, which determine the methods of Milton's poem. Just as in the original use of the sonnet the divisions and subdivisions between quatrains and tercets were observed by the diction and only transgressed for some special purpose, these divisions in the *canzone* were present to the writer and the reader and gave a distinctive emphasis and movement to the different parts of the stanza. And just as with the divisions of the sonnet, the divisions of the *canzone* were often deliberately overridden by sixteenth-century poets, but only because, even when the diction did not follow them, they remained in mind, and the effect was one of counterpoint between the rhyme-pattern and the diction, such as Milton reproduces in his sonnets. The divisions in both sonnet and *canzone* made possible a kind of rhetoric of rhyme: lines which rhymed had differing weight and emphasis according to their position

and function. It is impossible to follow Milton's methods in
Lycidas without perceiving that he makes use of such a rhetoric
of rhyme, combining it and contrasting it with the more usual
rhetoric of sentence-structure.

The most obvious feature which this method gives the poem
is the failure of Milton's sentences to correspond to the pattern of rhymes; the ebb and flow of statement, the pauses and
new departures, appear to be independent of any necessity but
their own. To give two examples:

Next *Camus,* reverend Sire, went footing slow,	a
His Mantle hairy, and his Bonnet sedge,	b
Inwrought with figures dim, and on the edge	b
Like to that sanguine flower inscrib'd with woe.	a
Ah; who hath reft (quoth he) my dearest pledge?	b
Last came, and last did go,	a
The Pilot of the *Galilean* lake,	c

Weep no more, woful Shepherds weep no more,	a
For *Lycidas* your sorrow is not dead,	b
Sunk though he be beneath the watry floar,	a
So sinks the day-star in the Ocean bed,	b
And yet anon repairs his drooping head,	b
And tricks his beams, and with new spangled Ore,	a
Flames in the forehead of the morning sky:	c

In the first of these passages there is a strong pause at the end
of the fifth line, yet the next line, introducing a new series of
rhymes, takes its own rhyme from those of the completed statement; in the second passage the first strong pause comes at
the end of the seventh line, yet this line introduces a new rhyme.
Everywhere in the poem we find such effects, and they are due
to the working of a positive principle, not to a mere negative
overriding of a casual rhyme-scheme. Milton has in mind the
chief principle resulting from the *stanza divisa* of the *canzone:*
that each new group or series of rhymes must be linked to its
predecessor by a key line. In the first example given, either the
fifth or sixth line (but preferably the latter) may be regarded
as such a key, taking up a rhyme from the first four lines. In the
second example the fifth line is such a key, though again it is
followed by a line which also takes up a rhyme from the first

four lines. A clearer example is the fifth line of the following
paragraph:

Return *Alpheus*, the dread voice is past,	a
That shrunk thy streams; Return *Sicilian* Muse,	b
And call the Vales, and bid them hither cast	a
Their Bels, and Flourets of a thousand hues.	b
Ye valleys low where the milde whispers use,	b
Of shades and wanton winds, and gushing brooks,	c

Milton is using the principle of articulation of the *canzone;*
and he has liberated it from its association with repeated *piedi*
or *versi* within his paragraphs. This principle of articulation
is therefore free to affect any part of his paragraphs, not only
certain transitions, like the *volta* or, as Dante calls it, the
"diesis."

The rhetoric of rhyme derived from the *canzone* has thus
provided Milton with an invaluable instrument—a type of
rhyme which looks both back and forward. His ear had been
so trained by the *canzone* as to appreciate this effect not only
in the key, or *chiave*, where it is most obvious, but in subtler
details. One of these is the use of the six-syllable lines, which
are also placed so as to give a sense of expectation: they not
only always rhyme with a previous longer line (thus looking
back), but they give the impression of a contracted movement
which must be compensated by a full movement in the next line
(which is always of full length), and they thus look forward.
This effect is most marked when, as in most cases, these short
lines rhyme with the line immediately preceding them.

Milton has constructed *Lycidas* by means of these very precise principles, though they are principles which not only allow
him a certain freedom of improvisation but even facilitate it,
in a way that would be impossible if the verse were not closely
controlled. He has made his own rules for this poem, but made
them out of his knowledge and enjoyment of the strictest Italian practice. Thus he appears to have decided that his rhymes
must not generally be separated by more than two lines. For the
scattered unrhymed lines he had sufficient Renaissance authority.
He has also accepted from Dante the preference for a couplet
to end his paragraphs; according to the *De Vulgari Eloquentia*,

"the endings of the last lines are most beautifully disposed if they fall with a rhyme into silence."

Indeed, the only true couplets in *Lycidas* are those which conclude verse-paragraphs; and one of the best ways to appreciate the articulation of the poem is to analyse the effect of those rhymes coming together elsewhere, which might appear to be couplets, but which are not, because the second rhyming line always looks forward to what comes next. The following examples illustrate this effect in varying degrees:

Begin then, Sisters of the sacred well,	a
That from beneath the seat of *Jove* doth spring,	b
Begin, and somwhat loudly sweep the string.	b
Hence with denial vain, and coy excuse,	c

It was that fatall and perfidious Bark	a
Built in th' eclipse, and rigg'd with curses dark,	a
That sunk so low that sacred head of thine.	b

Fame is no plant that grows on mortal soil,	a
Nor in the glistering foil	a
Set off to th' world, nor in broad rumour lies,	b
But lives and spreds aloft by those pure eyes,	b
And perfect witnes of all judging *Jove;*	c

To analyse *Lycidas* in the light of the *canzone* and the Italian eclogues is to realize with vividness that only a poet of Milton's intellectual energy could have devised and successfully applied such a formula. The poem is built upon movements of thought and emotion; Milton is able to use the methods of repeated transitions, of a continuous unfolding and developing, because his mind and emotions naturally moved with power and confidence, with a sustained strength. Even when other poets who have attempted solemn odes in English have had some of this capacity for embodying mental and emotional energy in verse, they have lacked a technical formula so appropriate to such a task. The discipline of *Lycidas* has left little mark on the tradition of the English ode; it has proved to be inimitable. And this is scarcely surprising, if the peculiarly combined forces described in this chapter are among those which went to its making.

Theme, Pattern, and Imagery in *Lycidas*

Rosemond Tuve

Lycidas is the most poignant and controlled statement in English poetry of the acceptance of that in the human condition which seems to man unacceptable. I do not of course refer simply to the calm ending of the elegy, but to its whole poem-long attempt to relate understandably to human life the immutable fact of death—the pain of loss, the tragedy of early death, the arraignment of the entire natural world that did not avert this unnatural concluding of what was unfulfilled, the passionate indictment of an order that sets a fatal stop upon even man's Orphean task and the good report that would crown it, the depositions one after another of those who carry out the higher commands in orderly fashion, the accusers who still press for an answer, and finally the center and heart of the matter: the questioning of a justice that would take the young and leave the ripe, take the devoted and leave the self-indulgent, so too would take the shepherd and leave the destroyer. What answer? What order? to what end a human life, struck down and ended by an immutable will even as it consecrates itself to God's own uses on an earth sick and famished under the hand of His enemy? Disorder, no answer, death is our answer; the slit life, the ravaged commonwealth.

From *Images and Themes in Five Poems by Milton* (Cambridge, Mass., 1957), pp. 73–111.

Indictments of the unfathomable total moral order, and answers to them, are matter of tragedy, not of pastoral, and Milton twice recognizes this and twice returns from that higher mode back into the different music of the pastoral. Each question has its answer before he makes this return. The questions are cognate. One is in terms of the folly of the poet's devotion (since Death ends it, irrelative of fulfillment), and one in terms of the flat impossibility of the priest's task, when an inscrutable power extinguishes those who alone would do its work here. The answers are not so much cognate as the same, that judgement is the Lord's. In each case the meaning of the answer transcends man's unaided wisdom, and it is properly spoken by an unearthly voice. This last is simply one aspect of the imagery which keeps each answer exactly suited to the nature and philosophical weight of the question.

In the first climax of question and answer Milton moves unobtrusively through related types of images: from the pastoral images which can signify to us all that is careless, not responsible for ends, in a life that sports with Amaryllis in the shade, all that is symbolized by "Delight" in a *Roman de la rose*, on through images with a sure romance connotation, spur and guerdon. The *guerdon* which as tangible token marks a course run with honor at the tournament or at the end of an entire knightly life [1] is not, I think, equated with the *spur* of honorable report (honor, not its by-product prestige) which impels to action. For a poet it impels to self-discipline and laborious days. Thence to the simpler figure used for what the care and labor bring forth, the *sudden blaze* of a poetic achievement worthy those years of fire tended and fostered; but instead of this comes the other suddenness, irretrievable, of Atropos' action. The terror that attends our powerlessness lies in the image, "*thin spun* life"; the ease of this end is an ironic comment on our attention to ends.

The secrets of the otherworld, of those who create and who judge, have been thought of as epic matters by Milton ever

[1] For example, Malory's last book was called by him "The Piteous Tale of the Morte Arthure *saunz Gwerdon*," and the reader will recall its import. *Blaze* in the next sentence is apparently an image from fire, not originating at any rate in the verb or noun *blazon, blaze*. The usual reading takes the *blaze* as *the becoming famous*. In support of my different one: the fire which smoulders or is tended in a poet bursts out at last in great poetry, only a smouldering *reputation* breaks forth into a blaze of *fame*.

since *Vacation Exercise*, 30–54. Yet it is fitting and necessary that the answer which enlightens his servant, and negates "the *thankless* Muse," should be fully spoken out here by shining *Phoebus*,[2] to whom the allegiance of all poet-shepherds is due, both him whose life is slit and the living ones who are left to write of it. In this answer, through the extended metaphor of the heavenly plant, which *lives and spreads* as the great final pronouncements echo through heaven, Phoebus extracts and throws away the irony and the powerlessness, reduces to instrument the inimical shears, redefines the spur, promises due guerdon when all real guerdons are given, "lastly." Not ignoble, the other conception had yet not been truly a conception of *Fame*. Artifice and vulnerability are the character of all garlands where soil is *mortal*, witness *im*perfect, eyes *im*pure; and "Fame" is neither rightly understood by men, nor conferable by them, nor measurable by their imperfect faculties, nor at all touchable by death; ineffable, unwithered, and immortal.

It is a perfect instance of subtle literary judgement that Milton did not phrase this, as he might have done, in the imagery of "And when the chief Shepherd shall appear, ye shall receive a crown of glory that fadeth not away" (1 Peter v. 4). He saved for his second great answer the overtly Christian terms of St. Peter's speech, by which time the sudden blaze and clear light of unequivocal terms is wanted. This is not a matter of "Christian" and "pagan" but of direction and indirection, of a less or a more figurative functioning in the language. Both are Christian. The question of Milton's pagan imagery in *Lycidas* here comes up in its first form, and we make the first answer to it, that such *terms* do not make images non-Christian. The additional element of indirection in the first question and answer was of a kind endeared to the Renaissance reader by long habit. Nor have Milton's Phoebus and Jove and amaranthine plant lost their classical suggestions to become exactly and solely what Peter and Paul talk about in God's conferred "crown of righteousness." The two terms of any metaphor both add meaning to that which is being given significance through its use. We must turn later to the full

[2] Milton's other uses of *Phoebus*, from *Elegy i* on, illuminate this one; the sense of a responsibility to poetry apparent here comes out especially in *Manso*, 35: "not profitless to Phoebus"; and the reminiscence of Virgil's Sixth Eclogue is pertinent. Modern over-personal readings are to be questioned.

importance of this, but the point that should be made before we leave Phoebus's *first* of the *three* overt "consolations" in *Lycidas* is this one concerning the metaphorical weight of classical allusion and figure. This does not deny the judgement that the unambiguously full statement of Christian consolation in Christian terms may shine out with a more splendid and luminous clarity, in Milton's own imagination and to us toward the end of the poem.

St. Peter both makes evident and answers the second great question which draws Milton into the epic and tragic realm, where doubts raised by resentful human bewilderment ask for ultimate answers, secrets known only to a wisdom above nature. Camus, though he is a river god like the rest, wears the clothing of grief and stands like the song itself among the mourners who question rather than among the accused who state their innocence, and it is he that asks the forthright "*Who* hath reft him?" which closes the inquiry; we hear no more of second causes, and nature is acquitted. The last personage is neither accuser nor accused, but the emblem of a just and final judgement, vicar of Christ. Peter speaks first as type, bishop, and head of all priests, of the living ones he could better have spared no less than of the faithful one cut off.[3]

From here onward the bitter, despairing and violent description, of "our corrupted Clergie then in their height," of its own weight poses the further accusation which the situation in fact in November 1637 had certainly brought Milton to make. It is Job's outcry against incomprehensibility in the moral order and in the "justice" of its Author; added, to turn the knife in the wound, is the irony of the death he here bewails, typifying all hopes cut off in the bud and all faithful devotion silenced. The indictment is expressed, not spoken; the very stones of these harsh facts cry out for reason and justice. After the rage and despair of the fierce "and nothing sed," Peter's answer is the terrible one of God's final doom, when all that is to be said will be said. He speaks little more

---

[3] Milton does not use precisely Dante's symbolism of Peter's gold and his white key, but there are interesting connections with the way Dante uses them (*Par.* v) in condemning private inconstancy to vows made to the Church; cf. also *Purgatorio,* ix. 127. *Paradiso,* xxvii, has Peter's own more famous diatribe, which also employs the common image of rapacious pastors as wolves, and also keeps to the tone of castigation that accompanies a still-anticipated judgement by the source of power that gave the keys.

of the divine justice than this, that judgement of evil is the
Lord's and that it will come; that is the answer, for man's
question in the face of the riddle of allowed evil is: WILL it?
It seems difficult to press the image, as many critics do, to
answer also the question "*when* will it?"; this is a vision of
judgement, not a picture of it, and if it "foretells the ruine"
of evil men for whom an earthly fall is even now preparing, it
also (or therefore) contains indubitable reference to the last
and perfect judgement. As the first climactic resolution in the
poem touched primarily the living greenness of an eternal justice accorded to faithful shepherds, heirs of Orpheus, by the
perfect witness of all-judging Jove, the second embodies that
other side of justice, when those upon the left hand shall know
the power of the sword that issues from the mouth of God.

These two apocalyptic lines [4] carry images, inseparable from
the Biblical imagery whence they spring, which make them
more than lines of triumph felt at the spectacle of just judgement, to be done at long last upon evil. Several considerations
make this trumpet note of prophetic vindication necessary.
But still—especially as we remember that we listen to Peter
not Milton—that fear which shakes also the "just" man when
he confronts the perfect judge, is felt too, if only in the power
of the image in the awful "at the door, *Stands ready*" and in
the dreaded finality:

>   Stands ready to smite once, and smite no more.

This inner tremor of even the less guilty, of every natural
creature, before the vision of doom, we know to be in the
poem, for the lines following are "Return, Alpheus, the dread
voice is past, That shrunk thy streams. . . ." The end of all
judging, when the sword shall smite *no more*, is the end of our
world, when by the dread voice announcing a final justice even
Alpheus' innocent streams shall indeed be forever shrunk, and
all the living rivers of the earth be dried up, when "the elements
shall melt with fervent heat, the earth also and the works that
are therein shall be burned up" (2 Peter iii. 10). The turn to
the reviving sweetness of the passage in which all fresh and
growing things give their loveliness to strew the hearse where
Lycid lies, is of an extreme beauty.

[4] [See the essays by LeComte, Howard, Robins, *et al.*, cited *infra*, p. 358.]

It is a turn from one kind of "consolation" to another, for all that. Milton never does turn in this poem from a non-Christian sense that death may be the only answer given for the riddle of life to a Christian belief in eternal life. He turns, more than once, from what seems senseless in death to death made tolerable. Where he must go outside the human world to find what makes endurable an "order" that commands the death of the unripe and the death of the consecrated, he leaves his chosen mode, but not his subject. Neither excursion is in the remotest degree digressive except in the first sense. There is no single "Christian consolation" in the poem; the whole texture of it is replete with these, and the imagery is the major voice carrying that constant burden. If it seem a fantastic misuse of words to call Peter's "dread voice" a consolation, the rest of the poem adds its witness to our own experience that the stab at the heart of loss is that it denies conceivable order. All that reaffirms order consoles. The image of life may seem to be more than balanced by the vision of death, the symbol of the mystical plant that lives and spreads to make a crown so different from the laurels and the myrtles brown may seem less adequate to its function than is the great engine of doom which metes out another due measure of "meed." However, not only is the poem a structure of cumulative, not contrasted, insights into the meaning of life and death, but also there is yet to come the vision of the nuptial union of the soul with the source of love, a third vision of judgement. Moreover, though it is notable that symbols are chosen at these three crucial points to convey great fundamental oppositions like growth and destruction, life and nothingness, union and sundering, fruition and annihilation, there is also the whole continuing web of the poem with its living and tender sense of imperishable sweetness in all moving and growing things. The affirmations of *Lycidas* begin with its first line.

The imagery within the great speech of St. Peter is different from any other in the poem. It has a different purpose: denigration, an almost magniloquent diminishing ("depraving") of its subjects—the exact formal parallel and the exact evaluative opposite of the "praise" or magnification which is the natural function of most images in Milton's as in any funeral elegy. This, combined with their satirical purpose and resultant "roughness," lowers the style violently (*within* the great symbolic parent image), paradoxically enough considering the elevation of subject. But for the one factor of their dependence, this would be intolerable, and is indeed some excuse for those who have called it digression. The crowd of lesser images, being all of one kind rhetorically (*meiosis*) set going so strong a current of defamation that the one line where this movement halts ("The hungry Sheep look up, and are not fed") derives thence an accent of most piteous blamelessness and vulnerability, and compassion converts to generosity what might have been arrogance. Comment can be spared on this group of images; their vitality, a series of direct shocks from a charged wire, is felt by any reader; the directness results from their pronounced logical simplicity (based on comparable quality: *lean, flashy, scrannel;* or compared manner of acting: *creep, devours, scramble*). The unifying pastoral figure which governs the passage gives their metaphorical depth and thence their universality to the terms within it. And this, not merely the type of particulars used, is the character of allegory.

The passage would be allegorical even if there were no topical reference to the events of the late 1630s in England; that simply doubles its allegorical reference. Since other treatments of *Lycidas'* "allegory" assume that it resides in these historical relationships, some general remarks are in order. They are best made with this passage under our eyes.

The gradual figurative amplification of the Good Shepherd in scores of pastoral figures throughout the Old and New Testament, the constant liturgical emphasis in all centuries and all churches, the accretions and interpretations through centuries of use, Petrarch, Mantuan, Spenser's powerful satirical use in May of *The Shepheardes Calender* (Milton quotes twenty-nine lines of it) [5]—these are what have given its allegorical power to Milton's figure, that is to say, made a metaphor of it. This is why rereading them makes us see more than history in it. Like all metaphor, the figure is "dark"; this re-

---

[5] In *Animadversions upon the Remonstrants Defence against Smectymnuus* (see Columbia *Milton* III, 165–166) Milton quotes lines 103–131 of *S. C.: May;* he is speaking of one's learning "to renounce the world and so give himselfe to God," and says that "our admired Spenser" "personates our Prelates, whose whole life is a recantation of their pastorall vow, and whose profession to forsake the World . . . boggs them deeper into the world. . . ."

sults from one term being left open, its meaningfulness left to
the experience and wit of the reader. Like all allegory, it is
continued metaphor. That is, in Spenser's phrase, "a dark conceit" in which profound conceptual meanings are gradually
figured forth (to be read only in the figures), providing thus
the deep-diving plunge into significance which the language
of discursive reason cannot provide. Such figures carry conceptions not propositions, essences not phenomena, and shadows
of that which we know the-substance-of only through its
shadows. The allegorical (contrast the illustrative, the exemplary) aspect of the figure of shepherd as type of Christ we
penetrate only through the figure's history, developing as it
did in intimate connection with all else that happened to pastoral poetry; Milton does not provide its metaphorical senses
but depends upon and uses them. A modicum of knowledge about
the life of a sheep, with its needs, perils, and protectors, will
tell us what sort of things the bad clergy did in 1637; but
only knowledge of what that allegorical figure was accustomed
to carry will make to shine out before our eyes the enormity
(to Milton) represented by what they did, and relate it to all
the other issues and griefs and joys of the poem. The enormity
because of the relation is Milton's point.

Such possible changes in sensibility (that is, of the receiving
mind in reading) can be pointed to but not really accomplished by explanations, and I shall dwell upon this figure only
long enough to clarify these general principles about the working of allegorical imagery through the poem's simplest example. Powerful as it is, St. Peter's arraignment of those who
by vow were Christ's shepherds pledged to lead his flock out
of death into life, for their treacherous betrayal of the idea
of Christlike love, is not the most complex or moving use of
the methods of allegory in the poem. One point which touches
this passage primarily and two which will be important later
may be made fairly swiftly.

The first concerns the relation of historical allegory to the
other figurative senses. Through its long Jewish and Christian
history, this Biblical figure of the shepherd had come to command ways of reading which are variously fruitful. Rather
simply parabolic sometimes, it was used in ways that ask a
tropological reading (that is, the metaphor leads to moral in-

sight and different conduct: *quid agas*); and an allegorical
reading in the strictest mediaeval sense (typological, with
Christ as the head of his hierarchical Church); and an anagogical reading (speaking, like the Shepherd's unfading crown in
1 Peter, quoted earlier, of last things and eternal life). Milton's *Lycidas* asks for all three kinds of reading. In addition a
less precise way of reading, which I believe may be included in
what was loosely referred to as taking the letter *spiritualiter*,
could open the way to ideas less homiletically moral or specifically Christian than metaphysical, Platonic or timeless. Milton early became a great master of the last (that is of writing
that asks it of us), but save for his very largest figures in
the long works, he is no match for his master Spenser in the
first, the creation of vast and extremely complex figures which
when read tropologically provide moral insight of unparal-
leled delicacy, and a universality unarrested by time.

Historical allegory is a special offshoot, which habit he borrowed not only specifically from Spenser's May and its like
but generally from the whole tradition of pastoral, to which
it now seemed indigenous because of mediaeval practice. Not
Dante's and Boccaccio's and Petrarch's eclogues alone (stem-
ming ultimately from Virgil) but dozens of Carolingian and
later pastorals enter the world of affairs thus, and give the lie
to any notions we in later ages may have of Arcadian "escape."
But historical allegory doubles the figure back upon itself to
provide a second *literal* reading, a way of making the metaphor give birth to an intended series of historically true significances, factual and interpretative. Spenser of course used
this, but only with the secondary importance of assisting clarity and inescapable convincingness in his universal meanings.
This Milton too has done in the passage in question. As readers interested in all the workings of his images, we have two
helpful courses to follow: when read not as sources *but as
pieces in their own right*, other literary works using any allegorical figure widen and deepen for us its metaphorical possibilities, for these possibilities are a common heritage, and
are often recognized through the merest color of specialized
diction or familiar allusion. This will be exemplified presently.
And secondly, because historical allegory is both literal history
(put figuratively) and active metaphor timelessly applicable,

we read history, in order that clear understanding of two sets
of literal terms may make this activity large and free. The
reading of ecclesiastical history during Laud's time reveals
without our taking thought for it the universality, more than
the historicity, of Milton's massive indictment.[6]

Two points touching the imaginative power of topical suggestions in allegorical figures are as relative to other parts of
the poem as to that here discussed. Only experience as direct
as possible of the second term of any metaphor provides both
the peculiar pleasure derived from the "translation" of terms
and the capacity to follow out the suggestions other than sensuous which are thus drawn in. Even "What time the Gray-
fly winds her sultry horn" remains a poorer thing if one has
never heard a horn, and the carefree languor and peace that
come with the music (metrical skill suiting) have changed the
thermal quality of *sultry*. In figures where many suggestions
enter, the avenues to such "direct experience" may sometimes
seem odd enough. An example is in the passage which begins
"Ay me! Whilst thee the shores, and sounding Seas / Wash
far away." It culminates in the headland where "the great vision of the guarded Mount" looks (from the Celtic tip of Britain that Druids and giants had guarded before Michael)
straight across the unbroken water to Spain; and it comes to
an end with the unexpected figurative turn in "Look homeward Angel now, and melt with ruth." "Direct experience"
here involves not only the imagined wash and murmur of the
cold seas down the whole western coast of Britain from the
Hebrides to Land's End. It asks that we should have thoughts
like those awakened in Milton by Drayton's *Polyolbion*, by
legends of Cornish might and of Orphean druidic seers pre-
figuring Christianity, by Spanish strongholds seen on Ojea's
map and recalling ecclesiastical tyrannies once escaped, by the

---

[6] Plentiful knowledge of contemporary events is not always so useful to
image-study as in this case, but the eclogue is a compressed form in Milton's
hands, requiring much inner particularization from a reader, and moreover
no antidote to a too-personalized way of taking Milton's vigorous style is
easier to take than the old-fashioned specific: Book iii in Masson's first
volume. (Strict correctness, in either writer, or our agreement, is not in
question here.) Another seemingly but not truly paradoxical result accrues:
a vivid sense of the parallels between *Lycidas*, 108–131, and our contemporary history, in this case secular. This is a normal result when reading historical allegory, unless of course it is not read as allegory but simply as
history.

events of the centuries during which the venerable unmoved Mount opposite had stood, guarded, with its angelic defender who looked only outward across the sea toward Namancos and Bayona's hold. It is with such reflections that we stand "where" Milton stood, conscious of the ancient integrities and remembering the ancient threats, to see the fragile body which he has made to typify England's frail integrity against present threat, and see it "*sleep*," inactive, unmarked, and pitiable, "by the fable of Bellerus old." In highly allusive poetry books must become our five senses, to make our experience direct.[7]

The second point is this. The reader must have noticed that it has proved almost impossible to avoid considering the whole theme of the poem whenever discussion of the functioning of any topically suggestive image was attempted. Each, no matter how small, was enmeshed in a web—which I have cut by simply not finishing the treatment of the full metaphorical meaning of any. Even the gray-fly's horn we left as if it were a line describing noonday, which nowhere nearly covers the matter; we allowed the Phoebus image to seem primarily a discussion of the poet's reward, whereas Lycidas' death *sans guerdon* has meanings that flow out of the image of Orpheus's unpreventable death, just before; we all but ignored St. Peter's speech as lament while noting it as diatribe. It is the metaphorical force of each image which was slighted. And the omission in the Hebrides-St. Michael's Mount passage was gross. For Lycidas is not only Lycidas, nor not only our own Edward Kings who die young; the passage speaks of the whole crushing human isolation and fragility, of the unreachable dumb body that goes out alone as it came, and of the slender thread of belief—in the loving and pitying superhuman "guard," in ideas of some meaningful harmony and order—which is all

[7] Therefore the debt of the student of *metaphor* to the annotator is not measurable, being an aesthetic debt. This is a linguistic point, and has little to do with a "historical" attitude or a "scholarly" reading. Full understanding of a poet's language is crucial for metaphor; diction affected by ancient conventions, and allusions no longer recognized as such, are words which are not quite in our vocabulary. To be sure, historical and scholarly criticism is oftenest responsible for our fully understanding the second terms of metaphors, when they are not primarily sensuous, and hence catching the relations which are the secret of their power. *Polyolbion,* Song i, and Selden's "Illustrations" discuss Christian use of a "Genius," the Druids, a speech by St. Michael's Mount; compare, with *Lycidas,* 53 ff., Songs ix, x, and Illustrations, and note 15 of this essay.

man has spun to secure him from the deep on which he wanders
undefended and as much in peril while he lives as when he dies,
unless the cry does indeed not echo back to mock his ideas of
meaning and of powerful allies, "Look *homeward* Angel *now*,
and melt with ruth. / *And, O ye Dolphins.* . . ." A rephrased
metaphor never keeps decorum, and Milton's statement does
not like mine seem to talk merely about whether angels and
dolphins exist and listen ; I have allowed the indecorum in order
to point out the major fact about the imagery of *Lycidas* : that
the entire poem is grounded in metaphor. It is figurative speech
from first to last.

This is the gift to Milton of the pastoral tradition. It means
that every group of images functions as a large figure, these
all within the largest ; that each of the so-called pastoral conventions is, like any metaphor, open at one end to allow interpretations that go as deep as a man's knowledge of life will
take him. It is time to see in a more deliberate way how this
operates. It cannot be seen very clearly (in our century) by
reading *Lycidas* alone, since we have lost a once truly widespread sophistication able to catch allusions far more numerous and subtle than the references normally so designated, and
we have lost the Renaissance and mediaeval and baroque habit
of following the multiple senses of long-continued metaphors—
for of course I am now speaking of the important kind of
allegory in pastoral. The history of the criticism of *Lycidas*
shows what happened as obscurity overtook first the habit
(eighteenth- and nineteenth-century criticism) and later the
knowledge (twentieth-century criticism). We are just beginning to get them back together again. Several kinds of recently
emphasized knowledge are involved, but all work primarily
to change a reader's expectations and presuppositions, and
thence his way of taking images rather than his capacity to
construe them.

The most important loss suffered by the general reader of
Lycidas since Milton's time is the loss of pleasure taken in a
familiar long procession of great pastoral elegies which preceded it. Study of sources and "classical background" have always received attention, but scholars have had to restore (and
chiefly to scholars) sympathetic knowledge of the great Italians and the prolific French and English writers of similar

elegies, and the reader is rare who brings to *Lycidas* that natural enjoyment of the form and immediate grasp of its modes
of feeling which come with wide and sympathetic reading—
of Castiglione and Sannazaro as well as Virgil, of Ronsard and
Spenser and Marot, of Petrarch and Boccaccio and nonelegiac
pastoral. Yet Milton wrote *Lycidas* in a continuing tradition,
for those to whom finding pleasure and emotional immediacy
in the similar works of just such famous predecessors was a
genuine and usual experience. It is more possible now than
it was fifty years ago to be such a reader.[8] I refer to something
considerably on the farther side of a mastery of parallels and
borrowings.

This essay cannot discuss the images of *Lycidas*, seriatim,
and that is not necessary or advisable. I should like instead
merely to suggest slowly by example the kind of reading of
pastoral imagery which comes naturally if we make use of its
inheritance. This inherited wealth was not created by Theocritus or Virgil but very slowly built. Milton's poem is the
supreme example of the fullest use of it; he misses nothing, he
wastes nothing. He fell heir to a way of reading as well as ways
of writing, and though the chief point about both is the seemingly simple one that his poem moves entirely on a metaphorical plane, this will prove to be (I think) the secret of that
mysterious attraction which has stirred readers of *Lycidas*
throughout the vicissitudes of three centuries. It is through
this power in the imagery that Milton can present, with the
greatest reticence, tact, power and depth, certain great and
moving conceptions, universally felt states of mind and meanings, not usually conveyable except in symbols; I point to this
power at work in a few instances. His method is not primarily
symbolic (differing here from that of the *Nativity Hymn*),
and no archetypal symbol such as those of purgation, rebirth,
love (water, fire, cave, garden, or the like) pervades or organ-
izes his poem. It is necessary to get into the poem by some
consideration of its first fourteen lines.

This is Milton's third English elegy, and all had put upon
him the irony of "*well* finished" to be said in the teeth of the
fact of early death, the interruption seemingly rather than

[8] See the fundamental study by J. H. Hanford [*supra,* pp. 31 ff.] and
the essays by Sandys, Norlin, *et al.* [cited *infra,* pp. 354–355].

the conclusion of life. It is through the imagery of the preceding lines, not line 8 ("dead, dead ere his prime . . .") that
we look at what bitter comment this death makes on human
aims. With a lasting garland men show honor to immortal
Poetry, crowning her mortal exemplar. But in this one shattered leaves displace those symbols long thought of as fit for
Poetry because it, too, matures *not* to die but live on. It is
Lycidas' garland which, like his poetic promise, is cut while
it is still harsh and unready; everything in the image is disrupted, plucked before it can ripen, finished before it can begin—but finished, ended, this crown or none. I do not read
in Milton's first lines the note of apology for his own unripe
verses familiarly referred to in commentary and criticism. This
poem brings honors, does not constitute them; the garland is
a symbol, and Milton does not pluck his *own* unripe honors.
He says overtly why he is compelled to disturb the due season
of leaves and berries destined thus never to ripen—"*For*" the
one whose poetic gift they exalt is dead ere his prime, and he
does not leave his like, to ripen the crown for. "Bring the
rathe Primrose that forsaken dies" (corrected from "unwedded
dies," 142) touches the same note; and throughout the poem
there are shadows of such ironic connections. These symbols
of "immortal" honor are at once too incongruous and too suit-
able to the fulfillment they signalize, torn from the plant and
made as mortal as what they crown. *Unripeness*—the flaw is
in our entire condition, and to read it as "my art as yet unready" seems too literal and too confined.[9] All is unperfected

[9] Even for line 18. The *Muses* are entreated to lament "loudly" even though
it be for a stripling youth rather than for one ripe in their service, not "deny"
their aid when *any* of their shepherd servants lie dead. When Milton hopes
that so too some gentle Muse will remember him, it is no longer, in this
second paragraph, of garlands and praises that he speaks, but of the "good
speed" of a companion, said where he in his turn will lie ready to be put
from men's sight. The usual very different interpretation of all these images
depends from an emphasis usual in Milton criticism since (roughly) the
period of Coleridge's "John Milton himself is in every line. . . ." Perhaps it
is we who intrude Milton's personality, not he; more than once this happens
in criticism when we underrate the largeness of reference that is an inherited
virtue of pastoral language (*human* ears must tremble, not just Milton's,
when Phoebus hears and answers our bitter accusation of the futility of
serving him; with "To morrow to fresh Woods, and Pastures new" we with
Milton take up again not The Epic but our human hopes—he too had others).
Possibly Tillyard's "the abnegation of self by the great egoist" [*supra*, p. 67]
has been more influential during the last twenty-five years of criticism, and
his careful reservations less so, than he intended.

still, one thing like another—but plucked, nevertheless. What can the unripe do but fade? "Who would not sing for Lycidas?" who indeed? when he is all that sorry load of human hopes, every early death, every quietus said too soon upon promise?

The title alone establishes certain delicate understandings with any reader even of English poetry, by Milton's time, and the chief of these is that Lycidas is both Edward King and all that he signifies. A death is one form of the whole danger; it is the principle of death in human life that is lamented. This is felt when, later, decay and disease, the worm that dooms the rose, all that destroys in the bud the promise of fruit, are "such" as was the news of this loss, *to Shepherds ear*. To the ear, that is, of the one who is guardian over "the weanling Herds," who sings the beauty of the white-thorn when first it blows, whoever in that group of Cambridge men thought that Orpheus' lyre could tame, and move, and make immortal, but who in a sudden event saw youth and beauty and dedication powerless against the hidden worm.

The pastoral figures for which so many critics apologize make it possible for Milton to engender in us the exact quality of feeling and the exact reference to universal realities with which men receive the first death that breaks rudely in upon any group, however loosely associated, who have lived together in youth. As Milton begins that pastoral day, "Together both, ere the high Lawns appear'd . . . ," we are not to make a one-to-one equation, detail by detail. That is not the way allegory works (lines 25–49 are a pure though simple example of the rhetorical figure *allegoria*). The most which is made of this passage usually is that it describes, "conventionally," a Cambridge association with King—unintimate to be sure but justifiably somewhat heightened for the occasion—in the borrowed cold pastoral terms of Greek, Latin, and Renaissance poetry, borrowed but decorous. But the image was not read this way (certainly of course not written this way); its "conventions" wake too many echoes to leave it so empty of passion. We may if we like read it so that something resembling the full feelings that are in it can appear. If we choose we may read it as did those who, weeping with Iolas, had mourned for Alcon that had borne the cold and heat of the day with him, worked, sung, talked, only to be taken by the fates in

the first flower of his youth. We may read as one who with
Simichidas has walked under the trees talking poetry with
Lycidas; one who has seen how Astrophel piped and danced at
the shearing feast, and has seen him untimely cropt, clean de-
faced; one who has remembered how the crowd of shepherds
had sat carefree a long day in the shade by the great cypress,
their craft of poetry protected by Argus, and how the cypress fell and they fled. Pastoral imagery did not remain a
game of allusions in minds familiarly accustomed to read thus
of Castiglione's friendship for a brother writer dead, of Theocritus comparing poems under an elm, of what English poets
looked forward to when Sidney, chief hope in certain high endeavors, would never write again, of how storms, intrigue and
murder, broke out for poets at the death of Petrarch's patron
Robert, of a score of other "shepherds" who had to leave the
flocks they battened. The pre-eminent result was then as now
that these figures for intellectual companionship fertile in life
or interrupted by death became inescapably, habitually, mov-
ingly metaphorical in their operation. "Battened their flocks"
is not a synonymn; it is a figure. Likewise all the rest.

Not the direct experience of a metaphor's terms is in question here but the habit of reading figuratively, of reading not
about history but about reality. (This is the habit the great
Doctor did not have, when he read pastorals.[10]) Since all our
experience of reality flows together, this has the further result
that these pastoral figures are not only pregnant with the feel-

[10] Dr. Johnson, in the passage on *Lycidas* which made "no flocks to batten"
so famous, clearly thinks of allegory as a set of synonymous correspondences,
and when he says "the true meaning is so uncertain and remote that . . . it
cannot be known when it is found," he marks as a vice what provides the
strength of allegory as it does a metaphor; that which speaks of things in
their universal consideration must of necessity present meanings not certainly
limited. It is *not* the associations, connoted second terms, of a metaphor which
are left free for a reader to assign as he fancies—hence the importance of
scholarly criticism, for here we should follow the author's slightest indication
—but the reality to which these point is necessarily undefined and limitless.
Dr. Johnson said some of the wisest and truest things of Milton which have
ever been said, but these are not they. It is idle to inflate into careful criticism
(as has become customary) his remarks on the pastoral mingling of pagan
"trifling fictions" with Christian "awful and sacred truths"; he indicates no
pagan-Christian conflict (rather deplores the absence of one), no tensions,
ambiguities—but quite simply does not realize that pastoral "fictions" are
metaphors in nature and function. They *became* thus through their history,
and he has not sympathetically lived through that history. The sympathy
again possible, if we add the history we may see again one of the faces of
truth which was turned aside from the eighteenth century.

ing and thought their own authors had and we experience
with them; metaphor plunges the arrow of its very precise
meaning into our own present selves and situations. I have
called what Milton wrote in this typical passage an *allegoria*
—not continued equations, but continued metaphor. Whether
there were high lawns near Cambridge, an inn at Grantchester
for cakes and ale after some village revel, is not of moment
except as our knowing some real or fancied detail makes it
all happen again, wearing its meanings in its face; and metaphor, by which we think about all real things together in the
one thought, brings back to life as well our own picnics at our
own Grantchesters. This is not the aim of the image, but only
the way it works; metaphor no more imprisons one in one's
own history than another's, but makes us look at the meanings
which give experience its quality. All the adventure and freshness of Milton's morning, all the endless noons when the gray-
fly's languorous horn stops only to start over—these all say
with one voice *life without time*, man without his mortality, the
rose without the thorn and the garden before what happened in
it. Nothing so sentimental as that youth *is* this; only that in
those moments, when with others "upon the self-same hill"
young poets saw in Orpheus' tasks and delights the highest
use of a life, nothing in the universal framework of things
spoke of the thorn, not on their rose. "But O the heavy change."
It was spoken of.

The monstrousness of death is stressed at first in the un-
naturalness of this death, and stressed at first in the imagery
alone. It appears in certain longer subtler images besides those
mentioned of the unripe honors and the denial of nature's
rhythm (frosts out of season, the young of the herd not the
old poisoned where they fed). It is stressed also in all the multitudinous intimations of man's questioning in the face of every
form destruction takes. Earlier in the poem this questioning
has the shape of "why must man go unready," and a man's fear
that he may die too soon is surely no stronger than the fear
and the pity for that which he loves and loses too soon. But
the question is absent from few lines of the poem. It dwells in
the cadences and inhabits the frail and lovely figures. We are
shaken because we know the fear—by the shadow of the un-
suspected death to come which darkens one figure among those

who drove out under the opening eyelids of the morn, by the vine that overgrows the unkempt woods the shepherd meant to keep, by the blind hands which hold the abhorred shears. The monstrousness of the fact that death the unmanageable (*"What could the Muse her self?"*) should be our single certainty is in the early part of the poem heightened by the wild incalculableness of this death at once early and by "accident."

The subject of all this first portion of *Lycidas* is what King's death meant (still means); not "King's death" nor "Milton's fears of death" nor "his poetic aspirations," but the pathos, unnaturalness, disorderliness, and impotence, hidden and revealed, in the fact of all early death. As Milton pursues the subject, it comes closer to the tragedy than the pathos of the destruction of promise, for the poem almost defines this as the nature of human life. The pursuit will not only integrate this theme with all the tragic human questionings discussed in my first pages, but will arrive at them through poignant considerations of the nature of loss, considerations of the obscure reasons why tribute paid to the dead eases grief, of the scheme of nature which includes man—whether inimical to him, indifferent, or loving, and of the relation of humane and natural; and finally will transform the questions into affirmations through a stronger opposing principle than that of death —and when this is stated we perceive it to be at one with that sweetness which has run underneath all the poem like a strong current, flooding these lines and those, now at the end running open and clear. It is a travesty thus to restate crassly what the poem says so delicately and fully, almost entirely through the metaphorical force of its figures. They could not do this were they not pastoral figures.

What is the nature of the loss? Reserve, dignity, and full expression with neither risk of bathos nor slighting of personal intensity of feeling are but the first gifts of metaphor; greater still is its universalizing power. It is the pastoral tradition that allows *Lycidas* to be a lament for the death of Poetry. So stated, this frightens no man. But metaphor does not state it so. Again we see this for what it means when a particular stance of the mind is habitual. I do not refer only to the fact that we expect the theme when we recall Spenser's October and Theocritus 16, though our doing so restores to

Lycidas a breadth it possesses but lost for a time in some eyes.
I mean rather that (for example) we cannot miss the tragedy
of what Milton says by looking at the point upside down,
when we are told that King was but a poor poet; and that we
cannot think the matter is esoteric, or see Milton as a self-
conscious poetaster, managing his clashes and planning his
ironies yet dismayed lest his own garland also wither. We cannot in fine read images without seeing the full depth and time-
lessness of the ancient themes they carry, if we have sorrowed
for the death of song when music itself dies in the death of
Bion its exemplar, known why Apollo left the fields and thorns
grew in them when Virgil's Daphnis died, wept that with
Adonis all things die (the beauty of Love herself becoming un-
fruitful), believed that order goes to wrack when the eddying
flood washed over the man beloved of the Muses, the first
Daphnis. This image has never meant that song stops, poets
never sing more, creatures never couple again, meadows never
become green—only that they do so in vain. It means that
deathless poetry is not deathless, that nothing is. The death
of any the humblest exemplar of that "civilization" man has
wrested from disorder tells us that Orpheus will die, and order
with him; nothing is exempt, not man's dearest hope or highest
achievement; the principle of death in the universe has worsted
what he thought confirmed his immortality, and nothing can
outwit, nothing negate, that dark power. "What could the
Muse her self that Orpheus bore?"—not even the mother and
source of that which allied him to the creating gods. All alike;
down the swift Hebrus. "Persephone," says Love out of whom
all things spring, "thou art stronger than I, and every lovely
thing must descend to thee."

How, starting from all this, should Milton not go on to
consider the mortality of Poetry, and the withering that awaits
all its laurels? And when the Protectors themselves are powerless, and the Poets put to a check, and dozens of poems down
the centuries point as does life itself to good that dies, and to
evil, decay, all death's lieutenants that take over the flock and
the fields, how should Milton not go on to the Bad Shepherds
and the sheep that rot inwardly? Men could not have seen
these as digressions except by not taking seriously the poets
Milton read with an intensity that burns through his language.

The pastoral images in Lycidas point to men's deepest trusts
and despairs; time had got them ready to mean all Milton
was able to say.

No claims of a critic can thus get them ready. But when,
reaccustomed to the old habits, we no longer think of all pastoral in terms of Arcadian "fancy," a related late-born mis-
understanding will likewise disappear. We remove from the
images of *Lycidas* the obscuring distortions they have worn
because a late Romantic separation of man from "Nature"
supplanted that living continuity in the fabric of all created
things whence, in *Lycidas* as in its predecessors, spring the
deepest pain of the lament and the noblest sublunar echoes
of a final and divine consolation.

Almost all pastoral elegies ask man's permanent question,
"Was this death Natural?" Sometimes with angry amazement,
as of Petrarch's Argus, "Did earth dare this?"; or with sad contrasts as in Castiglione's *Alcon* ("the rude husbandman does
not pluck the unripe fruit"); sometimes obliquely as in Marot's accusation: *"Hà Mort facheuse! onques ne te meslas Que
de ravir les excellentes choses."* It takes no poem to make a
man ask these questions; he asks them of every death that
touches him. But the answers are another matter. Milton has
learned, and uses, them all, and it is all but impossible to tell
some of the "pagan" ones from the other Christian ones, as it
had been for many hundreds of years. The answers are complicated, ranging from the merest color on an image to great
figures occupying fifty lines. We have noticed the simplest appearance of the question, the un-Naturalness of decay that is
untimely. And in all those images the human death and the
others were seen as like flaws, in the one fabric.

One later image might seem to place man in a "Nature"
hostile or indifferent to him, until we remember that the sea
beyond the stormy Hebrides is no more "Nature" than the
daffodils, the willows, or the singer himself. It is the human
pain over the remembered body wandering untended and un-
strewn that gives the sense of wild displacement to that image
which most mixes grief with pity: "Whilst thee the shores, and
sounding Seas / Wash far away . . . ." The cold indifferent
blows of "where ere thy bones are hurl'd" are only less powerful to give this sense than are the two lines:

> Where thou perhaps under the whelming tide
> Visit'st the bottom of *the monstrous world*.

That underseas world is peopled by creatures which carry their primitive alienation in their names (monsters: outside nature) and the irony of the intimate communication in *visit'st* is less grim than piteous. The body comes, goes again, not even a prey, not "at the mercy of," but a thing with no place, unheeded, meaningless, and alone. This rightly appears just before the tenderness of "And, O ye Dolphins, waft . . . ," so that a flood of sweetness accompanies the double assurance of a nonhuman concern for man. The love and rescuing pity which had long been thought of as the beauty of Arion's story [11] are like in character to the saving heavenly Love that walk'd the waves; but with the allusion to Arion's enchanting song Milton puts a close to the lament for the death *of poetry* more specifically, and the consolation (paralleled in "Look homeward Angel") is that assurance of natural and supernatural powers on the side of those the Muses loved which is in every pastoral elegy, pagan or Christian.

The ancient figures through which man's death is lamented as a great flaw in the fabric of nature are structurally used by Milton, by his attaching them to the other ancient motif fixing responsibility for a particular death. Because it is so familiar an echo, his "Where were ye Nymphs?" [12] can and does carry all its old weight of a sympathy that extends throughout the great frame, and that connects natural powers specifically with poets. We accepted the sympathy when we recognized the genre, for it is perhaps the greatest and most moving conception pastoral has borne down the ages. That this is true in *Lycidas* will appear gradually; here we but notice how Milton can count upon this meaning and make double structural use

[11] I see little reason for excluding Palaemon from this reference but none for substituting him. Parallels in fact (Palaemon died and Arion did not) make less difference to poetry than parallels in significance; both the echo of Orpheus, and Arion's winning harmonies that won the dolphins' love, are too valuable for Milton to forego them; Arion's dolphin was familiar in graphic arts.

[12] Echoing Theocritus 1, Virgil 10, Baïf 2, Alamanni 1, and others less exactly. I do not usually cite title or numbers of earlier elegies, since I confine my references to the great stream of well-known pastorals to which scholars have pointed as Milton's sources in articles I have cited; I have made them easily identifiable, in, for example, Harrison and Leon's anthology [cited *infra*, p. 353], whence I usually take translated phrases.

of the lamenting natural creatures and powers. His procession is not quite, or not only, a procession of mourners, but of innocent underlings who make depositions that exonerate great Neptune, and exonerate Natura herself. Yet it is partly the long history of these and all aspects of the natural world *as mourners* (the rivers and woods and winds that weep and sigh, the spirits of all places that join shepherds in laments, the myriad fruitful creatures that will no longer bear nor blossom) that rules out here in *Lycidas* any sense of a framework of "Nature" inimical or indifferent to "Man" or from which he is separable; a pure gentleness like cool balm breathes through all these passages. That is, as usual, the acceptances to which pastoral has accustomed its readers allow Milton to speak all by indirection. He prefers not to say outright as does Spenser and many another, "Ay me that dreerie Death should strike so mortall stroke, / That can undoe Dame natures kindly course" (kindly: deriving from her own essential nature; Nov., 123). But twice his images state this: in the poet's death which "Universal nature did lament"; in the perfidious Bark that sank where Panope in quiet played. The despairing sense of a whole powerful creation powerless before one ultimate threat is the ground of the final vision of love's conquest of death. Not truly sudden, or new, not opposed by but joined underneath to the image of the strewn flowers, this consolation—the only one Milton finds—has been shadowed throughout the poem. The ebb and flow of love and hostility in the universe is the secret of *Lycidas'* obscure and almost primitive power.

Such conceptions and such poetic powers remind us that we do not deal with an author whose sole remaining testament regarding the meaning of human life lies in the single text before us. The complication and the restraint of the images we have now to speak of more fully suggest that it is well to speak first of certain other kinds of assistance, besides a deepened understanding of pastoral poetry, to a fuller comprehension of *Lycidas*. It is one result of the subtlety of Milton's organization and the restraint of his style that the imagery resists a consideration in separation from more general matters; we have repeatedly come to a halt before points which are so related to the rest of our knowledge about Milton, or so recurrent in general criticism of this poem and others, that they ought to be made with recognition of that background rather than with the seeming innocence of plain exegesis.

Another kind of knowledge which like studies of the pastoral mode has received recent emphasis, is important to imagery for the steady balance it provides, hence for depth without waywardness in interpretations: the study of chronologically related poems of Milton's and of relations to some single other one, notably in this instance the *Epitaphium Damonis*.[13] As in the case of the poet Yeats, Milton himself wrote—in his earlier and later poems—some of the most important commentary on the images of *Lycidas*. There is a marked present tendency to criticize by the analysis of imagery within the single poem, but when studies with this approach (including the present one) are allowed to supplant more general studies of the kinds I have mentioned, profound understanding of the figurative language of the poem is not a result.[14] Some exception must be made for studies of the history of single great images, such as that of Orpheus.[15] But only the large substructure of recent extensions of knowledge in general scholarship on Milton and his period can protect the analysis of imagery from irresponsibility (both in its reader and its writer), or from turning into a mere "reading the poem *for* one" in a sort of question-begging paraphrase embodying explication of image. Even the explication necessary in order to relate themes to the formal nature of figures can be the bane of a discussion emphasizing imagery, and this I also am not able to escape entirely. But the following points, like some earlier ones, deal constantly with

[13] See especially A. S. P. Woodhouse, "Milton's Pastoral Monodies" [cited *infra*, p. 366].

[14] J. E. Hardy on *Lycidas* in Brooks and Hardy, *Poems of Mr. John Milton* [*supra*, pp. 140 ff.] contributes an occasional careful detail rather than a fully trustworthy reading, and at least three studies of the poem's imagery since 1949 base interpretations on overreading "lines concerned with water." An exception to these strictures is Barker's analysis [cited *infra*, p. 358]. D. C. Allen's chapter in *The Harmonious Vision*, which I read after this essay was written, avoids various abuses through critical use of many kinds of learning.

[15] See particularly D. P. Walker, "Orpheus the Theologian and Renaissance Platonists," *Journal of the Warburg and Courtauld Institutes*, XVI (1953), 100–120 (the druids also belong to *prisca theologia*). C. W. Mayerson [see *supra*, p. 116] brings together references from Sandys, Fletcher, Drayton, etc., and shows Orpheus as poet-prophet, symbol of civilizing order. But Milton draws upon yet other connotations of Orpheus as a symbolic figure, such as the denial of death through soul or form (of civilizing forces or of individuals), and cf. the ascetic self-discipline of the "aged Orpheus" in *Elegy vi*.

images whose *bases* in Milton's thought and poetic habits have
received comment in very many discussions; their wider general concerns, and knowledge, underlie any reading of the imagery proper which wishes to avoid starved or capricious interpretations. I touch upon all the cruxes which have caused
much debate, but generally incorporate answers to the questions thus raised without describing the arguments. Breadth
of knowledge pre-eminently affects our sense of a poet's tone
of voice, and with the point made in the last paragraph but
one this factor began to show as crucial.

The sensitivity to Milton's own suggested themes and patterns, with which we can come prepared through the help of
recent comparative and chronological studies, aids especially
our sense of direction, as we find ourselves carried unobtrusively along by certain hidden tides of comfort and of desolation which meet violently several times within *Lycidas*. One
sort of imagery which persistently carries the consolatory
stream of generosity, alliance, and love is rather obscurely
figurative. All the images *that present tributes* flow in one
stream with the final vision of the blest kingdom of joy and
love (this last a favored kind of figure in Milton's other elegies). Something more "natural" than Death, in the universe of
which man is one member, has been stressed since the first *he
must not float unwept*.

The poem is a tribute, is like some but not like all elegies
in that it is not an object but an act, offered, and speaking allegiance; and a tribute to the dead is part of a rite that as-
suages and reaffirms. Milton calls his poem, by the time-honored *metaphor*, a "tear," a public tear that goes down into the
grave with the body, and signifies sorrow for a loss of something that body once signified which still deserves undying
honor and receives unquenchable love; nothing more damaging
than to read this image *literaliter* as "water imagery," nor are
tears water symbols, nor chiefly wet. They are chiefly salt and
bitter; but this one is whatever the metaphor asks, and is what
Milton calls it elsewhere, a "vow." Symbols do not work through
mentionings, but through believed meanings.[16] Symbols that

---

[16] On the other hand, line 175 ("With Nectar pure . . .") does seem to me
a use of those symbolic meanings of water with reference to purification, rebirth, giving of life, of which we have heard so much in *Lycidas* criticism of

work naturalistically in this poem are few and simple, and archetypal significances working otherwise are generally so deep-caught in a web of historically understood meanings (classical and Christian) that these are the best way into them. This is early apparent, and the web itself is very moving.

It is as poet, first, that Lycidas must not go unwept (unsung); the Muses must know their own, and all poets have drunk with those heavenly companions of the well whose source is Deity. But also, all images wherein Milton sees Lycidas' physical self (as here on his watery bier) are touched with a deep human pity, and that sense of human community by which our tributes deny the aloneness of the dead makes each such tribute by him an affirmation of love, of strong and responsible ties. The tribute is due (*meed*, 14) not as praise but as memorial is due; and the obscure consolation that is handed down from human creature to human creature by this ritual remembrance of the human tie is deliberately strengthened in "So may some gentle Muse. . . . And as he passes turn, / And bid fair peace be to my sable shroud."

"Obscure" consolation—even primitive; and certainly both pagan and Christian. To be sure, the classical clothing reminds us of particular songs born of special ties between poets, and certain echoes—"fair peace to Daphnis," "peace to Gallus," fair peace to Alcon, to Astrophel—sound with sweetness in our minds to bulwark them against "What boots it with uncessant care" when the hostile tide sweeps in. A simpler sweetness lies in the universal human act so directly phrased: *and, as he passes—turn.* The pause which the living make for the dead is made in tribute to what has not died. But they make it in sorrow; Milton's next image following without paragraph break—the reason why, like that other fellow-servant of the Muses later, *he* must turn as he passes—is pierced through with that poignancy which loss has when it breaks open earliest unities: "*For* we were nurst upon the self-same hill, / Fed the same flock; by fountain, shade and rill." These lines are com-

---

the last ten years. Whether or not language is being symbolically used can often be detected by applying the principle: that such use always "presents" something the poem, as written, can use, and in that precise place. Symbols do not get in the way, in great poets; the relation to stated meanings may be obscure, ironic or unexpected, but it is real. On the possibly connected sun-sunk-beneath-water, see n. 21 of this essay.

pletely and perfectly metaphorical; they touch all earliest human allegiances, and shared endeavors which bind even scarce-
known men in unity, and they are at once so particular that a
single speaking voice seems to dwell upon the alliterative and
rhetorically intensified phrases, and yet so universal that the
pastoral landscape comprises our human world. The affirmative
force of these declarations of loyal relationship and responsibility (for there are others) flows on to the image of heavenly
love seen not in shadow but in essence, where all the saints in
paradise sing tributes of joy to the new soul, "And wipe the
tears for ever from his eyes." The fountains, shades, and rills
of this incomplete and transient place have their transcendent
counterpart in those "other groves, and other streams"; the
loving guardianship of heavenly beings which has appeared at
intervals throughout the poem continues now secure and sure,
and Lycidas' "large recompense" is felt to be with no sense of
dissonance or incongruity both the angel's propitious watch and
the grateful love returned to earthly petitioner by Genius or
Muse or any of Jove's sacred company.[17]

I have dealt especially with human tributes. There is a more
subtly tender feeling in certain other images with this same
avowed function—of which we may take the so-called flower
passage as typical—and the reasons for their consoling power
lie more deeply hidden. This passage is less accurately termed
"metaphorical" than simply a portion of the poem where the
great metaphors that underlie the whole pastoral conception,
as it developed more than as it originated, must govern our
reading or we read with a most unhappy superficiality. Its
place is deliberately just after the great vision of judgement
upon human evil, the self-aggrandizing betrayal of the flock
by those who were to have been the earthly types of the Good
Shepherd himself, that is of love which throws itself away for
the sheep. The reasons why our grief *even for this* is assuaged

---

[17] As with Sannazaro's Androgeo or Ronsard's Henriot. The latter is *"un
Ange parfait"* in heaven—*un ange* to whom green turf altars are to be built,
on which *"comme . . . Aux Faunes, aux Satyrs, te ferons sacrifice."* If such
"fusion" is to be called "baroque," the term loses its meaning—for a Boccaccio, too, merely expects to be *read* as cultivated men of the Middle Ages had
grown accustomed to reading, when he sings in Eclogue 14 of Christ sent
from Olympus into the Virgin's womb to bring back the Golden Age, and of
the fields of Elysium where Mary, *alma Iovis genitrix*, is honored by virgins
and martyrs, nymphs and fauns and Apollo himself (this is dependent on
Dante's Earthly Paradise, of course).

by the twenty-five lines which follow, "Return Sicilian Muse, /
And call the Vales, and bid them hither cast / Their Bells . . . ,"
are not so much complicated as deep. Pastoral has its ways of
reasserting a fundamental and harmonious sympathy, and of
proclaiming that not decay and death but life and creativity
and love is the universal principle, one which is seen (especially,
but not solely, as pastoral was Christianized) as having the
strength of a divine intention.

No person brings in tribute these heaped and countless
flowers, but the fresh and shady vales bring them to make the
same acknowledgement as the other tributes. They are the
precisest possible counterpart of the offered-up verses which
men strew upon a laureate hearse; all alike mourn for the
death of a part (as poet, an Orphean part) of that fabric to
which all belong, and all alike, reaffirming life, make an answer
to death's power. The valleys are bid by the Muse (the Muses
have always spoken through men of these harmonies and these
mysteries) to bring all their flowers, to cast here every flower
that can weep; this passage is for good reason elaborate with
tiny particulars, as are all images where significance is not
to be said outright, and the actual effect of assuagement depends much upon tone. For the sense that there is such a
thing as loving pity in the natural universe (of which evil men
and good are a part), seeping in after the inimical violence
which preceded, becomes a calm strong tide carried by the generous abandon of these lines. This sense, "consolation" almost
by definition, is at its height when Milton writes a line which
gives so quietly the sudden shock often produced by extreme
beauty in music that one is tempted to use the word "occult":

> Bid *Amaranthus* all his beauty shed . . .

The sudden depth of the image is unexpected; amaranth is
the deathless flower, later to be used by Milton as a symbol
of the flawless world before the Fall, but long known as the
immortal plant, that one blossoming thing whose "beauty" is
never quenched or withered [18]; and he is bid to give over his

---

[18] The verb whence the flower's Greek name was formed appears to make
it carry the sense not-quenched-light-or-flame, and the red spires revive in
water long after plucking and last many years (as Pliny describes, xxi. 23, or
Gerard's *Herball*, ii. 42: Floure-gentle or Floramor). The attendants of
Persephone in *Fasti*, iv. 39, picked amaranth.

exemption from the mortality which all natural things share
with Lycidas, and lay his red spires in symbolic tribute on
the bier to go down with it.[19] This is not hyperbole of praise,
but a glint of light upon the subterranean river that runs
under the long image making a connection between sacrifice
and immortality born of death—in a way which my explanation travesties almost unpardonably, except that it may shed
light on why and how these whole multitudes of plucked and
offered flowers do indeed interpose the "ease" Milton says they
give.

They are to strew the bier "where Lycid lies"—"Ay me!,"
where does he lie? This passage is very closely articulated with
the next one, and that Lycidas is "to our moist vows deny'd" is
not a simple grief, as the pain of the following passage shows.
How can we not come with tributes, though there is no place
to lay them? The much-discussed "For so . . . Let our frail
thoughts dally with false surmise" seems to me to have this
clear reference, and not to be an indication that Milton re-
pudiates the truth of preceding reflections—because he finds
that his "pagan" and his Christian comforts conflict and therefore asks us to throw away, as "false surmise," solace we have
all felt to be real as we read. There is not much evidence that
Milton was a man to let even innocent counterfeit stand because he had once thought it provided "a little ease." The two
contrasted passages of imagery work upon a very deep level
of feeling.

In the flower passage, it is indubitable that we respond,
and that he did, to symbolisms immemorially ancient, not only
feeling life in essence symbolized peculiarly by the moment of

---

[19] It should be stressed that consciousness of the kind of thing I speak of
in these paragraphs is at a minimum (in *writer* and *reader:* these relations
are nothing like so "known" within the thinking mind as description of them
must be) and there is much pleasure in these images for those who love at
lower rate. I do not think Milton consciously related this line to the spreading
heavenly plant which symbolizes immortal honor in lines 78 ff., nor perhaps
that he had yet the idea (image) in *Paradise Lost,* iii. 353 ff., where the
angels cast down their crowns inwove with amaranth.
Cf. also xi. 78: the blissful bowers "Of *Amarantin* Shade, . . . By the
waters of Life" where sit the angelic Sons of Light. He was probably *having*
the idea; symbolic images grow slowly, like all ideas involving complicated
relationships of much experience. The relations hold so solidly, as with a kind
of inner truth, that we can as it were see them coming—this characteristic I
believe Milton would have referred not to his originating mind but to the
structure of "reality"; perhaps such revealing (Invention, uncovering) is
what one asks for from a "Heavenly" Muse.

blossoming (promise of fruit, not fruit), but equally feeling
the necessity of giving over to death these symbols of life-to-be-
born-of-death. This is far from being unrelated to the dear
might of him that walk'd the waves. It is also indubitable that
part of the valid sense of assuagement which human beings feel
in symbolic actions that asssert the continuity of life despite
the fact of death does disappear when the action is not possible.
This did not make nonsense of the symbol. It made another form
of the assertion more consoling, and to that Milton proceeded.
He proceeded by way of another of those passages—here, the
body under the whelming tide—of imagery like direct experience of the reality of death (decay, evil, impermanence).
Throughout the poem these bitter tides meet, and are drowned in,
the full-flowing stream of symbolized life, faithfulness, creativity, eternal flowering, earthly and heavenly pity, aid, sacrifice,
and love. The vision in heaven, his last such answer to the inimical principle in all its forms—for that is the theme of *Lycidas*
—touches the "tender stops" of all these various Quills, and
when the singer's "eager thought" is closed in the tranquil light
of an ordinary dying day human life is once again "fresh
Woods, and Pastures new," a harmony accepted, hopeful, and
dear.

It is now possible to see with more exactness and force that
we disturb and nullify this entire design of images that discuss meaning and destiny in the universe when we import into
pastoral even subconsciously that special and quite recent way
of thinking which takes "Man" out of "Nature." The very
ground of the imagery in pastoral writing is the integrity of
the great fabric of created nature, and a chief contribution
of reading to saturation in Milton's predecessors and fellows
is a posture of the mind, an immediate and unreflecting readiness to feel this assumption true. If Ruskin's term, "pathetic
fallacy," accurately represents our subconscious presuppositions, it is folly to expect understanding of this poetry except
in ways which stand coldly outside it. The very simplest form
of imagery which assumes a living tie between all creatures
including man is used sparingly by Milton, but he uses complicated forms of it at every point in his poem. Such complica-
tions of structure and feeling as I have touched on are erected
upon the same assumption that gives us the simple "Thee

Shepherd, thee the Woods, and desert Caves, / With wild Thyme and the gadding Vine o'regrown, / And all their echoes mourn."

Why do the woods mourn for human deaths in pastoral poems? the vines lament in their untended wildness? Several accustomed meanings of such images provide for Milton the very conceptions of the universal order without which others of his great metaphorical figures could not move and work. I speak from examples. Other natural things mourn with men in pastorals for the death of the Orphean singer, of the order-bringer, the one who teaches men and quiets animals and prunes vines and moves rocks (all four the same thing), of the theologue who knows the nature of the creator and preserver of life—all those he delights and all those he instructed mourn; they mourn for the protector and helper, the Wise Shepherd; they mourn for the death of their peace, because thorns choke growth, and sterility and drought possess the land where death has intruded.

"The Shepherd" is poet and priest, certainly, but *these* figure forth, *being shepherds*, something more still. Especially this is true as Christian ideas transmuted the ancient ideas and extended them; man brought in death, as "shepherd" he helps to mend it. We have not finished reading when we read how Marot's Loyse, *la bergère de paix*, had wisdom to protect *"Contre le temps obscur et pluvieux"*—and see its reference to troublous persecutions. Or when we read Alamanni's *"Ahi quanto con ragion piangon . . . e greggi"* for that if the shepherd had remained alive their young might be safe from *rapaci pastor e feri lupi*—and see therein a reference to why he mourned Cosimo Rucellai. The universal use of figurative terms from the pastoral life for these literal historical meanings makes our *history itself present* to us much profounder significances of storm and wild ravager, and we read constantly in pastoral of two worlds, both that of our particular human disasters and that which we can organize only through our symbols of a Waste Land, of Garden given over to thorns, Harmony become chaos—and, of the Garden of Adonis, the Earthly Paradise, and the perfect music of the spheres. When Boccaccio's Olympia says, "All of us who are created in the woodlands are born to death," she speaks in the language of pastoral as well as in Dante's metaphor, and of the whole vast universe of created things. When Milton writes (*PL*, ix. 782) how at the instant of Eve's deed "Earth felt the wound, and Nature from her seat / Sighing through all her Works gave signs of woe, / That all was lost," and how the roses of Adam's garland faded as they dropped, he says what the pastoral woods mourn for. For the flaw, and mourn again for all who die mending it.

The harmony among the creatures is by no means necessarily pagan even when its terms are so; the point around which the matter turns is rather whether the metaphors which express it are believed or not. Figures which adumbrate it use the so-called pathetic fallacy as their natural language, but they mean what they say. Such language neither denies a hierarchy among creatures nor a special tie between man and divinity; its giving man's form of sentience or will or *pathos* to other creatures is a metaphorical way of putting unity not identity.[20] The phrase that makes pastoral trivial is "*a mere* metaphor." For, as pastoral developed, all its greater figures clearly call for the kind of reading termed "allegorical," and such reading is only possible to men who believe that metaphor does present the real.

Milton of course did not "write an allegory" in *Lycidas*. The phrase is fruitful of misconceptions; "allegorically" refers primarily to a way of understanding, reading, a thing. Proof that this way had become habitual and secular lies in what men wrote, over several hundred years and extending well into Milton's time and to his own work. An *allegoria* is a figure asking such reading for its comprehension, and a whole poem can be one, but *Lycidas* is not. And we find in it few of the most usual sort—moral allegories; we have not been reading tropologically, and the chief wisdom in *Lycidas* has little directly to do with "how men should act."

Much of the classical imagery of Christian pastorals ask to

[20] Nor is the unity in a sympathetic harmony contradicted by the famous figure of the "riddle" of man's short earthly life (his never coming again contrasted with the cyclical renewal of other creatures); Man is no more seen as outside "Nature" because he does not sprout again like the tree than the tree is fallaciously made "Man" when the metaphor of human responses (it sighs, mourns) is used. The conceptions really antipathetic to these ways of thinking and using language are nominalistic conceptions of metaphor, or naturalistic or positivistic conceptions of what meanings can be real. Milton did not share them.

be read allegorically in the stricter mediaeval sense, for classical figures retain their truth in being read as types of a later revelation. There would be some truth in saying that the Middle Ages made of classical literature one great old testament, for the New Dispensation is with little sense of displacement read in the figures of an older shadowed truth; so read, man sees from it "what to believe," as readily and truly as one could from reading the great book of the universe itself. And, one might add, as uncalculatingly, unself-consciously, and delightfully, for the forms in which we are meeting these habits of mind are only solemn because they are elegiac; no Planned Movement was needed to "save the classics" in the eras we speak of, and a good deal of exuberant gaiety accompanies the mediaeval and Renaissance pleasure in plurality of meanings. Reading allegorically for moral meanings merged with the stricter kind, and as Dante pointed out in the Letter to Can Grande, all these functions fall together in the supreme distinction between literal and figurative ("allegorical"). Pastoral early isolated itself as a genre which by reason of a basic figure for presenting universal harmonies and discords was fundamentally and formally "continued figure"; the largely mediaeval development toward historical allegory and satire in disguise was an expectable result, and Milton builds images on all these accepted forms of indirection.

The use of anagogy—which is writing that when read figuratively yields ideas of ultimate destiny, of the eschatological, of the other world—is equally natural to the form. Milton uses it for just the function it serves in his predecessors: to express in symbols the ultimate triumph of life over death. Such imagery is archetypal wherever we find it; the soul's home is that place where the conditions of our exile do not obtain. The place where Harmony, Love, Peace (all the same) are not threatened by Discord or Mutability or Death (all one enemy) is an otherworld where the details of music and growing things and endless spring and living waters simply tell over and over the same tale of the conquest of that one unconquerable flaw whence spring all the others. In Milton's anagogical figure for the complete victory of that principle which he has shadowed forth in all the consolations throughout his poem, the terms are largely Christian, and one Christian

symbol, a usual one, is basic—the marriage between the human
soul and Heavenly Love. He does not choose to use the symbol
of Light save in the reference to the saints "in their glory,"
and his simile of the Sun (which like Lycidas rises from the
waters to flame in the forehead of the morning sky) is probably not to be symbolically extended.[21] At any rate he does not
choose to use the great numbers of Earthly Paradise details
familiar from Dante, Boccaccio, Ronsard, Marot; in these as
in Spenser or Sannazaro the homogeneity of classical and Christian details is assumed, and Milton had himself assumed it in
those Latin elegies whose visions of paradise are among the
best commentaries upon this in *Lycidas*. Where symbols are
archetypal these differentiating terms lose their meaning. Spenser is not baroque but simply nursed on old habits when he
says his Dido "raignes a goddesse now emong the saintes," but
when he calls his paradise the Elysian fields he is, more simply
still, just in the right. There is no incongruity and certainly
no surprise in the classical close of Milton's image.

The close of the poem is properly kept strictly within pastoral bounds in language and imagery, even to the degree of
a quite usual final realism in the Coventry-blue of the shepherd's mantle. Restraint and tranquillity are native possessions
of writing which by definition shadows further meanings but
does not say them. In one last quiet and delicate image of the
shepherd, intentionally as well as deceptively pictorial, Milton
makes the vast human world which pastoral writing can denote
with so economical a pen seem to us that tranquil place which
his vision of man's end makes of it.

What we call "pastoral imagery" was a great achievement of

---

[21] Of course it speaks metaphorically of resurrection, life born of death;
but it is difficult in fact to tell whether it includes what we might well expect:
that it rose again because it sank into the water. There are many difficulties
with it as a naturalistically based rebirth symbol (familiar as this must have
been to Milton, since natural-philosophy meanings offer one of the common-
est forms of allegorical interpretation throughout Middle Ages and Renaissance). Among these difficulties are the emphasized literal meaning in line 167
("Sunk though he be beneath the watry floar"; there is no special rebirth for
the drowned); and the immediate other symbolic use of water in "walk'd the
waves." The unextended simile (as ostensibly written) avoids what I should
call a *true* incongruity otherwise present: i.e. that the only Sun-figure large
enough for this context would have been God-as-Light. On these old and
common images and on the language of other poets in the King volume see
R. Wallerstein, *Studies in 17th Century Poetic* (Madison, 1950), for example
pp. 104–105.

the human imagination. In eighteen centuries no man used it with more power and grace than Milton in *Lycidas*.

Literature as Context: Milton's *Lycidas*

Northrop Frye

I should like to begin with a brief discussion of a familiar poem, Milton's *Lycidas*, in the hope that some of the inferences drawn from the analysis will be relevant to the theme of this conference. *Lycidas*, then, is an elegy in the pastoral convention, written to commemorate a young man named Edward King who was drowned at sea. The origins of the pastoral are partly classical, the tradition that runs through Theocritus and Virgil, and partly Biblical, the imagery of the twenty-third Psalm, of Christ as the Good Shepherd, of the metaphors of "pastor" and "flock" in the Church. The chief connecting link between the traditions in Milton's day was the Fourth or Messianic Eclogue of Virgil. Hence it is common enough to have pastoral images echoing both traditions at once, and not surprising to find that *Lycidas* is a Christian poem as well as a humanistic one.

In the classical pastoral elegy the subject of the elegy is not treated as an individual but as a representative of a dying spirit of nature. The pastoral elegy seems to have some relation to the ritual of the Adonis lament, and the dead poet Bion, in

From *Fables of Identity: Studies in Poetic Mythology* (New York, 1963), 119–29; first published in *University of North Carolina Studies in Comparative Literature* 23 (1959): 44–55.

Moschus's poem, is celebrated with much the same kind of imagery as Bion himself uses in his lament for Adonis. The phrase "dying god," for such a figure in later pastoral, is not an anachronism: Virgil says of Daphnis, for example, in the Fifth Eclogue: "*deus, deus ille, Menalca.*" Besides, Milton and his learned contemporaries, Selden, for example, or Henry Reynolds, knew at least as much about the symbolism of the "dying god" as any modern student could get out of *The Golden Bough*, which depends mainly on the same classical sources that were available to them. The notion that twentieth-century poets differ from their predecessors in their understanding or use of myth will not bear much scrutiny. So King is given the pastoral name of Lycidas, which is equivalent to Adonis, and is associated with the cyclical rhythms of nature. Of these three are of particular importance: the daily cycle of the sun across the sky, the yearly cycle of the seasons, and the cycle of water, flowing from wells and fountains through rivers to the sea. Sunset, winter, and the sea are emblems of Lycidas' death; sunrise and spring, of his resurrection. The poem begins in the morning, "Under the opening eyelids of the morn," and ends with the sun, like Lycidas himself, dropping into the western ocean, yet due to rise again as Lycidas is to do. The imagery of the opening lines, "Shatter your leaves before the mellowing year," suggests the frosts of autumn killing the flowers, and in the great roll-call of flowers towards the end, most of them early blooming flowers like the "rathe primrose," the spring returns. Again, the opening invocation is to the "Sisters of the sacred well," and the water imagery carries through a great variety of Greek, Italian, and English rivers to the sea in which the dead body of Lycidas lies.

Lycidas, then, is the "archetype" of Edward King. By an archetype I mean a literary symbol, or cluster of symbols, which are used recurrently throughout literature, and thereby become conventional. A poetic use of a flower, by itself, is not necessarily an archetype. But in a poem about the death of a young man it is conventional to associate him with a red or purple flower, usually a spring flower like the hyacinth. The historical origin of the convention may be lost in ritual, but it is a constantly latent one, not only in literature but in life, as the symbolism of the scarlet poppies in World War I shows. Hence in *Lycidas* the "sanguine flower inscrib'd with woe" is an archetype, a sym-

bol that recurs regularly in many poems of its kind. Similarly
Lycidas himself is not only the literary form of Edward King,
but a conventional or recurring form, of the same family as
Shelley's Adonais, the Daphnis of Theocritus and Virgil, and
Milton's own Damon. King was also a clergyman and, for Milton's purposes, a poet, so, having selected the conventional archetype of King as drowned young man, Milton has them to
select the conventional archetypes of King as poet and of King
as priest. These are, respectively, Orpheus and Peter.

Both Orpheus and Peter have attributes that link them in imagery with Lycidas. Orpheus was also an "enchanting son" or
spirit of nature; he died young, in much the same role as Adonis,
and was flung into the water. Peter would have drowned too without the help of Christ; hence Peter is not named directly, but
only as "The Pilot of the Galilean Lake," just as Christ is not
named directly, but only as "Him that walked the waves." When
Orpheus was torn to pieces by the Maenads, his head went float-
ing "Down the swift Hebrus to the Lesbian shore." The theme
of salvation out of water is connected with the image of the
dolphin, a conventional type of Christ, and dolphins are called
upon to "waft the hapless youth" just before the peroration
begins.

The body of the poem is arranged in the form ABACA, a main
theme repeated twice with two intervening episodes, as in the
musical rondo. The main theme is the drowning of Lycidas in
the prime of his life; the two episodes, presided over by the
figures of Orpheus and Peter, deal with the theme of premature
death as it relates to poetry and to the priesthood respectively.
In both the same type of image appears: the mechanical instrument of execution that brings about a sudden death, represented
by the "abhorred shears" in the meditation on fame and the
"grim two-handed engine" in the meditation on the corruption
of the Church. The most difficult part of the construction is the
managing of the transitions from these episodes back to the main
theme. The poet does this by alluding to his great forerunners
in the pastoral convention, Theocritus of Sicily, Virgil of
Mantua, and the legendary Arcadians who preceded both:

> O fountain Arethuse, and thou honour'd flood,
> Smooth-sliding Mincius, crown'd with vocal reeds . . .

and later:

> Return, Alpheus, the dread voice is past
> That shrunk thy streams: return, Sicilian Muse.

The allusion has the effect of reminding the reader that this is, after all, a pastoral. But Milton also alludes to the myth of Arethusa and Alpheus, the Arcadian water-spirits who plunged underground and reappeared in Sicily, and this myth not only outlines the history of the pastoral convention, but unites the water imagery with the theme of disappearance and revival.

In pastoral elegy the poet who laments the death is often so closely associated with the dead man as to make him a kind of double or shadow of himself. Similarly Milton represents himself as intimately involved with the death of Lycidas. The theme of premature death is skilfully associated in the opening lines with the conventional apology for a "harsh and crude" poem; the poet hopes for a similar elegy when he dies, and at the end he accepts the responsibilities of survival and turns "To morrow to fresh woods, and pastures new," bringing the elegy to a full rich *tierce de Picardie* or major chord. By appearing himself at the beginning and end of the poem, Milton presents the poem as, in a sense, contained within the mind of the poet.

Apart from the historical convention of the pastoral, however, there is also the conventional framework of ideas or assumptions which forms the background of the poem. I call it a framework of ideas, and it may also be that, but in poetry it is rather a framework of images. It consists of four levels of existence. First is the order revealed by Christianity, the order of grace and salvation and of eternal life. Second is the order of human nature, the order represented by the Garden of Eden in the Bible and the Golden Age in classical myth, and which man in his fallen state can, up to a point, regain through education, obedience to law, and the habit of virtue. Third is the order of physical nature, the world of animals and plants which is morally neutral but theologically "fallen." Fourth is the disorder of the unnatural, the sin and death and corruption that entered the world with the Fall.

Lycidas has his connections with all of these orders. In the first place, all the images of death and resurrection are included in and identified with the body of Christ. Christ is the sun of

righteousness, the tree of life, the water of life, the dying god
who rose again, the saviour from the sea. On this level Lycidas
enters the Christian heaven and is greeted by the "Saints above"
"In solemn troops, and sweet societies," where the language
echoes the Book of Revelation. But simultaneously Lycidas
achieves another apotheosis as the Genius of the shore, corresponding to the Attendant Spirit in *Comus*, whose habitation
is said to be a world above our own, identified, not with the
Christian heaven, but with Spenser's Gardens of Adonis. The
third level of physical nature is the world of ordinary experience,
where death is simply a loss, and those who mourn the death
have to turn to pick up their tasks again. On this level Lycidas
is merely absent, "to our moist vows denied," represented only
by the empty bier with its flowers. It is on this level too that the
poem is contained within the mind of the surviving poet, as on
the Christian level it is contained within the body of Christ.
Finally, the world of death and corruption holds the drowned
corpse of Lycidas, which will soon come to the surface and "welter to the parching wind." This last is an unpleasant and distressing image, and Milton touches it very lightly, picking it up
again in an appropriate context:

> But swoln with wind and the rank mist they draw,
> Rot inwardly . . .

In the writing of *Lycidas* there are four creative principles
of particular importance. To say that there are four does not
mean, of course, that they are separable. One is convention, the
reshaping of the poetic material which is appropriate to this
subject. Another is genre, the choosing of the appropriate form.
A third is archetype, the use of appropriate, and therefore recurrently employed, images and symbols. The fourth, for which
there is no name, is the fact that the forms of literature are
autonomous: that is, they do not exist outside literature. Milton
is not writing an obituary: he does not start with Edward King
and his life and times, but with the conventions and archetypes
that poetry requires for such a theme.

Of the critical principles illustrated by this analysis, one
will be no surprise to the present audience. *Lycidas* owes quite
as much to Hebrew, Greek, Latin, and Italian traditions as it
does to English. Even the diction, of which I have no space to

speak, shows strong Italian influence. Milton was of course a
learned poet, but there is no poet whose literary influences are
entirely confined to his own language. Thus every problem in
literary criticism is a problem in comparative literature, or simply of literature itself.

The next principle is that the provisional hypothesis which
we must adopt for the study of every poem is that that poem
is a unity. If, after careful and repeated testing, we are forced
to conclude that it is not a unity, then we must abandon the
hypothesis and look for the reasons why it is not. A good deal
of bad criticism of *Lycidas* has resulted from not making enough
initial effort to understand the unity of the poem. To talk of
"digressions" in *Lycidas* is a typical consequence of a mistaken
critical method, of backing into the poem the wrong way round.
If, instead of starting with the poem, we start with a handful of
peripheral facts about the poem, Milton's casual knowledge of
King, his ambitions as a poet, his bitterness against the episco-
pacy, then of course the poem will break down into pieces corresponding precisely to those fragments of knowledge. *Lycidas*
illustrates, on a small scale, what has happened on a much bigger
scale in, for example, the criticism of Homer. Critics knowing
something about the fragmentary nature of heroic lays and bal-
lads approached the *Iliad* and the *Odyssey* with this knowledge
in mind, and the poems obediently split up into the pieces that
they wished to isolate. Other critics came along and treated
the poems as imaginative unities, and today everyone knows that
the second group were more convincing.

The same thing happens when our approach to "sources"
becomes fragmentary or piecemeal. *Lycidas* is a dense mass of
echoes from previous literature, chiefly pastoral literature.
Reading through Virgil's Eclogues with *Lycidas* in mind, we can
see that Milton had not simply read or studied these poems:
he possessed them; they were part of the material he was shaping. The passage about the hungry sheep reminds us of at least
three other passages: one in Dante's *Paradiso,* one in the Book
of Ezekiel, and one near the beginning of Hesiod's *Theogony.*
There are also echoes of Mantuan and Spenser, of the Gospel
of John, and it is quite possible that there are even more striking parallels with poems that Milton had not read. In such cases
there is not *a* source at all, no one place that the passage "comes

from," or, as we say with such stupefying presumption, that the poet "had in mind." There are only archetypes, or recurring themes of literary expression, which *Lycidas* has recreated, and therefore re-echoed, yet once more.

The next principle is that the important problems of literary criticism lie within the study of literature. We notice that a law of diminishing returns sets in as soon as we move away from the poem itself. If we ask, who is Lycidas? the answer is that he is a member of the same family as Theocritus' Daphnis, Bion's Adonis, the Old Testament's Abel, and so on. The answer goes on building up a wider comprehension of literature and a deeper knowledge of its structural principles and recurring themes. But if we ask, who was Edward King? What was his relation to Milton? How good a poet was he? we find ourselves moving dimly in the intense inane. The same is true of minor points. If we ask, why is the image of the two-handed engine in *Lycidas?* we can give an answer, along the lines suggested above, that illustrates how carefully the poem has been constructed. If we ask, what is the two-handed engine? there are forty-odd answers, none of them completely satisfactory; yet the fact that they are not wholly satisfactory hardly seems to be important.

Another form of the same kind of fallacy is the confusion between personal sincerity and literary sincerity. If we start with the facts that *Lycidas* is highly conventional and that Milton knew King only slightly, we may see in *Lycidas* an "artificial" poem without "real feeling" in it. This red herring, though more common among third-rate romantics, was dragged across the study of *Lycidas* by Samuel Johnson. Johnson knew better, but he happened to feel perverse about this particular poem, and so deliberately raised false issues. It would not have occurred to him, for example, to question the conventional use of Horace in the satires of Pope, or of Juvenal in his own. Personal sincerity has no place in literature, because personal sincerity as such is inarticulate. One may burst into tears at the news of a friend's death, but one can never spontaneously burst into song, however doleful a lay. *Lycidas* is a passionately sincere poem, because Milton was deeply interested in the structure and symbolism of funeral elegies, and had been practising since adolescence on every fresh corpse in sight, from the university beadle to the fair infant dying of a cough.

If we ask what inspires a poet, there are always two answers. An occasion, an experience, an event, may inspire the impulse to write. But the impulse to write can only come from previous contact with literature, and the formal inspiration, the poetic structure that crystallizes around the new event, can only be derived from other poems. Hence while every new poem is a new and unique creation, it is also a reshaping of familiar conventions of literature, otherwise it would not be recognizable as literature at all. Literature often gives us the illusion of turning from books to life, from second-hand to direct experience, and thereby discovering new literary principles in the world outside. But this is never quite what happens. No matter how tightly Wordsworth may close the barren leaves of art and let nature be his teacher, his literary forms will be as conventional as ever, although they may echo an unaccustomed set of conventions, such as the ballad or the broadside. The pretence of personal sincerity is itself a literary convention, and Wordsworth makes many of the flat simple statements which represent, in literature, the inarticulateness of personal sincerity:

> No motion has she now, no force:
> She neither hears nor sees.

But as soon as a death becomes a poetic image, that image is assimilated to other poetic images of death in nature, and hence Lucy inevitably becomes a Proserpine figure, just as King becomes an Adonis:

> Rolled round in earth's diurnal course
> With rocks, and stones, and trees.

In Whitman we have an even more extreme example than Wordsworth of a cult of personal statement and an avoidance of learned conventions. It is therefore instructive to see what happens in *When Lilacs Last in Dooryard Bloomed*. The dead man is not called by a pastoral name, but neither is he called by his historical name. He is in a coffin which is carried the length and breadth of the land; he is identified with a "powerful western fallen star"; he is the beloved comrade of the poet, who throws the purple flower of the lilac on his coffin; a singing bird laments the death, just as the woods and caves do in *Lycidas*.

Convention, genre, archetype, and the autonomy of forms are all illustrated as clearly in Whitman as they are in Milton.

Lycidas is an occasional poem, called forth by a specific event. It seems, therefore, to be a poem with a strong external reference. Critics who cannot approach a poem except as a personal statement of the poet's thus feel that if it says little about King, it must say a good deal about Milton. So, they reason, *Lycidas* is really autobiographical, concerned with Milton's own preoccupations, including his fear of death. There can be no objection to this unless Milton's conventional involving of himself with the poem is misinterpreted as a personal intrusion into it.

For Milton was even by seventeenth-century standards an unusually professional and impersonal poet. Of all Milton's poems, the one obvious failure is the poem called *The Passion*, and if we look at the imagery of that poem we can see why. It is the only poem of Milton's in which he is preoccupied with himself in the process of writing it. "My muse," "my song," "my Harp," "my roving verse," "my Phoebus," and so on for eight stanzas until Milton abandons the poem in disgust. It is not a coincidence that Milton's one self-conscious poem should be the one that never gets off the ground. There is nothing like this in *Lycidas*: the "I" of that poem is a professional poet in his conventional shepherd disguise, and to think of him as a personal "I" is to bring *Lycidas* down to the level of *The Passion*, to make it a poem that has to be studied primarily as a biographical document rather than for its own sake. Such an approach to *Lycidas* is apt to look most plausible to those who dislike Milton, and want to see him cut down to size.

One more critical principle, and the one that I have written this paper to enunciate, seems to me to follow inevitably from the previous ones. Every poem must be examined as a unity, but no poem is an isolatable unity. Every poem is inherently connected with other poems of its kind, whether explicitly, as *Lycidas* is with Theocritus and Virgil, or implicitly, as Whitman is with the same tradition, or by anticipation, as *Lycidas* is with later pastoral elegies. And, of course, the kinds or genres of literature are not separable either, like the orders of pre-Darwinian biology. Everyone who has seriously studied literature knows that he is not simply moving from poem to poem, or from one æsthetic experience to another: he is also entering into a coherent and progressive discipline. For literature is not simply an aggregate of books and poems and plays: it is an order of words. And our total literary experience, at any given time, is not a discrete series of memories or impressions of what we have read, but an imaginatively coherent body of experience.

It is literature as an order of words, therefore, which forms the primary context of any given work of literary art. All other contexts—the place of *Lycidas* in Milton's development; its place in the history of English poetry; its place in seventeenth-century thought or history—are secondary and derivative contexts. Within the total literary order certain structural and generic principles, certain configurations of narrative and imagery, certain conventions and devices and *topoi*, occur over and over again. In every new work of literature some of these principles are reshaped.

Lycidas, we found, is informed by such a recurring structural principle. The short, simple, and accurate name for this principle is myth. The Adonis myth is what makes *Lycidas* both distinctive and traditional. Of course if we think of the Adonis myth as some kind of Platonic idea existing by itself, we shall not get far with it as a critical conception. But it is only incompetence that tries to reduce or assimilate a poem to a myth. The Adonis myth in *Lycidas* is the structure of *Lycidas*. It is in *Lycidas* in much the same way that the sonata form is in the first movement of a Mozart symphony. It is the connecting link between what makes *Lycidas* the poem it is and what unites it to other forms of poetic experience. If we attend only to the uniqueness of *Lycidas*, and analyze the ambiguities and subtleties of its diction, our method, however useful in itself, soon reaches a point of no return to the poem. If we attend only to the conventional element, our method will turn it into a scissors-and-paste collection of allusive tags. One method reduces the poem to a jangle of echoes of itself, the other to a jangle of echoes from other poets. If we have a unifying principle that holds these two tendencies together from the start, neither will get out of hand.

Myths, it is true, turn up in other disciplines, in anthropology, in psychology, in comparative religion. But the primary business of the critic is with myth as the shaping principle of a work of literature. Thus for him myth becomes much the same thing as Aristotle's *mythos*, narrative or plot, the moving formal cause which is what Aristotle called the "soul" of the work and assimilates all details in the realizing of its unity.

In its simplest English meaning a myth is a story about a god, and Lycidas is, poetically speaking, a god or spirit of nature, who eventually becomes a saint in heaven, which is as near as one can get to godhead in ordinary Christianity. The reason for treating Lycidas mythically, in this sense, is conventional, but the convention is not arbitrary or accidental. It arises from the metaphorical nature of poetic speech. We are not told simply that Lycidas has left the woods and caves, but that the woods and caves and all their echoes mourn his loss. This is the language of that curious identification of subject and object, of personality and thing, which the poet has in common with the lunatic and the lover. It is the language of metaphor, recognized by Aristotle as the distinctive language of poetry. And, as we can see in such phrases as sun-god and tree-god, the language of metaphor is interdependent with the language of myth.

I have said that all problems of criticism are problems of comparative literature. But where there is comparison there must be some standard by which we can distinguish what is actually comparable from what is merely analogous. The scientists discovered long ago that to make valid comparisons you have to know what your real categories are. If you're studying natural history, for instance, no matter how fascinated you may be by anything that has eight legs, you can't just lump together an octopus and a spider and a string quartet. In science the difference between a scientific and a pseudo-scientific procedure can usually be spotted fairly soon. I wonder if literary criticism has any standards of this kind. It seems to me that a critic practically has to maintain that the Earl of Oxford wrote the plays of Shakespeare before he can be clearly recognized as making pseudo-critical statements. I have read some critics on Milton who appeared to be confusing Milton with their phallic fathers, if that is the right phrase. I should call them pseudo-critics; others call them neo-classicists. How is one to know? There is such a variety of even legitimate critics. There are critics who can find things in the Public Records Office, and there are critics who, like myself, could not find the Public Records Office. Not all critical statements or procedures can be equally valid.

The first step, I think, is to recognize the dependence of value-judgments on scholarship. Scholarship, or the knowledge of literature, constantly expands and increases; value-judgments are produced by a skill based on the knowledge we already have. Thus scholarship has both priority to value-judgments and the power of veto over them. When Thomas Rymer called *Othello* a bloody farce, he was not making a bad value-judgment; he was making a correct value-judgment based on impossibly narrow scholarship. Most of the famous howlers of criticism are of this kind. The second step is to recognize the dependence of scholarship on a coordinated view of literature. A good deal of critical taxonomy lies ahead of us. We need to know much more than we do about the structural principles of literature, about myth and metaphor, conventions and genres, before we can distinguish with any authority a real from an imaginary line of influence, an illuminating from a misleading analogy, a poet's original source from his last resource. The basis of this central critical activity that gives direction to scholarship is the simple fact that every poem is a member of the class of things called poems. Some poems, including *Lycidas*, proclaim that they are conventional, in other words that their primary context is in literature. Other poems leave this inference to the critic, with an appealing if often misplaced confidence.

Five Types of *Lycidas*

M. H. Abrams

Most modern critics base their theories on the proposition that a poem is an object in itself. And all critics endorse enthusiastically at least one statement by Matthew Arnold, that the function of criticism is "to see the object as in itself it really is." The undertaking is surely valid, and laudable; the results, however, are disconcerting. For in this age of unexampled critical activity, as one poetic object after another is analyzed under rigidly controlled conditions, the object proves to be highly unstable, and disintegrates. In the pages of the critics we increasingly find, under a single title, not one poem but a variety of poems.

Milton's *Lycidas* is a convenient case in point, because it is short enough to be easily manageable, has been explicated many times, and is almost universally esteemed. If not every reader goes all the way with Mark Pattison's judgment that it is "the high-water mark of English Poesy," still critics agree about its excellence as closely as they ever do in evaluating a lyric poem. My point is that, on the evidence of their own commentaries, critics agree about the excellence of quite different poems. They present us not with one *Lycidas* but with discriminable types of *Lycidas*—five types, I have announced in my title. I feel confident that with a little more perseverance I could have distinguished at least seven, to equal William Empson's types of ambiguity. But in these matters distinctions, as Mr. Empson's pro-

---

This essay is based on a lecture given at the Columbia Graduate Union in 1957 and elsewhere.

cedure demonstrates, can be rather arbitrary. And even five
types of *Lycidas* are enough to confront the literary theorist
with an embarrassing problem: Is a poem one or many? And if
it is one, how are we to decide which one?

I

For the first type, take *Lycidas* as it was commonly described
in the period between the first volume of Masson's monumental
Life of Milton (1859) and the critical age ushered in by T. S.
Eliot and I. A. Richards a generation ago. This traditional
reading (in which I was educated) was conveniently epitomized
by J. H. Hanford in his *Milton Handbook*. Individual discussions varied in emphasis and detail; but when in that lost paradise of critical innocence readers looked at *Lycidas*, they agreed
that they saw an elegiac poem about Edward King, a contemporary of Milton's at Christ's College, who had been drowned when
his ship suddenly foundered in the Irish Sea. To depersonalize
his grief and elevate its occasion, Milton chose to follow the
elaborate conventions of the pastoral elegy, as these had evolved
over the 1800 years between the Sicilian Theocritus and the English Spenser; he ended the poem with a traditional consolation
at the thought of Lycidas resurrected in heaven, and found in
this thought the strength to carry on his own concerns. In two
passages, many commentators agreed—they often called them
digressions—Milton uttered his personal concerns in a thin fic-
tional disguise. In one of these Milton expressed his own fear
that "th' abhorred shears" might cut him off before he could
achieve the poetic fame to which he had dedicated his life. In the
other Milton, through St. Peter, voiced a grim warning to the
corrupt English clergy of his time.

Writing in 1926, on the extreme verge of the New Criticism,
Professor Hanford was so imprudent as to close his discussion
with the statement that "*Lycidas* bears its meaning plainly
enough on its face." It contains, to be sure, a minor verbal crux
or two, such as the nature of the "two-handed engine at the
door"; but, he roundly asserted, "there has been little room for
disagreement regarding its larger features."

Only four years later E. M. W. Tillyard published in his *Milton* an analysis of *Lycidas* which in its opening tucket sounded
the new note in criticism:

> Most criticism of *Lycidas* is off the mark, because it fails to
> distinguish between the nominal and the real subject, what the
> poem professes to be about and what it is about. It assumes that
> Edward King is the real, whereas he is but the nominal subject.
> Fundamentally *Lycidas* concerns— [1]

But before we hear what *Lycidas* is really about, we ought to
attend to Tillyard's distinction between "nominal" and "real"
poetic meaning. For this modern polysemism, which splits all
poems—or at least the most noteworthy poems—into two or
more levels of meaning, one overt and nominal (which other
readers have detected) and the other covert but essential (whose
discovery has usually been reserved for the critic making the
distinction) is extraordinarily widespread, and we shall find it
repeatedly applied to *Lycidas*. The lamination of poetic significance is variously named. Tillyard elsewhere distinguishes between conscious and unconscious, and direct and oblique meanings. Other critics make a parallel distinction between manifest
and latent, ostensible and actual, literal and symbolic, or particular and archetypal significance. And at the risk of giving
away a trade secret, it must be confessed that most of the time,
when we critics come out with a startling new interpretation of
a well-known work, it is through the application of this very
useful interpretative stratagem.

The procedure is indispensable in analyzing works for which
there is convincing evidence that they were written in the mode
of allegory or symbolism. But it is worth noting that the distinction was developed by Greek commentators, interested in establishing Homer's reputation as a doctor of universal wisdom,
who dismissed Homer's scandalous stories about the gods as
only the veil for an esoteric and edifying undermeaning. The
same strategy was adapted by Philo to bring the Old Testament
into harmony with Greek philosophy, and by the Church Fathers
to prove that the Old Testament prefigured the New Testament,
and by medieval and Renaissance moralists in order to disclose,
behind Ovid's pagan and ostensibly licentious fables, austere
ethical precepts and anticipations of the Christian mysteries.
From the vantage of our altered cultural prepossessions, it appears that the distinction between nominal and real meaning has

[1] Quotations without page references are from essays reprinted in this
volume.

not infrequently been used as a handy gadget to replace what an author has said with what a commentator would prefer him to have said.

We are braced now for Tillyard's disclosure of the real subject of *Lycidas*. "Fundamentally *Lycidas* concerns Milton himself; King is but the excuse for one of Milton's most personal poems." The main argument for this interpretation is that *Lycidas* is generally admitted to be a great poem, but "if it is great, it must contain deep feeling of some sort"; since this feeling is obviously not about King, it must be about Milton himself. Milton, Tillyard maintains, expresses his own situation and feelings and attitudes, not only in the obviously allegorical passages about driving afield and piping with Lycidas, or in the passages on fame and the corrupt clergy which had been called personal by earlier critics, but from beginning to end of the poem. How radical Tillyard's formula is for translating objective references to subjective equivalents is indicated by his analysis of the poem's climactic passage:

> The fourth section purports to describe the resurrection of Lycidas and his entry into heaven. More truly it solves the whole poem by describing the resurrection into a new kind of life of Milton's hopes, should they be ruined by premature death or by the moral collapse of his country. . . . Above all the fourth section describes the renunciation of earthly fame, the abnegation of self by the great egotist, and the spiritual purgation of gaining one's life after losing it.[2]

Only such an interpretation, Tillyard claims, will reveal the integrity of the poem, by making it possible "to see in *Lycidas* a unity of purpose which cannot be seen in it if the death of King is taken as the real subject." Furthermore, the value of the poem really resides in the ordered and harmonized mental impulses for which the objective references are merely a projected correlative: "What makes *Lycidas* one of the greatest poems in English is that it expresses with success a state of mind whose high value can hardly be limited to a particular religious creed."

From this interpretation and these grounds of value John Crowe Ransom (to speak in understatement) disagrees. His premise is that "anonymity . . . is a condition of poetry." Mil-

[2] See also Tillyard's analysis of *Lycidas* in *Poetry Direct and Oblique*, revised edition (London, 1948), pp. 81–84.

ton very properly undertook to keep himself and his private
concerns out of his memorial verses, and to do so assumed the
identity of a Greek shepherd, the "uncouth swain" of the last
stanza, who serves as a dramatis persona, a "qualified spokesman" for the public performance of a ritual elegy. As for the
problem with which Tillyard confronted us—if the passion is not
for King, for whom can it be except Milton himself?—Ransom
solves it by dissolving it. There is no passion in the poem, and so
no problem. "For Lycidas [Milton] mourns with a very technical piety." The pastoral conventions are part of the poetic
"make-believe," and the whole poem, whatever more it may be,
is "an exercise in pure linguistic technique, or metrics; it was
also an exercise in the technique of what our critics of fiction
refer to as 'point of view.' "

This is the poem, at any rate, that Milton set out to write
and almost succeeded in writing. But his youth and character
interfered and forced into the writing three defiant gestures of
"rebellion against the formalism of his art." One of these is the
liberty he took with his stanzas, which are almost anarchically
irregular and include ten lines which do not rhyme at all. Another
is St. Peter's speech; in Ransom's comment on this passage, we
hear a voice out of the past—the Cavalier critic gracefully
but firmly putting the stiff-necked and surly Puritan in his place:
it expresses, he says, "a Milton who is angry, violent, and perhaps a little bit vulgar . . . Peter sounds like another Puritan
zealot, and less than apostolic." The third instance of Milton's
self-assertion is his "breach in the logic of composition"; that
is, he shifts from the first-person monologue with which the poem
opens to dialogues with Phoebus and others, then abruptly to
the third person in the last stanza, where the uncouth swain is
presented in "a pure narrative conclusion in the past [tense]."
It follows that Ransom's concluding evaluation turns Tillyard's
precisely inside-out. The sustained self-expression, on which Tillyard had grounded both the unity and excellence of the elegy,
according to Ransom breaks out only sporadically, and then
so as to violate the integrity and flaw the perfection of the poem.
"So *Lycidas*, for the most part a work of great art, is sometimes
artful and tricky. We are disturbingly conscious of a man behind the artist."

One might, of course, demur that given Ransom's own criteria,

two of the items he decries as arrogant gestures of Milton's
originality are exactly those in which he closely follows established conventions. The scholarly annotators—at whom, as he
passes, Ransom turns to smile—tell us that the models for Milton's stanzas, the elaborate *canzone* employed by several Italian
lyrists of the sixteenth century, were not only variable in structure, but also included unrhymed lines for the sake of that seeming ease and freedom which is the aim of an art that hides art.
As for St. Peter's diatribe, Milton inherited the right to introduce rough satire against the clergy into a pastoral from a widespread convention established by Petrarch, who was hardly vulgar, nor a Puritan, nor even a Protestant. In Ransom's third
exhibit, one element—Milton's putting the elegy into a narrative
context in the conclusion, without a matching narrative introduction—is not, apparently, traditional. But it is at any rate
odd to make Milton out to assert his own egoism in the passage
which specifically assigns the elegy to another person than himself; a person, moreover, who is the entirely conventional rural
singer of a pastoral elegy.

But this begins to seem captious, and does not represent
the measure of my admiration for the charm and deftness of Mr.
Ransom's essay, which thrusts home some important and timely
truths about the dramatic construction of *Lycidas* by the artful
device of overstatement. It is, one might hazard, a virtuoso exercise in critical point of view.

Let the commentary by Cleanth Brooks and John Hardy, in
their edition of Milton's *Poems* of 1645, represent *Lycidas*, type
four. At first glance it might seem that to these explicators the
poem is not really about King, nor about Milton, but mainly
about water. They turn to the first mention of water in lines
12–14 and discover at once the paradox that the "tear" which
is the "meed" paid to Lycidas by the elegiac singer is of the
same substance, salt water, as the "wat'ry bier," the sea on which
the body welters. As the poem develops, they say, "the 'melodious
tear' promises to overwhelm the 'sounding Seas.' " For the tear
is the elegy itself, which derives its inspiration from the "sacred
well" of the muses, and flows on through a profusion of fountains, rivers, and streams, in richly ambiguous interrelations of
harmonies, contrasts, and ironies, until, by the agency of "resurrection images," all of which "have to do with a circumvention

of the sea," we are transferred to a transcendent pastoral realm where Lycidas walks "other streams along" and the saints wipe the tears forever from his eyes.

The base of the critical operation here is the assumption that "the 'poetry' resides in the total structure of meanings." The primary component in this structure is "imagery," of which the component parts are so organically related, through mutual reflection and implication, that it does not matter where you start: any part will lead you to the center and the whole. The key to both the form and value of *Lycidas*, then, which Tillyard had found in the ordering of mental impulses, and Ransom in the all-but-successful maintenance of impersonal elegiac conventions, Brooks and Hardy locate in the evolution and integration of the imagery: "*Lycidas* is a good poem not because it is appropriately and simply pastoral and elegiac—with . . . all the standard equipment—but because of its unique formal wholeness, because of the rich 'integrity' of even such a single figure as that in the lines 'He must not flote upon his wat'ry bear / Unwept. . . .'" [3]

It turns out, however, that these images are only provisionally the elements of the poem, since in Milton they are used as vehicles for a more basic component, "certain dominant, recurrent symbolic motives." The fact, hitherto mainly overlooked, is that "Milton is a symbolist poet to a considerable extent." [4] Accordingly we must again, as in Tillyard's essay, penetrate the ostensible meaning to discover the real meaning of *Lycidas*, though a real meaning which in this case is an abstract concept. "What," they ask, "is the real subject" of *Lycidas?*

> If Milton is not deeply concerned with King as a person, he is deeply concerned, and as a young poet personally involved, with a theme—which is that of the place and meaning of poetry in a world which seems at many points inimical to it.

Specifically, the early part of the poem presents the despairing theme that nature is neutral, emptied of the old pastoral deities ("to say nymphs are ineffectual is tantamount to denying their existence"); and this concept is transcended only by the movement from philosophic naturalism to Christian supernaturalism, in the pastoral imagery of the conclusion in heaven.

[3] *Poems of Mr. John Milton* (New York, 1951), p. 259.
[4] *Ibid.*, pp. 256, 250.

inded reader, constitute the essential poem M
te.

out—in the sense that it presents as the poe
s elected fiction—a nameless shepherd, sitti
vening in a rural setting and hymning the dea
pastor, who is not Edward King but, specifical
eason all our interpreters except Ransom tre
st rather casually, if at all, is that they tend
that a poem is an object made of words, or
anings." So indeed it is. But as a starting poi
would be more inclusive and suggestive to s
made of *speech*, because the term "speech" e
r speaker. In *Lycidas* the speaker is an unnam
ose speech refers to a state of affairs, describ
and quotes the statements of other speakers, i
s, Camus, and St. Peter, expresses his ov
hanging mood, and conveys, by immediate ii
hing of his own character. The poem is ther
amatic lyric, with a setting, an occasion, a chi
several subordinate characters (who may, hov
d as representing the speaker's own thought
dramatic purposes as standard personae of tl

rely right, as against Ransom (and earlier, D
ding deep feeling in the poem, but he confront
ious alternative that the feeling must be eithe
about Milton himself. The feeling is occasione
Lycidas and the thoughts plausibly evoked b
it is experienced and expressed not by Miltor
Milton is at considerable pains to identify a
than himself. Precisely what Milton himsel
t during the many hours—probably days—ii
l over *Lycidas*, despite Tillyard's assurance, i
he most tenuous conjecture; although it is saf
ong other things, he was thinking how he migh
best possible pastoral elegy. But we know pre
uncouth swain thought and felt, because the
thoughts and feelings constitutes the poem, from
s, "Yet once more, O ye Laurels . . . ," up to
ng, the closing eight lines, when the author

Perhaps other readers share my disquiet at this discovery. Leaving aside the validity of assuming that *Lycidas* is essentially a symbolist poem of which the real subject is a theme, there remains the difficulty that the theme seems to be startlingly anachronistic. Milton, we are told, writing in 1637, and echoing a complaint about the nymphs which is as old as Theocritus' first Idyll, presents us with the world-view involving "an emptied nature, a nature which allows us to personify it only in the sense that its sounds seem mournful. . . . The music of nature . . . has also been stilled." But wasn't it Tennyson who said this, in an elegy published in 1850?

> And all the phantom, Nature, stands—
> With all the music in her tone,
> A hollow echo of my own,—
> A hollow form with empty hands.

As for the concept imputed to Milton, with respect to the place of poetry in an inimical world, that "Nature is neutral: it is not positively malignant, but neither is it beneficent"—isn't this exactly the thesis laid down in 1926 by I. A. Richards in a very influential little book, *Science and Poetry?* In our own age, Mr. Richards said,

> the central dominant change may be described as the *Neutralization of Nature,* the tranference from the Magical View of the world to the scientific. . . . There is some evidence that Poetry . . . arose with this Magical View. It is a possibility to be seriously considered that Poetry may pass away with it.[5]

At any rate, it is by a notable sleight of explication that Brooks and Hardy convert to the real meaning that Nature does not sympathize with the poet's sorrow and "has no apparent respect for the memory of Lycidas" the very passage in which Milton explicitly states the contrary: that nature, which had responded joyously to Lycidas' soft lays when he was alive, now mourns his death:

> Thee Shepherd, thee the Woods, and desert Caves,
> With wilde Thyme and the gadding Vine o'regrown,
> And all their echoes mourn.

We go on to the fifth type of *Lycidas*, the archetypal version, which entered the critical ken after the vogue of the writings

[5] *Science and Poetry* (London, 1926), pp. 47–48.

in comparative anthropology of James G. Frazer and in analytical psychology of C. G. Jung. This mode of criticism, like the last, begins by isolating images or patterns of imagery; now, however, the focus is on images which reflect the agents and events of myth or folklore. The favorite legends are those which (according to some folklorists) concern beings who were once nature deities—the dead and risen gods of Syria, Egypt, and Greece associated with the dying or reaping of the crops in the fall and their revival in the spring.

Richard P. Adams, investigating "The Archetypal Pattern of Death and Rebirth in *Lycidas*," discovers that the poem is throughout "a remarkably tight amalgam of death-and-rebirth imagery." These images begin with the initial reference to the evergreen plants, the laurel, myrtle, and ivy, and continue through the allusions to the hyacinth, the rose, and the violet, which had their mythical genesis in the blood of a mortal or deity. The many water-images are here interpreted as fertility symbols; the allusion to the death of Orpheus is said to bring in a myth whose similarities to "the deaths of Adonis, Attis, Osiris, and other fertility demigods have been pointed out by modern scholars"; while the poet's speculation that the body of Lycidas perhaps visits "the bottom of the monstrous world" parallels the descent into water and the dragon fight "which is often a feature of death-and-rebirth cycles." [6]

Adams is content with a fairly traditional interpretation of the subject of *Lycidas:* Milton's concern was not with Edward King, but "with the life, death, and resurrection of the dedicated poet, and specifically with his own situation at the time." Northrop Frye, however, in his essay on "Literature as Context: Milton's *Lycidas*," contends that the "structural principle" of the poem, the formal cause which "assimilates all details in the realizing of its unity," is "the Adonis myth," and that "Lycidas is, poetically speaking, a god or spirit of nature, who eventually becomes a saint in heaven." The archetypal reading here provides us with a new principle of unity, a new distinction between ostensible and implicit meaning, and a new version of what the poem is really rather than nominally about. In an earlier essay, Frye put the matter bluntly: "Poetry demands, as Milton saw

[6] I have cited the original, extended form of this essay in *PMLA*, LXIV (1949), 183–188.

it, that the elements of
archetypes. . . . Hend
about his archetype, *A*
Lycidas in Milton's pc

It will not do to se
five versions of *Lycida*
selected aspects and d
or emphasis, but in ess
poem; each claims to I
tural principle, which
terrelations of the pa
the meaning, unity, an
Humpty Dumpty tog
sometimes hear, to cor
criticism which has t
none. To provide a co
itself be coherent; it c
principles. A syncreti
not an integral poem,

When there is such r
the real but nonliter
best hope of remedy, I
and reading it with a
clear evidence that so
symbolically. This is
In a way, this puts n
writing as a new criti
out with an old readin
set out to labor the
number of earlier criti

Looked at in this w
although in some case
about Milton, about
in an inimical world;
God (Christ) who di
these in the central wa

[7] "Levels of Meaning in

to the literal-m
ton chose to wi

First, it is a
datum, Milton
from morn to
of a fellow poet
Lycidas. The :
the stated eleg
take as premis
structure of m
for criticism, i
that a poem is
tails a particul
rustic singer w
the appearance
cluding Phoeb
thoughts and
plication, some
fore clearly a d
character, and
ever, be regard
objectified for
pastoral ritual

Tillyard is s
Johnson), in fi
us with the spu
about King or
by the death of
that event; and
but by a singe
someone other
thought and fe
which he labor
beyond all but
to say that, am
put together th
cisely what the
expression of hi
the bold openin
but not includ

takes over as omniscient narrator: "*Thus* sang the uncouth Swain. . . ."

Readers of the poem at its first appearance knew that it was one of thirteen *Obsequies to the Memorie of Mr. Edward King*, and undoubtedly some also knew that the J.M. who signed the last obsequy was John Milton, whose circumstances and relations to King bore some resemblance to those presented in the poem. Such knowledge, however, does not displace but adds a particular historical reference to the two chief persons of the literal poem. *Lycidas* is not simply "about" King; it is a public ceremonial on the occasion of King's death, and the decorum of such a performance requires that the individual be not only lamented but also honored. And how could King be honored more greatly than to be made an instance of the type of poet-priest, identified by the traditional name "Lycidas," and to be lamented by a typical pastoral singer—in Ransom's phrase, a "qualified spokesman" for the public performance of a ritual elegy—whose single voice is resonant with echoes of poets through the ages mourning other poets untimely cut off? My insistence here may seem to be much ado about trivia, and, provided we are ready to fill out the details when pertinent, it can be a harmless critical shorthand to say that it is Milton who sings a lament for Edward King. But entirely to disregard these elementary circumstances may be the beginning of critical arrogance, which can end in our substituting our own poem for the one Milton chose to write.

The pastoral singer sets out, then, both to lament and to celebrate Lycidas. But consideration of this particular death raises in his mind a general question about the pointless contingencies of life, with its constant threat that fate may slit the thin-spun thread of any dedicated mortal prior to fulfillment and so render profitless his self-denial. This doubt, it should be noted, is not an ulterior "theme" beneath the ostensible surface of the poem. It is, explicitly, a topic in the thought of the lyric speaker, a stage in his soliloquy, which the speaker's continued meditation, guided by the comments of other imagined characters, goes on to resolve. This turn away from Lycidas to the circumstance of those who have survived him is not insincere, nor does it constitute a digression or an indecorously personal intrusion. It is entirely natural and appropriate; just as (to borrow a parallel from J. M. French) it is altogether fitting and proper for Lin-

coln, in the course of the *Gettysburg Address,* to turn from "these
honored dead" to concern for "us the living." [8] After all, the
doubts and fears of the lyric speaker concern the insecurity of
his own life only in so far as he, like Lycidas, is a member of the
genus Poet, and concern the class of poets only in so far as they
share the universal human condition.

While initially, then, we may say that the presented subject
of *Lycidas* is a pastoral singer memorializing the death of a
dedicated shepherd poet-and-priest, we must go on to say that—
in a second and important sense of "subject" as the dynamic
center, or controlling principle, of a poem—its subject is a question about the seeming profitlessness of the dedicated life and
the seeming deficiency of divine justice raised by that shocking
death in the mind of the lyric speaker. That the rise, evolution,
and resolution of the troubled thought of the elegist is the key
to the structure of *Lycidas,* Milton made as emphatic as he
could. He forced it on our attention by the startling device of
ending the elegy, in a passage set off as a stanza in ottava rima,
not with Lycidas, but with the elegist himself as, reassured, he
faces his own destiny with confidence. But there is no occasion
for Lycidas to feel slighted by this dereliction, for has he not
been left in heaven, entertained and comforted by a chorus of
saints, and given an office equivalent to St. Michael's, as guardian
of the western shore?

III

If this, in barest outline, is the subject and the structural
principle of the poem, what are we to make of the thematic
imagery which, in the alternative interpretation by Brooks and
Hardy, motivate and control its development?

Lycidas indeed, as these critics point out, incorporates many
water and sheep-and-shepherd images; it also has song-and-
singer images, flower images, stellar images, wide-ranging geographical images, even a surprising number of eye, ear, and
mouth images. The usual strategy of the imagist critic is to pull
out a selection of such items and to set them up in an order
which is largely independent of who utters them, on what occasion, and for what dramatic purpose. Freed from the controls

[8] See J. M. French, "The Digressions in Milton's *Lycidas,*" *Studies in
Philology,* L (1953), 486.

imposed by their specific verbal and dramatic contexts, the selected images readily send out shoots and tendrils of significance, which can be twined into a symbolic pattern—and if the critic is sensitive, learned, and adroit, often a very interesting pattern. The danger is, that the pattern may be largely an artifact of the implicit scheme governing the critical analysis.

From our elected point of view, the images in *Lycidas* constitute elements in the speech—some of it literal and some figurative, allegoric, or symbolic—which serve primarily to express the perceptions, thoughts, and feelings of the lyric speaker. These images constitute for the reader a sensuous texture, and they set up among themselves, as Brooks and Hardy point out, various ambiguities, contrasts, and harmonies. But in *Lycidas*, the procession of images is less determining than determined. If they steer the meditation of the speaker, it is only in so far as they cooperate in doing so with more authoritative principles: with the inherited formulas of the elegiac ritual, and with these formulas as they in turn (in Milton's inventive use of pastoral conventions) are subtly subordinated to the evolving meditation of the lyric speaker himself. In effect, then, the imagery does not displace, but corroborates the process of feelingful thought in the mind of a specified character. This, it seems to me, is the way Milton wrote *Lycidas;* there is no valid evidence, in or out of the poem, that he constructed it—as T. S. Eliot might have done—out of a set of ownerless symbols which he endowed with an implicit dynamism and set to acting out a thematic plot.

For the mythic and archetypal interpretation of *Lycidas*, as it happens, there is a more plausible basis in Milton's ideas and characteristic procedures. As a Christian humanist of the Renaissance, Milton was eager to save the phenomena of classical culture, and thus shared with the modern archetypist an interest in synthesizing the ancient and modern, the primitive and civilized, pagan fable and Christian dogma, into an all-encompassing whole. And Milton knew, from divers ancient and Renaissance mythographers, about the parallel to the death and resurrection of Christ in ancient fables and fertility cults— about what in *Paradise Lost* he called the "reviv'd Adonis" (IX, 440), and the "annual wound" of Thammuz, identified with Adonis by the Syrian damsels who lamented his fate "in amorous ditties all a Summer's day" (I, 446–452). But these facts are not adequate to validate a reading of *Lycidas* as a poem which is really about Adonis, or any other pagan fertility god. In *Lycidas* Milton makes no allusion whatever to Adonis, and he refers to Orpheus only to voice despair that even the Muse his mother was helpless to prevent his hideous death. In his references to these fables in *Paradise Lost*, Milton specifies that the story of the Garden of revived Adonis is "feign'd," lists Thammuz-Adonis among the "Devils [adored] for Deities," and describes the mother of Orpheus as "an empty dream" (VII, 39). For though a humanist, Milton is a Christian humanist, to whom revelation is not one more echo of archetypal myths but the archetype itself, the one Truth, which had been either corrupted or distortedly foreshadowed, "prefigured," in various pagan deities and fables. There is a world of difference between Milton's assumption that there is only one religion and Blake's archetypal assertion that "All Religions are One."

By conflating Christian and non-Christian story into equivalent variations on a single rebirth pattern, the tendency of an archetypal reading is to cancel dramatic structure by flattening the poem out, or even—in the extreme but common view that we get closer to the archetype as we move back along the scale toward the vegetational cycle itself—by turning the poem inside out. For if we regard the rebirth theme as having been revealed in the opening passage on the unwithering laurel, myrtle, and ivy, and as merely reiterated in later passages on Orpheus, on water, on sanguine flowers, and in the allusion to Christ and the risen Lycidas, then the denouement of the poem lies in its exordium and its movement is not a progress but an eddy.

The movement of *Lycidas*, on the contrary, is patently from despair through a series of insights to triumphant joy. We can put it this way: read literally, the elegy proper opens with the statement "Lycidas is dead, dead ere his prime"; it concludes with the flatly opposing statement "Lycidas your sorrow is *not* dead." Everything that intervenes has been planned to constitute a plausible sequence of thoughts and insights that will finally convert a logical contradiction into a lyric reversal by the anagnorisis, the discovery, that for a worthy Christian poet-priest a seeming defeat by death is actually an immortal triumph.

Milton achieves this reversal by a gradual shift from the natural, pastoral, and pagan viewpoint to the viewpoint of Chris-

Perhaps other readers share my disquiet at this discovery. Leaving aside the validity of assuming that *Lycidas* is essentially a symbolist poem of which the real subject is a theme, there remains the difficulty that the theme seems to be startlingly anachronistic. Milton, we are told, writing in 1637, and echoing a complaint about the nymphs which is as old as Theocritus' first Idyll, presents us with the world-view involving "an emptied nature, a nature which allows us to personify it only in the sense that its sounds seem mournful. . . . The music of nature . . . has also been stilled." But wasn't it Tennyson who said this, in an elegy published in 1850?

> And all the phantom, Nature, stands—
> With all the music in her tone,
> A hollow echo of my own,—
> A hollow form with empty hands.

As for the concept imputed to Milton, with respect to the place of poetry in an inimical world, that "Nature is neutral: it is not positively malignant, but neither is it beneficent"—isn't this exactly the thesis laid down in 1926 by I. A. Richards in a very influential little book, *Science and Poetry?* In our own age, Mr. Richards said,

> the central dominant change may be described as the *Neutralization of Nature,* the tranference from the Magical View of the world to the scientific. . . . There is some evidence that Poetry . . . arose with this Magical View. It is a possibility to be seriously considered that Poetry may pass away with it.[5]

At any rate, it is by a notable sleight of explication that Brooks and Hardy convert to the real meaning that Nature does not sympathize with the poet's sorrow and "has no apparent respect for the memory of Lycidas" the very passage in which Milton explicitly states the contrary: that nature, which had responded joyously to Lycidas' soft lays when he was alive, now mourns his death:

> Thee Shepherd, thee the Woods, and desert Caves,
> With wilde Thyme and the gadding Vine o'regrown,
> And all their echoes mourn.

We go on to the fifth type of *Lycidas*, the archetypal version, which entered the critical ken after the vogue of the writings

[5] *Science and Poetry* (London, 1926), pp. 47–48.

in comparative anthropology of James G. Frazer and in analytical psychology of C. G. Jung. This mode of criticism, like the last, begins by isolating images or patterns of imagery; now, however, the focus is on images which reflect the agents and events of myth or folklore. The favorite legends are those which (according to some folklorists) concern beings who were once nature deities—the dead and risen gods of Syria, Egypt, and Greece associated with the dying or reaping of the crops in the fall and their revival in the spring.

Richard P. Adams, investigating "The Archetypal Pattern of Death and Rebirth in *Lycidas*," discovers that the poem is throughout "a remarkably tight amalgam of death-and-rebirth imagery." These images begin with the initial reference to the evergreen plants, the laurel, myrtle, and ivy, and continue through the allusions to the hyacinth, the rose, and the violet, which had their mythical genesis in the blood of a mortal or deity. The many water-images are here interpreted as fertility symbols; the allusion to the death of Orpheus is said to bring in a myth whose similarities to "the deaths of Adonis, Attis, Osiris, and other fertility demigods have been pointed out by modern scholars"; while the poet's speculation that the body of Lycidas perhaps visits "the bottom of the monstrous world" parallels the descent into water and the dragon fight "which is often a feature of death-and-rebirth cycles." [6]

Adams is content with a fairly traditional interpretation of the subject of *Lycidas:* Milton's concern was not with Edward King, but "with the life, death, and resurrection of the dedicated poet, and specifically with his own situation at the time." Northrop Frye, however, in his essay on "Literature as Context: Milton's *Lycidas*," contends that the "structural principle" of the poem, the formal cause which "assimilates all details in the realizing of its unity," is "the Adonis myth," and that "Lycidas is, poetically speaking, a god or spirit of nature, who eventually becomes a saint in heaven." The archetypal reading here provides us with a new principle of unity, a new distinction between ostensible and implicit meaning, and a new version of what the poem is really rather than nominally about. In an earlier essay, Frye put the matter bluntly: "Poetry demands, as Milton saw

[6] I have cited the original, extended form of this essay in *PMLA*, LXIV (1949), 183–188.

it, that the elements of his theme should be assimilated to their archetypes. . . . Hence the poem will not be about King, but about his archetype, Adonis, the dying and rising god, called Lycidas in Milton's poem." [7]

II

It will not do to say, as one is tempted to say, that these five versions of *Lycidas* really give us the same poem, in diversely selected aspects and details. The versions differ not in selection or emphasis, but in essentials. Each strikes for the heart of the poem; each claims to have discovered the key element, or structural principle, which has controlled the choice, order, and interrelations of the parts, and which establishes for the reader the meaning, unity, and value of the whole. Nor will it help put Humpty Dumpty together again to carry out the proposal we sometimes hear, to combine all these critical modes into a single criticism which has the virtues of each and the deficiency of none. To provide a coherent reading, a critical procedure must itself be coherent; it cannot be divided against itself in its first principles. A syncretic criticism is invertebrate, and will yield not an integral poem, but a ragout.

When there is such radical and many-sided disagreement about the real but nonliteral and esoteric meaning of the poem, the best hope of remedy, I think, lies in going back to Milton's text and reading it with a dogged literalness, except when there is clear evidence that some part of it is to be read allegorically or symbolically. This is what I propose, very briefly, to attempt. In a way, this puts me in a favorable position. A drawback in writing as a new critic is that it would be embarrassing to come out with an old reading; while I can plead that I have deliberately set out to labor the obvious, and can take comfort from the number of earlier critiques with which I find myself in agreement.

Looked at in this way, *Lycidas* turns out to be in some sense—although in some cases a very loose sense—about Edward King, about Milton, about water, about the problem of being a poet in an inimical world; and it is undoubtedly about at least one God (Christ) who died to be reborn. But it is about none of these in the central way that it is about certain other things that,

[7] "Levels of Meaning in Literature," *Kenyon Review*, XII (1950), 258.

to the literal-minded reader, constitute the essential poem Milton chose to write.

First, it is about—in the sense that it presents as the poetic datum, Milton's elected fiction—a nameless shepherd, sitting from morn to evening in a rural setting and hymning the death of a fellow poet-pastor, who is not Edward King but, specifically, Lycidas. The reason all our interpreters except Ransom treat the stated elegist rather casually, if at all, is that they tend to take as premise that a poem is an object made of words, or "a structure of meanings." So indeed it is. But as a starting point for criticism, it would be more inclusive and suggestive to say that a poem is made of *speech*, because the term "speech" entails a particular speaker. In *Lycidas* the speaker is an unnamed rustic singer whose speech refers to a state of affairs, describes the appearance and quotes the statements of other speakers, including Phoebus, Camus, and St. Peter, expresses his own thoughts and changing mood, and conveys, by immediate implication, something of his own character. The poem is therefore clearly a dramatic lyric, with a setting, an occasion, a chief character, and several subordinate characters (who may, however, be regarded as representing the speaker's own thoughts, objectified for dramatic purposes as standard personae of the pastoral ritual).

Tillyard is surely right, as against Ransom (and earlier, Dr. Johnson), in finding deep feeling in the poem, but he confronts us with the spurious alternative that the feeling must be either about King or about Milton himself. The feeling is occasioned by the death of Lycidas and the thoughts plausibly evoked by that event; and it is experienced and expressed not by Milton, but by a singer Milton is at considerable pains to identify as someone other than himself. Precisely what Milton himself thought and felt during the many hours—probably days—in which he labored over *Lycidas*, despite Tillyard's assurance, is beyond all but the most tenuous conjecture; although it is safe to say that, among other things, he was thinking how he might put together the best possible pastoral elegy. But we know precisely what the uncouth swain thought and felt, because the expression of his thoughts and feelings constitutes the poem, from the bold opening, "Yet once more, O ye Laurels . . . ," up to, but not including, the closing eight lines, when the author takes over as omniscient narrator: "*Thus* sang the uncouth Swain. . . ."

Readers of the poem at its first appearance knew that it was one of thirteen *Obsequies to the Memorie of Mr. Edward King*, and undoubtedly some also knew that the J.M. who signed the last obsequy was John Milton, whose circumstances and relations to King bore some resemblance to those presented in the poem. Such knowledge, however, does not displace but adds a particular historical reference to the two chief persons of the literal poem. *Lycidas* is not simply "about" King; it is a public ceremonial on the occasion of King's death, and the decorum of such a performance requires that the individual be not only lamented but also honored. And how could King be honored more greatly than to be made an instance of the type of poet-priest, identified by the traditional name "Lycidas," and to be lamented by a typical pastoral singer—in Ransom's phrase, a "qualified spokesman" for the public performance of a ritual elegy—whose single voice is resonant with echoes of poets through the ages mourning other poets untimely cut off? My insistence here may seem to be much ado about trivia, and, provided we are ready to fill out the details when pertinent, it can be a harmless critical shorthand to say that it is Milton who sings a lament for Edward King. But entirely to disregard these elementary circumstances may be the beginning of critical arrogance, which can end in our substituting our own poem for the one Milton chose to write.

The pastoral singer sets out, then, both to lament and to celebrate Lycidas. But consideration of this particular death raises in his mind a general question about the pointless contingencies of life, with its constant threat that fate may slit the thin-spun thread of any dedicated mortal prior to fulfillment and so render profitless his self-denial. This doubt, it should be noted, is not an ulterior "theme" beneath the ostensible surface of the poem. It is, explicitly, a topic in the thought of the lyric speaker, a stage in his soliloquy, which the speaker's continued meditation, guided by the comments of other imagined characters, goes on to resolve. This turn away from Lycidas to the circumstance of those who have survived him is not insincere, nor does it constitute a digression or an indecorously personal intrusion. It is entirely natural and appropriate; just as (to borrow a parallel from J. M. French) it is altogether fitting and proper for Lincoln, in the course of the *Gettysburg Address,* to turn from "these honored dead" to concern for "us the living." [8] After all, the doubts and fears of the lyric speaker concern the insecurity of his own life only in so far as he, like Lycidas, is a member of the genus Poet, and concern the class of poets only in so far as they share the universal human condition.

While initially, then, we may say that the presented subject of *Lycidas* is a pastoral singer memorializing the death of a dedicated shepherd poet-and-priest, we must go on to say that— in a second and important sense of "subject" as the dynamic center, or controlling principle, of a poem—its subject is a question about the seeming profitlessness of the dedicated life and the seeming deficiency of divine justice raised by that shocking death in the mind of the lyric speaker. That the rise, evolution, and resolution of the troubled thought of the elegist is the key to the structure of *Lycidas,* Milton made as emphatic as he could. He forced it on our attention by the startling device of ending the elegy, in a passage set off as a stanza in ottava rima, not with Lycidas, but with the elegist himself as, reassured, he faces his own destiny with confidence. But there is no occasion for Lycidas to feel slighted by this dereliction, for has he not been left in heaven, entertained and comforted by a chorus of saints, and given an office equivalent to St. Michael's, as guardian of the western shore?

III

If this, in barest outline, is the subject and the structural principle of the poem, what are we to make of the thematic imagery which, in the alternative interpretation by Brooks and Hardy, motivate and control its development?

Lycidas indeed, as these critics point out, incorporates many water and sheep-and-shepherd images; it also has song-and-singer images, flower images, stellar images, wide-ranging geographical images, even a surprising number of eye, ear, and mouth images. The usual strategy of the imagist critic is to pull out a selection of such items and to set them up in an order which is largely independent of who utters them, on what occasion, and for what dramatic purpose. Freed from the controls

[8] See J. M. French, "The Digressions in Milton's *Lycidas,*" *Studies in Philology,* L (1953), 486.

imposed by their specific verbal and dramatic contexts, the selected images readily send out shoots and tendrils of significance, which can be twined into a symbolic pattern—and if the critic is sensitive, learned, and adroit, often a very interesting pattern. The danger is, that the pattern may be largely an artifact of the implicit scheme governing the critical analysis.

From our elected point of view, the images in *Lycidas* constitute elements in the speech—some of it literal and some figurative, allegoric, or symbolic—which serve primarily to express the perceptions, thoughts, and feelings of the lyric speaker. These images constitute for the reader a sensuous texture, and they set up among themselves, as Brooks and Hardy point out, various ambiguities, contrasts, and harmonies. But in *Lycidas*, the procession of images is less determining than determined. If they steer the meditation of the speaker, it is only in so far as they cooperate in doing so with more authoritative principles: with the inherited formulas of the elegiac ritual, and with these formulas as they in turn (in Milton's inventive use of pastoral conventions) are subtly subordinated to the evolving meditation of the lyric speaker himself. In effect, then, the imagery does not displace, but corroborates the process of feelingful thought in the mind of a specified character. This, it seems to me, is the way Milton wrote *Lycidas;* there is no valid evidence, in or out of the poem, that he constructed it—as T. S. Eliot might have done—out of a set of ownerless symbols which he endowed with an implicit dynamism and set to acting out a thematic plot.

For the mythic and archetypal interpretation of *Lycidas,* as it happens, there is a more plausible basis in Milton's ideas and characteristic procedures. As a Christian humanist of the Renaissance, Milton was eager to save the phenomena of classical culture, and thus shared with the modern archetypist an interest in synthesizing the ancient and modern, the primitive and civilized, pagan fable and Christian dogma, into an all-encompassing whole. And Milton knew, from divers ancient and Renaissance mythographers, about the parallel to the death and resurrection of Christ in ancient fables and fertility cults— about what in *Paradise Lost* he called the "reviv'd Adonis" (IX, 440), and the "annual wound" of Thammuz, identified with Adonis by the Syrian damsels who lamented his fate "in amorous ditties all a Summer's day" (I, 446–452). But these

facts are not adequate to validate a reading of *Lycidas* as a
poem which is really about Adonis, or any other pagan fertility
god. In *Lycidas* Milton makes no allusion whatever to Adonis,
and he refers to Orpheus only to voice despair that even the
Muse his mother was helpless to prevent his hideous death. In
his references to these fables in *Paradise Lost*, Milton specifies
that the story of the Garden of revived Adonis is "feign'd," lists
Thammuz-Adonis among the "Devils [adored] for Deities," and
describes the mother of Orpheus as "an empty dream" (VII, 39).
For though a humanist, Milton is a Christian humanist, to whom
revelation is not one more echo of archetypal myths but the
archetype itself, the one Truth, which had been either corrupted
or distortedly foreshadowed, "prefigured," in various pagan
deities and fables. There is a world of difference between Milton's
assumption that there is only one religion and Blake's archetypal
assertion that "All Religions are One."

By conflating Christian and non-Christian story into equivalent variations on a single rebirth pattern, the tendency of an
archetypal reading is to cancel dramatic structure by flattening
the poem out, or even—in the extreme but common view that
we get closer to the archetype as we move back along the scale
toward the vegetational cycle itself—by turning the poem inside out. For if we regard the rebirth theme as having been
revealed in the opening passage on the unwithering laurel, myrtle, and ivy, and as merely reiterated in later passages on Orpheus, on water, on sanguine flowers, and in the allusion to Christ
and the risen Lycidas, then the denouement of the poem lies in
its exordium and its movement is not a progress but an eddy.

The movement of *Lycidas*, on the contrary, is patently from
despair through a series of insights to triumphant joy. We can
put it this way: read literally, the elegy proper opens with the
statement "Lycidas is dead, dead ere his prime"; it concludes
with the flatly opposing statement "Lycidas your sorrow is *not*
dead." Everything that intervenes has been planned to constitute
a plausible sequence of thoughts and insights that will finally
convert a logical contradiction into a lyric reversal by the anagnorisis, the discovery, that for a worthy Christian poet-priest
a seeming defeat by death is actually an immortal triumph.

Milton achieves this reversal by a gradual shift from the natural, pastoral, and pagan viewpoint to the viewpoint of Chris-

tian revelation and its promise of another world, the Kingdom of Heaven. He carefully marks for us the stages of this ascent by what, to contemporary readers, was the conspicuous device of grading the levels of his style. For as Milton said in the treatise *Of Education*, issued seven years after *Lycidas*, decorum (including "the fitted stile of lofty, mean, or lowly" to the height of the matter) "is the grand master peece to observe." The problem of stylistic decorum had been particularly debated in connection with the pastoral, which had troubled Renaissance theorists by the duplicity of its stylistic requirements, since it typically dealt with high matters under the lowly guise of a conversation between two uncouth swains. Milton's comment on the fitted style probably was an echo of Puttenham's statement that "decencie," or "decorum"—the just proportioning of the "high, meane, and base stile"—is "the chiefe praise of any writer"; and Puttenham had also pointed out that, though the normal level of pastoral was the "base and humble stile," the form was often used "under the vaile of homely persons and in rude speeches to insinuate and glaunce at greater matters." [9]

Accordingly Milton's singer opens the poem with a style higher than the pastoral norm: "Begin, and somewhat loudly sweep the string" is what he bids the muses, echoing the *"Sicelides Musae, paulo maiora canamus"* with which Virgil had elevated the pitch of his Fourth, or "Messianic," Eclogue. (Puttenham had remarked concerning this pastoral that, because of its lofty subject, "Virgill used a somewhat swelling stile" and that under the circumstances, "this was decent." [10]) The initial level of *Lycidas* suffices for the early pastoral and pagan sections on sympathizing nature, the nymphs, and the death of Orpheus. But this last reference evokes the despairing thought: what boots the ascetic life for those who, like Lycidas, stake everything on a treacherous future? The immediate comfort is vouchsafed the

[9] George Puttenham, *The Arte of English Poesie* (1589), in George G. Smith, ed., *Elizabethan Critical Essays* (New York, 1904), II, pp. 155, 27, 40.

[10] *Ibid.*, p. 156. In his Epistle and gloss to Spenser's *Shepheardes Calender*, one of the chief models for *Lycidas*, E. K. had also emphasized the question of stylistic decorum in the pastoral. He observed of the October Eclogue, which concerns poetry, that the style is properly "more loftye than the rest" and that at its inspired close Spenser's "verse groweth so big, that it seemeth he hath forgot the meanenesse of shepheards state and stile." (Ernest De Selincourt, ed., *Edmund Spenser: Minor Poems* [New York, 1910], pp. 101, 104.)

singer in a thought in which the highest pagan ethics comes
closest to the Christian: the distinction between mere earthly
reputation and the meed of true fame awarded by a divine and
infallible judge. The concept is only tangentially Christian, however, for the deities named in this passage, Phoebus and Jove,
are pagan ones. Nevertheless "that strain," the singer observes,
"was of a higher mood," and he therefore readdresses himself
to Arethuse and Mincius, waters associated with the classical
pastoralists, as a transition back to the initial key: "But now
my *Oat* proceeds. . . ."

The next modulation comes when St. Peter raises by implication the even more searching question why a faithful shepherd
is taken early, while the corrupt ones prosper. He himself gives
the obscurely terrifying answer: the two-handed engine stands
ready to smite at the door; infallible justice dispenses punishment as well as rewards. This time the "dread voice" has been
not merely of "a higher mood," but of an entirely different ontological and stylistic order, for it has "shrunk" the pastoral
stream and frightened away the "Sicilian Muse" altogether. It
is not only that the voice has been raised in the harsh rhetoric of
anger, but that it belongs to a pastor, and expresses a matter,
alien to the world of pagan pastoral. A Christian subject is
here for the first time explicit. The appearance and speech of
Peter, although brought in, as Milton said in his subtitle, "by
occasion," is far from a digression. It turns out, indeed, to be
nothing less than the climax and turning point of the lyric
meditation, for without it the resolution, inadequately grounded,
would seem to have been contrived through Christ as a patent
Deus ex machina. The speech of Peter has in fact closely para-
phrased Christ's own pastoral parable (John 9:39–41; 10:1–
18), addressed to the Pharisees, in which He too had denounced
those who remain blind to the truth, who climb into the sheepfold,
and who abandon their sheep to the marauding wolf, and had then
identified Himself as the Good Shepherd who lays down His life
for His sheep—but only, He adds, "that I might take it again."
Once Christ, the shepherd who died to be born again, is paralleled
to the dead shepherd Lycidas, though by allusion only, the resolution of the elegy is assured—especially since Peter, the Pilot
of the Galilean Lake, is the very Apostle who had been taught by
Christ, through faith and force of example, to walk on the water

in which he would otherwise have drowned (Matthew 14:25–31). The elegiac singer, however, is momentarily occupied with the specific references rather than the Scriptural overtones of Peter's comment, with the result that the resolution, so skillfully planted in his evolving thought, is delayed until he has tried to interpose a little ease by strewing imaginary flowers on Lycidas' imagined hearse. But this evasion only brings home the horror of the actual condition of the lost and weltering corpse. By extraordinary dramatic management, it is at this point of profoundest depression that the thought of Lycidas' body sinking to "the bottom of the monstrous world" releases the full implication of St. Peter's speech, and we make the leap from nature to revelation, in the great lyric peripety:

> Weep no more, woful Shepherds weep no more,
> For *Lycidas* your sorrow is not dead,
> Sunk though he be beneath the watry floar . . .
> So *Lycidas,* sunk low, but mounted high,
> Through the dear might of him that walk'd the waves. . . .

This consolation is total, where the two earlier ones were partial. For one thing, we now move from the strict judgment of merit and demerit to the God who rewards us beyond the requirements of justice by the free gift of a life eternal. Also, the elegist has had the earlier promises of reward and retribution by hearsay from Apollo and Peter, but now, in a passage thronged with echoes from the Book of Revelation and soaring, accordantly, into an assured sublimity of style, he has his own imaginative revelation, so that he, like St. John in that Book, might say: "And I saw a new heaven and a new earth." His vision is of Lycidas having lost his life to find a better life in a felicity without tears; in which even that last infirmity of noble mind, the desire for fame, has been purged "in the blest Kingdoms meek of joy and love," the earthly inclination to Amaryllis and Neaera has been sublimated into the "unexpressive nuptial Song" of the marriage of the Lamb, and the pastoral properties of grove, stream, and song serve only to shadow forth a Kingdom outside of space and beyond the vicissitude of the seasons. But the meditation of the lyric singer, as I have said, is ultimately concerned with the dead as they affect the living; so, by way of the Genius of the shore, we redescend to the stylistic level of plain utterance and conclude with the solitary piper at evening, facing with restored confidence the contingencies of a world in which the set and rise of the material sun are only the emblematic promise of another life.

IV

We are all aware by now of a considerable irony: I undertook to resolve the five types of *Lycidas* into one, and instead have added a sixth. But of course, that is all a critic can do. A critique does not give us the poem, but only a description of the poem. Whatever the ontological status of *Lycidas* as an object-in-itself, there are many possible descriptions of *Lycidas*—as many, in fact, as there are diverse critical premises and procedures which can be applied to the text.

In the bewildering proliferation of assumptions and procedures that characterizes the present age, we need a safeguard against confusion, and a safeguard as well against the sceptical temptation to throw all criticism overboard as a waste of time. I would suggest that we regard any critique of a poem as a persuasive description; that is, as an attempt, under the guise of statements of fact, to persuade the reader to look at a poem in a particular way. Thus when a critic says, with assurance, "A poem means X," consider him to say: "Try reading it as though it meant X." When he says, "*Lycidas* is really about Milton himself," quietly translate: "I recommend that you entertain the hypothesis that *Lycidas* is about Milton, and see how it applies." From this point of view, the best interpretation of *Lycidas*—we can say, if we like to use that philosophical idiom, the reading which approximates most closely to *Lycidas* as an object-in-itself—is the one among the interpretations at present available which provides the best fit to all the parts of the poem in their actual order, emphases, and emotional effects, and which is in addition consistent with itself and with what we know of Milton's literary and intellectual inheritance and his characteristic poetic procedures.[11]

The persuasive description of *Lycidas* which I have sketched must be judged by the degree to which it satisfies these criteria

[11] See R. S. Crane's analysis of critical interpretations as hypotheses for investigating the structures of poems, *The Languages of Criticism and the Structure of Poetry* (Toronto, 1953), pp. 164–183.

of correspondence and coherence. To be sure it has a serious handicap, when measured against the startling discoveries in recent years of what *Lycidas* is really about. It is singularly unexciting to be told at this date that *Lycidas* is really what it seems— a dramatic presentation of a traditional pastoral singer uttering a ritual lament and raising in its course questions about untimely death and God's providence which are resolved by the recognition that God's Kingdom is not of this world. But surely this is the great commonplace in terms of which Milton, as a thoroughly Christian poet, inevitably thought. We cannot expect his innovations, on this crucial issue, to be doctrinal; the novelty (and it is entirely sufficient to make this an immense feat of lyric invention) consists in the way that the pastoral conventions and Christian concepts are newly realized, reconciled, and dramatized in the minute particulars of this unique and splendid poem.

I would not be understood to claim that the alternative readings of *Lycidas* I have described are illegitimate, or their discoveries unrewarding. They freshen our sense of old and familiar poems, and they force readers into novel points of vantage that yield interesting insights, of which some hold good for other critical viewpoints as well. I am as susceptible as most readers to the charm of suddenly being brought to see a solidly dramatic lyric flattened into an ornate texture of thematic images, or to the thrill of the archetypal revelation whereby, as Jane Harrison described it, behind the "bright splendors" of "great things in literature" one sees moving "darker and older shapes." But in our fascination with the ultra-violet and infra-red discoveries made possible by modern speculative instruments, we must take care not to overlook the middle of the poetic spectrum. The necessary, though not sufficient condition for a competent reader of poetry remains what it has always been—a keen eye for the obvious.

"Eager Thought": Dialectic in *Lycidas*

Jon S. Lawry

Lycidas may well be the most excellent poem in English. Dr. Johnson notwithstanding, it may also be the most "sincere" and convincing. However, despite parallels with a work such as "To His Coy Mistress," in which a wistful proposition is confuted by "fact," and so yields a conclusion that seems logically inescapable, *Lycidas* does not persuade by means of ordinary argument. If the elegy were to justify faith in life by staging a virtual death and resurrection, something more than a version of syllogism would be needed. The poem instead works to win what Newman would call assent. Its consolation is earned by the prior concession of desolation. Its text engages the hard fact of drowning as well as registering intimations of immortality. Because the speaker must look on a corpse before he can listen to a saint, his words often become self-subverting, using reversions, such as "Ay me, I fondly dream" and "Let our frail thoughts dally with false surmise." Yet all the while, the work was to constitute a "melodious tear."

It can be objected that *Lycidas* finally gains assent not by any rational means whatsoever, but only by music; and that the movement from "*Lycidas* is dead" to "*Lycidas* your sorrow is not dead" is neither a progress in conviction nor even a leap of

From *Publications of the Modern Language Association* 77 (1962): 27–32; revised for this book by the author.

faith, but only a concession to poetic beauty. But surely it is nearer the truth to say that the only kind of "argument" possible for so searching an elegy was a version of the Great Argument of *Paradise Lost*. It would be an agon, rather than a logical exercise. It would justify the ways of God to everything that is implied in the figure of Lycidas. And in doing so, it would only make use of some two hundred all but flawless verses, rather than the enormous expanse of epic.

In the broad structure designed to accomplish that process, *Lycidas* has long since been considered to be much like a musical suite of three mirroring sections, which are introduced and resolved by closely related framing passages. When our attention is concentrated mainly upon the process of thought which moves within and throughout those parts, the poem may be considered to be triadic in another way, that of Hegelian dialectic : an initial dogmatic proposition (thesis) is opposed by a skeptical second (antithesis) ; from their encounter arises a third statement, one of mystic certainty (synthesis). Within *Lycidas*, the major subject of this process is poetry itself. The timeless, serene, and objective attitudes of pastoral, impassioned only in formal artistic imitation of loss, are opposed by the skeptical affronts of death, temporal corruption, and several failures of consolation, all of which are impassioned in and through actual experience. However, each of these two modes of awareness or response is found to be incomplete in the course of the work, and a consummate statement, greater than either but partaking of both, gradually evolves. Put another way, the general issue is that of the possibility of poetry and, more particularly, of Christian poetry. Within the données of *Lycidas*, the attitudes and materials of the pastoral sequences are held to be ideally poetic— ideal in both the popular and the philosophic senses, being both the personal preference of the speaker and also an imaginative construct. They are also elements in a traditionalized and almost impersonal "poetic" response to death. But the "digressions" that follow enforce actuality upon this ideal, threatening to destroy it exactly as actuality had destroyed Edward King. That the apparently destructive argument of actuality has been cast in poetry is, of course, an indication that its force is limited, and that poetry will prove its power even within the supposedly hostile hold of actuality. However, the resolution of these seeming opposites—pastoral vs. local engagement, timeless poetry vs. experience, art vs. actuality—produces a reconstituted possibility of poetry which in part grows out of the formerly opposed modes, *both* of which have seemed, whether by impotence or by antagonistic assault, to signal the defeat of poetry.

Although such a process seems demonstrable in *Lycidas*, it would be a mistake to think of the poem as a straightforward dialectical sequence. It does not follow partitioned steps within a triadic strategy, either within each of the three movements or among them. Instead, it is pervasively dialectical, dialectical in almost every line. Not only are potentialities of synthesis lodged in the early stages of the work, but also pastoral details appear in the digressions, and pressures of actuality in the pastoral sections, thereby continuously suggesting the immense reconciliation that is to come. Because the three internal sections are closely related both to one another and to the opening and closing lines, the total statement must be present by suggestion or implication in every part. Furthermore, actuality is not finally considered to be alien to poetry, even though in particular passages it is presented as an agency of defeat for both poet and poetry. In short, neither the occasional concentration upon divisive particulars in the following discussion, nor the general use of the seemingly sequential Hegelian model, should be taken as an argument for true contrarieties within the poem. The purpose of the study is to adduce exactly the opposite.

From the viewpoint of its general dialectic, the poem clearly is not about Edward King, save as the conditions of his life and death intersect the ideal pastoral attitude in *Lycidas*. Nor, by the same token, is it about John Milton. Instead, it is about poetry and the poet, generally conceived, and about the conditions impelled by existence upon the poet and his works. It is with this concern that the dialectical process begins. On the one hand, King's death (and the death of any person, but especially of any poet) is objective material for poetic expression, the "ideal" form of which is the pastoral elegy. The conditions of poetry are so far "pure," any real sense of loss having been transmuted into the beautiful imitation of such a sense. The poet to this point is involved only as a singer; his commitment is a "melodious tear." On the other hand, the death of the individual poet, King, implies the real death of the poet generally and the consequent death of poetry. Melodious artistic lament—the essential concern of which is neither King nor Milton but the expression itself within the formal determinations of the genre—is confronted by the anguished recognition of real physical loss, of defeated promise, and of corrupt society. Lament veers sharply away from the provinces of "pure" art as the vulnerable poet himself and his equally vulnerable creations become its subject.

Although *Lycidas* begins upon some sense of an implied protest, the initial apology for premature entry into demanding poetry is in part conventional, and vestiges of the pure pastoral possibility remain in the description of elegy as a "melodious tear." But the apology becomes somewhat more than conventional, and other than pastoral, by the nature of the protest against too early exercise of poetry. King's untimely death *forces* expression. By implication, reality, with its conditions of death and unripeness, stands opposed to the evergreen laurel, myrtle, and ivy symbolic of poetry, which are "never sere." Experiential intensity repeatedly breaks into the conventional apology in oxymoron and paradox: "Sad occasion *dear*," "melodious *tear*." The occasion is "dear" poetically, "sad" actually; even more precisely, the occasion is "dear" both in the sense of evoking a purely poetic token of affection and in that of exacting, at great cost, personal grief from the speaker. Similarly, an actual "tear" obeys the demand of existence, but in the pastoral attitude the tear as poetic lament may be "melodious." The initial announcement of the poem—"Lycidas is dead"—also looks both to the reality of death and to imaginative pastoral beauty by the use of an "unreal," transmutative name. The name "Lycidas," that is, can objectify Edward King into the unaffecting; his actual death can receive no such distancing.

The pastoral convention is maintained in the invocation to the muses, but a dominating point of opposition is again reached in the immediate connection of the lost Lycidas with poetry ("he knew/ Himself to sing, and build the lofty rhyme"). Lament for Lycidas will necessitate lament for poetry—by implication, for the very poetry of the present elegist. Such association of the dead poet with the living appears more fully in the speaker's hope for a like memorial:

So may som gentle Muse
With lucky words favor my destin'd Urn,
And as he passes turn,
And bid fair peace be to my sable shroud.

The term "lucky words" at this point in the poem reflects (with
perhaps a shade of irony) a pastoral objectivity, but it is opposed at once by the term "destin'd Urn," which reverberates
with the same recognition of loss—including loss of poetry—
as had the earlier notice of the death of Lycidas. In memory,
pastoral reasserts itself by objectifying Cambridge into a scene
like those in *L'Allegro*, but that scene is at once swept away
by the heavy real change inflicted by actuality. The sense of
the loss of Lycidas, partially held off again for a time by conventional pastoral images of desolated nature—which, however,
bear their own grim sense of mortality—returns sharply with
"Such, *Lycidas*, thy loss to Shepherds ear": again the threat
of reality to poetry overcomes the pastoral attitude.

Ensuing conventional appeals to pastoral deities are inter-
sected by the same sense of destruction, and for a time the pastoral convention is nearly surrendered. The saving pastoral
nymphs are gone, particularly from the nearly objective British
scene: they are not where the Druids lie, nor on Mona, nor at the
Dee. The pastoral attitude and legendary British subjects are
alien to the real scene and would be in any case helpless before
actuality: "Had ye bin there . . . what could that have don?"
The materials of "pure" poetry seem useless or unusable, denied by death.

This unwilling but progressive surrender of the pastoral attitude moves directly from the recognition that Orpheus's voice,
too, was stopped in death, to the first so-called "digression,"
that concerning the certain defeat of the "slighted Shepherd's
trade" by the "blind *Fury* with th'abhorred shears." The speaker recognizes a double defeat of poetry and of the honorable
fame due the poet: inattention from a corrupt world, which
sports with Amaryllis in the shade, and destruction in death. A
hint of the possible reconciliation of "pure" poetry with existence
is made by Phoebus: praise of poetry and of the poet is not so
much denied by reality as lodged elsewhere than in the world.
Both poet and poetry must be considered *sub specie aeternitatis*,
within the "artifice of eternity." For the first time in the poem,

synthesis—in the partly disclosed theme of resurrection and right judgment—tentatively reveals itself.

However, Phoebus's lofty and not immediately comforting statement is left suspended as the poem returns to pastoral conventions ("now my Oat proceeds"), which have already shown themselves unequal to the thrust of reality. The pastoral world, through Triton and other water figures, is found innocent of Lycidas's death by water, but was, however, impotent to prevent it. Reality, in "that fatal and perfidious Bark," is *necessarily* "guilty"; Atropos's abhorred shears again glint savagely across the pastoral scene. Then suddenly St. Peter, a water figure for the moment alien to the pastoral world, appears, shivering the helpless pastoral scene completely for the time. Like the progression from Orpheus to the poet in the first "digression," the movement from Camus to St. Peter in the second is logical in terms of imagery, but, like the earlier progression, it also intersects and contradicts the whole pastoral framework. St. Peter speaks not through the imaginative and beautiful pastoral convention but through stern theological "realities," judging the contemporary physical reality. His sweeping condemnation of the false clergy takes sharp note of the death of Lycidas, the true poet-priest who should have been spared. The synthesis will insist that he *has* been "spared," of course, but for the moment false poets and false priests, alive whereas Lycidas is dead, define the apparent nature of reality. Atropos's shears and the corrupt world's inattention still dominate the speaker's vision. Although the "two-handed engine," beyond human time, will somehow restore justice, little mitigation is offered for the present, in which poetry and pastoral seem helpless to prevent, to transcend, or to express reality (pastoral conventions do not appear directly in the "digressions"; the original "ideal" form cannot yet cope with seemingly antithetical materials). However, the second note of synthesis has been lodged, and a transformation of the pastoral attitude now begins. Transferred into Christian application, gradually adopting the Christian iconology of the shepherd as poet-priest, the pastoral materials can move into and beyond formerly antagonistic reality. Triton, helpless before the destructive wave, will be transformed into Christ, the savior who walks the waves, stills them, and makes them baptismal.

Such a change within pastoral is distantly figured as the poem returns from the second "digression" to the pastoral mode: the stream of Alpheus, shrunken by the "dread voice" of St. Peter, returns to fullness. In the preceding pastoral return, "Arethuse" had been the vehicle. The mythical Alpheus and Arethusa, by metamorphosis removed from the antagonisms of life into water seeking mysterious union, are in themselves a principle of reconciliation or synthesis. Furthermore, Alpheus—in *Arcades* called "divine"—in himself suggests the dialectic of the poem. Criminally involved in reality, he was granted a sea change whereby he became material for pastoral beauty (through association with Theocritus): he also may be included among the symbols of reconciliation, suggesting in his effort for union with Arethusa the "unexpressive nuptial Song" which is to come. The poem proceeds now in a mood of relative serenity, as if both real corruption and the apparent powerlessness of the pastoral were largely overcome.

Before the open synthesis is reached, however, there appears the lapidary flower section, in which pastoral impotence, if alleviated, is yet present. These memorial flowers do indeed bring color and a lightening of the grimmest sense of death, yet they offer only illusory ease and "false surmise" against the reality of loss. But "false surmise" looks ahead, as well, to the evident physical reality—the terrifying picture of King's body "hurl'd" or hidden in the destructive sea. That reality, too, begins to undergo a transformation, somewhat in the manner of the metamorphosis of Alpheus, for King's body also may mysteriously visit the bottom of the world or sleep within the protective (though physically unavailing) sight of Michael. The two seemingly irreconcilable attitudes of the poem here meet: pastoral poetry in and of itself is weak before the onslaught of actuality, but actuality itself gradually has been discovered to rest within a vastly larger aspect, that of eternity. The confrontation of the two modes, each of which has revealed weakness and incompleteness, together with the emergent Christianizing of both, permits the poem to move with certain confidence beyond the last eddy of doubt, in which both attitudes were caught in the suspense of "false surmise" and were thereby made ready for the reconciliation which follows.

The full architectural turn from "*Lycidas* is dead," and the fully achieved synthesis of modes, is announced with *"Lycidas your sorrow is not dead,/ Sunk though he be beneath the watry floar."* Except for the prophetic use of St. Peter as "pastor" on Galilee and the regenerative use of divine Alpheus seeking union across the abysses of ocean, water images in the poem had tended toward sterility, the unbearable reality of drowning, or the impotence of pastoral beauty. Now it becomes apparent that they had always had other attributes. The "sacred well . . . beneath the seat of *Jove*" in the invocation had always transcended both actuality and pastoral; its Jove-Jehovah always has produced, justified, and rewarded Christian poetry. To a lesser extent, Phoebus had also guaranteed poetry by Christianizing its conditions and rewards. Even at the start, then, the "sacred well" had intimated much of the argument of the poem: the union of pastoral with Christianity, the transformation of physical reality within the lens of divinity, and the eternal reconciliation of death with life that comes about in resurrection. Now such promise sweeps to its fulfillment. The seemingly dying daystar sinks in order to rise, just as Christ, who also triumphed over the waves and made them benign, "died" to a greater life. Lycidas now is offered in place of death by water the waters of baptismal anointment, and in place of a dirge the joy of the "unexpressive nuptial Song." The full choir of heaven takes the tears from his—and the speaker's—eyes, resolving the "melodious tear" into celebration. Lycidas in his way becomes transformed from victim to savior, like Christ; he is delivered beyond the lament either of pastoral or of reality.

There is a full return to pastoral convention at the end of the elegy, but that convention now has been shot through with Christian illumination. The "Swain" at the close is the poet in full command of both pastoral and actuality through the emergence of their transforming and reconciling third. The "tender stops" of pastoral are directed now to the celebration of resurrection, to Lycidas within the union of Christ and his church. The formerly agonized reception of reality now is altered as a higher vision leads the speaker into "eager thought." The resolved poet-priest, comfortably observing the daystar repeating the cycle of loss and return, serenely anticipates not loss of life and poetry but, for both, "Tomorrow . . . fresh Woods, and Pastures new." "Pastures" puts the final stamp upon the synthesis, for the reference can be "pastoral" in the sense of poetry and at the same time "pastoral" in the sense of a Christian pastorate, because poet and priest, singer and Christian song, have been united.

Our study of the poem has at times carried the discussion beyond its established limits, as Christian materials appeared. We may then recapitulate the terms of its argument. *Lycidas* begins with pastoral conventions which represent an ideal attitude toward poetry and the poet: melodious song produced by an uninvolved observer of the world, both song and singer being free of time and the passions of experience. Within this framework, the death of King might have remained nothing more than object for beautiful though somber lyrical imitation. But because King was a poet, his death impels reality upon poetry and the poet. Reality at first is felt to be wholly antagonistic, antipoetic: men are corrupt and inattentive; death destroys the poet; false poets and false priests live, whereas the true die. Thereafter a synthesis slowly emerges. The pastoral gains potency as Christian iconology is joined to it. Temporal reality is revealed in a far different light as Christian judgment and Christian confidence in resurrection bring corruption to account and death into increased life. The fully satisfied Christian "Swain" of the conclusion retains the pastoral beauty of "pure" poetry, but has through Christianity found for it new modes of powerful awareness: Theocritus has assumed the harp of David. Poetry will henceforth use any materials, bestow upon them the beauty of song, and find them in all ways glorious. The poet may now confront, receive, and finally surmount experience, combining pastoral or "pure" beauty with his expression of experienced realities; for those realities, when seen within God's eternally real purposes, are materials for holy song. Such reconciliation of song and existence is found repeatedly in the later Milton, where again the seeming antagonisms of poetry and personal experience are wrought into serene unity, almost as an extension of the imagery and dialectic of *Lycidas*:

> Thee *Sion* and the flow'ry Brooks beneath
> That wash thy hallow'd feet, and warbling flow,
> Nightly I visit: nor sometimes forget
> Those other two equall'd with me in Fate,

So were I equall'd with them in renown,
Blind *Thamyris* and blind *Maeonides*,
And *Tiresias* and *Phineus* Prophets old.
Then feed on thoughts, that voluntary move
Harmonious numbers. (*Paradise Lost*, 3:30–38)

Lycidas: The Poet in a Landscape

Isabel G. MacCaffrey

Lycidas is both a great and complex poem, and a short one. It is therefore particularly attractive to the critic, its brevity making possible a unified single view and its compact intricacy inviting us to marvel at the sureness of technique that produced so expressive an order. Milton, the greatest architect in English poetry, never exercised his power to better effect. It is hardly strange, then, that we would view *Lycidas* as we regard some small but perfect building, say the Tempietto of Bramante in Rome. Its reticulated allusions and cross-referenced images, its "rhetoric of rhyme"[1] uniting the verse-paragraphs, perhaps above all its total familiarity, persuade us as critics to see in *Lycidas* a wholly visible, completed pattern.

Let us recall, however, a curious fact: *Lycidas*, almost alone among Milton's important poems, does not suggest at the beginning how it will end. *Paradise Lost* unfolds its vast design in the Argument and again in the opening sentences, laying before us a fable whose concentric circles will widen steadily until all its implications have been explored. The *Nativity*, another vision, on a smaller scale, of a great nodal point of history, is also concentric in its structure, beautifully suspending time in

---

From *The Lyric and Dramatic Milton: Selected Papers from the English Institute*, ed. Joseph H. Summers (New York, 1965), 65–92.

[1] F. T. Prince, "The Italian Element in *Lycidas*," above, 157. Prince discusses both atemporal effects of Milton's rhyme patterns—"rhyme which looks both back and forward"—and the creation of forward momentum through rhyme, "a sense of expectation" (169).

a series of simultaneous visions. As we view it with a steadfast gaze, the sun's wonted speed flickers and dies before the power of time's maker and destroyer. *Comus*, like *Lycidas*, tells of a journey in time; but, unlike *Lycidas*, it is provided from the start with a cosmic setting in the opening speech of the Attendant Spirit. It is thus defined as allegorical and exemplary, the Spirit relating the poem to the audience's world and assuring us by his beneficent presence that the outcome will be happy. In *Paradise Lost* and the *Nativity*, again, Milton assumes the posture of a bard whose formal utterance presents the poem to an audience and who prophesies, in some degree, its conclusion.[2] All three poems are mediated by a speaker who is not, or is not only, an actor in the narrative. Even in *L'Allegro* and *Il Penseroso*, the poet approaches at a leisurely pace, reciting genealogies before permitting us to hear with him the lark and the nightingale.

The opening of *Lycidas* is by contrast brutally direct. Declining to observe the decorum of a public event, the poet in his Argument noncommittally recites the private occasion. His claim to the role of prophet is modestly confined to immediate history; he will foretell "the ruine of our corrupted Clergy." Of the poem's conclusion we are given no hint, either in a formal presentation or in the painful emotions of the introduction. Nor does Milton explicitly take his bearings in the tradition of pastoral elegy, though he could easily have done so. One of his major models was Vergil's tenth eclogue, which is introduced by an appeal to the Sicilian Muse, a passage symmetrical with the conclusion imitated in the coda of *Lycidas*. But Milton does not allow us at once to place his poem in a literary context of mourning and consolation, nor does he permit us at the beginning a glimpse of that supernatural realm from which consolation will descend. Though the focus is on bucolic detail, it is the world of pastoral in general that he wishes us to assume, not any example of its literary embodiment that might cause us too readily to draw conclusions about what will happen next. The title and the word *Monody* in the Argument certainly offer clues to the poem's mode, and in line 10 the Vergilian echo admits a literary analogue more openly. But the design deliberately prohibits a large view, contrasting in this respect with the

[2] See Anne D. Ferry, *Milton's Epic Voice: The Narrator in "Paradise Lost"* (Cambridge, Mass., 1963).

Epitaphium Damonis. There, Milton first invokes the *Himerides nymphae*, framing the picture of the poet under "the accustomed elm" with a formal introduction. The poem has a much less powerful forward momentum than *Lycidas*; the use of a refrain is one token that a movement of ebb and flow rather than sequence was intended. The voice speaks to us always from a little distance.

But in *Lycidas* we hear the unmediated exclamation of a speaker who is not yet identified as an uncouth swain. The mode is dramatic, hasting "into the midst of things," setting before us a moment of time in words that allude to prior events known to the speaker but not to us. "Yet once more" hints at other occasions on which laurel was plucked, but what occasions, whether personal or traditional, we are not told and we do not need to know. The opening words announce a proximate intention, insisting that we attend to a specific person about to perform a specific action. The details, while traditionally based, are minutely concrete and tactually realized in the modifiers *harsh* and *crude*. We view the action from close up, as it moves urgently forward in time. This perspective is a circumscribed one in comparison with the ample horizons natural to Milton's imagination. We are related to this poem's action as eavesdroppers, ignorant, like the speaker, of where we shall finally emerge. *Lycidas* is, in short, a poem bound to the wheel of time, which is made to revolve before our eyes; we observe events as they occur, unfolding in the fictive span of the Doric lay from "Yet once more" to the swain's last words, in the future tense: "Shalt be good/ To all that wander in that perilous flood."

The landscape, the spatial coordinate, is present to register time's movement, which for the speaker, as for all of us, becomes visible when changes occur in the place where we are. The importance of a firmly established spatial foreground can be demonstrated by glancing at Milton's first English elegy, *On the Death of a Fair Infant Dying of a Cough*, a poem which the author, an exacting judge, excluded from the 1645 volume. This poem foreshadows *Lycidas* in the immediacy of its opening and in its reference to vegetation untimely cropt:

> O fairest flower no sooner blown but blasted,
> Soft silken Primrose fading timelesslie.

This is, however, precisely a poem *without* a landscape. Despite references to the seasons, there is no country where their sequences can be observed. Nor is there any spot where the speaker can establish himself as chief actor. He speaks from no place, and so the range of effective eloquence is severely limited for him; though there is plenty of movement, it lacks focus and therefore point. The poet has also neglected to provide himself with a metaphorical base, a fictive geography enabling the reader to assess the figurative weight of the conceits. Lacking the feigned literalness of "Yet once more . . . I come," the opening metaphor fails to evoke a world in which Hyacinth, Astraea, Winter, and Truth can live together. The address at the end to "the mother of so sweet a child" is disconcertingly abrupt; such a sudden emergence from fiction to fact need not occur in pastoral because the fiction is the fact incarnate. Initially literal, though preeminently metaphorical, the pastoral convention can assume much while saying little and yet permit elaboration of detail in a concretely realized foreground when that is appropriate.

So far, I have been trying to describe the kind of poem *Lycidas* is, and how Milton defines its genre obliquely in his mode of presentation. It is dramatic, unmediated, unfolding in time and in the space of a recognizable but, at the beginning, incompletely realized pastoral landscape.[3] A second question is, of course, implied: Why must it be so? To describe a form is also to define a theme. In *Lycidas* is embodied one of the great themes of poetry, one of crucial concern to Milton—the loss of innocence. The prototype of this motif, as of so many others, is definitively rendered in *Paradise Lost*, but it must undergo a formal metamorphosis when treated on the private level in Milton's elegy. For fallen man, its essential meanings demand, and here receive, a temporal development, an exposure of the process, known to each one of us, by which innocence *becomes* experience. In *Lycidas*, the process is generated by the sudden invasion of the protagonist's consciousness by those great powers linked with Time in another poem of the 1645 volume. With the advent of "long Eternity," Milton wrote, we shall triumph at once "over

---

[3] "The poem is . . . clearly a dramatic lyric, with a setting, an occasion, a chief character, and several subordinate characters" (M. H. Abrams, "Five Types of *Lycidas*," above, 226).

Death, and Chance, and thee O Time."[4] But eternity is not yet.
Death and Chance, united in the terrible figure of the blind Fury,
provide the occasion for the sequences of *Lycidas*. The first
loss of innocence brought Death into the world, and hencefor-
ward death is cause and symbol simultaneously of those repeated
losses suffered by Adam's seed.[5]

Death is the occasion, lost innocence the theme; the poem
itself records the experience provoked by death and loss. The
true landscape of *Lycidas* is the speaker's consciousness; as
Northrop Frye has said, Milton "presents the poem as, in a
sense, contained within the mind of the poet."[6] The action is
epistemological before it is moral; the sin of the protagonist does
not figure directly in the action, as it does in *Paradise Lost*.
Rather, like Blake's singers, the shepherd awakens from the
dream of innocence to find himself living in a world of experience, a world of death, injustice, and sick roses, ruled by a blind
Fury. Such an awakening occurs, of course, in every fallen human life, and must occur if we are to grow toward truth; but it is
always painful. The speaker suffers, then, an unwelcome expansion of knowledge. How to cope with such knowledge is, indeed, a moral problem which the poem does not long evade.

Both the temporal and the spatial perspectives of *Lycidas* are
designed to convey the implications of this awakening. The
poem's threefold pattern has long been visible to critics: a
"poetry" section, a "church" section, and a resolution.[7] Many
readers have observed too that *Lycidas* is only intermittently
"pastoral"; the bucolic tone and rural setting are repeatedly
left behind as new ranges of awareness open in the speaker's

[4] *On Time*, ll. 11, 22. The text of Milton's poems, including *Lycidas*, is that
of Helen Darbishire's one-volume edition in the Oxford Standard Authors:
The Poetical Works of John Milton (Oxford, 1958).

[5] The relation between the subject matter of *Paradise Lost* and of *Lycidas*
is illuminated by several of the other contributions to the memorial volume
of 1638. For example, Henry King (brother of Edward) invokes Death as
"executioner to destinie," the product of Sin, like other "tormentours" which
also make part of the subject of Milton's two poems:

> Brought in by sinne, which still maintains thee here,
> As famines, earthquakes, and diseases were,
> Poore mans tormentours, with this mischief more,
> More grievous farre, his losse whom we deplore.   (7–10)

Justa Edouardo King, ed. E. C. Mossner (New York, 1939), 2.1.

[6] "Literature as Context: Milton's *Lycidas*," above, 207.

[7] The structure is clearly outlined by Arthur Barker in "The Pattern of
Milton's *Nativity Ode*," *University of Toronto Quarterly* 10 (1941): 171–72.

memory and imagination. This alternation of tones and landscapes reflects the two worlds of the poem: of innocence and of
experience. The second invades the first, with effects of violation
and distress, both emotional and aesthetic, that have caused commentators to speak of "digressions." This now old-fashioned
concept records a true response; in shifts of tone, setting, and
temporal planes, Milton imitates a basic pattern of consciousness, the emerging sense of loss in all its catastrophic significance. The speeches of Phoebus and St. Peter, first heard in an
unspecified past, are absorbed into the speaker's meditation,
and each is followed by a return to a later point in the temporal
"plot," as "now" moves forward to a new stage. There is a series
of parallel returns in space to the pastoral landscape where fountains, rivers, and Muses mourn the dead shepherd, offering consolation which becomes more poignant but less satisfying as
the poem develops.

   In the first paragraphs of *Lycidas*, Milton makes two initial
statements of the theme. The introductory lines put before us
the interference with "nature" that has been immemorially a
symbol of evil. In the proper order of things, berries ripen, leaves
fall in their season, the year revolves in a "due" round. Milton's
epithets—"harsh," "crude," "rude," "forc'd"—connote the disruption of macrocosmic decorum, insisted upon and indeed effected by a speaker accustomed to see his feelings reflected in the
world around him. His forced fingers compel the season to
recognize disaster. From this premature death, other disturb-
ances must follow, though Milton does not admit the traditional
extravagance of proclaiming that the young man's death *caused*
nature's decay. "With him all things have died, even as he, and
the flowers are all withered"; this is Bion's *Lament for Adonis*,[8]
but the conceit is inappropriate for *Lycidas*, where the loss of
innocence leads to a changed relationship between the speaker
and "nature." Further on in the first paragraph, the wild fallen
world beyond the pastoral island emerges, as we first glimpse the
sea where Lycidas welters. This ocean is a "property" in the
poem, a feature of the literal level; is is also connected, of course,
with Milton's feelings about the uncontrollable events of human
life.

   [8] Thomas P. Harrison, Jr., ed., *The Pastoral Elegy*, trans. H. J. Leon
(Austin, 1939), 35.

The two worlds thus established in the opening images are further defined in paragraphs 3 and 4. A passage of reminiscence recreates, precariously, the world of "then"—before death, change, and the canker in the rose. It is the most complete rendering of landscape which the poem offers, and *at this point* in the "plot" exists only in memory, a never-never land which (the speaker believes) has disappeared forever. In its place is the fallen world of heavy change described in the next passage. But what precisely has changed? Surely it is the speaker's state of mind—not the landscape, but what his newly acquired experience causes him to see in it. So Eve sees, observing the sunrise for the first time with fallen eyes:

> see the Morn,
> All unconcerned with our unrest, begins
> Her rosie progress smiling.   (*Paradise Lost*, 11.173–75)

The shepherd, even while he notes the sympathy of thyme and vine, strikes a similar (though not identical) chord.

> The Willows, and the Hazle Copses green,
> Shall now no more be seen,
> Fanning their joyous Leaves to thy soft layes.

Since Lycidas no longer sings, the willows cannot fan their leaves in harmony; but they are still *there*. The leaves may, even, still be joyous.[9] Two facts about "nature" become visible: a desolating unconcern with man, implicit in her ability to renew her life; and the fact that the only valid "sympathy" between macrocosm and microcosm must be based on their common corruption as fallen worlds.

The second of these insights is developed in a simile. Overt comparison is rare in this pervasively metaphorical poem. It suggests here a likeness between man and nature that is somewhat less complete than the identification of self and world recalled in the passage on the shepherds' unfallen pleasures. A new relationship, of similarity, not identity, is established. The literal landscape exhibits features *analogous* to the mind's landscape; its details are thus transformed into figures of speech.

---

[9] As James H. Hanford noted long ago, "He does not dwell on the fiction that the natural objects express grief. . . . It is the description that we remember, not the conceit" ("The Pastoral Elegy and Milton's *Lycidas*," above, 39).

> As killing as the Canker to the Rose,
> Or Taint-worm to the weanling Herds that graze,
> Or Frost to Flowers, that their gay wardrop wear,
> When first the White-thorn blows;
> Such, *Lycidas*, they loss to Shepherds ear.

The world of "nature" can provide the materials for poetry, for
the "melodious tear" that is the poem, because it shares with man
his fallen condition. But because it is unaware of its own state,
suffering but not perceiving its corruption, the song of nature
cannot adequately record the meaning of human death.

The loss is principally a "loss to Shepherds ear," an invasion
of consciousness, the subtly tuned ear of the mind. The death-
haunted anguish of time's passage is a human pain, and so Adam
speaks of it in *Paradise Lost:* "A long days dying to augment
our paine" (10.964). For the singer of *Lycidas*, as for Adam
and Eve, there is a poignant contrast between this long day and
the sequence of days that wheels through the pastoral paradise.
That was the world of innocence, the same as the one recalled
for Hermione by Polixenes in *The Winter's Tale:*

> We were, fair queen,
> Two lads, that thought there was no more behind,
> But such a day to-morrow, as to-day,
> And to be boy eternal.[10]

Milton's long sentence holds in suspension the dream of eternal
boyhood, a pattern, so he had thought, to be endlessly renewed.[11]

> Together both, ere the high Lawns appear'd
> Under the opening eye-lids of the morn,
> We drove afield, and both together heard
> What time the Gray-fly winds her sultry horn,
> Batt'ning our flocks with the fresh dews of night,
> Oft till the Star that rose, at Ev'ning, bright
> Toward Heav'ns descent had slop'd his westering wheel.

In the pastoral metaphor as Milton explores it in *Lycidas*,
something of the life history of the convention is visible, and

---

[10] 1.262–65. Ed. A. C. Quiller–Couch and J. D. Wilson, 2d ed. (Cambridge, 1950).
[11] See Rosemond Tuve, "Theme, Pattern, and Imagery in *Lycidas*," above,
183 ff. The present essay is heavily indebted to Miss Tuve's discussion of
Lycidas—one of the most expert readings the poem has received.

not only in the many traditional details. Nostalgia has often
been the sentiment that produces pastoral; almost since its
earliest appearance, an innocent bygone virtue has implied a
corrupt present sophistication, acquiring glamor by virtue of the
contrast. The pastoral world becomes remote in space or time,
or both, retreating to a legendary past or an imaginary country.
So Arcadia is born. In *Lycidas*, this remoteness develops before
our eyes, as the speaker's lost childhood is recreated in the past
tense of memory. Pastoral perfection recedes into a past innocent and unreturning.

In *Lycidas*, too, we can observe the development of a so-called
satirical element from the co-presence of harsh reality and benign past. Pastoral innocence provides an ethical measure for
judgment and a technical point of departure for analyzing the
ruined fallen world of experience. The beginning of such a process may perhaps be seen in Vergil's first eclogue, entitled in one
modern translation "The Dispossessed."[12] One of the speakers is
taking the rocky road to exile, stripped of his patrimony by a
ravenous and unjust state. The other shepherd, Tityrus, has
already endured voluntary exile in Rome, gained a protector,
and returned to his farm.[13] Meliboeus's speech to him evokes a
changeless peace:

> Time and again, as it has always done, the hedge there . . . will
> have its willow-blossom rifled by Hyblaean bees and coax you
> with a gentle humming through the gates of sleep. . . . You will
> hear the vine-dresser singing to the breezes, while all the time
> your dear full-throated pigeons will be heard, and the turtle-
> dove high in the elm will never bring her cooing to an end.

The ceaseless country sounds, the suspension in a friendly element, are rendered by Vergil in words denoting time's recurrence: *nota, semper, nec tamen interea.* Yet the peace is shown

---

[12] E. V. Rieu, trans., *Virgil: The Pastoral Poems* (London, 1949). The
translated passage from the *Eclogues* below is taken from p. 23 of Rieu's
edition. The Latin text is that of the Loeb Classical Library: *Virgil*, ed. H. R.
Fairclough, 2 vols. (Cambridge, Mass., 1946).

[13] An apparent allusion to this eclogue in *Epitaphium Damonis* suggests
that Milton took an interest in the pattern of exile and return. He speaks of
his Italian journey, including the visit to Rome, which is no longer "qualem
dum viseret olim, Tityrus ipse suas et oves et rura reliquet" (ll. 116–17);
even if a reference to Chaucer is intended, behind it is surely Vergil's poem.
In the *Epitaphium*, the journey coincides with the death at home of Diodati;
it is thus linked with the "discovery" of the rude facts of life and death.

to be precarious by the presence of the exile and references to wars in Africa, Scythia, Britain, even at home. Resolution, Vergil implies, is won not simply by retreat but by a prior excursion into and mastery of the "great world" outside. This reading of *Eclogue I* is perhaps an overreading, but it illustrates how readily in pastoral a suggestive contrast develops between a precious but vulnerable rural landscape and a ferocious if sometimes heroic world of history.

Lycidas reenacts, then, both the immemorial journey of the maturing spirit and the development of one of humanity's most resourceful metaphors for that journey. It is a poem "about" poetry *and* "about" human life—about the two in conjunction, man's vision of himself and the mirror of art in which he sees the vision. It can be read as a reassessment of the pastoral mode itself. Innocence is exchanged for bleak experience, in turn to be replaced by a wiser innocence. So "mere" pastoral—both the poetry and the view of the world it implies—is shown as too vulnerable and limited to account for the brutalities of life; but it is shown, finally, to contain the possibility of deeper, or higher, strains more faithful to "reality."

These intertwined threads of Milton's theme are visible in the details of the landscape picked out by the speaker. All four elements play a part in *Lycidas*, and all an ambivalent part, reflecting their divided allegiance in a fallen world where they may either serve as emblems of their Creator or become the playthings of satanic forces. Thus, Air is the "parching wind," the "gust of rugged wings," the figurative wind that bloats the sheep;[14] it is also the breezes in the willows, the "milde whispers" of valley winds. Earth puts forth the vegetation that can either flourish or wither. Fire is represented, on the one hand, by the counterfeit flare of fame's "sudden blaze," the "glistering foil" of worldly reputation; and, on the other, by the lofty light-bearing heavenly bodies: the evening star and Phoebus, who brings dawn and witnesses to the glory of the firmament. "Water

[14] John Ruskin's elaboration of ll. 125–27, developing the notion of *spiritus* or "wind" as breath, ought to be recalled: "There are two kinds of breath with which the flock may be filled; God's breath, and man's. The breath of God is health, and life, and peace to them, as the air of heaven is to the flocks on the hills; but man's breath—the word which *he* calls spiritual—is disease and contagion to them, as the fog of the fen." Lecture 1, *Sesame and Lilies* (New York, 1866), 32.

imagery" in *Lycidas* has been sufficiently explicated; its double-
ness should perhaps be more emphasized.[15] It is at once the
monster-harboring, formless ocean that was to symbolize Chaos
in *Paradise Lost* and the fountains, dews, and friendly rivers
that mourn for Lycidas in the unsullied pastoral world. In the
Alpheus/Arethusa references, the two strands meet but do not
merge, and the resurgence of Alpheus from the dark descent
beneath the ocean's floor bears witness to the ultimate deliverance
of creation from the dark forces that hold it enthralled. To look
at these elemental patterns in the light of the poem's development
is to see mirrored in them the movement of the speaker's mind.
He reaches a point where the demonic aspect of creation dominates his consciousness. Experience has supplanted innocence,
and the pastoral metaphor of a nature exactly congruent with
man's life, responsive to his hopes and fears, has been revealed
as inadequate.

In a passage from *Pericles* that was perhaps in Milton's mind
when he wrote *Lycidas*, the king speaks to the "scarcely coffin'd"
body of his wife, and in his grief it seems to him that "th' unfriendly elements/ Forgot thee utterly."[16] We ought not perhaps
to go so far as to speak of unfriendly elements in *Lycidas*. "Nature" is always "sympathetic" in the etymological sense, and
Rosemond Tuve has wisely reminded us that we must beware of
importing notions about man's alienation from nature into Renaissance poetry.[17] But just as the Muse can seem thankless, the
elements can seem unfriendly to the speaker. They are related
to us, we are made of them, yet they are powerless to help, just
as "the Muse herself that *Orpheus* bore" was helpless to save
him from death at the hands of arbitrary unintelligible forces.
But these forces are outside the original economy of nature and
cannot be ruled by it, as the speaker ultimately realizes. One of
the paragraphs following the passage on "heavy change" ex-

[15] The contrast between sea water and fresh water was noticed by Emerson
R. Marks, *Explicator* 9 (1951): Item 44.
[16] 3.1.57–58. Ed. J. C. Maxwell (Cambridge, 1956). T. H. Banks observed
that a manuscript phrase in *Lycidas*, l. 157—"humming tide" (altered to
"whelming")—echoes *Pericles*, 3.1.63: "And humming water must o'erwhelm
thy corpse." Pericles's speech powerfully evokes the journey of Thaisa's dead
body through the whales' "monstrous" realm. "A Source for *Lycidas*, 154–
158," *Modern Language Notes* 62 (1947): 39–40.
[17] "Theme, Pattern, and Imagery," above, 192.

onerates Nymphs and Muse of responsibility for Lycidas's fate;
another speaks in defense of the destructive element itself:

> The Ayr was calm, and on the level brine,
> Sleek *Panope* with all her sisters play'd.

This "level brine" is an innocent extension of pastoral fields, the
playground of nymphs. The accusation is diverted to the "fatall
and perfidious Bark," belonging to the world of the blind Fury
and her shears—a world of fallen, civilized, and unnatural con-
trivance and of mysterious subnatural hostilities alluded to in
the eclipse, which in *Paradise Lost* gives evidence of nature's
fall. These progressive exonerations are preparing for the final
movement of *Lycidas* into a "nature" hallowed and redeemed, a
pastoral mode deepened and reconfirmed.

If nature is excused in *Lycidas*, however, man is not. The
passages on Fame and the Church move away from the pastoral
foreground into the vicissitudes of history and the consequences
of our lost innocence. The embodiment of fallen society is the
ominous blind Fury, a Fate rechristened but still as blind as her
meaningless power.[18] In this section, as the poet's allusion to a
"higher mood" suggests, the style alters; and it can alter decor-
ously because the matter alters. Milton begins in the pastoral
present, referring to poetry as the "Shepherds trade." But the
action moves immediately into a no-time of eternal verities and
questions, an infinite space where the great antagonists of the
major poetry confront each other in the persons of the Fury
and Phoebus. It is a metaphorical space inhabited by the august
personages of sacred allegory, a world evoked at the opening of
the *Nativity* Hymn and of *Comus*, where meek-eyed Peace and
the Attendant Spirit make visible things ordinarily invisible to
mortal sight. This is, in short, the plane of vision and prophecy,
affording a glimpse of final verities ultimately to be affirmed in
the poem and in history.

The debate of the speaker with Phoebus defines an aesthetic
and moral issue. The lines on Fame, as Miss Tuve has said, use
the language of chivalric romance—"guerdon," "foil," "spur,"
"noble mind."[19] The ambition to win fame by composing the

---

[18] Cf. Marjorie H. Nicolson, *John Milton: A Reader's Guide to his Poetry*
(New York, 1963), 95, on the significance of the eyes of the Furies.
[19] "Theme, Pattern, and Imagery," above, 172.

poetry that celebrates earthly glory is shown by Phoebus to be a
false direction; this is the same Phoebus, after all, who plucked
Vergil's ear and reproved him for writing of "kings and battles"
in *Eclogue VI*.[20] This ambition can also be seen as a betrayal
of the values embodied in pastoral, which in Christian tradition
encompasses both the lowest and the highest subjects. The shepherd singer of the Psalms is one exemplar; another is "That Shepherd, who first taught the chosen Seed" (*Paradise Lost*, 1.8) in
the sacred poetry of Genesis. In *Paradise Regained*, Milton was
to contrast Sion's songs with the "swelling Epithetes" of pagan
poetry (4.343). The contrast is confirmed in his rejection of traditional epic in favor of a heroic mode that would treat of virtues
at once grander and humbler. The middle realm, the realm of
history and its monotonous disasters, is the fallen world in the
power of the Fury, recorded in an epic poetry corrupt though
brilliant. Perhaps we should not press this point, which depends
partly on our knowledge of the author's future, invisible to him
in 1637. But the infirmity of ambition rebuked in *Lycidas*,
whether poetic or heroic, is conceived in terms inconsistent with
the pastoral metaphor.

A second vision of history is developed in the Church passage.
As in the one just examined, this section is separated in time
and space from the pastoral foreground. We move back or away
from the "literal" landscape of rivers—Sicilian or English—and
the classical allusions that enforce the pastoral mode, into a development of the convention's *metaphorical* dimensions, principally through the theological associations of *pastor*. The
figure of St. Peter emerges out of the pastoral world (like the
"pastor" metaphor itself); it is continuous with the pageant of
witnesses to nature's innocence: the Herald of the Sea, Hippotades, Camus, and then the Galilean Pilot. But the pageant, as it
concludes, merges with an envisaged past and the spaces of imagination, and the style of Peter's speech, like that of the Fame
meditation, is allusive and oblique, as the two-handed engine and
its multitudinous glosses suggest. References to flocks and herds-
men link the speech metaphorically, indeed, with the paragraph

---

[20] It is interesting that, in the sixth eclogue, Vergil goes on to write, in
Silenus's song, of subjects loftier and more permanently significant than
battles: Creation, the Deluge, and the shifting shapes of mythological history.
This poem, like *Eclogue IV*, provided Milton with a classical precedent for
his development of "high pastoral."

early in the poem on the diseased landscape. This later passage
sternly explains how that death-pervaded world of experience
came into being. The source of contagion in flower and flock is
not "innocent nature" but sin-ridden human beings, here mon-
strously reduced to "blind mouthes." The safe world of the
"faithful Herdman" is invaded by their rapacity. Their grating
songs contrast with Lycidas's soft lays, their hungry diseased
sheep with the flock battened on the "fresh dews" of the water of
life. The potent lines on inward contagion recall the "killing"
canker that lays waste the shepherd's heart, or "ear." But while
at that early stage no consolation beyond Nature's lament could
be proposed, the dread voice of the Pilot here speaks in condemnation and prophecy, of the sword's readiness and a heavenly
meed.

In the final paragraphs of the song, resolution and consolation are achieved and the validity of the pastoral mode is confirmed. But these certainties, like the other hard-won insights of
the swain, emerge only at the end of the process which Milton
called elsewhere "the perpetual stumble of conjecture and disturbance in this our dark voyage."[21] *Lycidas* imitates the painful, unsteady effort of imagination which alone, in our mortal
state, can lead to vision. The sense of moving forward among
the half-lights of the dark voyage is nowhere felt more powerfully than in the poem's last stages. We turn from a minute and
loving attention to the details of pastoral landscape in close-
up to the gigantic horizons of distant seascapes, from the bottom of the monstrous world to the heavenly hosts singing in their
glory. The sequence embodies those grand shifts of perspective
which Milton was to exploit in *Paradise Lost*.[22] It also renders
metaphorically the fundamental pattern of Christian literature,
a movement through the tragic phase to an ultimately comic
vision.

Accompanying this process is a sequence of imagery that
supports the movement of insight won, lost again, and rewon.
The kinetic and auditory images of Peter's speech are succeeded
by the "flower passage," a landscape rich in visual detail. Blind

[21] *The Reason of Church Government* in *The Student's Milton*, ed. F. A.
Patterson (New York, 1933), 506.
[22] This use of rapidly shifting points of view is discussed and related to
Mannerist styles by Roy Daniells, *Milton, Mannerism and Baroque* (Toronto, 1963), 41.

Fury and blind mouths are replaced by a healthier world whose moral value is symbolized by its appeal to the eye, though these quaint enameled flower-eyes do not see as far as the "pure eyes" of all-judging Jove, nor is the vision they symbolize finally valid. In these low valleys, the gentle "nature" of the opening sections emerges again: shades, gushing brooks, fresh fields. The "swart Star" reminds us, however, of the flowers' frailty and their melancholy fates—the primrose forsaken, the cowslips wan, even Amaranth shedding his beauty in tribute to Lycidas. Since the mortal sin, this is no plant that grows on mortal soil; it resembles rather the plant of true fame that "lives and spreads aloft." In *Paradise Lost*, Amaranth after the Fall is removed from Eden to Heaven, where it "grows/ And flours aloft shading the Fount of Life" (3.357). Its failure to thrive on earth marks the final failure of unconsecrated pastoral in *Lycidas*, confirmed by the speaker's acknowledgment that the whole vividly evoked scene has been "false surmise," though its falseness to fact need not negate the measure of imaginative consolation it provides.[23] Pastoral as the dream of an actual earthly paradise is about to be finally abandoned, but pastoral as a holy fiction foreshadowing a heavenly meed is about to be confirmed.

The song's conclusion is composed in two movements. The first expresses the poem's deepest terror in a series of sensory impressions that appeal to the dumb, blind responses of the helpless body—not vision, but inhuman sounds and eyeless kinetic forces: "wash," "hurld," "stormy," "whelming." The speaker does not withdraw his earlier assent to Neptune's plea of innocence; he does not accuse, but merely records the facts of Lycidas's condition as they assault the anguished imagination. Then, almost without warning, the perspective shifts again, from the blind depths to "the great vision of the guarded Mount," the angel who fixes the sea's boundary and wields a two-handed sword.

In *Paradise Lost*, Michael reveals to Adam the triumph of Chaos in history, symbolized by the Deluge when the sea is

---

[23] In the Trinity MS, Milton first wrote "sad thoughts" in line 153. The alteration to "fraile" (one of the crucial words in *Paradise Lost*) introduces the notion of human weakness, in this case perhaps the habit of clinging to consoling fictions which we know to be untrue.

allowed to regain its power over the forces of order. Following
the vision he unfolds its meaning:

> So willingly doth God remit his Ire,
> Though late repenting him of Man deprav'd,
> Griev'd at his heart, when looking down he saw
> The whole Earth filld with violence, and all flesh
> Corrupting each thir way.   (11.885–89)

Violence and the corruption of all flesh: these have been revealed, with relentless insistence, to the swain in *Lycidas*. But
the rainbow speaks, in the epic, of reestablished order:

> Day and Night,
> Seed time and Harvest, Heat and hoary Frost
> Shall hold thir course, till fire purge all things new,
> Both Heav'n and Earth, wherein the just shall dwell.
>   (11.898–901)

In Books 11 and 12, Milton develops on a grand scale the movement from disaster to redemption adumbrated in *Lycidas*. The
vision that completes the cycle of history in the epic completes
the cycle of meditation in the elegy.

The hinge of the transition from the infernal underworld to
the heaven of heavens is the Sun image, the second of the two
major similes in *Lycidas*. The ground of the analogy is the
circular solar movement, concentric with that of the dead shepherd, from ocean bed to morning sky. This parallel is profoundly reassuring in its context—chiefly, I think, because it denies
the most poignant disparity between man and the nonhuman
world: while seasons, stars, and vegetation move in cyclical patterns, a man's life pursues an unreturning course downward to
darkness. This distressing fact is lamented, of course, everywhere in elegiac poetry: in Catullus's reminder that "one ever-
during night" awaits us, in Spenser's *November* eclogue, in
Castiglione's *Alcon*, where the sun comparison contrasts with
that in *Lycidas*:

> Behold, the declining sun now sinking in the heavens is setting,
> and as it dies, kindles the stars in the sky; still, when it has
> bathed its chariot in the western waves, it will again revisit the
> lands with orient light. But when once we have bathed in the

black waters of cruel death and the door of that relentless
realm has been shut, no way leads ever to the upper light.[24]

But Milton's conclusion reaffirms the congruence between nature's cycle and man's: Lycidas, *like* the daystar, is "sunk low
but mounted high." The daystar itself functions in the poem not
as a symbol but as an analogue; Milton wishes us to hold apart
in imagination the various realms of being—natural, human,
supernatural—precisely so that we can admire the marvelous
correspondences between them. Therefore he makes the comparison overt, a simile, not an identifying metaphor. The diurnal
cycle reminds us that something similar occurs for the youth
sunk beneath ocean's floor, as earlier it occurred in the death and
resurrection of God himself, who assumed the burdens and
necessities of "nature" when he entered our darksome house of
mortal clay. The simile, like the rose figure of an earlier section,
at once affirms a distinction between ourselves and "nature" and
reaffirms its ultimate relationship to us. We are able, owing to
the song's last paragraph, to look back to earlier sections, especially the flower passage, and see them in a new light: the pathos
and consolation did after all have a "real" basis; the flowers in
their annual cycle are after all in harmony with the life of men.
In this new perspective of analogy, "nature" is seen to possess a
metaphorical relevance to human concerns; its availability for
Christian pastoral poetry is implied. But it *becomes* sentient and
expressive only in the light of the poet's transforming vision.

The force that accomplishes these metamorphoses is the same
that translates Lycidas: "the dear might of him that walk'd the
waves." The redemptive power is figured in an image Milton
had used earlier; in the *Nativity*, nature's most unruly force is
hallowed by the Redeemer's coming, and "Birds of Calm sit
brooding on the charmed wave" (st. 5). The ruling of the waves
was heralded in that mythic event when the creative Word ruled
Chaos:

> Silence, ye troubl'd waves, and thou Deep, peace.
> *(Paradise Lost*, 7.216)

Christ's walking the waves possesses every kind of aptness in a
poem about a drowned youth whose brief life embodied the

[24] Harrison, *The Pastoral Elegy*, 114–15.

forces of order implicit in his vocations of poet and priest. In eschatological terms, it defines the relationship between the Redeemer and redeemed Creation that permits the Christian poet to prefigure in his earthly landscapes those "other groves and other streams" of true paradise.

In the poem's temporal scheme, however, the redemption of nature is not final, and the speaker, who has descended and reascended in imagination, must be returned to his native element of life in time, like the Red Cross Knight after his vision of the New Jerusalem or Calidore when the Graces vanished. The metamorphosis of Lycidas effects this return. He becomes, as Mr. Frye has said, a figure "corresponding to the Attendant Spirit in *Comus*, whose habitation is said to be a world above our own, identified . . . with Spenser's Gardens of Adonis." [25] As the Genius of the shore, he will mediate between the still fallen world of the perilous flood and the realm of redeemed nature glimpsed by the speaker in vision. He is the third, and most consoling, of the "heavenly messengers" who descend to the protagonist of *Lycidas*. [26] He will serve as a reminder that the wilderness of the world can be ordered and transcended.

The speaker in *Lycidas* has traveled from a preoccupation with the "melodious tear" of his song as the only possible "meed" to the vision of redemption where there are no tears, where the earthly shepherds weep no more and the song will cease, stilled by the unexpressive heavenly harmonies. The song ceases, but it has not been sung in vain. Its meaning is confirmed in the receding perspective of the coda, which offers us, now more distantly but also more distinctly, a figure in a landscape, long familiar but now transfigured, *because* the song has been sung and the vision realized. The pastoral scene is recreated; now it is informed by the presence of the poets who first made these details into poetry and by the redeemed imagination that has come gradually to understand their meaning. The ancestor of the coda is Vergil's tenth eclogue, concluding traditionally with a return home and the arrival of the evening star. Line 190 of

---

[25] "Literature as Context," above, 208.

[26] Thomas M. Greene, *The Descent from Heaven* (New Haven, 1963), treats the "heavenly messenger" as a recurrent motif in epic. In *Lycidas*, the three "messengers"—Phoebus, Peter, and the dead shepherd as Genius—enter the poem just at those points where the "old" pastoral idiom is left behind and a new perspective into the heroic finalities of Providence is opened.

Lycidas echoes the conclusions of two other eclogues, where the sun stretches out the hills:

> et sol crescentis decedens duplicat umbras.[27]

These deliberate allusions to literary tradition underline the function of the stanza as a "return": a return to the pastoral landscape and the poetry based on it, now made potent as a vehicle of human meaning because its patterns are seen to be reproduced in the divine plan of the universe. Like the young shepherds of the poem's third section, this uncouth but more experienced swain has piped through the wheel of a day, from still morn to westering sun. The last line is not to be read only as a personal reference to sea voyaging or a promise of the turn to epic poetry. "Fresh" and "new" surely reaffirm those self-renewing powers of "nature" that legitimately figure our own survival and revival. As for "tomorrow," it marks the return of a world where the future once again exists full of promise, not a long day's dying, but "such a day tomorrow as today," a process endlessly renewed by the covenant of God himself. In this world will flourish, not eternal boyhood, but a wise innocence that has absorbed and transcended experience. So Spenser's Colin Clout, after the manner of Tasso's shepherd, came home again from court. This new wisdom understands the pastoral world for what it is—a foreshadowing, not an echo. In this peaceful order, "Seed time and Harvest, Heat and hoary Frost/ Shall hold thir course," until the kingdom which the metaphor anticipated is established to succeed the cycles of history.

A decade or so before *Lycidas*, Milton in a Latin poem had celebrated the regular cycles of the universe and affirmed the eternal youth of great Nature, the perpetual flame of bright Phoebus in his strength: "floridus aeternum Phoebus juvenile coruscat." The poem concludes with an anticipation of Michael's revelation:

> Sic denique in aevum
> Ibit cunctarum series justissima rerum.[28]

"The righteous course of all things": it is precisely this sense of control and ultimate rightness that Milton seeks to establish

---

[27] Vergil, *Eclogue II*, l. 67. The other echo, regularly noted by editors, is of *Eclogue I*, l. 83: "maioresque cadunt altis de montibus umbrae."

[28] *Naturam non pati senium*, ll. 41, 65–66.

in the final cadences of *Lycidas*. The voice that asserts it is impersonal. Many reasons for Milton's shift to the third person in the coda can be reconstructed by the ingenious critic. Among them is the fact that his subject at this point has transcended the personal. Two others are pertinent to this discussion.

The first concerns the redefinition of pastoral convention. The two similes, as I have suggested, are strategically placed in the fourth and last paragraphs of the song; they record a development in the speaker's treatment of his metaphor, from the naive assumption that it represents actuality, to the recognition of it as one of man's great symbols for ultimate reality, securely rooted in the imagination's life. This insight is confirmed by the ostensive gesture of the poet in the coda. He can now name the poem's "kind" explicitly: it is a "*Dorick* lay" sung by a swain. In thus specifying its genre, Milton insists that pastoral be taken seriously. Like the swain, we must readjust our notions of what "pastoral" can mean. It is to be recognized as a serious *fiction*, a mode of the imagination, not a self-deluding fancy. The lowest of forms has been demonstrated to be capable of articulating the loftiest insights, embodying that vision of final things from which Milton was to make *Paradise Lost*. This "high pastoral" is akin to the metamorphosed epic form which Milton later devised for an action more heroic than any known to Homer. In the prologue to Book 9, he was to announce his intention, defining the "Heroic name" of his poem as once he had directed attention to a new meaning of the Doric lay. The habit of transcending and transforming genres is most dazzlingly manifested, in the 1645 volume, in *Lycidas*.

Finally, the coda demonstrates the relevance, not only of the poem's form, but of its theme, to ourselves. As the impersonal voice addresses us, we become co-listeners, and as the foreground recedes into the middle distance, we find ourselves paradoxically in a more intimate relation to it. This sensation is effected—I do not say intended—when the poem's frame unexpectedly widens to include the "real" speaker and ourselves, on the same footing because we have heard the same song. The poem's world becomes our world, the song's pattern a paradigm of our experience. In the final lines there is a fusion of worlds created by a confusion of temporal planes, phrased in syntax that unites past and present: "now had stretch'd," "now was dropt." Past and present are one, the song continuing though the singer has ceased. The last line refers ambiguously to the singer's thought, the poet's comment on his future, the author's prospects, and our own hopes.

> To morrow to fresh Woods, and Pastures new.

It is not unmistakably located "in" the mind or spoken by the voice of either the real or the fictive speaker, and can therefore sum up a pattern now possible for all those who, by listening, have participated in the song.

Lycidas: The Shattering of the Leaves

Balachandra Rajan

Ever since Dr. Johnson forced us to recognize that *Lycidas* was about something more than Edward King, the depths of the poem have been variously sounded. *Lycidas* has been interpreted biographically, historically, musically and archetypally; as the climax of a tradition, as the casting aside of tradition by the individual talent and as a precarious mannerist balancing of the two forces; as a poem from which personality is virtually smoothed out and as one into which personality all but explodes.[1] Fortunately, the critic is left at the end not with the picture of confusion which this description suggests, but rather with a tangible though elusive sense of richness. No approach to *Lycidas* can be dismissed as wholly irrelevant; and yet none seizes the quintessence of a poem which continues to walk disconcertingly intact across the sounding seas of commentary.[2] If this map of partial successes teaches us anything it is that *Lycidas* is a poem built out of conflict. Criticism falls short of the whole, when it

---

From *The Lofty Rhyme: A Study of Milton's Major Poetry* (London, 1970), Chap. 4, first published in *Studies in Philology* 64 (1967): 51–64.

[1] See the essays above, and in particular, "Five Types of *Lycidas*" by M. H. Abrams, 216ff. For Baroque and Mannerist interpretation, see Daniells, Nelson, and Sypher (cited below, 359–365) and Rosemond Tuve's cautions in "Baroque and Mannerist Milton," in *Milton Studies in Honor of Harris Francis Fletcher* (Urbana, 1961), 209–25.

[2] The image is offered in response to the fears expressed by R. M. Adams in *Ikon: John Milton and the Modern Critics* (Ithaca, N.Y., 1955), 160–62.

regards one term or other of the conflict as paramount; it is
more likely to succeed when it recognizes how the struggle
which is the poem's substance is created and pressed forward at
a series of interlinked levels and then made to subside as the
poem works out its peace.

Educated innocence is not easy to achieve but one should make
the effort to see *Lycidas* under the morn's opening eye-lids and,
if one may vary another poet's metaphor, to take the poem as
its suddenness resists one. Perhaps the impact of that suddenness is best suggested by going back to what may have been
Milton's encounter with it. When Milton sat down in 1637 to
write the poem we know as *Lycidas* in the Trinity manuscript
he may not have been writing the poem for the first time but
rather transcribing and revising a previous draft.[3] Be that as
it may, the poem as he wrote it, fell naturally and without disturbance into the reticent tones of the pastoral lament.

> yet once more O ye laurells and once more
> ye myrtl's browne wth Ivie never sere
> I come to pluck yo[r] berries harsh and crude
> before the mellowing yeare.[4]

At this point Milton struck out the fourth line and replaced it
by the line we know—"and wth forc't fingers rude"—a line which
subtly imports a new note of violence into the poem. He then
went back to exemplary pastoral diction—"and crop yo[r] young"
—and then striking the half-line dramatically out, yielded the
poem to the power of its suddenness.[5]

> shatter yo[r] leaves before y[e] mellowing yeare
> bitter constraint, and sad occasion deare
> compells me to disurbe yo[r] season due

[3] For the view that *Lycidas* is transcribed, see *The Poems of John Milton*,
ed. H. J. C. Grierson (London, 1925), 1.14–17, and Ants Oras, "Milton's
Early Rhyme Schemes and the Structure of *Lycidas*," *Modern Philology* 52
(1954): 17n.
[4] Quotations from the Trinity MS are from Harris F. Fletcher's facsimile
in *John Milton's Complete Poetical Works* (Urbana, 1943), vol. 1.
[5] These changes occur in the "trial-sheet" of the MS, which follows *Comus*.
It is assumed that Milton, having recast the first lines, then wrote out
the main text which incorporates these changes and subsequently returned
to the trial-sheet to further revise the "Orpheus" and "flower" passages. Helen
Darbishire's view, in her edition of Milton's poetry (Oxford, 1955), 2:336n,
that "this famous 'flower-passage' was an afterthought" is too easily reached.
The deletion in the main text may mean that Milton was dissatisfied with
his language and not that he had jettisoned his idea.

> for Lycidas is dead, dead ere his prime,
> young Lycidas and hath not left his peere

Language is the poet's most basic resource and it is here, in the body and movement of the language, that we find the contentions of *Lycidas* at work. The explosive force of "shatter," its harsh chime with "bitter" into an assonance of anguish, are balanced against the gradualness, the organic decorum of "mellowing." Controlled by this interplay, the striking force quietens into "disturb," to strengthen again in the repeated "dead," with the caesura subtly spacing the drum-beat of grief. When we come to "young," the word is stressed not only by its metrical position but by the lyric context in which it is made to reverberate. It is not simply a matter of untimely death; the whole theme has been stated with a tormented power that opens the lonely road to the blind fury. Looking back to the fourth line we now see that the "forc't fingers rude" are more than the disclaimer of a young poet, writing before his time and under the pressure of circumstances. What is being "forced" is ultimately the decorum of the poem, a decorum which as we shall come to recognize, is not simply formal but also elemental, powerfully symbolic of the sense of design in reality. *Lycidas* is the shattering of the leaves, not simply in the passage from innocence to experience, but in the angry challenge of the poem to the tradition which it inherits and finally, to its own security and indeed survival.

Inferences from the evolution of a poem can be treacherous and most of us have been obliged to learn that more than one conclusion can be drawn from manuscript changes. In the passage just discussed for instance, it can be argued that Milton's first two changes merely correct two errors of anticipation resulting from the transcribing of a previous draft and that the dramatic change to "bitter" strengthens a design already in Milton's mind rather than one which springs to life on the page. Neither hypothesis can be disproved but fortunately acceptance of the less favourable hypothesis would not greatly affect the substance of this chapter; it would merely reduce what has been said so far to the status of an enlightening, prefatory myth. All that is suggested is that the view of *Lycidas* being developed here is consistent with the changes made by Milton and perhaps provides a perspective in which to see them.

As is well-known, the passages which are worked over most
heavily in the Trinity manuscript are the "Orpheus" passage,
which is revised in the main text, rewritten in the margin and
rewritten again in the "trial-sheet," and the flower passage,
which is struck out in the main text and rewritten in the trial-
sheet. The first passage is *expanded* from four to seven lines;
that menacing line "downe the swift Hebrus to the Lesbian
shore" is added to the marginal revision; its effect is intensified
by the addition of "when by the rout that made the hideous roare"
in the trial-sheet; and the avalanche of horror is given further
momentum as Orpheus's "divine head" becomes his "goarie visage." In the flower passage, the number of lines is *reduced* by
two; a certain amount of mythological exposition is discarded;
and the passage takes on the quality of a procession with each
flower given a distinct and vividly focused presence. The movement in one case is towards ferocious elementality; in the other
it is towards conventionality in the best sense, the pastoral mood
wrought to the height of its beauty. If Milton knew his business
and everything in *Lycidas* suggests that he knew it considerably
better than we do, revision in opposite directions can only
mean that he wished deliberately to intensify rather than to
diminish the oppositions that dominate the poem; he realized
clearly that it was out of the struggle of contraries that the
creative pattern had to be forged and won.

Professor Nicolson in her eloquent remarks on *Lycidas*, has
threatened to haunt those who speak of digressions in the poem.[6]
The word is certainly one which has unfortunate connotations
and most of us would agree that it is not in the interests of accuracy to employ it. Nevertheless there is an interplay in the
poem which Professor Nicolson herself treats as the intertwin-
ing of laurel and myrtle[7] but which is perhaps better described
for our purposes as the attack mounted by the higher mood
against the pastoral form. Convention and elementality are the
basic forces of contention in the poem and the struggle between
them is not one for supremacy, but rather for a vision which
can include both, which can accept the shock of reality, without
sacrificing the sense of design. Professor Barker who, with dis-

[6] Marjorie Nicolson, *John Milton: A Reader's Guide to his Poetry* (New
York, 1963), xv.
[7] Ibid., 107 ff.

concerting ease, has taught us how to read *Lycidas*, in an essay which is actually about another poem,[8] has suggested a three-part structure for Milton's monody which is by now, universally accepted; it only remains to be added that each part begins with a statement that the pastoral convention has been or is about to be violated. Two of these admissions have been noted;[9] the intention of the third ("Begin, and somewhat loudly sweep the string") has been obscured because it is a reminiscence of Virgil's Fourth Eclogue; but once the strategy of Milton's poem has been grasped, the kind of notice being served will be plain. After attention has been drawn to the previous or impending violation of decorum, a conventional passage follows: the remembrance of idyllic days spent in the fields, the procession of mourners and the procession of flowers. The assault of experience on the convention then develops and chaos beats against the wall of the poem's order, until an equilibrium is restored. There are of course, variations upon this pattern, as might be expected with an artist of Milton's subtlety and power of musical ordering. The long first section contains not one but two waves of assault, with the reworked "Orpheus" passage functioning as the first wave. In the second section the brevity of the pastoral interlude gives force to the apocalyptic resolution. In the third section the pastoral mood is restored to a kind of intense fragility in which every detail is worked over with an almost caressing finesse. Then as the sounding seas muster for what threatens to be their most dangerous assault, the poem, instead of yielding once again to chaos, passes through it and is piloted to its peace. These variations help to remind us that we face in *Lycidas* a poet of supreme accomplishment writing a poem that is totally and tautly controlled. But we also face a poet who has moved beyond those academic groves that once formed the dark wood of *Comus*, who has decided to confront the anger of his poetry and to discover the truth on the lips of the blind fury. There is a difference between the "honour'd flood" of the Mincius and

[8] "The Pattern of Milton's *Nativity Ode*," *University of Toronto Quarterly* 10 (1941): 171–72.

[9] See J. Milton French, "The Digressions in Milton's *Lycidas*," *Studies in Philology* 50 (1953): 486, 489; M. H. Abrams. "Five Types of *Lycidas*," above, 216 ff; and A. S. P. Woodhouse, in *Studies in Honour of Gilbert Norwood*, ed. M. E. White (Toronto, 1952), 273. Woodhouse observes that the first two parts of *Lycidas* culminate in passages that "shatter the pastoral tone, while the third does not shatter but rather transcends it."

that "perilous flood" over which Lycidas comes to preside; the achievement of Milton's pastoral is that it is conscious of both of these forces, that it is able to outlive their perilous encounter and to absorb their struggle in a profounder sense of reality.

Some gathering of the threads is called for by now and perhaps one can suggest that there is involved in *Lycidas*, an assault upon the poem's own assumptions, which the poem in the act of making itself, recognizes and progressively strengthens. This attack is exemplified, both in the kind of microcosmic enactment of language that was studied at the beginning of this chapter and in the larger tactical manoeuvre of the pastoral spectacle, thrice set up to be undermined. The total attack, both formal and linguistic, can be thought of as the stylistic correlative to the deeper assault of experience upon the sense of order; and the restoration of equilibrium in convention and language corresponds to, validates and intensifies the deeper restoration of a sense of design in reality. It is because of this inclusive and highly sophisticated strategy that the poem to quote Douglas Bush "is at once an agonized personal cry and a formal exercise, a search for order and a made object, an affirmation of faith in Providence and an exploitation of pastoral and archetypal myth." [10] One more paradox can be added to the description of this unprecedented poem in which everything has a precedent. It is both a powerfully allusive essay in a convention and a highly controlled denial of that convention.

Because *Lycidas* is so completely both a pattern and a process and because the pattern has so often been misunderstood, it has been necessary to run ahead of the poem and to suggest some of the definitions it achieves. It is time to resume the poem's own voyage of discovery and to note how the fringe of darkness grows out of pastoral peace, how from the very beginning the canker is in the rose and how the incipient suggestion is stirred at the outset that the sadness of things is also the fitness of things. The frost attacks all flowers including those of poetry but in what should be the open mind of the reader, seasonal death points also to seasonal rebirth. Not too much should be made of these implications; they are set up largely to ensure that the main current of assertion dominates but does not overwhelm the poem.

[10] *John Milton* (New York, 1964), 62.

These consolations of the pastoral decorum, the coupling of life and death to the rhythm of nature, are designed so that the violence which follows can sweep them aside; but they also remain alive for the eventual restoration. So, the traditional "Where were ye Nymphs" blazes into the recognition that protection is useless, that the poet's fate is to be doomed like Orpheus. Large reechoes are stirred by the powerful image. Since Orpheus was a symbol of the force of civilization, his death connotes a reversion to barbarity and the dimensions of his defeat are given depth because in the sombre power of the verse, the fury that overwhelms him is now wholly uprooted from any rational order; the mourning of the woods and caves has broadened into the lament of universal nature and indeed in an earlier version of the passage both heaven and hell had joined in the chorus of grief. At the same time the context works, as always, in more than one direction: Orpheus as a type of Christ, keeps our minds open to that upward movement which the poem is eventually to achieve.[11] For the time being however, the nihilist momentum is dominant and it is against this threatening background that the first temptation to irresponsibility evolves. It is a temptation particularly striking for the immediacy it achieves within the pastoral tone. The buoyant consonants lend their sprightliness to sporting with Amaryllis and the line on Neaera's hair—surely one of the most voluptuous in all literature—is almost tactile in its quality of ardent entanglement. A few lines later, as the sudden blaze of fame is throttled down to the thin-spun whisper of frustration, we are made aware again of Milton's confident power to achieve what is currently called enactment. But something more than enactment is involved. If the verse is fully responsive to the immediate eddy it also sweeps on in the larger tide. As the higher temptation of fame succeeds the lower (in that ironical call of the clear spirit), we relinquish the world of casual living only to realize that dedication creates its own dangers. To live for the moment is to lose only the moment. But the commitment to a vocation, however warped by the pressures of earthly glory (the language is care-

[11] For the history of the image see Caroline F. Mayerson, "The Orpheus Image in *Lycidas*," 116 ff., and Don Cameron Allen, "Milton and the Descent to Light," in *Studies in Honor of Harris Francis Fletcher* (Urbana, 1961), 10–13.

fully judged to cover what it dismisses), opens, by its very
seriousness, the door into a world of anti-meaning. The word
"slit" placed with almost malignant accuracy in the halting
march of the monosyllabic line, is potent in evoking a calculating power of destruction, all the more challenging because it is
driven by blindness.[12]

With the question posed, the answer has to follow. Professor
Daiches has rightly stressed the tentative character of Phoebus's
reply, though it is an exaggeration to describe it as a "deliberately false climax."[13] Professor Daniells agrees with Professor
Daiches and uses the occasion to assure us that the "refusal to
promulgate a resounding resolution" is characteristic of mannerist restlessness.[14] This may be true but if the poem is successfully making itself, the weight of reassurance that is here
offered must be precisely what the evolving logic demands; the
justification is perhaps better sought in an inner necessity rather than in a current style. In any event, the resolution of the two-
handed engine should be resounding enough for any taste and
the poem, whether or not it is mannerist, does not at this point,
cease to be itself. In fact neither resolution is sufficient and the
difference in their quality is significant for precisely this reason.
Both are temporary truces in the onslaught of questioning and
both must give way to a different and superior order of recognition before the poem can attain its peace.

In the procession of mourners which initiates the second section Lycidas's death is once again made to stand apart from
nature. All winds are imprisoned and the very phrase "sleek
Panope" reflects the mirror-like gloss of the sea's surface. The
calamity is no part of the order of life; it emanates from a world
of arbitrary destructiveness and the Fury's true function is to
slit the thread of design. Thus, the natural logic of doubt is

[12] Marjorie Nicolson reminds us (*John Milton: A Reader's Guide to his
Poetry*, 95) that it is the Fates, not the Furies, who cut the thread of life
and that the Furies are not notable for their blindness. Milton's alteration
is, as always, significant. Death is removed from the realm of order, however inscrutable, to that of arbitrary punishment; the Furies, calculating
in their victimization, are blind in the choice of their victim.

[13] David Daiches, from *A Study of Literature*, above, 103.

[14] Roy Daniells, *Milton, Mannerism and Baroque* (Toronto, 1963), 45.
Christ's equally quietist dismissal ("For what is glory but the blaze of
fame," *Paradise Regained*, 3.47) echoes *Lycidas* but is made from the far
side of a sea which the earlier poem is only beginning to enter.

encouraged to flourish and one irrationality opens into another.
If the fate of the innocent is to be struck down in the "perfidious
Bark" that carries them through life, then by the same injustice,
the destiny of the wicked is to prosper. We are in fact making
the first exploration of that world which Michael describes in
Paradise Lost as "To good malignant, to bad men benigne." The
second irresponsibility is now presented to us, neatly balancing
the first, the personal questioning of one's vocation versus the
public abandonment of one's calling. Complaint against ecclesi-
astics is not uncommon in late pastoral poetry and is indeed a
fairly typical expression of that mode's social content. One
might add that Virgil's Ninth Eclogue in which one of the speakers is Lycidas, includes a passing reference to social injustice.
The muster of precedents should, however, serve to inform us
that there are no precedents for the crescendo of indignation
which the poem develops. In using what Professor Allen calls
"the inherited right of the pastoralist to be both satirist and
allegorist" Milton is achieving effects which are far more than
satirical.[15] Once again if an explanation is to be sought, it must
take account of the poem's internal necessities, of the rage for
order which has become a condition of its questioning. It is the
mounting violence of that rage, pressed forward inexorably by
the poem's dynamics that seems to reach up to and almost to
call down the responsive thunder of the two-handed engine.

The return to the pastoral mood is now particularly fervent,
as if the two previous breakdowns have made more anxious the
search for security. Yet the caressing care with which the illusion is built up does not prevent it from being revealed as an
illusion. The false surmise is not only that there is no laureate
hearse; it is also the assumption that absorption in a ritual
however ardent, can serve to protect one against the assault of
reality. This is the third irresponsibility: the dalliance not with
Amaryllis, or with the spoils of a desecrated office, but with that
frail and precious sense of order out of which the poem has no
choice but to advance. The forces of chaos muster for their assault and Milton in three daring revisions, makes clear not only
his uncompromising sense of direction but the imaginative risks
he knows he can negotiate. The "floods and sounding seas" be-

[13] *The Harmonious Vision*, enl. ed. (Baltimore, 1970), 57.

come the "shores and sounding Seas" as if to destroy any residual sense of security and to suggest inexorably that, for those
who ask ultimate questions, neither land nor ocean can provide
a place of refuge. "Sad thoughts" become "frail thoughts," to
stress the precariousness of the defence against chaos; and the
"humming tide" becomes the "whelming tide," giving additional
strength to the attacking forces.[16] Even nature which mourned
Lycidas and lamented Orpheus, now seems committed to the
"monstrous world" of the enemy. As the pastoral mood faces its
peril for the third time it appears to be confronted by annihilation; and precisely because of the poem's unitive power, a formal
defeat must be also a failure of life. What is at stake in the inner
world of the poem is nothing less than that sense of order and
design in reality without which no man can survive in this perilous flood.

What happens next is of course known to every reader of
Lycidas but bears repeating because it is so plain. In seven lines
the poem is manoeuvred with startling authority from the des-
peration into which it has been deliberately plunged into an
almost exultant recovery. "Weep no more, woful Shepherds weep
no more" is a line alive with both serenity and joyousness; the
conviction that rings in it is not merely declared but achieved.
This transformation is accomplished by an image which according to T. S. Eliot is for sheer magnificence of sound unsurpassed
in the English language.[17] Little penetration is needed to see,
however, that sumptuous noises alone cannot bring about what
is accomplished here. It is also not sufficient to suggest that
everything is contained in Mercator's atlas or that the angel
looking towards Spain, is being advised to turn its attention to
England's internal enemies. The image is clearly the turning
point of *Lycidas*[18] and some attempt to elucidate how it works
is necessary both to understand the poem better and to test those
critical approaches that claim to possess it.

Lycidas, as one comes to realize progressively, is full of sig-

[16] The revisions to lines 153 and 154 are in the Trinity MS, that to line 157
in the 1645 text. However, both the Cambridge University copy of 1638 and
one British Museum copy have *humming* replaced by *whelming* in what is
regarded as Milton's hand.

[17] "Milton I," in *On Poetry and Poets* (New York, 1961), 163–64.

[18] Allen (*Harmonious Vision*, 68 ff.), however, locates the turning point in
the flower passage.

nificant symmetries arranged as affirmations of its three part structure. The three forms of irresponsibility have already been noted and it is well-known that the outburst of questioning in each part is stilled on each occasion by a form of divine reassurance. The relationship between these reassurances is not undisputed. Professor Abrams considers that they disclose "a gradual shift from the natural, pastoral and pagan viewpoint to the viewpoint of Christian revelation" while Professor Nicolson considers that the answers from above are uniformly Christian.[19] Perhaps it is best to say that each part discloses a different face of God or more precisely, a different form of man's recognition of God's nature. The God who calms the first wave of doubt is the god of justice and emphasis is laid on his impartiality, his "perfect witnes," and on the "all-judging" power that weighs all things fully and impartially in its balance. The god of the second part is the apocalyptic god of retribution whose single blow is sufficient to crush the armies of the godless. To make understanding doubly clear Milton defines the specific quality of each reassurance, immediately after the reassurance has been offered. Significantly, these definitions occur in those two crucial passages that admit the violation of the pastoral decorum. We return to normality from the "higher mood" of justice; we return again to it from the "dread voice" of retribution.

The third recognition of God is the one recognition that can truly answer man's agony. It is the consciousness not of justice but of the power beyond justice, not the might of him who wields the two-handed engine but instead the "dear might of him that walk'd the waves." To quote the language of another poem, it is the "rigid satisfaction, death for death" which has dominated the first two "resolutions" in *Lycidas*. The third resolution transcends the law and so reminds us that there are energies in this poem which even the law cannot silence. If peace is to be won it can be won only through the higher satisfaction of redemptive love. The angel mediates the movement into this recognition. Against the menace of the "sounding seas" it stands steadfastly protective, guarding and yet guarded, vigilant and unassailable, looking out not only on a geographical panorama

[19] Abrams, "Types of *Lycidas*," above, 230 ff.; Nicolson, *John Milton: A Reader's Guide to his Poetry*, 96n; French, "Digressions in *Lycidas*," 489.

but also on the wide landscape of man's questioning and searching. The "great vision" here is evocative of the blaze of understanding while the "guarded mount" with its evocations of paradise, suggest distantly it is true, but strongly enough to give resonance to the verse, the redemption of man's nature and the protective finality with which God's grace surrounds that redemption. Finally, the angel looking homeward is not asked to wield the weapons of retribution but is implored instead to "melt with ruth." Just as power has modulated into protective strength, protective strength now modulates into mercy. Though legendary, archetypal and even political associations surround this great image, it lives also in a specific world of embattlement, drawing the self-wounding strength of the poem's conflict, into the conviction of design and peace. As the dolphins waft Lycidas to Byzantium,[20] they surely guide us also to the recognition that salvation lies not with the god of hosts, nor with the exact dispenser of Olympian justice, but in "the blest Kingdoms meek of joy and love"[21] which establish both our dignity and dependence. The god of compassion will not be seen again with such tenderness in the sterner movements of Milton's later poetry; and though in an earlier poem, heaven had stooped towards a feeble but upward-climbing virtue, that, as befitted a masque, was a choreographic gesture, exquisitely felicitous, rather than a cry out of the heart of experience. The moment of comprehension in *Lycidas* is unique; it is not merely called but implored into being by the poem.

The unrhymed lines of *Lycidas* are no longer evidence that the poem is not quite anonymous.[22] Nevertheless, it is significant

[20] The line is usually interpreted as an allusion to Arion. T. O. Mabbott, in "Milton's *Lycidas*, ll. 164 and 183–85," *Explicator* 5 (1947):26, follows Richardson and Newton in reading it as alluding to Palaemon. Michael Lloyd in "The Two Worlds of *Lycidas*," *Essays in Criticism* 11 (1961):397–98, notes that in "Servius's version of the myth, Phoebus Apollo himself in the guise of a dolphin rescued his drowning son Icadius and carried him to Mount Parnassus." This interpretation of the myth would fit best the pattern here suggested.

[21] The omission of this line in the 1638 edition is presumably accidental. It appears in the MS and in the 1645 and 1673 texts and is restored in two copies of 1638.

[22] See John Crowe Ransom, "A Poem Nearly Anonymous," above, 68 ff. Precedents for Milton's rhyme and stanzaic structure are found by F. T. Prince in the canzone ("The Italian Element in *Lycidas*," above, 157 ff.), by Ants Oras in the madrigal ("Milton's Rhyme Schemes," 20), and by Gretchen Finney in the *dramma per musica* ("A Musical Background for *Lycidas*," *Huntington Library Quarterly* 15[1952]:325–50).

that the resolution contains no unrhymed lines.[23] The regularity is expressive of other mergings that are taking place: of the pastoral with the Christian, of the rhythm of nature with the death of man, of the poem itself with the forces of doubt which have invaded it and all but brought it to its destruction. It is also one more reminder of the fully-shaped economy with which the poem moves on its various levels of disturbance and achievement so that all that happens in it, however microscopic, acquires its full meaning in more than one dimension. In the end, even the shore and sounding seas are joined in a pattern of purpose, not a chaos of nihilism. Lycidas the genius of the one is also, through the hard-won achievement of the poem, an example to all those who fare forward upon the destructive element of life. All is in order now. If there is a time for grief there is a time to put grief behind one and to see the world made green again in the power of God's blessing. As the westering wheel of the poem sinks to its rest in the brisk finality of its last *ottava rima* a position has been established, a recognition achieved and the point has now been reached when even the poem must be put into its framework. The subtle shift from first to third person is a beautifully judged manoeuvre, distancing the poem, depersonalizing it and leaving it decidedly behind. The performance is over and a new day will begin.

If this examination of *Lycidas* is not wildly erroneous, we are facing a poem more intricately articulated than even the most elaborate dissections of it suggest. Every point on its surface inherits a long tradition to which it is competitively and creatively responsive. This is as it should be; since the singing match is a root convention of the pastoral, a late pastoral should have in abundant measure, the *élan* and the *brio* of performance. But *Lycidas* is always and inescapably more than a technical accomplishment of extreme sophistication. It is a voyage towards

[23] Oras, in "Milton's Rhyme Schemes," 17, notes that the design of the paragraphs of *Lycidas* "closely mirrors the broader architectonics of the poem as a whole, beginning regularly and clearly, then becoming more and more intricate and involved and eventually reverting to transparent regularity." A study of repetitions of phrase in the poem bears out this conclusion. Such repetition, particularly when it occurs with the first or second syllable of successive or closely linked lines (as in 8, 9; 15, 17; 162, 163; 167, 168; and 190, 191) strengthens the impression of pastoral performance. Phrase repetition is most frequent in the first forty-nine lines of the poem (when the pastoral convention has not yet been undermined) and in the last twenty-nine (when the convention is reestablished).

recognition, a poem that resolutely faces itself, that opens all windows upon the storm of reality and takes all assaults into its ultimate order. What gives the questioning its singular strength and the final resolution its inclusive validity, is the complete integration of experience, structure and language; few poems can have embodied and made alive their substance so fully, both in the large strategy and the minor manoeuvres of style. It is because of this total authenticity that the poem is able to accommodate and eventually to unify a range of dissension that would otherwise tear it apart. Rosemond Tuve is right in regarding *Lycidas* as "the most poignant and controlled statement in English poetry of the acceptance of that in the human condition which seems to man unacceptable."[24] But if the unacceptable is brought within the framework of order it is only by taking risks which are uniquely comprehensive. It is this perilous openness that gives *Lycidas* its character, that enables it to remain inclusively honest in its fidelity to experience, yet imbued throughout with a passionate sense of the *genre*.

[24] "Theme, Pattern, and Imagery in *Lycidas*." above, 171.

Lycidas: The Swain's Paideia

Donald M. Friedman

Lycidas has provoked debates and disagreements because so many of the questions it asks remain unanswered or receive inadequate or irrelevant answers; the experience of reading *Lycidas* is, I suspect, more like Milton's in writing it than is the case with most other poems. And it is an important part of Milton's central conception of his pastoral persona to show him in the midst of a roiling sea of uncertainty, anger, despair, and bewilderment. Out of these weltering moods come the challenges, the demands, the questionings of fate, the gods, the self, which constitute so much of the actual texture of the poem. Responses come from the gods, from nature, from the saints; but these responses—explanations and utterances meant to quiet and reassure—are not only often shown to be unhelpful but are actually ignored by the questioner. He seems to be neither informed nor reassured, but merely determined to go on with his frustrating pursuit of resolution.

However one views what once were called "digressions" in the poem, explanations of its structure and of the thematic interrelations of its parts lead inevitably to the idea of a poem based on a dynamic of conflict—sometimes between classical and Christian myth, sometimes between innocence and experience, but always between major principles of poetic allegiance which Milton is striving to reconcile. An important consequence for *Lycidas* of

From *Milton Studies* 3 (1971):3–34; condensed for this book by the author.

its pattern of successive impact and recoil is that it allows Milton to render the experience of the poem's speaker as one of active struggle. The pastoral persona is not swept up in the poem's large movements of debate and abortive harmonies; typically, he fights *against* the knowledge that floods the serene "high Lawns"[1] of his mental landscape in the hortatory voices of Phoebus and St. Peter. The struggle is not carried on forensically; the inspired arguments are not refuted; the lamenting shepherd simply sweeps, or tries to sweep, them away, urging himself on through the disordered countries of his mind, while demanding all the time an explanation that never comes. The further reach of Milton's skill, in this portrait of a consciousness defending itself against the knowledge it knows to be necessary and saving, is his ability to show us the gradual, very gradual, growth of understanding that accompanies and emerges from the tides of conflict which shape the surface and structure of the elegy. The final consoling vision is neither conceived nor spoken from a predetermined position of revealed or human wisdom; it does not follow from the elegist's understanding or from his role at the beginning of the poem; nor is it a knowledge held in suspense, a potentiality implicit in the pastoral and in the mind of the shepherd persona. Rather, it is a knowledge whose realization depends from moment to moment on his ability to grasp and accept what the experience of the poem is teaching him.

At each stage of this development in the persona, changes in consciousness are reflected in the speaker's language as he challenges the fate that governs the pastoral elegy, and as he reacts to the literary and religious doctrines that are given voice in the poem to meet his challenges. Lowry Nelson, Jr., has described this process as "a kind of self-education";[2] it is not presented, however, as a slow and unperturbed ascent of that "hill side" Milton speaks of in *Of Education*, than which "the harp of *Orpheus* was not more charming."[3] *Lycidas* is a dramatization of the first steps in the ascent of that hill, which Milton calls "laborious indeed." Knowing that as fallen creatures our ele-

---

[1] Milton's poetry is quoted from the edition by Merritt Y. Hughes (New York, 1957); his prose, from the Yale edition of his *Complete Prose Works* (1953 ff.). The present passage is from *The Reason of Church-Government*, in *Prose*, 1:816–17.

[2] *Baroque Lyric Poetry* (New Haven, 1961), 149.

[3] *Of Education*, in *Prose*, 2:376.

ment is "the perpetuall stumble of conjecture and disturbance
in this our darke voyage," Milton insists also that "the darknes
and the crookednesse is our own," that "our *understanding* [has]
a film of *ignorance* over it," is "blear with gazing on . . . false
glisterings," "The very essence of Truth is plainnesse, and
brightnes";[4] that men cannot perceive that essence is not the
result of mere inability, but of their active struggle not to accept
truth, a struggle carried on by human energies perverted in the
service of self-deception, egotism, sloth, and the "frail thoughts"
that would "dally with false surmise."

At the very beginning of the poem we are troubled by allusions to a past we know nothing of. "Yet once more," says the
voice we do not yet know as the swain's. The events he recalls
are never specified; they exist in the poem as symbolic gestures
invoking, perhaps, previous exercises in the same formal genre,
or simply other poems, or even other moments of crisis and loss
in the putative history of the mourning shepherd. His address
to the emblematic, honorific plants combines reverent apology
and a grinding, reluctant distaste for his enforced task. We cannot help noting that the thoroughly conventional disclaimer of
the traditional elegist—the pretense that he is unqualified to
praise the subject of his elegy adequately—is here transformed
into a trope that is both wider in reference and more intensely—
almost crudely—personal than the tradition would seem to allow.
This poet is unready, not because King's virtues are beyond his
powers to celebrate (the phrase, "hath not left his peer," is
strangely ambiguous in context), but because he has not yet arrived at a desired state of "ripeness." We are made to feel the
force of his desire for that ripeness without being told in what
it consists or how it will be recognized. With the pervasive obliquity of the opening part of the poem, the ideal state is defined
for us largely by images of negation and qualification. Although
the berries the swain comes to pluck are "harsh and crude,"
emblematic both of his unpreparedness and of the act he is
forced to perform, the stressed rhymes also draw our attention
to "never sere" and "the mellowing year," sounds that contra-
dict the violence of the action in the foreground of the poem
and set up a standard of permanence and serenity by which to
judge what follows. In this way Milton begins to shape one of

[4] *Of Reformation*, in *Prose*, 1:566.

the fundamental patterns of the poem: the dramatic *events* we witness and hear described are rendered in a language that simultaneously suggests a reinterpretation of those events; the meanings the swain attaches to them are subsumed in larger and truer meanings that reveal themselves to him only as he submits to the apparently random course of his experience.

Another way to make much the same point is to observe that the voice we hear in the *ottava rima* coda, the voice that guides us to look back at the swain and to consider what he has said and learned during the recitation of *Lycidas*, is in control of the poem's diction from the beginning. He allows us and helps us to see more than the swain does, at the same time that we listen to the swain's speech. Thus, while we translate "forc'd fingers rude" and "Shatter" into perceptions of the speaker's pain and dissatisfaction, we also become aware that "the mellowing year" represents a reality that comprehends, and promises ultimately to justify, the particular "perturbations of the mind" that are being displayed. The symbolic plants that receive the swain's first address have their "season due"; that prophetic concept governs the development of the poem as it moves through many misapprehensions and false versions of that promised ripeness. Similarly, the first ten lines or so of the poem, as they insist on the idea of death and disruption that come too early, also create the necessary notion of "due season," the stable, knowable criterion by which maturity is judged. Thus the swain, in his very first words, speaks truer than he knows, and the language of pastoral begins to generate the terms of a redefinition of the pastoral mode.

If the pastoral key signature tells us immediately that the poem will have something to say about poetry itself, it is typical of Milton to embody that familiar idea in a sequence of passages ordered by the importance of *sound*. Thus, the "logic" of the opening fourteen lines of the poem says that the "bitter constraint" of Lycidas's death forces the swain to disturb the laurels of poetry prematurely *because* Lycidas was a singer and must not be left to the winds and waters without the "meed" of a mournful song. In the fictive world of Milton's swain, silence is a threat, an unspeaking sign of death, disorder, unnaturalness. So, when the muses are implored to "sweep the string," one strenuous activity of the poem is begun, the act of filling the

silence wrought by too early fatality with the music of the
"Sphere-born harmonious Sisters, Voice and Verse"; and the
necessary continuity of sound is established as the swain looks
forward to the silence of his "destin'd Urn," hoping for the propriety of "lucky words" spoken for *him* by another poet.

Miss Tuve made much the same point, by her italics, when she
remarked that "decay and disease . . . are 'such' as was the news
of . . . loss, *to Shepherd's ear*."[5] But this ellipsis needs to be
expanded; and the task is made light and easy by Milton's
scrupulous insistence, in the early stages of the poem, on the
figural importance of natural and artificial sound in the composition of the pastoral world. As the "eyelids" of the morn open
to perceive the two shepherd-figures making their way onto the
serene and fertile plains of youth and early, carefree song, the
swain testifies to the quality of their common experience by remembering the sultry horn of the Gray-fly, and by showing us
the power of their "Rural ditties" to stir the fauns and satyrs
to dance, the excellence of the "glad sound" that could please
those presumably sterner and better-trained sensibilities of
"old *Damoetas*."

The momentary vision of delight that has passed, then, is
sketched so that our familiar image of the pastoral landscape is
suffused with minor harmonies and lively tunes, appropriate
both to innocent immaturity and to its dawning and uncomplicated ambitions. We are then returned to a present transformed
by a "heavy change," and denied the comfort, not of a promised
future glory, but of the simplicities and satisfactions of a ravaged past. The bereaved shepherd is circumscribed both by events
and by the limits of his understanding of them. One way in which
the limits of that understanding are made clear is the variation
Milton works on the conventional "pathetic fallacy"; the natural scene described by the swain does not mourn actively. The
trees do not cast down their fruit, the ewes' udders do not wither,
cattle do not refuse to drink, nor do any Libyan lions roar with
grief, fountains do not dry up, nor does the earth give forth only
darnels;[6] the "heavy change" is defined for us, rather, as the
absence of a musical sound which once gave order, dancelike pat-

---

[5] "Theme, Pattern, and Imagery in *Lycidas*," above, 185 ff.
[6] Cf. Moschus, *The Lament for Bion*; Virgil, *Eclogue V*; Castiglione,
Alcon. The texts of these poems, with translations, are conveniently assem-
bled in the collections by Elledge and Harrison (cited below, 359, 353).

tern, and pleasure to the natural world. The willows fan their
leaves "no more" to Lycidas's songs, and the woods and caves
mourn the dead shepherd with their "echoes" that can now only
reverberate silence. Milton drives the point home unmistakably
by having the lines rise in a rhythmic climax to the definition of
all disruption and sorrow as a loss to the ear. And as a yet more
refined intensification of his dominant idea, that loss is compared to the effect of *premature* death, the cutting-off of "weanling" herds, the "blasting" of flowers which put on their "gay
wardrobe" in the earliest days of spring.

The lament thus takes us back to the tonality of the poem's
opening lines, the bewildered and dismayed contemplation of an
unexpected fate that has overtaken a poet whose youthful harmonies had given life and beauty to an appreciative world. At
this point "denial vain and coy excuse" have been swept away
not only by the necessary proprieties of elegizing a fellow poet
but also by the "sight" of the scars his death has left on the
charming and comfortable world sketched for us in lines 25–36.
The movement of the entire elegy is rehearsed in the confrontation between the memory of that world and the undeniable
present reality. The transformation has been worked, and the
swain is trying to accommodate himself to its meaning. He defines what is by referring it to what has been, and can go no
further than to realize that death has shown itself to be inimical
not only to beauty and simplicity but to the potentiality of
creation implicit in the figural poet. Still, it is the *shepherd's ear*
that has been deprived, just as it had been the swain who was
forced to shatter the laurel's leaves too soon.

And it is still that swain who is unable to grapple his mind
to that reality for very long. His next thought, sanctioned by
pastoral elegiac tradition, is to question the gods, to try to discover a complicity that will explain the death of Lycidas. He
chooses the indigenous legendary figures, supposed to stand in
a tutelary relation to bardic, prophetic poetry. But the attempt
is abandoned as soon as it begins, not because the swain is too
clear-sighted to place any faith in such Celtic nonsense, but
because he knows that the great Muse, the mother of the true
poet's guardian and genius—Orpheus—could do nothing to save
her precious charge. Thus he exchanges one myth for another,
but in that exchange he has moved toward the acceptance of an

emblematic meaning larger than any he has yet acknowledged. "Universal nature did lament" Orpheus's death, and the contemplation of "his gory visage" effectively bars the reentrance to the world of "high Lawns" and "Rural ditties." Nor was it simply a silent and inexplicable act of fate that destroyed *this* myth; Orpheus's "enchanting" powers were drowned by the "hideous roar" of that "rout" whose type was the mad Bacchants but whose embodiments recur throughout human history. They are the forces that crush poetry and the sympathetic alliance with nature that generates it.

Having gone this far toward the recognition of a universal predicament, the swain cannot retreat unthinkingly into the reassuring formulas that had served him. Milton signals this by bringing his mind once again back to the present; but, as before, it is a present transformed by what he has learned in the lines that precede it. What was a memory of two brother poets "nurst upon the self-same hill" becomes an inquiry into the justification of the métier of poetry itself. Once the swain had recalled the pleasure and approval of the fauns and Damoetas; now he speaks of the "homely slighted Shepherd's trade." It is important to realize that nothing has been said in the poem to change our knowledge or opinions of the poet's calling; what the new characterization of poetry reflects is the swain's changing awareness. The atmosphere of pastoral ease and delight which surrounded the image of those glad sounds and carefree dances has been darkened by the memory of Orpheus's fate, and as a consequence the calling of poetry, which then seemed natural and unbidden, is now seen as burdensome and problematical. Furthermore, the swain's questioning of his own relation to his calling is not phrased in nostalgic terms, but clearly alludes to actual contemporary poets, fashionable styles, and immediate rewards. In short, the pastoral pretense begins to dissolve into a discussion of what it means to be a poet in England in 1637. The alternatives are set up in terms of effort and ease. The vision of *otium* usually associated with the pastoral tradition out of which Milton had fashioned the first picture of his youth at Cambridge is now transferred to the naturalists, the erotic poets who "sport with *Amaryllis* in the shade"; and so the expressive figure of pastoral poetry no longer remains unitary, but divides into true and false, or at least worthy and slothful, song. And the former is attributed to those who pursue their calling with "uncessant care," who "meditate" the muse "strictly." These are not the concepts of an untroubled shepherd piping "unpremeditated" tunes to an audience of pagan hedonists; they reveal the grave dedication to a holy and demanding art that has been observed in Milton's own youthful writings. The question he asks himself is not simply whether one kind of poetry is better than another, but whether the kind of poetry he knows to be better is worth pursuing if his labors and his achieved excellence are never to be given due praise.

However noble the Renaissance concept of fame may have been, however different from its usual connotations of reputation and public applause, Milton is at pains to show here that it is inadequate to the reassurance the swain is seeking. If it is the "last infirmity of Noble mind," it is nevertheless an infirmity. And the point is underlined by the swain's hoping to "find" it, thinking to "burst out into sudden blaze," thinking, in other words, of a spectacular, unexpected, almost unearned reward of glory and admiration. The very terms belie the characterization of the poetic calling as a strict, thankless, uncessant devotion to the highest standards of personal and artistic integrity. The lines ring with ambition, and their passion is rendered even more compelling by the tight-lipped contempt poured upon the "blind *Fury*" in the phrase, "slits the thin-spun life." But this complex burst of energy is checked by the voice of Phoebus, who replied to the swain's question by telling him that he should expect fame only in heaven, that its plant, unlike the laurels and myrtles, does not grow in mortal soil. The change of tense breaks the time sequence that has been established in the poem thus far and begins to suggest a mental past in which this examination has been carried on previously. It both clarifies some of the implications hinted at by "Yet once more" and looks forward to the coda in which Milton subsumes the entire experience of the swain in his closing comment.

The deliberate blurring of the narrative line is Milton's way of creating a fictive time in which the elegy exists, and it functions in much the same way as the suggestive backward glance of the opening words of the poem. The discomfort we feel as a result of such disorientation is a vital part of the experience of the poem, for it reminds us in subtle ways that both the occasion

and the statement of *this* pastoral elegy vibrate between the
poles of particularity and universal meaning. The strained
speculation through which the swain forces himself enacts, but
also reenacts, a mental history through which Milton himself,
and any serious poet, has lived many times. And so he can immediately return to the waiting current of pastoral imagery, as
his "Oat proceeds" in the present time of the poem; the "higher
mood" of Phoebus's speech, although it necessitates a decorous
invocation of the appropriately legendary Arethusa and Mincius,
does not disturb the flow of pastoral conventions in the swain's
repertory. The procession of mourners, which Milton might have
found in elegies by Moschus, Castiglione, Sannazaro, and others
and in Virgil's Tenth Eclogue, carries us back not only to the
familiar traditions of the elegy, but also to the questioning mood
of the address to the nymphs in lines 50–55. It is as if the swain
has forgotten that both the inquiry into causes and the notion
of the protective muses have been discovered to be fond dreams.
But these figures—"the Herald of the Sea" and Hippotades—
come unbidden; the sea and the winds send their answer to questions unasked by the swain, as the classical deities of nature
exculpate themselves. The important point here is that what they
have to say is no answer to the underlying question about Lycidas's death. Even Camus, the allegorical figure who recalls for
the last time in the poem the fading pastoral emblem of early
life at Cambridge, brings only another empty question; his
venerable age and his aura of semimystical wisdom cannot offer
knowledge or resolution.

At this stage in the poem it seems as if the machinery of conventional pastoral has seized the initiative from the swain. With
the exception of the lines on the "perfidious Bark," which seem
an explanation *faute de mieux*,[7] he merely reports and describes;
the personal tones of anguish and bitterness diminish and are
powerfully subdued by the angry, craggy denunciation voiced
by St. Peter.

The conventional procession of mourners, then, erupts from
within, as the swain reports an incursion more violent and un-
assimilable than any that have occurred thus far. The speech
of Phoebus might have been a version of any young poet's con-

[7] See Michael Lloyd, "The Fatal Bark," *Modern Language Notes* 75
(1960): 103–9, for a different reading.

cerned musings; but this diatribe, if only because of the many
ways in which it violates the rhetorical manners of the elegy, is
meant to make us feel that a power hitherto unacknowledged
and untapped by the swain's mind has now thrust into the fragile
framework in order to speak a truth that cannot be softened or
distanced by literary technique. The point is made to the ear by
a new vocabulary, which includes the sounds and judgmental
images of "flashy songs," "scrannel Pipes," and the "hungry
Sheep" rotting "inwardly." This is a language that has been
only tentatively drawn upon in the lines that spoke of the
"homely slighted Shepherd's trade"; but it achieves its full impact now, not simply by sound, but by the way it converts the
swain's defensive pastoral mode into a way of revelation. Peter
speaks of the same contemporary conditions the swain had deplored in lines 64–69, but in his mouth the figure of the shepherd is no longer an airy and elegant allusion to the life of art.
While the swain has been attempting to understand and control
the implications of Lycidas's death for his own commitment to
poetry, he has been ignoring the significance of the young cleric's
death for the health of the English pastorate. Peter's speech
reminds him of what he has forgotten, but not in the solicitous
manner of Phoebus. Indeed, Peter does not even speak *to* the
swain; he simply defines what has been lost by describing the
"corrupted clergy" that remain, and foretells retribution. As
at every marked turning point in *Lycidas* the bearing of the
passage, its relation to the developing elegiac pattern, is left
unspecified. Milton provides no easy or obvious way to decide
what we or the swain are to understand from Peter's speech;
what is to be *done* is even more problematical.

This troubled indecision is underlined by the swain's response.
Peter's clarification of the true meaning of "shepherd" is referred to as "the dread voice"; the swain acknowledges only a
sound whose harsh veracity has disrupted the orderly, plaintive,
nostalgic gestures to which he is trying to attune his own
thoughts. And so the return to convention, as Peter's words
have been more difficult to accommodate than Phoebus's, is here
more poignant, more detailed; we may even say more desperate.
The flower catalogue was as clearly a standard part of the archetypal pastoral elegy as the mourning procession; and we know
from the Trinity manuscript that Milton labored carefully

over it, meaning it to stand for all similar attempts to find
respite from grief and bewilderment in the passive and numerable
beauties of a sympathetic nature. Alpheus and the Sicilian Muse
are called once again into their mild and uncomplicated relationship with the swain; they are asked to "call the Vales" and
ask them to cast their flowers on the imaginary "Laureate
Hearse" of the dead shepherd. This request, at least, is answered; for immediately the swain turns to address the "valleys
low" himself, and his imagination responds to the comforting
"mild whispers" that issue from the gushing brooks of this newly
surmised landscape. The flower catalogue sketches for us a
locus amoenus quite different from the remembered, autobiographical setting the swain described initially. Here there are
no "high Lawns," no gaily piped tunes, no dancing pagan deities.
Rather, in the extremity of shock wrought by Peter's tirade,
the swain conjures the healing and restorative landscape of the
literary pastoral, as if the convention itself of the flower catalogue had the power to wipe out the memory of what he has just
heard. No longer is he in full command of his chosen poetic mode;
no longer does he speak of King and himself as shepherds, assured of the stable meaning of that usage. Peter has bereft him
of that simple and complacent equation, and he is driven back
to its elemental, underlying pretense of an animate and em-
pathetic nature. The swain tries, by exercising his command
of an artificial literary mode, to grasp the consolation that may
be distilled from it.

But the grasp is loosening even as it is attempted, for the
very beauty of the things described is tempered and shadowed.
The elaborate pastoral panoply that Milton draws, we must notice, is at the same time an indirect witness of its helplessness
to stave off the effects of Peter's speech, if we conceive that as
a new kind of statement, bringing with it a new kind of knowledge. The ambition and confidence adumbrated in the vision of
shepherds' life on those high lawns of youth surrender to the
mood of the flower catalogue. And that mood is attuned to the
"valleys low" and their "mild whispers"; these lines are a demonstration of the pastoral's commitment to a life of ease, dis-
engagement, even immaturity and a denial of responsibility. The
flowers belong to the spring season, appropriate still to the
theme of Lycidas's early death, but also to the stage of personal

development in which the mind and spirit are shielded from the fierce, inevitable onslaught of destructive experience. The "swart Star sparely looks" on *this* pastoral scene; but it is impossible for the shepherd-poet who has faced the apparently random and indifferent harshness of life in the world to avoid emerging into the full blaze of that sun of maturity. The "wanton winds" may blow softly and playfully through these imagined dales, but the heights of poetic achievement that tempt the swain's "clear spirit" are buffeted by "every gust of rugged wings / That blows from off each beaked Promontory." The swain, the poet, the man can wander contentedly in the landscape of *otium* only so long as his mind can accept the literary mode as a real and satisfying substitute for the mode of active responsibility, in whose nature he has been instructed both by the death of Lycidas and by the words of St. Peter. Once the meaning of the true pastorate is understood, or even recognized, the low valleys must become an eternally desirable but finally uninhabitable region of the mind.

And so the magnificence, the brilliant detail, the lovingly fashioned colors and sounds of the flower passage must ultimately be dismissed as a "false surmise," and the swain must show, to himself as to us, that he understands the intrinsic meaning of the temptation he has overcome by exposing his motives with frank but tender honesty: "For so to interpose a little ease, / Let our frail thoughts dally with false surmise" (152–53). The sting is removed from the charge implicit in "false" by the conscious admission of the frailty of all human thoughts, among which the imagination of pastoral is one of the most beautiful and most fragile. Milton does not mute the notes of lingering nostalgia in these lines, but neither does he allow them to sound with transparent simplicity. The little ease supplied by this dimming glimpse of honied showers and vernal flowers is merely interposed between the acts of unillusioned contemplation that confront the truths of Peter's attack and the facts of King's death. The dalliance is interrupted brutally by the self-aware and resigned expletive, "Ay me!"; with the utterance of that brief appeal the swain is swept forward finally into the great concluding movements of the poem. Even syntax contributes to our sense of rising and climactic rhythm; we do not grasp the scope of "whilst" until nine lines later, when Michael is asked to "look homeward" while the body of Lycidas follows its uncouth path through the unfathomable waters. But "whilst" also looks backward to the flower passage, as the swain opens himself to the realization that the artistry he has devoted to the invocation of an "enamell'd" and animate nature has neither appeased his grief or confusion, nor stayed the flow of intractable experience, imaged here as the hurling of Lycidas's bones among the monsters of the unimaginable ocean depths. At this point the poetic imagination, in its role as a shaper of forms of language intended to soften, reinterpret, and give pattern to the formless succession of events we call experience, falters and proves to be inadequate. Milton tells us this, in one way, by juxtaposing the "fable" of Bellerus with the "great vision" of the guardian archangel; and the swain's response to his own discovery of the limits of his poetic power is to turn from lamentation and self-recrimination to prayer. He asks for no aid from the muses nor from symbolic rivers and fountains, for to do that would be to maintain the empty fiction of the centrality of the elegiac poet, to insist on the importance of the interpreting voice. Rather, he surrenders those illusory notions of competency, and in doing so surrenders as well the theme of the dead shepherd to the tutelary powers of St. Michael and the legendary dolphins. And that surrender is not entirely an act of conscious choice; he has been led to the discovery of Michael's guardianship by the current of imagination which, as it follows the dreadful vision of Lycidas's body lost beneath the sea, is brought back to the actual place at which knowledge stops, the Irish Channel, and to the actual presence of the "guarded Mount." Once again a question is answered, but not in an expected way. At the moment when the swain's consciousness of inability and ignorance is most profound, both ability and insight are *provided*; not because he has asked for them, but because he has admitted his lack.

The same pattern, the answer that comes unexpectedly and in terms that seem incomprehensible to the questioner, seems to me to govern the speech of consolation that follows the appeal to Michael. The swain has given up the apparently fruitless task of demanding explanations from nature and the gods; his

rending doubts about the worth and purpose of poetry have
been stilled, if not satisfied. His ambitious sallies into the world
of confusion and disappointment that surrounds the various pastoral attempts at order and intelligibility have been reduced to
a single, painful speculation on the true whereabouts of the body
of his dead friend. And that speculation is resolved, not by yet
another voice from outside the frame of the elegy, but by the
creation of a new voice for the swain. The first clear demarcation
of that new voice is the fact that for the first time in the poem
the swain addresses himself to a human audience.[8] He casts aside
the obliquity inherent in speaking to muses, nymphs, laurels, and
myrtles and turns to a silent group of fellow mourners whose
presence we have not been allowed to suspect. And for the first
time in the poem he neither questions, nor challenges, nor debates with himself, but simply *tells* what he knows to be true.
It is crucial that we realize Milton forbids us to feel we understand how the swain has come to this knowledge of truth. The
transformation he undergoes has nothing to do, in the poem,
with a logical or sequential argument or demonstration; nothing he is told, nothing he hears, can account for his grasp of
the new truth he promulgates to the listening shepherds. The
transformation lies in the speech itself that we hear; and the
effect of that speech depends as heavily on its function as on its
content. The swain's consoling vision of Lycidas comforted in
"other groves" is the only passage in the elegy which is directed
to the enlightenment of men other than himself. It is neither a
private revelation, as is Phoebus's lesson, nor a scarifying indictment of historical reality, as is Peter's; it is, precisely, an
example of the service poetry performs which Milton described
in *The Reason of Church-Government*, "to allay the perturbations of the mind, and set the affections in right tune, to celebrate
in glorious and lofty Hymns the throne and equipage of Gods
Almightinesse." It fulfills these tasks by embodying the obligations of the true pastor in poetry divinely inspired. It commu-
nicates saving truth in lines whose music is a reflection of the
bright vision which is not the reward of study and preparation
but of the proper rectification of the will. The swain's ability

[8] Lowry Nelson, Jr., makes much the same point in his *Baroque Lyric
Poetry*.

to speak the lines of consolation is Milton's dramatization of the infusion of grace.[9]

It is not an accident that these lines occur immediately after the swain has reached the deepest levels of sorrow, self-abnegation, and self-knowledge. Not until he has admitted to himself that the noblest ideas of poetry he has held are but false surmises can he receive the gift of true poetry which, as other critics have observed, does not abandon the pastoral mode as a pagan fiction, but transmutes it into a Christian mode of apprehending reality.[10] The classical idea of pastoral is not wrong, but incomplete; and in the poem it serves not only as a conventional allegorical frame, but also as a way of representing the incompleteness of mind and spirit that handicaps all human endeavors that grow from an unexamined assumption of the self-sufficiency of the imagination. The power of this assumption has been demonstrated to us in *Lycidas* in many ways: the serene complacency of the memories of the youthful "high Lawns" of Cambridge; the bitter musings over the comparative rewards of Amaryllis and the "thankless Muse"; the strivings to blot out the "higher mood" of Phoebus and the "dread voice" of Peter by calling up the liquid sounds of Mincius and the Sicilian Muses; the tapestry work of the flower passage; and the last, despairing clutching at the little ease that all such surmises promise. In each case the inability, or the refusal, to face and accept the inexplicable fact of death, the unbearable fact that dedication and talent are not guaranteed recognition—in each case the swain's struggle against the knowledge that will force him into maturity is cast in the form of an attempt to maintain the flow of the pastoral elegy. The conventions of the genre are used as examples of the mind's defensive impulses; and while

[9] William G. Madsen in "The Voice of Michael in *Lycidas*," *Studies in English Literature* 3 (1963): 1–7, argues that the consolation speech is delivered by the archangel Michael. For a number of reasons I find Madsen's argument unconvincing; most obviously, Madsen has difficulty in explaining why the *ottava rima* coda refers to the swain having sung the final verse paragraph, and is forced to divide the paragraph to allow for the swain's sudden reappearance in line 182; nor can he explain why Michael, alone of all the speakers identified specifically in the poem, is introduced without comment or identification.

[10] See Rosemond Tuve, "Theme, Pattern, and Imagery in *Lycidas*," above, 171 ff., Jon S. Lawry, " 'Eager Thought': Dialectic in *Lycidas*," above, 236 ff. and Isabel G. MacCaffrey, "*Lycidas*: The Poet in a Landscape," above, 246 ff.

they reveal the swain's artistry, they also show the hollowness of that artistry when it is used to falsify the reality that true poetry should embody.

Some years ago Michael Lloyd wrote a short piece to show that the position of *Lycidas* in the volume known as *Justa Edovardo King* was not without significance.[11] Lloyd does not comment on the fact that, of all the poems in *Justa Edovardo King*, *Lycidas* is the only pastoral elegy. Milton's choice of the genre must have appeared to his contemporaries an act of conscious archaism, or an instance of his scholarly traditionalism, or even a kind of homage to his "teacher," Spenser. The death of a young shepherd serves as the formal occasion and frame for the poem; but the death of a way of conceiving the roles of poet and priest is the action that *Lycidas* truly imitates.

As in so many places in Milton's work, the death of an immature or inadequate idea is wrought by the incursion of a new kind of knowledge into a consciousness that wants to preserve its familiar sense of security, but cannot deny the power of truth to change its way of seeing the world. And in all those places Milton does not tell us *how* that change is accomplished; he shows us the results of the change. Adam never speaks about the *experience* of disobedience; what Milton shows us is the change in Adam's speech and behavior after he has eaten of the apple. Samson may speak of "some rousing motions" stirring within him, but the moment of regeneration occurs offstage, away from our view, and in silence. We are not privy to Christ's inner debates in *Paradise Regained*; we listen to the results of that debate as he turns Satan's questions and offers back against him, and we watch Christ's actions. Milton asks always that we learn from the contemplation of his heroes' deeds; and the implicit command is that we try to understand their inward spiritual progress by testing our responses to their situations against theirs. It is in this sense that Milton's major poems are didactic, as well as in the more limited sense of conveying knowledge or doctrine to his audience. The epics and the closet drama teach by submitting us to the experience of trial; they guide our rational understanding by the example of dramatic figures who undergo trial and are moved to act on what they learn in consequence.

[11] *"Justa Edovardo King,"* *Notes and Queries*, n.s. 5 (1958):423–24.

Lycidas may, I think, be compared in some degree to these greater poems because the major instrument of its consolation is not the mere recounting of the swain's climactic vision of Lycidas's "large recompense," but the entire, complex process through which he both raises himself and is raised to the vantage point which grants him that vision. I have said that he delivers the consoling speech to the shepherds only after his imagination has surrendered its stiff self-will and allowed itself to follow the idea of Lycidas's corpse to the bottom of the sea. That surrender of the will elicits immediately the assurance of a corrective vision, which sees that Lycidas, "Sunk though he be beneath the wat'ry floor," is not dead because,

> So sinks the day-star in the Ocean bed,
> And yet anon repairs his drooping head,
> And tricks his beams, and with new-spangled Ore,
> Flames in the forehead of the morning sky.

Analogy as a means of discovering truth had been discredited in the progressive disarming of pastoral symbols and language; the equation of shepherd and poet, the swain had realized, does not suffice to explain or justify the true relationships between the poet and his world, or between the poet and the art to which he is called. What is at fault is not the idea of such relationships, but the misrepresentation of that idea inherent in the use of metaphor. Metaphor makes it seem that different realities can be fused by language; the swain realizes, however, that such fusion is brought about by the enlightened understanding, which uses language to reveal both differences and likenesses. And so in these lines the swain comes upon an analogy that brings into consonance the meaning of Lycidas's mortal tragedy, the psychic experience the swain himself is undergoing, and the traditional emblem of that power which guarantees the truth of the analogy and yokes all spiritual histories with their archetype, the "dear might of him that walk'd the waves." The elements of pastoral metaphor, which have been shown to be an incomplete picture of reality, are unfolded and exposed in a simile: "So sinks the day-star ... So Lycidas." The swain now sees, controls, and explains an identity that exists in natural and supernatural phenomena, rather than in the literary language he has inherited.

Thus it is important to notice that, as a part of the elegy, the

description of heaven's "other groves," "the blest Kingdoms
meek of joy and love," is no less an imaginative fiction than the
fields that first appeared "under the opening eyelids of the
morn." Here, as there, are companionship, music, sunlight, and
soothing liquids. The difference in our response to this setting
is not accountable simply by the deliberately muted presence
of Christ, but by the tone of the swain's speech. He speaks in a
timeless present, describing firmly and clearly what is, not what
once was or what is gone. And, finally, he takes upon himself
the cloak of prophecy and tells Lycidas what is to come out of
the grief and loss with which the poem began. Nor is the prophecy
complete without a gesture toward the swain's newly found responsibility to all shepherds, to "all that wander in that perilous flood." The dead shepherd will receive the meed of creation
as a tutelary "Genius," but the living poet is granted, and assumes, the charge of explaining the meaning of that uncertain
journey to all men who will embark upon it.

To assume such a charge requires both humility and confidence, and the tone of the speech displays both. The poet knows
that the "solemn troops, and sweet Societies" to which Lycidas
has been assimilated "sing, and singing in their glory move,"
but the song itself is beyond his powers to imitate. Nevertheless,
he accepts the burden, which must have been deeply vexing
for Milton, of sustaining both the memory and the prophetic
vision of that song in poetry which he knows to be only a shadow
of its harmonious source. The combination of confidence and
humility in his speech is exactly parallel to the ambiguous gifts
of knowledge the swain accepts as he assumes the obligations of
the true shepherd. The calling of priestly poetry confers special
powers and special responsibilities. The swain as the grieving
pastoral elegist had been conscious only of the talents that
separated him from other men, even from other poets. Peter's
speech had reminded him of the more important burdens of
the pastorate; but his response was a retreat, even if momentarily, into the fictive world of beauty and *otium*. Now, with the
acknowledgment of both his ability and his duty to speak of
true Christian consolation to "woeful Shepherds" whose salvation lies partially in the power of his inspired voice, he is given
a language adequate to the task he agrees to perform, a language both "answerable" and "in strictest measure ev'n" to the

"lot" toward which time and the course of the elegy have led him.

We can recognize in Milton's works throughout his life—from Sonnet VII to *Samson Agonistes*—a grating tension between his will to create the proof of his singular powers and his will to believe that acts of poetic creation should be and would be prompted by "some strong motion" instilled in him by "Time ... and the will of Heav'n." This tension is exhibited most clearly in Sonnet VII and in the figure of Samson; it is exposed and resolved in the invocations in *Paradise Lost*. But *Lycidas* is Milton's one attempt to dramatize the experience of that tension and to show how transcending it leads to the attainment of the poetic voice which alone can sustain the continuing act of creation which is the epic poem.

It is as a teacher, of course, that the swain speaks finally, and he teaches a truth that has not been uncovered by his reason in the course of the poem, but that has been borne in upon him by the action of the poem, as it responds to the guiding pressure of divine will. Milton is certainly playing on the word *uncouth* in the coda, for while the swain had been both uninstructed and unknown as he first laid his hands unwillingly upon the evergreen laurels, he is no longer ignorant. Nor, we are made to feel, will he be long unknown; the address we have just heard does not fit the characterization of a *"Doric* lay," and its majestic rhythms can be described as "warbling" only by the poet who knows fully how far his persona has traveled and what heights of wisdom and poetic brilliance he has attained. I find as much humor as serenity in the coda, because Milton is relying on our shocked rediscovery of the pastoral setting to remind us of the scope of the journey we have just undergone. We now find that the swain has been singing for the length of the imagined day, but that we have been raised out of the cycle of time in which we began; the magnificent, telling symbol of the "daystar" flaming "in the forehead of the morning sky" is once again simply the sun, now "dropt into the Western bay." The sensation is that of returning to a familiar, natural, real world; and we can appreciate the flourish of Milton's delighted skill when we remember that the reality to which we have been restored is the world of the literary pastoral, completely mastered and controlled by the poet whose voice we hear for the first time. This fiction has opened the way to a truth that can be expressed only in fictions; yet the discovery of that truth renders us, and the swain, forever unable to mistake fiction for what it is intended to represent.

That same discovery, the result of the process of self-education at the center of *Lycidas*, is, I think, the key to Milton's renovation of the conventional epic beginning, and to his successive re-creations of himself in the speakers of the several invocations in *Paradise Lost*. In the initial address to his "Heav'nly Muse," he defines her part in the process of writing the epic as assisting him to surpass the highest reaches of the classical epic, and to carry him toward the hitherto unattained excellences of Christian epic. I take that assistance to be conceived, at least in the first fifteen lines of the poem, as primarily stylistic. Milton asks the heavenly muse, in short, for the power to sustain a song that will tell man's history from the creation to the final triumph of Christ; to be more precise, he asks the muse to inspire and sustain a language the poet has already formed, during the patient and devoted years of study and practice.

But when he turns, in line 17, to what we may call the second invocation, we should be warned by his use of "chiefly" that Milton does not mean this to be the lesser request, an afterthought; quite the contrary. With that typical softening of focus that overtakes Milton's theological arguments as they move from *The Christian Doctrine* to *Paradise Lost*, the lines we are examining are addressed to a "Spirit" whose nature and rank are unspecified. But his function is clear and entirely consonant with the view of the Holy Spirit as the channel of saving knowledge. He is asked to "instruct"; the emphatic positioning of the word in line 19 is a sign that Milton is not simply appealing for the radical degree of knowledge demanded by *this* epic, but that he has also gone to the root meaning of the word, realizing that any human vessel, in order to contain such knowledge, must be remade. To follow the metaphor, he must be rebuilt, inherently constructed out of the knowledge infused in him by the Spirit. Thus, in another way Milton supports the notion, implicit in the Spirit's preference for the "upright heart and pure" "Before all Temples," that even the sanctity of Zion, the delight of the "Heav'nly Muse" whose aid he has so recently implored, is a less certain guarantee of prophetic truth than the actual regeneration of a soul by the truth conveyed by the Spirit.

The "great Argument" of *Paradise Lost*, of course, is truth —the truth of man's condition seen under the aspect of "Eternal Providence." In this opening invocation Milton prays for the kinds of assistance appropriate to the task of asserting that providence *while* revealing its justice to the audience of men. Although he places heavy emphases in the passage on his need for help, on that in him which is "low" and "dark," he speaks as if there is no doubt that, given the power to tell truth, he will inevitably succeed in the conjoint goal of creating assent to that truth. This air of untroubled confidence, which blends so unnoticeably with the suppliant tone of the invocation, may be accounted for, at least in part, by the fact that Milton chooses from the outset to implicate himself in the condition of the audience he is addressing. He speaks immediately of "our woe," looks forward to Christ's coming to "Restore us," and begins the narrative by referring to "our Grand Parents." This is not merely a variation of the familiar Miltonic device of "placing" the narrator and his listeners in the poem; it is also a declaration of Milton's solution to the unique problems facing a poet who chooses to sing to other men of divine and prophetic truths that no man can know simply by taking thought.

There are only the faintest suggestions of the garland and the singing robes in the figure of the poet Milton adumbrates in these lines. The grandeur and power of the epic role, qualities which had obsessed him in his youth, are muted and replaced by the weight of obligation he willingly assumes, his responsibility to "the chosen Seed." Milton's awareness of the change in his idea of the poet's role is shown, I think, in his deliberate identification of himself with Moses. The identity is asserted by the central term, *shepherd*, and through that term is extended to all the members of the line whose glory consisted in being burdened with the task of witnessing, explaining, justifying. In the consolation passage in *Lycidas* the swain had assumed a similar burden. But his audience were shepherds only by virtue of literary convention; the swain began as one of them and ended as a true shepherd, his state defined largely by his differences from them. Milton begins *Paradise Lost* in a voice that combines the hard-earned understanding of the swain and the stable, compassionate wisdom of the coda of *Lycidas*. That meaning of *shepherd* which is created by the long and intricate *agon* of *Lycidas* is the starting point of the epic. And once that meaning has been absorbed into the poet's idea of his relation to his subject, it leads unerringly to the massive, sustained, flexible, infinitely various union of sound and sense that is the music of *Paradise Lost*. Its keynote is the blending of humility and assurance that we hear in the first twenty-six lines, that incredibly exact rendering of the mind and impulses of a man praying to the Holy Spirit for gifts with which to instruct and solace his fellow men. In the climactic speech of consolation in *Lycidas* Milton drew a sketch for the full portrait he achieved in *Paradise Lost*.

Lycidas in Christian Time

Edward W. Tayler

"Thus sang the uncouth swain . . . " Thus begin the astonishing last lines of *Lycidas*, signifying that the poet has attained, in the course of writing the monody, the artistic distance that may be conferred only on those who have become fully a part of the tradition in which they write. The opening lines of the poem appear to sound by contrast an almost purely personal note:

> Yet once more, O ye Laurels, and once more
> Ye Myrtles brown, with Ivy never sere,
> I come to pluck your Berries harsh and crude.

Surely there is more to this "I" than the convention requiring the pastoral poet to represent himself as lisping in numbers? Surely (we think) this must be the young Milton, uncertain of his craft; his "forc'd fingers" are "rude," and he is again reluctant to test his powers before the "season due." Since the myrtles and the laurels symbolize immortal poetry, the words "yet once more" would seem to point toward earlier poetic creations: *Comus* perhaps? the Nativity Ode? or even the "Fair Infant Dying of a Cough"? And certainly I have no wish to argue that this pastoral monody wrote itself, no inclination even to imply that Milton failed to sense a parallel between Edward King, young priest and poet, and himself, young poet-priest.

From Milton's Poetry: its Development in Time (Pittsburgh, 1979), chap. 2; first published in *Huntington Library Quarterly* 41 (1978): 103–17; condensed for this book by the author.

But since the poet writes in special relation to his predecessors, the artistic—as distinct from the biographical—significance of the opening lines may be ascertained from the uses to which Milton has put the pastoral traditions. The poet in the pamphleteer confesses in the famous digression in *The Reason of Church-Government* that he aspires to do for England "what the greatest and choicest wits" of Greece and Rome as well as "those Hebrews of old did for their country"—"with this over and above," he adds, "of being a Christian."[1] Emphasis on Milton's "classicism" and "humanism" has led to neglect of the Christian pastoral of the Middle Ages as well as two even more important traditions of pastoral: that of "those Hebrews of old" and that which is "over and above" the Hebrew, the pastoral of the New Testament. Canticles, Psalms, the Prophets, and the Gospels are of course all deeply permeated by what James Holly Hanford, following Dr. Johnson, refers to as "inherently absurd" imagery.[2] The Lord is my shepherd, I shall not want. Ignoring the scriptural models also obscures one (Renaissance) aspect of classical pastoral itself, for medieval and later Christians habitually read the "choicest wits" in their own terms—rejecting in part, modifying in part, or even supposing that Vergil's Fourth Eclogue had prophesied the coming of the Messiah. In the sixteenth century Puttenham had these developments partly in mind when he acknowledged that the eclogue does not attempt merely to "counterfait or represent the rusticall manner of loues and communication: but vnder the vaile of homely persons, and in rude speeches to insinuate and glaunce at greater

---

[1] *John Milton: Complete Poems and Major Prose*, ed. Merritt Y. Hughes (New York, 1957), 668.

[2] James Hanford is of course concerned with defending the genre, though his masterly essay concludes with the rather forlorn hope that eventually we will "find ourselves forgetting that the pastoral imagery is inherently absurd" ("The Pastoral Elegy and Milton's *Lycidas*," above, 59). But no imagery is *inherently* absurd, and if we attend to Christian transformations of pastoral imagery, aesthetic amnesia will be unnecessary. Although Hanford notes that the genre was "to a certain degree changed in essence by its contact with Christianity," he does not seek to define the crucial changes because he feels (with W. W. Greg and others) that medieval pastoral "need detain us but a moment" (see, however, my *Nature and Art in Renaissance Literature* [New York, 1964], esp. 73–101). Hanford mentions the medieval "identification of the two kinds of 'pastor'," but he does not distinguish the traditions or appear to be aware that it is, crucially, identity with difference. Johnson's comments about the "inherent improbability" of pastoral will be found in the excerpt from *The Life of Milton*, above, 60.

matters."[3] Theocritus and Vergil in this context take their
clearly assigned places within the "greater matters" of Christian history, which means that in an important sense Milton had
not one but three "traditions" on which to draw and that their
relation each to the other rested on theological premises derived
from the language of biblical exegesis: Vergil, obscurely, and
"those Hebrews of old," less obscurely, shadowed forth the
"chief Shepherd" (1 Peter 5:4) of the New Testament.

And here, in this triple progression from antiquity through
the Old Testament to the New, lies part of the artistic significance of the opening lines of the poem: "Yet once more . . . and
once more." Probably because she had in mind only a "literary
context," Isabel MacCaffrey mistakenly felt that *Lycidas*, "almost alone among Milton's important poems, does not suggest
at the beginning how it will end."[4] But if we ignore for the moment the biographical and literary contexts, we are free to attend to the scriptural force of the allusion, which points unmistakably to Hebrews 12:22–28:

> Ye are come unto mount Sion, and unto the city of the living
> God, the heavenly Jerusalem, and to an innumerable company
> of angels . . . and to the spirits of just men made perfect. . . .
> See that ye refuse not him that speaketh. . . . Whose voice then
> shook the earth: . . . Yet once more I shake not the earth only,
> but also heaven. And this *word*, Yet once more, signifieth the
> removing of those things that are shaken . . . that those things
> which cannot be shaken may remain. Wherefore we receiving a
> kingdom which cannot be moved, let us have grace.

The relevance of these verses to the end as well as to the beginning of *Lycidas* will perhaps be obvious, but to appreciate the
full purport of these oracular utterances it helps to consult the
exegetes. The commentators understood the Apostle to be dis-
tinguishing two kinds of judgment—that under the Old from
that under the New Dispensation—and accordingly they explain that he

> commenteth vpon the Testimonie of Haggai, Chap. 2.6. and
> from this word *Once*, concludeth, That Heaven and Earth shall

---

[3] *The Arte of English Poesie*, ed. G. D. Willcock and A. Walker (Cambridge, 1936), 38.
[4] *"Lycidas*: The Poet in a Landscape," above, 246.

passe away. . . . That these chaungeable Heavens and Earth
being removed, Hee may make a Newe Heaven and a Newe
Earth . . . but *Once More*, and no oftener, is CHRIST to shake
the same. . . . All thinges made, shall be shaken: but CHRIST's
Kingdome, and the Salvation of His Subjectes, shall never bee
shaken.

The reference to Haggai reveals that the Apostle had first in
mind "the terrible quaking of the Earth, and burning of Mount
Sinai," secondly the way God's wrath "at the Daye of Iudge-
ment, may be seene in that little Resemblance of Mount Sinai."[5]
The mode of exegesis is typological, moving "from shadowy
Types to Truth" (*Paradise Lost*, 12.303); the author of Hebrews finds in the thunders and lightnings upon Sinai a type of
the Last Judgment, just as Milton in the Nativity Ode saw in
the "thunder" of the "trump of doom" the antitype of the "hor-
rid clang" on "mount Sinai."

All this helps to explain, insofar as explanation may be
needed, why this place in Hebrews is invariably compared with
2 Peter 3 ("new heavens and new earth") and with the Book of
Revelation, which heralds the New Jerusalem, "a new heaven and
a new earth," where God shall "wipe away all tears from their
eyes; and there shall be no more death . . . : for the former things
are passed away." (The conclusion of *Lycidas* draws heavily on
Revelation, especially 7:17, 19:9, and 21:4.) The symmetry of

[5] David Dickson, *A Short Explanation of Hebrewes* (Aberdeen, 1635),
306–7. Or see the compendious summaries in Matthew Poole, *Annotations
Upon the Holy Bible*, 2 vols. (3rd ed., corrected and enlarged by Sam Clark
and Edward Veale [London, 1696]), I, Kkkk2v–Kkkk3r. Cf. John Pearson, et
al., *Critici Sacri*, 9 vols. (London, 1660), 7. 4387. Thomas Wilson, *A Complete
Christian Dictionary*, 8th ed., additions by Bagwell and Sympson (London,
1678; 1st ed., 1612), under the heading "Shake Heaven and Earth," cites
Hebrews, connects the passage with 2 Peter, and contrasts the two Dispensa-
tions; cf. William Gouge, *A Learned . . . Commentary . . . Hebrewes* (Lon-
don, 1655), 369 of second pagination of second volume, and *A Commentarie on
Hebrewes by M. Iohn Calvin*, trans. Clement Cotton (London, 1605), 313.
David S. Berkeley, "A Possible Biblical Allusion in 'Lycidas'," *Notes and
Queries* 206 (1961): 178, first identified the passage in print, but the allusion
may have been turned to better uses by Louis Martz, "Who is Lycidas?,"
Yale French Studies 47 (1972): 170–88; and by Joseph Anthony Wittreich,
Jr., "A Poet Amongst Poets," *Milton and the Line of Vision*, ed. Wittreich
(Madison, Wis., 1975), 97–117. More recently, Mother M. Christopher
Pecheux, "The Dread Voice in *Lycidas*," *Milton Studies* 9 (1976): 221–41,
has made use of the phrase in arguing that the "voice" is not exclusively that
of St. Peter but a composite of Moses, Christ, and Peter. Although this kind
of syncretism is of course common enough, I hope my argument makes clear
that what counts in *Lycidas* is the *progression* from Apollo through St.
Peter to Christ.

the allusions emerges clearly: *Lycidas* begins with "Yet once more . . . and once more"; it proceeds to the "two-handed engine" (the Last Judgment seen under the aspect of Old Testament justice, the antitype of "that little Resemblance of Mount Sinai"), which "stands ready to smite once, and smite no more"; and it ends with "ruth" and "joy and love" (Judgment seen under the aspect of New Testament mercy), with the "unexpressive nuptial Song" of Revelation when the shepherds shall "weep no more . . . weep no more . . . weep no more," and "all the Saints above" shall "wipe the tears for ever from his eyes." In *Lycidas* the dread voice shakes the earth yet once more "so that those things that cannot be shaken may remain," and so that Lycidas himself may receive "grace" and a "kingdom that cannot be moved": "In the blest Kingdoms meek of joy and love." The word *more* sounds and sounds throughout the poem and, as is usual in Milton, the beginning of the poem prefigures its ending.

The network of allusion does more than connect the parts of the poem: "yet once more" defines the arrangement of the three main parts of the poem, for the phrase suggests, to the reader of *Lycidas* who is also a reader of Hebrews, the *way* in which "those things that are shaken" may be removed so that "those things which cannot be shaken may remain." And, finally, the allusion may be used to explain Milton's distinctive use of genre, for the three pastoral traditions not only relate specifically to each of the three main parts of the poem but also provide the means by which the poet modulates his singing voice.

The first fourteen lines define the situation and prefigure the major themes: "For *Lycidas* is dead, dead ere his prime." The first of the three main sections (ll. 15–84) begins by invoking the muses and reiterates the note of loss—"now thou art gone, and never must return." This lament for the shepherd-as-poet occasions the ineffectual appeal ("Ay me, I fondly dream") to the Nymphs and Calliope, which prompts the appropriate question about the value of strictly meditating the "thankless Muse" and finds the answer in the "perfect witness of all-judging *Jove*" who "pronounces lastly on each deed." The second section (ll. 85–131) repeats the pattern, beginning with an invocation and then reiterating the fact of loss: "That sunk so low that sacred head of thine." This lament for the shepherd-as-priest includes the ineffectual questions of Triton and brings up the relevant

problem of the good pastor in a corrupt church, locating the
answer this time in the "two-handed engine at the door." The
third section (ll. 132–85) also begins with an invocation and
also "dallies" with an ineffectual "surmise" (the flower passage),
then repeats the fact of loss—but this time only to reverse it.
Lycidas, here the shepherd-as-poet-and-pastor, who was "dead,
dead ere his prime," now "is not dead"; and Lycidas, who was
no more than "sunk so low," is now "sunk so low, but mounted
high." This section likewise ends in judgment, the merciful
judgment of the angel who "melts with ruth" and of him "that
walk'd the waves."[6] The last eight lines, invariably referred to as
ottava rima but perhaps more properly called *strambotto*,
conclude the poem. The movement of the three main parts, from
death to life, from sinking to mounting, and from despair to
consolation, may be easily reduced to the Christian commonplace
that we must lose life to gain it. Yet the order and relation of
the three movements is so calculated as to compel the reader to
reacknowledge the truth of the truism.

The forward movement of the monody may be viewed in one
of its aspects as an exercise in the critical history of literature,
for Milton has in the first two sections dealt with classical and
Old Testament "pastorals" in such a way that they find their
proper fulfillment in the "pastoral" of the New Testament. I
do not mean, of course, that there are no allusions, say, to the
New Testament in the second section (there are many, and they
preponderate) or that the first section is devoid of Christian
implications—only that the solutions to the problems presented
in each part must be associated, in turn, with classical consolation, with Old Testament vengeance, and with New Testament
mercy. It is this tripartite movement, identified in the minds of
Milton and his "fit . . . audience" with the rhythm of time "from
shadowy Types to Truth," that orders the ongoing momentum
of the poem and lends it its distinctive rhythm of anticipation
("yet once more") and fulfillment ("weep no more"). The shepherd is first the classical poet whose hope for immortality rests

---

[6] Arthur Barker, in a brilliant paragraph of his "The Pattern of Milton's
Nativity Ode," *University of Toronto Quarterly* 10 (1941): 171 ff., first drew
attention to the three-part pattern that has since received wide acceptance.
I owe a less obvious debt to Josephine Miles, whose subtle observations about
the way repeated words reveal the "motion from low to high" appears,
revised, in "The Primary Language of *Lycidas*," above, 86 ff.

on the fame of his pastoral verses ("that last infirmity of Noble mind"), which at first appears to be lost through premature death, though finally the solution is to understand that true fame is "no plant that grows on mortal soil" but is rather the "praise" of "all-judging Jove": "Of so much fame in Heav'n expect thy meed." This is to anticipate the end, but it is not yet the end. The shepherd is next the biblical pastor, whose trade is not to meditate the muse but to feed the "hungry Sheep," and whose preoccupation is not with poetic immortality but with eternal salvation or damnation, with the "massy Keys" of heaven and hell ("The Golden opes, the Iron shuts amain"). His practice of the "faithful Herdman's art" is threatened not by the blandishments of Amaryllis in the shade but by the corrupt clergy, whose "lean and flashy" pastorals "grate on their scrannel Pipes of wretched straw." His consolation lies not in the praise of Jove but in his reliance upon Old Testament justice, the judgment of the iron key:

> But that two-handed engine at the door
> Stands ready to smite once, and smite no more.[7]

This is of course the end, but it is not the entirety of the end; for we know that at the Second Coming Christ will temper justice with mercy, will use the golden key of the New Dispensation as well as the iron of the Old. The engine that remains ready to "smite once, and smite no more" in this way becomes part of the greater movement within the poem of "yet once more," which can be perfected only with the third, and last, of the three main sections. Lycidas, finally both the pastor and poet, "receiving a kingdom which cannot be moved," wanders the fields of eternal pastoral, "where other groves, and other streams along," and hears the pastoral verses of eternity as the saints above "sing, and singing in their glory move." Milton has, in effect, recapitulated the history of the pastoral genre.

[7] The "two-handed engine" refers to the "two massy Keys," though only one, that of iron, is fully relevant here. The keys of St. Peter were known in the controversial literature of the time as an *Engine*. In *Of the Power of the Keyes* (London, 1647), for example, Henry Hammond decries the use of the keys as *"engine of State"* (A1r) or as "an engine in the shape of a spiritual institution" for "secular advantage" (120–21), explaining that the power of the keys ought never to be "look't on as a meer engine," for he "that can take any *carnal* or *sensual* pleasure in the exercise of those Keyes, in the using of that sharp engine of surgery, or ever draw it," except in proper use, is one of the "sonnes of bloud" (A1v–A11).

The "Fair Infant," like *Lycidas*, consists of eleven stanzas;
and, like *Lycidas*, the "Fair Infant" sees the fact of death from
the twin perspectives of classical and Christian consolation. But
the "Fair Infant" fails, not only because the Spenserian diction
seems mannered and awkward but also because the poet appears
to have discovered no way as yet to integrate the two kinds of
consolation. In *Lycidas*, on the other hand, Milton perfectly
adjudicates the potentially conflicting claims of the two. It is
as if the poet had asked himself how classical pastoral, with its
implicit concern for immortality through poetic fame, might be
related to Christian pastoral, with its concern for immortality
through Christ. And the answer proceeds in an order that reflects
the characteristic movement of Christian time "from shadowy
Types" to the "Truth" of eternity.

Proleptic patterns appear even within sections, as when the
"Herald of the Sea" prepares us for the "Pilot of the *Galilean*
Lake." Had Milton specified Triton and St. Peter, the relation
would vanish, and it is in this sense that the amplitude of The
Grand Style may be viewed without contradiction as an instrument of poetic condensation. Although it is true and doubtless
important to recognize that *Lycidas* is moist with water imagery
(King did indeed die at sea, and the poem is appropriately a
"melodious tear"), the connection between the classical "Herald
of the Sea" and the "Pilot of the *Galilean* Lake" is not merely
associative, the result of poetic revery, for there is a qualitative
difference between the two, the first being a "little Resemblance"
of the other. "Identity," observes Wallace Stevens, "is the vanishing point of resemblance"; and if we argue—it has been
argued—that the pilot *is* Christ, then we lose the surge of fulfillment that derives from our seeing how the "Pilot of the *Galilean* Lake" has shadowed the truth of "him that walk'd the
waves." Identity, rather than "little Resemblance," would mean
that the poem had in a basic way "finished," completed its design, before the third section. (Similarly, if we take "all-judging
Jove" simply as Renaissance shorthand for "God," the poem
is in the same way completed before the second section.) But
Lycidas must be allowed its distinctive temporal dimension, as
the poet assimilates without rejecting the kinds of judgment appropriate to classical "immortality" and Old Testament vengeance. Phoebus Apollo may adumbrate the Son but cannot

provide a place for the virtuous heathen in a classical "heaven";
the god of the sun and of song can guarantee only an everlasting
meed of praise. And the justice of the Old Testament remains imperfect until fulfilled by the mercy of the Son. The movement is
dynamic, from the shadows of Time to the truths of Eternity.

More important is the *use* to which the poet puts the pastoral
genre in relation to the Christian end he contemplates for Edward King. Lycidas, who was *dead* and *sunk*, becomes Lycidas
who "is not dead," "sunk though he be beneath the wat'ry floor."
Lycidas is "sunk low, but mounted high," and it is this oscilla-
tion between low and high that defines the manner in which the
pastoral singer modulates his voice.

The allusion to Vergil's Fourth or Messianic Eclogue in the
third line of the opening invocation—

> Begin then, Sisters of the sacred well,
> That from beneath the seat of *Jove* doth spring,
> Begin, and somewhat loudly sweep the string—

advertises Milton's intention to imitate the Latin poet in rising
above the low style, supposed (purely by convention) to be appropriate to pastoral, and to sing of greater matters.[8] Milton
accordingly somewhat loudly sweeps the string, rising to consider the blind Fury and the witness of Jove. Imitating the imitation (Vergil's) of still another of the "choicest wits" of
antiquity (Theocritus), Milton uses the norm of classical pastoral in order to transcend it. And precisely the same motive
governs the invocation that begins the second section:

> O Fountain *Arethuse*, and thou honor'd flood,
> Smooth-sliding *Mincius*; crown'd with vocal reeds,
> That strain I heard was of a higher mood:
> But now my Oat proceeds . . .

Since Arethuse, the spring near the birthplace of Theocritus,
points to the Greek pastoral poet, and Mincius, the river near the
birthplace of Vergil, alludes to the Latin writer, Milton is con-
versing across the centuries with the "choicest wits" of Greece

---

[8] Vergil (*Sicelides Musae paulo maiora canamus*) had invoked his own
great predecessor to "take a higher flight" (so rendered by John Ogilby, *Works*
[London, 1654], 19). Ogilby's annotation is standard: "alluding to *Theocritus*
the Sicilian Poet, whose Imitatour our Author in these Eclogs professes
himself to be."

and Rome, first to acknowledge that he has in his turn violated the decorum of pastoral ("That strain I heard was of a higher mood") and then to submit that he is once more observing the literary amenities ("now my Oat proceeds"). Yet the poet promptly modulates again, rising to the vision of the pilot of the Galilean lake and the dreaded engine at the door.

The third section repeats the pattern precisely:

> Return *Alpheus*, the dread voice is past,
> That shrunk thy streams; Return Sicilian Muse . . .

Alpheus, the river of Arcady, alludes to Vergil and corresponds to Mincius in the preceding section; the Muse of Sicily, Theocritus, here takes the place of the earlier Arethuse; and the "dread voice" parallels the "higher mood" of the earlier section. Once again Milton maintains decorum (the flower passage) for only a moment, rising from the low style of the oaten pipe and reaching for a strain of higher mood—not this time a voice of greater dread but one of immeasurable mercy, the "great vision of the guarded Mount" and the "dear might of him that walk'd the waves."

From the moment that Milton begins somewhat loudly to sweep the string, he is engaged in a conscious, even self-conscious, dialogue with his illustrious precursors, and the dialogue grows in complexity as he proceeds. Much has been written of the speakers and their dramatic contexts in *Lycidas*; but the most important speaker is, after all, the pastoral singer himself, and it may be that the most important dramatic situation defines Milton's relation to the "choicest wits" of pagan antiquity. Milton speaks to his predecessors, calling them by name in the language of pastoral allusion; he invokes their presence neither to legitimize, nor to preside over, his present endeavor, but rather to show that their vision of nature, while lovely enough "to interpose a little ease," remains at best a "fond," at worst a "false surmise." Return, Alpheus (speak again, Vergil), says Milton, knowing that readers of Ovid had learned how in another sense Alpheus had already "returned."

Alexander Ross retails the geographical facts: "*Alphaeus* is a river of Elis in Arcadia, through secret passages running under the earth & sea, it empties it self in the spring *Arethusa* in

Sicilie; which though Strabo denyeth it, it cannot be otherwise, seeing so many witnesses confirm that whatsoever is cast into *Alphaeus* is found in *Arethusa*."[9] The river god Alpheus had fallen in love with Arethusa, a wood nymph, she, transformed into a subterranean stream, fled to Ortygia, where she rose as a fountain, but Alpheus, the Arcadian stream, pursued her underground to mingle his waters with hers in Sicily. All of this not only explains Ross's "facts"; it also indicates the complexity of Milton's dialogue with antiquity. As by mythological allusion Vergil (Alpheus) pursued the streams of pastoral to its fountain or source in Theocritus (Arethuse),[10] so by literary allusion Milton turns to his own fountains or sources, that is, to Theocritus by way of Vergil. This elaborate conversation with antiquity testifies to Milton's attempt to do what the "choicest wits" of Greece and Rome and "those Hebrews of old" had done—but "with this over and above" of being a Christian.

The nature of the dialogue points to the artistic function of pagan pastoral. It is the standard from which the poet varies, the stable medium from which he may rise to "greater matters" and to which he may then return. It is "imitation"—but only in the Renaissance sense of *overgoing*; Theocritus and Vergil are guides, not commanders. Analogous to meter in poetry, the pastoral genre is the norm against which the reader measures variations, the means by which he can grasp the significance of the singer's modulations. This particular norm, with just such variations, must have seemed singularly appropriate to readers before Dr. Johnson: the pastoral genre, as Renaissance critics never tired of repeating, occupies the lowest degree in the hierarchy of literary *kinds*, and Christianity, many still repeat, is the religion of the humble, of the meek who shall inherit the earth. Since the pastoral care of the chief shepherd was not for the proud but the humble, many Christian writers, most notably Augustine, tended to invert not only the pagan hierarchy of social values but also the classical hierarchy of styles. In Christian theology

---

[9] *Mystagogus Poeticus* (London, 1648), 16–17.
[10] In annotating the Tenth Eclogue Ogilby observes that Vergil "invokes his Muse, *Arethusa* the Sicilian Nymph in relation (as more than once already) to *Theocritus*."

man gains life by losing it and rises by being "lowly wise," which is one of the better reasons Milton can use the lowest of the genres to utter the highest truths.

In using the pastoral as a standard from which to depart significantly, Milton reanimates the Christian commonplace that is the consolation for the loss of Lycidas. *Lycidas* is so constructed that as a poem it does exactly what Lycidas himself is described as doing; the pastoral poem sinks in order to mount, just as the pastoral figure sinks in order to mount, with the result that structure reflects theme, structure mirrors meaning. From the beginning ("Yet once more") we have anticipated the end, though we do not arrive there immediately but in three successive waves, the crest of each being "higher" than the one before; we are required to stand and wait two times before fulfillment. Once in the first section Milton somewhat loudly sweeps the string; once more in the second section; and yet once more in the third. The poet, that is, sinks yet once more to rise to the final affirmations: "So Lycidas sunk low, but mounted high." In terms such as these we may see that the poem not only recapitulates the history of pastoral but also, and more significantly, uses that history as a mimetic reinforcement of its main theme. Both *Lycidas* and Lycidas sink in order to mount. By what may be thought of as an almost muscular effort of the verse itself—the successive movements of the three sections—Milton readies us to acknowledge yet once more the truth of the Christian truism, for this pastoral monody owes a large part of its artistic success to its having been constructed in imitation of itself. *Lycidas* endures, triumphantly, as a work of art that *is* what it *says*.

The *commiato* or coda reverts to the pastoral norm with astounding abruptness: "Thus sang the uncouth Swain . . . . " Uncouth indeed! In the introductory epistle to Gabriel Harvey, E. K. applies Chaucer's "uncouthe, unkiste" to "this our new poete" Spenser (and his pastorals), "who for that he is uncouthe (as said Chaucer) is unkist, and unknown to most men . . . ."[11] But while the word may mean *unknown*, there is no way that either a seventeenth- or twentieth-century reader can isolate

[11] Edmund Spenser, *Complete Poetical Works*, ed. R. E. Neil Dodge (Cambridge, Mass., 1936), 5.

the connotations of ignorant and rude and seal them hermetically under a bell jar—which must have afforded the poet some mild amusement. The use of the past tense and the third person, as the "I" of line 3 suddenly becomes the "uncouth Swain" of line 186, has intensified our sense of shocked surprise; the pastoral singer becomes persona, receives his generic designation only with the final lines, just as the monody proper receives its generic status as a song within a narrative frame only with the concluding lines. "As the impersonal voice addresses us," says Isabel MacCaffrey, "we become co-listeners, and as the foreground recedes into the middle distance we find ourselves paradoxically in a more intimate relation to it," for "we have heard the same song." [12] It is as though we had been forced to look through the wrong end of the telescope, for first we watch the first-person singer, the "I" of line 3, recede suddenly, now an "uncouth Swain," into the pastoral landscape occupied by the "young swain" Lycidas; but then the artistic distance narrows once more, not only because we have heard the same song but also because the coda itself so much resembles the song. The "still morn" goes out with "sandals gray," as if human; the shepherd's pipe has "tender stops," as though sentient. The swain's "lay" is *Doric*," in allusion to Theocritus; and the sun stretches out the hills, in a line that imitates the last verse of Vergil's First Eclogue. We have heard the same song, and now we share the same landscape.

The opening lines of *Lycidas* establish two resonant parallels: first, that between the natural circle of the days and seasons ("mellowing year") and the circle of human life, though the point is at first to lament that one human life—Lycidas "dead ere his prime"—failed of "season due." The second parallel is between the poetic act, the writing of the poem, and the subject of the poem, the death of Lycidas—both of which are assumed, at first, to be premature, "crude" or unripe (*crudus*), though the once-reluctant swain will at last come to sing with "eager thought." The circle of the seasons and of the day somehow resembles the cycle of human life, and in some way resembles the act of poetic creation. But since the resemblances are not identities, there is occasion for discomfort and grief. The

[12] "Lycidas: The Poet in a Landscape," above, 265.

natural cycles are at first imperfectly understood; specifically, we presume too much if we suppose that Lycidas did not in some way find his "season due." As Sir Thomas Browne says, "Let them not therefore complaine of immaturitie that die about thirty," for there is "some other hand that twines the thread of life than that of nature."[13] Milton's task must be to reveal that the circle of poetic creation in art can only be truly completed through reference to a realm that includes and transcends nature. The task must be to show—poetic and theological resolution require it—that the cycles of nature and time may be truly understood only in relation to the realm of grace and eternity. To think otherwise (with Theocritus and Vergil) is to "fondly dream," is to dally with "false surmise"; the flower passages and the appeal to the nymphs of nature represent the norm of the oaten flute, nature as it is depicted in the beautiful but partial truths of Theocritus and Vergil. The analogy between nature and grace, time and eternity, truly exists, but it was hidden in types and shadows until the coming of "him that walk'd the waves." We as readers must at last be enabled to recognize, with Jesus in *Paradise Regained*, that God is "He in whose hand all times and seasons roll." It is what Abdiel tries to tell Satan, whose obduracy blinds him to the vanishing points of resemblance, in *Paradise Lost*: "God and Nature bid the same."

Lycidas is an idyll or picture that lacks one half of its frame. Since the narrative frame appears only with the coda, there is a sense in which the poem itself is at first not ripe, its pastoral singer a shadowy type not yet seen in true perspective—a singer nearly anonymous, piping before his "season due." In time the singer will receive a name, a generic designation consonant with his literary predecessors and his present purpose. But meanwhile we as readers, lacking the artistic distance conferred by the device of the narrative frame common to so many eclogues, become directly implicated in the movement of the poem, following the "I" of line 3 in sweeping the string—once, once more, and yet once more. Twice the pastoral singer defers the true consolation, then without transition (because it must carry something of the force and immediacy of revelation) there comes the lyric peripety in the form of the rhetorical charge to the shepherds, that is, to all of us who are natural, fallen men, we who must,

[13] *Religio Medici*, 1:43, ed. L. C. Martin (Oxford, 1964), 41.

like Adam and Eve, drop "some natural tears": "Weep no more, woeful Shepherds weep no more." With the singer, we have been sinking in order to rise, until finally we have been readied to experience the true meaning of the circles of nature:

> So sinks the day-star in the Ocean bed,
> And yet anon repairs his drooping head,
> And tricks his beams, and with new-spangled Ore,
> Flames in the forehead of the morning sky:
> So *Lycidas*, sunk low, but mounted high . . .

Here is transformed the "Star that rose, at Ev'ning, bright," here is the true surmise of what occurs "under the opening eyelids of the morn." Nature, as depicted by Theocritus and Vergil, can only mourn and can reveal only that Lycidas is sunk beneath the watery floor; but as the great vision looks homeward with mercy, we perceive the true relation of nature to grace. The natural cycle that had been interrupted within nature and time before the season due has been perfected in the eternal realm. Three times, following the efforts of the pastoral singer, we have sought the greatest vision, each time mounting higher than the time before, until at last we see the analogy of the sun made good by the Son—no fond dream, no false surmise. It is the "season due."

"Thus sang the uncouth swain . . . " And the song has moved from the personal to the impersonal, from the vision bounded by time to the vision of eternity. The swain, no longer merely unknown and rustic, may now bear as well the other meanings of *uncouth* that were current at the time: marvelous, uncommon, strange, wonderful—as in the "uncouth Revelations" of St. Bridgit (1648; cited OED). And Milton may conclude in accord with the revelation given those who have heard the same song, shared the same landscape:

> And now the Sun had stretch't out all the hills,
> And now was dropt into the Western bay;
> At last he rose, and twitch't his Mantle blue:
> Tomorrow to fresh Woods, and Pastures new.

The swain gets up—though as natural men we legitimately might have expected him to lie down—and firmly secures (twitches) his mantle against the chill of evening. But "Sun" is in fact the nearest grammatical antecedent of the "he" in

"he rose," and of course we know that the sun drops into the
western bay only to arise at last attired in its blue mantle.[14]
We may expect that in the evening the swain will lie down and
that the sun will do no more than drop into the bay, but in the
economy of *this* poem one sinks only to mount yet once more,
at long last to the "fresh Woods, and Pastures new" of the
Chief Shepherd. The uncouth swain, like Lycidas and the sun
and the Son and (hopefully) the reader, sinks in order to rise
"at last"; that these parallels "work" seems to imply a rare
kind of imaginative integrity in the poet. Milton, with "this
over and above of being a Christian," speaks across the years to
the "choicest wits" of pagan pastoral and exemplifies what it
means to pronounce "yet once more" in the poetic syntax of
Christian time, moving from "shadowy Types to Truth."

[14] As in lines 169–70 where "*his*" refers exclusively to the "day-star" or sun.
(*His* was the original genitive neuter, and while *its* was coming into general
use during the early seventeenth century, it was apparently regarded as
rather colloquial or newfangled, for it was avoided by the writers of the
King James version of 1611. In his poetry Milton tends to avoid *its*.) The
"we" of line twenty–three also reveals functional ambiguity, although it
refers, logically, to the pastoral singer and Lycidas, its nearest grammatical
antecedent is "he" ("some gentle Muse"), which means that "we" includes
past and future, as well as present, pastoral singers, emphasizing the con-
tinuities that are the subject of the passage and, ultimately, the poem as a
whole.

Lycidas: A Poem Finally Anonymous

Stanley E. Fish

I. THE SWAIN SPEAKS

Much of *Lycidas* criticism is an extended answer to those who, in the tradition of Dr. Johnson, see the poem as an "irreverent combination" of "trifling fictions" and "sacred truths," or as a lament marred by intrusive and unassimilated digressions, or, more sympathetically, as "an accumulation of magnificent fragments,"[1] or simply (and rather notoriously) as a production more "willful and illegal in form" than any other of its time.[2] This last judgment—it is John Crowe Ransom's in his famous essay "A Poem Nearly Anonymous"—indicates the extent to which the poem has been brought before the bar. The indictment has included, among others, the following charges: the tenses are inconsistent and frustrate any attempt to trace a psychological progression; there are frequent and unsettling changes in style and diction; the structure is uncertain, hesitating between monologue, dialogue, and something that is not quite either; the speaker assumes a bewildering succession of poses; the lines on Fame are poorly integrated; the procession

---

From *Glyph: Johns Hopkins Textual Studies*, 8, ed. Walter B. Michaels (Baltimore, 1981), Ch. 1.
[1] G. Wilson Knight, *The Burning Oracle* (London, 1939), 70.
[2] "A Poem Nearly Anonymous," above, 75; first published in 1933.

of mourners is perfunctory; the Pilot's speech is overlong and overharsh; the flower passage is merely decorative; the Christian consolation (beginning "Weep no more, shepherds") is unconvincing and insufficiently prepared for; the shift to the third person in the final lines is disconcerting and without any persuasive justification. Together and individually, these characterizations constitute a challenge to the poem's unity, and it is as an assertion of unity that the case for the defense is always presented.

Typically, that defense proceeds by first acknowledging and then domesticating the discontinuities that provoke it. Thus William Madsen observes that the voice that says "Weep no more, shepherds" at line 165 does not sound at all like the voice we have been listening to; but no sooner does he note this breach in the poem's logic then he mends it by assigning the line and what follows to the angel Michael,[3] although he fails to explain, as Donald Friedman points out, why among all the speakers in *Lycidas*, Michael is the only one who "is introduced without comment or identification."[4] Friedman himself is concerned with another moment of disruption, occasioned by the voice of Phoebus whose unexpected appearance as a speaker in the past tense blurs the narrative line and creates a "confusion about the nature of the utterance we are listening to." That confusion, however, is only "momentary," at least in Friedman's argument, where it is soon brought into a relationship with "the coda in which Milton subsumes the entire experience of the swain." That coda, of course, brings its own problem, for as Stewart Baker observes, the appearance, after 185 lines, of a third person narrator constitutes a "surprise"; but after acknowledging the surprise in the opening sentence of his essay, Baker proceeds to accommodate it, and by the time he finishes, it has been removed, along with St. Peter's dread voice, as a possible threat "to the poem's unity."[5] Defending the poem's unity is also the concern of H. V. Ogden, who writes in part to refute G. Wilson Knight's characterization of *Lycidas* "as an effort to bind and clamp together a universe trying to fly off

[3] *From Shadowy Types to Truth* (New Haven, 1968), 13.
[4] *"Lycidas*: The Swain's Paideia," *Milton Studies* 3 (1971): 33 (condensed above, 281 ff.).
[5] "Milton's Uncouth Swain," *Milton Studies* 3 (1971): 35–50.

into separate bits."[6] Ogden cannot but acknowledge that the poem abounds in "abrupt turns in new directions," but these turns are explained or explained away by invoking the seventeenth-century principle of "aesthetic variety," and one can almost hear Ogden's sigh of relief as he declares triumphantly that "*Lycidas* is a disciplined interweaving of contrasted passages into a unified whole."[7]

Examples could be multiplied, but the pattern is clear: whatever *Lycidas* is, *Lycidas* criticism is "an effort to bind and clamp together a universe trying to fly off into separate bits." It is, in short, an effort to put the poem together, and the form that effort almost always takes is the putting together of an integrated and consistent first person voice. Indeed, it is the assumption that the poem is a dramatic lyric and hence the expression of a united consciousness that generates the pressure to discover a continuity in the narrative. The unity in relation to which the felt discontinuities must be brought into line is therefore a *psychological* unity; the drama whose coherence everyone is in the business of demonstrating is mental. In the history of the criticism that coherence has been achieved by conceiving of the speaker as an actor in one of several possible biographical dramas: he may be remembering a past experience from a position of relative tranquility (the position of the last eight lines); or he may be performing a literary exercise in the course of which he creates a naive persona (the uncouth swain); or he may be in the process of breaking out of the conventional limitations imposed on him by a tradition; or he may be passing from a pagan to a Christian understanding of the world and the possibilities it offers him. The readings are written in opposition to one another, but in fact they all share an assumption that is made explicit by John Henry Raleigh when he declares that "*Lycidas* is an existential poem. . . . It is about 'becoming,' the emergence of the ego to its full power."[8] Given this assumption, the poem can only be read as one in which the first person speaker is a seventeenth-century anticipation of a Romantic hero.

[6] Knight, *The Burning Oracle*, 70.
[7] "The Principles of Variety and Contrast in Seventeenth-Century Aesthetics and Milton's Poetry," *Journal of the History of Ideas* 10 (1949): 159–82.
[8] "*Lycidas*: 'Yet Once More,'" *Prairie Schooner* 42 (1968): 317.

The notorious exception to this way of dealing with *Lycidas* is John Crowe Ransom, who explains the discontinuities in the poem as evidence of a failure to *suppress* the ego, a failure to realize the proper poetic intention of remaining "always anonymous." In Ransom's account, the "logical difficulties of the work," the shifts in tense, the changes in tone, the interpolations of different speakers, the roughness of verse, are the intrusive self-advertisements of a poet who cannot keep himself out of his poem, who is "willful and illegal" so that "nobody will make the mistake of not remarking his personality." In general the Milton establishment has not been impressed by Ransom's argument which is now viewed as something of a curiosity. In what follows, I will attempt to revive it, but with a difference. Ransom is right, I believe, to see that the shifts and disruptions in the poem reflect a tension between anonymity and personality; but I do not think, as he seems to, that the personality in the poem is triumphant because it is irrepressible. Indeed, it will be my contention that the suppressing of the personal voice is the poem's achievement and that the energy of the poem derives not from the presence of a controlling and self-contained individual, but from forces that undermine his individuality and challenge the fiction of his control. If the poem records a struggle of personality against anonymity, it is a struggle the first person speaker loses, and indeed, the triumph of the poem occurs when his voice can no longer be heard.

That voice, when we first encounter it, is heard complaining about the task to which it has been called by "sad occasion." The complaint is all the more bitter because it takes the form of an apology. "I am sorry to have to do this to you," the speaker says to the apostrophized berries, but what he is really sorry about is something that has been done to him. The double sense of the lines is nicely captured in the ambiguity of "forc'd" in line 4 ("And with forc'd fingers rude"), which can be read either as a characterization of his own action or as an indictment of that which has made the action necessary (he is forced to do the forcing). In the same way, "rude" is at once a deprecation of his poetic skills and an expression of anger at having to exercise them prematurely: his fingers are rude because they have been forced to an unready performance. The pretense of an apology is continued through line 5, where it is once again undermined by the phrase "the mellowing year." Thomas Warton objected to an "inaccuracy" here because the " 'the mellowing year' could not affect the leaves of the laurel, the myrtle, and the ivy . . . characterized before as 'never sere.' "[9] Just so. The "inaccuracy" is there to call an ironic and mocking attention to the inappropriateness of the apology: the laurel, the myrtle, and the ivy have no "mellowing year" to shatter; what has been shattered, in different ways, are the mellowing years of Lycidas and the speaker; and it is in response to the violence (interruption) done to them that these lines are spoken. By the time we reach line 7 it is impossible to read "disturb your season due" as anything but a bitter joke. It is the speaker's season that has been disturbed and by a disturbance (the death of Lycidas) even more final; and it is with the greatest reluctance that he is compelled to give voice to this "melodious tear" (14).

This posture of reluctance is one often assumed by Milton's characters, most notably by the Attendant Spirit in *Comus*, who is more than a little loath to leave the "regions mild of calm and serene air" (4) for the "smoke and stir of this dim spot, / Which men call earth" (6). It is also the posture in which Milton likes to present himself in the prose tracts, so that, typically he will declare with what small willingness he leaves the "still time" of his studies to engage in "tedious antiquities and disputes,"[10] or he will announce that only in response to the "earnest and serious conjurements" of a friend has he been "induc't" to break off pursuits "which cannot but be a great furtherance . . . to the enlargement of truth."[11] The labor to which he is called in these tracts is always an *interruption*, something that comes between him and a preferred activity, a discontinuity that threatens the completion of his real work.

This is especially true of *The Reason of Church Government*, in which his situation, as he characterizes it, exactly parallels that of the speaker in *Lycidas*. He writes, he tells us, "out of mine owne season when I have neither yet compleated to my minde the full circle of my private studies."[12] "I did not," he

    [9] *Milton's "Lycidas"*, ed. Scott Elledge (New York, 1966), 259.
    [10] *An Apology against a Pamphlet* in *The Complete Prose Works of John Milton*, gen. ed. Don M. Wolfe (New Haven, 1953 ff.), 1:953.
    [11] *Of Education* in *Prose Works*, 2:363.
    [12] *Prose Works*, 1:807. The ensuing quotations are from 808, 810, 820, and 821–22.

says, "choose this manner of writing, wherin knowing myself
inferior to myself . . . I have the use . . . but of my left hand."
He would rather be "soaring in the high region of his fancies
with his garland and singing robes about him," where, in response to the "inward prompting" of thoughts that have long
"possest" him, he "might perhaps leave something so written to
aftertimes, as they should not willingly let it die." It is from
those exalted "intentions" that he has been "plucked" by the
"abortive and foredated discovery" of the present occasion
("sad occasion dear") and he knows that the reader will understand how reluctant he is "to interrupt the pursuit of no less
hopes than these . . . to imbark in a troubled sea of noises and
hoars disputes, put from beholding the bright countenance of
truth in the quiet and still air of delightful studies." In *Lycidas*,
the still and quiet air of studies is punctuated by the "Oaten
Flute" and by the song beloved of "old Damoetus," but as in *The
Reason of Church Government*, this is a lost tranquility now
recollected from the vantage point of a present turmoil, of a
"heavy change" (37). In both contexts the change is the occasion for premature activity, for the hazarding of skills that are
not yet ready in the performance of a task that is unwelcome.

There is one great difference however. The Milton of *The Reason of Church Government*, like the Attendant Spirit in *Comus*,
is soon reconciled to that task because he is able to see it not
as an interruption, but as an extension of the activity from
which he has been called away. He may be "put from beholding
the bright countenance of truth," but it is as a witness to the
same truth that he takes up the labor forced upon him by the
moment. All acts performed in response to the will of God are
equally virtuous, and "when God commands to take the trumpet
and blow a dolorous or a jarring blast, it lies not in man's will
what he shall say." Indeed, "were it the meanest underservice, if
God by his secretary conscience enjoin it," then it is impossible
for a man to draw back. It is the same reasoning that leads him
in *Of Education* to accede to the entreaties of Hartlib, for although the reforming of education is not the pursuit to which
the love of God was taking him, he is able to see the present assignment as one "sent hither by some Good providence" and
therefore as an opportunity to manifest that same love. In *An*

Apology, he has decided, even before he descends to the dis-
agreeable business of replying to slanders and calumnies, that it
is his duty to do so, lest the truth and "the religious cause" which
he had "in hand" be rendered "odious." "I conceaved myself," he
declares, "to be not now as mine own person, but as a member
incorporate into that truth whereof I was perswaded."

This conception of himself as "not . . . mine owne person" is
essential to his ability to see the disrupting activity as an instance or manifestation of the activity from which he has been
unwillingly torn. That is, the disruption looms large only from
the perspective of his personal desires—he would rather be
writing poetry, or reading the classics, or furthering some long-
term project—but from the vantage point of the truth whereof
he is but a member incorporate, there is no disruption at all,
simply a continuity of duty and service. It is here that the point
of contrast with the speaker in *Lycidas* is most obvious: he takes
everything *personally*, and as a consequence, whatever happens
is seen only as it relates to the hopes he has for his own career.
This, of course, is the great discovery of twentieth-century criticism, that in *Lycidas* Milton "is primarily taking account of
the meaning of the experience to himself";[13] but for Milton to
be *primarily* doing this is for him to be doing something very
different from what he does in the prose tracts where egocentric
meanings are rejected as soon as they are identified. That is, the
stance of the speaker in *Lycidas* is anomalous in the Milton
canon; for rather than relinquishing the conception of himself
as "his owne person," he insists on it, and by insisting on it he
resists incorporation into a body of which he is but an extending
member.

Indeed, insofar as the poem can be said to have a plot, it
consists of the speaker's efforts to resist assimilation. He does
this in part by maintaining an ironic distance from the conventions he proceeds to invoke. As we have seen, that irony is com-
pounded largely of bitterness, and it takes the form both of
questioning the adequacy of the conventions to the occasion and
of claiming a knowledge superior to any the conventions are able
to offer. Irony is itself a mode of superiority: the ironic voice always issues from a perspective of privilege and presents itself

[13] James H. Hanford, *A Milton Handbook* (New York, 1926).

as having penetrated to meanings that have been missed by the naive and the innocent. The ironic voice, in short, always knows *more*.

In this case it knows more than the traditions of consolation; it knows that they are fictions, false surmises. The method in the opening sections is to let these fictions have their say, only so that the speaker can enter to expose their shallowness. "He must not float upon his wat'ry bier" seems as we read it to be the sentiment of someone who believes that there is something to be done, but that belief is dismissed and mocked by the first word of line 13, "Unwept." He will, in fact, continue to float on his watery bier, and the only thing that will be done is what the speaker is doing now, producing laments in the form of "some melodious tear" (14). This characterization of his own activity is slighting, but it does not mean that he is assuming a stance of modesty or self-deprecation; the criticism extends only to the means or tools, and not to the workman who finds them inadequate. It is their failure and not his that is culpable; and indeed, his recognition, even before he employs them, that they will not do the job, validates the superiority of his perception.

Even when the pastoral conventions are invoked they are invoked in such a way as to call into question their capacities. The elegy proper begins with an echo of Virgil's messianic eclogue: "Begin . . . and somewhat loudly sweep the string." That eclogue, however, specifically promises to transcend the genre, and therefore to invoke it is already to assume the insufficiency of the tradition in the very act of rehearsing its tropes. One of those tropes is the recollection of past delights, and it is given an extended, even lingering evocation in lines 25–36 (the lines to which Dr. Johnson so objected); but even as we listen, in the place of "old Damoetas," to this song, we are aware, with Douglas Bush, that it is "a picture of pastoral innocence, of carefree youth unconscious of the fact of death."[14] We therefore hear it with *condescension* and with an expectation that it will be succeeded by a perspective less naive. As a result, when the speaker breaks in with "But O the heavy change" (37), the tone may be elegiac, but the gesture is a triumphant one, made by someone who is able to present himself as "sadder, but wiser." What he

[14] A. S. P. Woodhouse and Douglas Bush, eds., *A Variorum Commentary on the Poems of John Milton* (London and New York, 1972), 2:2.647.

is wiser than is the pastoral mode and all of the ways by which it attempts to render comfortable what is so obviously distressing. One of those ways is the doctrine of natural sympathy, which would tell us that in response to the death of Lycidas, "the Willows and the Hazel Copses green / Shall now no more be seen" (42–43) ; but that assertion is allowed to survive only for the moment before the succeeding line at once completes the syntax and, in an ironic reversal, changes the meaning: "Shall now no more be seen / Fanning their joyous Leaves to thy soft layes." The willows and the hazel copses green will in fact be seen, but they will be seen fanning their joyous leaves to someone else's soft lays, for it is Lycidas who will be "no more." This new meaning does not simply displace, but mocks the old: "how foolish of any one to believe that nature takes notice of the misfortunes of man." Obviously, the speaker is not such a one, and as always, the superimposition of his perspective on the perspective of the convention has the effect of establishing him in a removed and superior position. He maintains this position even when he appears to be turning on himself. "Aye me, I fondly dream" (56) has the form of a self-rebuke, but the fondness is displaced onto the tradition and its representative figures, the nymphs, the bards, the druids, the Muses, Orpheus, and even Universal Nature. It is their ineffectiveness that has led the speaker to break off his performance and to exclaim, "for what could that have done; / What could the Muse herself that Orpheus bore" (57–58). What *he* can do, and very effectively, is to see and say just that and so disassociate himself from the failures he continues to expose.

I am aware that in the more orthodox accounts of the poem this questioning of pastoral efficacy has received another reading, and is seen not as evidence of egocentricity, but as a kind of heroism. B. Rajan, for example, reads the poem as the anguished discovery by the first person voice that ritual and tradition are inadequate when confronted by the "assault of reality." [15] The poem is thus an attack on "its own assumptions," an attack that is "mounted by the higher mood against the pastoral form." In the struggle that ensues, "convention and elementality are the basic forces of contention," and for "elementality" we may read the personal voice, characterized by Rajan,

[15] *"Lycidas:* The Shattering of the Leaves," above, 275.

as the "cry out of the heart of experience." His argument is more finely tuned than Raleigh's, but its point is the same: *Lycidas* is about becoming, the emergence of the ego to its full power; or in Rajan's more guarded vocabulary, "it is a voyage toward recognition," a recognition that is won to some extent at the expense of the claims to adequacy of pastoral and other ritual or public forms.

For Rajan, then, the contest between the conventional and the real or personal is the story the poem tells; what I am suggesting is that it is a story *the speaker* tells, and that he tells it in an effort to situate himself in a place not already occupied by public and conventional meanings. It is less "a cry out of the heart of experience" than a *strategy*, a strategy designed to privilege experience, and especially *individual* experience, in relation to the impersonality of public and institutional structures. That is why the efficacy of the pastoral is called into question so that the efficacy of the speaker, as someone who stands apart from conventions and is in a position to evaluate them, can be that much more firmly established. In other words, the characterization of the pastoral is deliberately low and feeble in order to display to advantage the authority and prescience of the speaker when he pronounces in his own voice, as he does at line 64: "Alas, what boots it with incessant care." Here, and in the lines that follow, the speaker is at the height of his powers, in the sense that he seems to have earned the questions he hurls at the world, questions whose force is in direct proportion to the claim (silently, but effectively made) to sincerity. Here is no mediated pastoral voice, heard through a screen of tradition and ritual; here is the thing itself, the expression of a distinctive perspective on a problem that many have considered ("Yet once more"), but never with such poignancy and perceptiveness. It is precisely what Rajan says it is, a cry out of the heart of experience, a cry which emerges from the wreckage of failed conventions to pose the ultimate question: in a world like this, what does one do?

II. THE SWAIN IS SILENCED

It is all the more startling, then, when that cry is interrupted by the voice of Apollo, a moment characterized by Ransom as "an incredible interpolation" and "a breach in the logic of composition." These are strong words, but they are in response to a very strong effect given the extent to which the speaker has, to this point, asserted his control over the poem and its progression. Here the control is taken from him in so complete a way that we as readers do not even know when it happens. The identification of Apollo's voice occurs at the beginning of line 77 ("Phoebus repli'ed"), but the identification is after the fact, with the result that there is no way of determining who has been speaking. Many editors add punctuation to make it "clear" that Phoebus enters with "But not the praise"; but as we read Milton's unpunctuated text, "but not the praise" seems to be part of a dialogue the first person voice is having with himself on the nature of Fame and its relationship to effort ("incessant care"). The correction supplied by "Phoebus repli'ed" does not result in a simple reassignment of the half line, but blurs, retroactively, the assignment of the lines preceding. When does Phoebus begin to speak? Is this his first reply, or has he begun to respond to the first person complaint at line 70: "*Fame* is the spur . . ."? The first person would then return in line 73—"But the fair Guerdon when we hope to find"—and *then* Phoebus would be heard to reply "But not the praise." My point is not to argue for this particular redistribution of the lines, but to demonstrate that it is possible; and because it is just one among other possibilities, and because the matter cannot be settled once and for all, the question of just who is in charge of the poem becomes a real one.

This is not the only question raised by Apollo's intervention. Because "repli'ed" is in the past tense, what had presented itself as speech erupting in the present is suddenly revealed to be recollected or reported speech. As Ransom observes, "dramatic monologue has turned . . . into narrative"; and the result, in Friedman's words, "is a momentary confusion about the nature of the utterance we are listening to." [16] The confusion is not only generic (monologue or narrative), but extends to the kind of hearing we are to give to that utterance, for "if the memory of Phoebus's words is reported by the swain as part of the elegy, then what has happened to the pretense of spontaneity and present creation?" Friedman's question contains its own answer (although it is not

[16] Ransom, "A Poem Nearly Anonymous," above, 83; Friedman, "Swain's Paideia," 33.

the one he eventually gives) : it is here that the spontaneity begins to be exposed precisely as a pretense, as a claim elaborately
made by the speaker from his very first words: "Yet once more."
Although these words acknowledge convention (by acknowledging that this has been done before), they are themselves uncon-
ventional, because they are not produced within the frame or
stage setting that traditionally encloses the pastoral lament.
From Theocritus to Spenser, elegiac song is introduced into a
situation that proclaims its status as artifice, as a piece of cur-
rency in a social exchange (song for bowl), or as a performance
offered in competition. In *Lycidas*, however, the frame is omitted,
and what we hear, or are encouraged to hear, is an unpremeditated outpouring of grief and anger. When Apollo's reply is
reported in the past tense, the pastoral frame is introduced retroactively, and the suggestion is that it has been there all the
while. Immediately the spontaneity of the preceding lines is
compromised, and compromised too are the claims of the speaker
to independence. At the very moment he dismisses the pastoral,
he is revealed to be a narrated pastoral figure, no longer the
teller of his tale, but told by it, identified and made intelligible,
as it were, by the very tradition he scorns. Moreover, he is identified in such a way as to call into question his identity. When
Apollo plucks his trembling ear, he repeats an action already
performed in response to another poet who also has dreams of
transcending the pastoral conventions :

> When I tried a song of kings and battles, Phoebus
> Plucked my ear and warned, "A shepherd, Tityrus,
> Should feed fat sheep, recite a fine-spun song.
>   (Virgil, *Eclogue VI*, trans. Paul Alpers)

Apollo, in short, puts Virgil in his place, and by doing so establishes a place (or commonplace) that is now occupied by the
present speaker. That is, the desire of the poet to rise above the
pastoral is itself a pastoral convention, and when the speaker
of *Lycidas* gives voice to that desire, he succeeds only in demonstrating the extent to which his thoughts and actions are already
inscribed in the tradition from which he would be separate. Not
only are his ambitions checked by Apollo,[17] but they are not *his*

---

[17] Friedman, "Swain's Paideia," 13.

ambitions, insofar as he is only playing out the role assigned him in a drama not of his making.

It is not too much to say, then, that the intervention of Apollo changes everything: the speaker loses control of his poem when another voice simply dislodges him from center stage (where he had been performing in splendid isolation), and, at the same time, the integrity of his own voice is compromised when it becomes indistinguishable from its Virgilian predecessor. Apollo poses a threat to the speaker not only as a maker, as someone who is in the act of building the lofty rhyme, but a self-contained consciousness, as a mind that is fully present to itself and responsible for its own perceptions. The speaker meets this twin threat by rewriting, or misreading, what has happened to him in such a way as to reinstate, at least for the moment, the fiction of his independence:

> O fountain *Arethuse,* and thou honour'd flood,
> Smooth-sliding *Mincius,* crown'd with vocall reeds,
> That strain I heard was of higher mood:
> But now my oat proceeds. (85–88)

The picture in these lines is of someone who has paused to listen, no doubt politely, to the opinion of another before proceeding resolutely on *his* way (the strong claim is in the *my* of "my oat"). There is no acknowledgment at all of the violence of Apollo's entrance, of his brusque and dismissive challenge to the speaker's sentiments, of the peremptory and unceremonious manner in which he seizes the floor. Moreover, the action Apollo performs is misrepresented when it is reported as an action *against* the pastoral ("That strain was of a higher mood"). In fact, it is an action against the speaker, a rebuke, as Mary Christopher Pecheux observes, to his "rebellious questioning."[18] If Apollo's words are higher, they are higher than the speaker's own; rather than supporting his denigration of the pastoral, they are precisely pastoral words and mark the moment when the tradition interrupts the "bold discourse"[19] of one who scorns it and exposes the illusion of his control.

It is in order to maintain the illusion that the speaker sets

[18] "The Dread Voice in *Lycidas,*" *Milton Studies* 9 (1976): 238.
[19] See *Paradise Lost,* 5:803 ff.: "Thus far his bold discourse without control / Had audience, when, among the Seraphim, / Abdiel . . . / Stood up."

Apollo against the pastoral, for he can then present himself as
the judge of their respective assertions. But no sooner has he
reclaimed the central and directing role ("But now my oat
proceeds") than it is once again taken from him:

> But now my oat proceeds,
> And listens to the Herald of the Sea
> That came in *Neptune's* plea. (88–90)

Suddenly the voices competing for attention, and for the position of authority, multiply and become difficult to distinguish.
Triton comes, but he comes in Neptune's plea, and therefore
when we read of someone who "ask'd" the waves and felon winds
(91), it is not clear whether that someone is Triton or Neptune,
nor when that someone speaks (it could be that Triton reports
the investigative queries of Neptune—he "ask'd"—or that
Triton *now* asks in the present of the narrative, but is reported as
having done so in the present of the narrator, i.e. the voice that
tells us Phoebus "repli'ed"). The one thing that is clear is that
the questioner is not the speaker, who is now reduced to the role
of a listener, as someone else conducts the investigation. Again,
that someone else could be Triton or Neptune or the yet unknown third person voice of whose existence we have had only
hints, or, after line 96, it could be the "sage Hippotades" who
brings someone's (it seems to be everyone's) unsatisfactory answers. By the time we reach the most unsatisfactory answer of
all—"It was that fatall and perfidious Bark"—there is absolute-
ly no way of determining who delivers it. A poem that began as the
focused utterance of a distinctive personal voice is by this point
so diffused that it is spoken, quite literally, by everybody.

Not only is the original speaker now indistinguishable from a
chorus, but he is not even the object of direct address, as he was
when he listened to Apollo. Whoever it is that indicts the fatal
and perfidious bark, he directs his remarks to Lycidas: "That
sunk so low that sacred head of *thine*." Moreover, the indictment
and the entire investigation are once again proceeding in a narrated past. The fading of the speaker from the scene of his own
poem coincides with the almost imperceptible slide into the past
tense, and both movements are complete when we hear (we have
displaced the speaker, who is no longer even a prominent lis-

tener) that "last came, and last did go / The Pilot of the Galilean
lake" (109).

It would seem that with this figure the poem is once again
dominated by a single controlling presence, but his identity (in
two senses) is perhaps not so firm as we have been taught to
think. Taking up a suggestion first made by R. E. Hone, Mary
Pecheux has argued persuasively that the Pilot of the Galilean
lake (who significantly is not named) is not Peter, but a composite of Peter, Moses, and Christ. The speech thus dramatizes
Milton's assertion in *Christian Doctrine* that revelation was disclosed in various ages by Christ even though he was not always
known under that name: "Under the name of Christ are also com-
prehended Moses and the Prophets, who were his forerunners,
and the Apostles whom he sent."[20] This splitting of the "dread
voice" has the advantage, as Pecheux points out, of being "consonant with the extraordinary richness and ambivalence" of the
poem, with the sense one has "of having heard a multitude of
overtones difficult to disentangle from one another." The details
of her argument are less important than the fact that it can be
made (and others are now making it), for this means that the
question is now an open one, and that the Pilot's speech too proceeds from a source that is not *uniquely* identified.

That speech is also addressed to Lycidas ("How well could
I have spar'd for thee, young swain"), and its "stern" message
further shifts attention away from the first person voice by re-
placing his very personal concerns with the concerns of the
church as a whole. That is, the complaint one hears in these lines
is quite different from the complaint that precedes Apollo's
interruption: it is not an answer to the speaker's questions
("What boots it . . ."), but a "higher" questioning in which the
ambitions of any one shepherd or singer are absorbed into a more
universal urgency, as rot and foul contagion spread (127). The
focus of the Pilot's words is continually expanding, until it opens
in the end on a perspective so wide that all of our attempts to
name it are at once accurate and hopelessly inadequate. Whatever the two-handed engine is—and we shall never know—the
action for which it stands ready will not be in response to any
cry out of the heart of experience, and in this moment of apoca-

[20] "The Dread Voice in *Lycidas*," 235.

lyptic prophecy, the private lament that was, for a time, the poem's occasion is so much transcended that one can scarcely recall it.

This movement away from the personal is a structural component of Milton's work from the very beginning. It is seen as early as the Nativity Ode, where the poet begins by desiring to be first, to stand out ("Have thou the honor first thy Lord to greet"), and ends by being indistinguishable from the others (animals, angels, shepherds) who "all about the Courtly Stable / . . . sit in order serviceable." The glory he had hoped to win by being first is won when, in a sense, he no longer is, and is able to pronounce the glorious death of his own poetic ambitions ("Time is our tedious Song should here have ending"). While the career of the speaker in *Lycidas* is parallel, it is also different because he does not relinquish his position voluntarily. He holds tenaciously to his own song and must be forcibly removed from the poem by voices that preempt him or displace him or simply ignore him until at the end of the Pilot's speech he seems to have disappeared.

Indeed, so long has it been since he was last on stage (line 90) that when he suddenly pops up again he seems an interpolation more incredible than Apollo. He seems, in fact, a digression, a departure from what we have come to recognize as the poem's true concerns; and as a digression his gesture of reassertion is, in every sense, reactionary:

> Return *Alpheus* the dread voice is past
> That shrunk thy streams; Return *Sicilian* Muse,
> And call the Vales and bid them hither cast
> Their bells and Flourets of a thousand hues. (132–35)

Once again the return of the speaker is marked by a rewriting that is a misrepresentation. He acts as if all had been proceeding under his direction, as if the voices in the poem require his permission to come and go, a permission he now extends to the pastoral, which is characterized as if it were a child that had been frightened by the sound of an adult voice. His strategy is two pronged, and it is familiar. He opposes the pastoral to the speech of the Galilean Pilot (as he had earlier opposed it to Apollo) and thus denies it the responsibility for documenting ecclesiastical abuses, a responsibility it was given in the Scriptures. In effect, it is he, not the Pilot, who shrinks, or attempts to shrink, the pastoral stream, and he does it, characteristically, in a denial of the extent to which his own stream has been shrunk in the course of the poem. In a classic form of displacement he attempts, for the last time, to project a story in which he is a compelling and powerful figure. It is as part of that story that he calls the role of flowers, a gesture intended not so much to "interpose a little ease" as to set the stage for still another assertion of pastoral inadequacy:

> Let our frail thoughts dally with false surmise. (153)

As before, what is presented as self-deprecation is an act of self-promotion. The "frail thoughts" are detached from the speaker —he merely dallies with them—and identified with the failure of the convention: if, in some sense, he can do no better, at least he is able to recognize a false surmise when he sees one, and that ability in itself is evidence of a vision that is superior even if it is (realistically) dark:

> Ay me! Whils't thee the shores and sounding Seas
> Wash far away, where ere thy bones are hurl'd. (154–55)

This is, of course, exactly what he has said before, when he breaks off his address to the nymphs to exclaim, "Aye me, I fondly dream," and again, when his rehearsal of Orpheus's death (he also was hurled by shores and sounding seas) is followed by a bitter question: "Alas! What boots it with incessant care?" What is remarkable about the speaker is how little he is affected by those sections of the poem that unfold between his intermittent appearances. Higher moods and dread voices may come and go, but when he manages to regain the stage, it is to sing the same old song: Ay me, alas, what am I to do? What's the use? it's all so unfair. As the poem widens its perspective to include ever larger considerations (eternal fame, the fate of the Church, the condition of the Christian community, the last judgment), he remains within the perspective of his personal disappointment, remains very much "his owne person," and therefore he becomes, as I have said, a digression in (what began as) his own poem. While he has been busily exposing the false surmises of pastoral consolation, the poem has been even more insistently exposing the surmise that enables him (or so he thinks) to do so, the surmise that his vision is both inclusive and conclusive, that he sees what there is to see and knows what there is to know.

What he sees is that there is no laureate hearse (only the "wat'ry bier" he saw at line 12), and what he knows is that there is neither justice nor meaning in the world. He seems to have heard in the Pilot's speech none of the resonances that have been reported by so many readers. His words remain determinedly bleak, and therefore, they are all the more discontinuous with the call that is sounded at line 165:

> Weep no more woful Shepherds, weep no more,
> For *Lycidas* your sorrow is not dead.

These are entirely new accents spoken by an entirely new voice. It is a voice that counsels rather than complains, that turns outward rather than inward, a voice whose confident affirmation of a universal benevolence could not be further from the dark and self-pitying questioning of the swain. Everything, in short, has changed, and it has changed not even in a line, but in the space between lines. It is at this point that the orthodox reading of the poem, in which "the troubled thought of the elegist" traces out a sequence of "rise, evolution, and resolution," founders.[21] There is no evolution here, simply a disjunction, a gap, and the seekers of unity are left with the problem of explaining it. In general, their explanations have taken one of two forms. Either the change is explained theologically as "a leap from nature to revelation"[22] and "a dramatization of the infusion of grace,"[23] or it is explained away by assigning the lines to another speaker. This is the solution of William Madsen, who notes the abrupt transition from the "plaintive" and "ineffectual" to the authoritative and concludes that the consolation is spoken not by the swain, but by Michael, who responds in a fuller measure than might have been expected to the speaker's appeal ("Look homeward, Angel, now and melt with ruth"). Madsen offers his emendation as an alternative to the theological reading; but in fact there is very little difference between them, since in either reading this point marks the appearance in the poem of "a new voice."

[21] M. H. Abrams. "Five Types of *Lycidas*," above, 228.
[22] Ibid., 233.
[23] Friedman, "Swain's Paideia," 19.

For Madsen that voice is Michael's; for Abrams and Friedman (among others) it is the voice of a regenerated (made new) swain. In either case there is agreement that the voice we had been hearing is heard no more, and that what takes its place is something wholly different. This is of course not the first time this has happened, and it is only because in Madsen's reading the event is unusual that he feels moved to assign the new voice a specific name (it is that assignment that has been objected to). In the reading that has been developed here, however, the appearance of new voices and the merging of old is occurring all the time; the speaker is repeatedly dislodged or overwhelmed or absorbed, and his disappearance at line 164 is just one in a series.

There is, however, a difference. This disappearance is the last; the speaker is never heard from again. Or if he is heard from again, it is not as his "owne person" but as a "member incorporate" of a truth from which he is now indistinguishable. That is to say, Madsen is right to hear the voice as different, but he is wrong to hear it as anyone's in particular. The accents here, as Marjorie Nicolson has observed, are "choral" as "all voices combine in virtuous crescendo."[24] If the speaker is among them, he is literally unrecognizable, since what allowed him to stand out was the "dogged insistence"[25] with which he held on to the local perspective of his own ambitions. In the end he is not even distinguishable as an addressee: the choral voice responds not to one, but to a mass of complaints; the consolation is for "woful Shepherds," the plural noun silently denying the speaker even the claim to have been uniquely grieving; the grief is as general as the consolation, and it simply doesn't leave room for anything personal. The distance that has been travelled is the distance from the melodious tear of line 14 to the "unexpressive nuptial Song" of line 176. The tear falls from a single eye; it is the poem as the product of one voice that demands to be heard, if only as an expression of inconsolability; but the nuptial song is produced by everyone and therefore *heard* by no one, in the sense that there is no one who is at a sufficient distance from it for there to be a question of hearing. That is why it is called "unexpressive," which means both inexpressible (can't be said) and

[24] *John Milton: A Reader's Guide to his Poetry* (New York, 1963), 110.
[25] The phrase is Madsen's, *From Shadowy Types*, 13.

inaudible (can't be apprehended) : both speaking and receiving assume a separation between communicating agents; but this song is not a communication at all, but a testimony to a joy which, since it binds all, need not be transmitted to any. The mistake of the first person voice has been his desire to speak, to proclaim from an analytic and judgmental distance a truth he only sees; but in the great vision of these soaring lines the truth proclaims, because it fills, its speakers, who are therefore not speakers at all but witnesses. They are in the happy condition for which Milton prays at the end of *At a Solemn Music* :

> O may we soon again renew that song
> And keep in tune with heaven, till God ere long
> To his celestial consort us unite
> To live with him and sing in endless morn of light.

The wish that we may join that choir is the wish that we *not* be heard as a distinctive and therefore alienated voice, the wish that we might utter sounds in such a way as to remain silent (unexpressive). It is a wish that is here granted the would-be elegist, whether he wants it or not, as finally, he is no longer his own person, but a member incorporate into that truth whereof he has been persuaded.

I am aware that this might seem a back door way into the usual reading of *Lycidas*, for just like any other critic I have gotten the swain into heaven or at least into a position where a heavenly vision is available to him. But if he is now one of those who sing and singing in their glory move, he could not be picked out from among the other members of troops and societies, and therefore his "triumph," if one can call it that, is not achieved in terms that he would understand or welcome. As Friedman remarks, the speaker "fights *against* the knowledge" offered by the poem's higher moods; his experience is "one of active struggle." My point is that it is a struggle he loses, and that the poem achieves its victory first by preempting him and finally by silencing him. Rather than the three part structure traditionally proposed for *Lycidas*, I am proposing a structure of two parts: a first part (lines 1 through 75 1/2), where the first person voice proceeds under the illusion of independence and control, and a second, longer part, where that illusion is repeatedly exposed and finally dispelled altogether. In place of an interior lyric punctuated by digressive interpolations, we have a poem that begins in digression—the first person voice is the digression—and regains the main path only when the lyric note is no longer sounded. We have, in short, a poem that relentlessly denies the privilege of the speaking subject, of the unitary and separate consciousness, and is finally, and triumphantly, anonymous.

It is anonymous twice. The last eight lines of *Lycidas* have always been perceived as problematic, because they insist on a narrative frame that was not apparent in the beginning, because the frame or coda is spoken by an unidentified third person voice, and because that voice is so firmly impersonal. One advantage of the reading offered here is that these are not problems at all: if the introduction of a narrative perspective suggests that everything presented as spontaneous was in fact already spoken, this is no more than a confirmaton of what has long since become obvious; if the new voice is unidentified, it is only the last in a series of unidentified voices or of voices whose single identities have long since been lost or blurred; and if the unidentified voice is impersonal, it is merely a continuation of the mode the poem has finally achieved. In fact, the crucial thing about these lines is that there is no one to whom they can be plausibly assigned. They are certainly not the swain's, for he is what they describe, and they describe him significantly as someone who is "uncouth," that is, unknown, someone who departs the poem with less of an identity than he displayed at its beginning; nor is there any compelling reason to assign them to any of the previous speakers, to the Pilot, or Hippotades, or Triton, or Neptune, or Cambridge, or Apollo. The only recourse, and it is one that has appealed to many, is to assign the lines to Milton, but of all the possibilities, this is the least persuasive. No voice in English poetry is more distinctive than Milton's, so much so that the characters he creates almost always sound just like him. But these lines do not sound like anyone; they are perfectly, that is unrelievedly, conventional, and as such they are the perfect conclusion to a poem from which the personal has been systematically eliminated. Indeed, if these lines were written in accents characteristically Miltonic, they would constitute a claim exactly like that which is denied to the poem's first speaker, the claim to be able to pronounce, to sum up, to say it conclusively, and once and for all. Instead, Milton gives over the conclusion of the poem to a collection of pastoral commonplaces which are not even structured into a summary statement, but simply follow one another in a series that is unconstrained by any strong syntactical pressures. (The lines are markedly paratactic and conform to what Thomas Rosenmeyer has called the "disconnective decorum" of the pure pastoral.)[26] In short, Milton silences himself, just as the first person voice is silenced, and performs (if that is the word) an act of humility comparable to that which allows him to call his nativity ode "tedious" at the very moment when its intended recipient falls asleep. Rosemond Tuve once observed that in Herbert's career we can see a lifelong effort to achieve the "immolation of the individual will." This has not usually been thought to be Milton's project, but the determined anonymity of *Lycidas* should remind us that the poet's fierce egoism is but one-half of his story.

[26] *The Green Cabinet* (Berkeley and Los Angeles, 1969), 33.

Postscript
M. H. Abrams

In the essay I wrote a quarter century ago (above, 216 ff.), I emphasized the drastic changes effected in our reading of *Lycidas* by alternative critical perspectives—in other words, by diverse hypotheses as to the principle which controls the choice, order, and interrelations of the parts of the poem and serves to account for the nature and degree of its poetic success. In the present critical climate, however, in which we hear frequent claims that all literary texts disseminate themselves into a range of undecidable and inescapably contradictory meanings, one needs to emphasize the other side of the matter; and that is, the uniformity of the interpretive premises that are shared by all the critics represented in this volume, whatever the diversity of their critical hypotheses, and including the authors of the six essays, published during the last two decades, which have been added to the present edition.

The most important of these premises is that the sentences of Milton's poem have a determinable meaning—even though in some instances that meaning is determinably ambiguous or multiplex—which qualified readers are capable of understanding in approximately the same way. To this view the essay by Stanley Fish might be regarded as an exception by those who know Fish's claim, in his theoretical writings, that there are a number of possible "interpretive strategies," each of which creates its own distinctive text by "constituting" both the formal prop-

erties and the meanings of the sequence of verbal signs on a page.
In the course of evolving his theory, however, Fish has gone on to
assert that in his applied criticism, such as his essay on *Lycidas*,
he operates—he in fact suggests that he cannot help but op-
erate—as a member of a particular "interpretive community,"
specified as the community of "academic literary criticism,"
whose shared assumptions and procedures make possible a common understanding of the meanings of a text.[1] To this latter
view I, and perhaps the writers of the other essays in this volume,
agree—with the important proviso, however, that there is abundant evidence that the practice of the English language that we,
as an "interpretive community," have inherited is continuous
enough with the practice that Milton had himself inherited to
provide adequate assurance that our understanding of the language of *Lycidas* can approximate the meanings that Milton expressed and intended his readers to understand.

The issue is confused by the fact that what we call "the interpretation of a poem" involves two discriminable though interrelated processes. One of these is *linguistic* interpretation : making
sense of the English sentences (or in a current parlance, "the
speech acts") that compose a text, in the order of their occurrence.
The other is *critical* interpretation : making sense of *Lycidas* as
a poem, by applying to it an artistic hypothesis concerning the
principle which controls the poem's overall structure and specifies the relations between its component elements. The matter is
complicated by the phenomenon that linguistic interpretation
and critical interpretation are co-responsive and interdependent,
with the result that (as I tried to show in my essay) linguistic
meanings are altered by the particular critical hypothesis that
a reader brings to bear on the poem. But what the critics in this
volume say about *Lycidas* demonstrates that linguistic meanings, while to a considerable degree acquiescent to different
artistic hypotheses, are nonetheless recalcitrant to demands
which are inordinate. The common core of recalcitrant linguistic
meanings, established by the shared practice, or "strategy," that
constitutes what we call understanding the English language, is

---

[1] Professor Fish has collected his theoretical essays, written over a span of
ten years, in *Is There a Text in This Class?* (Cambridge, Mass., 1980). For
his discussion of the evolution in his views during that period, see especially
the "Introduction," 1–17.

adequate to disqualify some critical interpretations of the poem as too strained to be tenable, and also to provide a common ground on which critics can share insights and argue reasonably about interpretive disagreements, not only within the same critical perspective, but to a lesser extent between diverse critical perspectives.

To cite one instance: In line 8 Milton writes, "For Lycidas is dead, dead ere his prime." In line 166 he writes, "For Lycidas your sorrow is not dead." Taken as isolated assertions, these sentences signify a flat logical contradiction. All the critical essayists manifest their common understanding of the assertive meaning of these sentences. What they undertake is to demonstrate, by a critical interpretation applied to the intervening sentences—each in terms appropriate to his or her proposed artistic hypothesis—that these contradictory assertions in fact express a lyric peripety, either by virtue of a change of view in the lyric speaker attendant on a discovery or on a breakthrough to a higher mode of knowledge, or else by the triumph of one side in a conflict of opposing forces.

This brings me to another important premise which is shared by the interpreters of the poem: the critical assumption that we should undertake to read a poem as a unified whole—that is, as having an apt beginning and a middle section that leads coherently to a resolution which, since it requires nothing to follow it, satisfies us that the poem is complete. The degree to which the poem is a coherent and sufficient unity serves as a prime, though not a sufficient, criterion of its poetic value. If a critic, like G. Wilson Knight in his essay on Milton in *The Burning Oracle*, discovers that *Lycidas*, while "exquisite in parts," is "an accumulation of magnificent fragments," then the poem is deemed to be deficient in an essential aspect of its artistry.

The essayists added to this edition all assume and apply this presumption of artistic unity—most of them, presumably, on the implicit ground that Milton in all probability undertook to write a unified poem. They also concur that, whatever the seeming dislocations and disruptions between one and another of its parts, *Lycidas*, when read from the appropriate critical viewpoint, turns out to have an adequate integrity. The principle and locus of this integrity, however, differs according to the kind of hypothesis posited by the critical expositor. It is found, for ex-

ample, to consist in the plausible sequence of consciousness
through which the lyric speaker, by rising gradually through
the Old Testament doctrine of vengeance to the Christian revelation of mercy and redemptive love, comes to accept in his life
(and to resolve for the writing of his poetry) the violent on-
slaughts of reality upon the pastoral dream. Alternatively, the
unity is located in an intricately modulated three-part evolution; this evolution is variously described as a movement of the
speaker's state of mind, and of his view of the content of poetry,
from innocence through experience of a fallen world to a wiser
innocence, or as an Hegelian dialectical process, involving the
possibility of writing poetry, from thesis through antithesis to
synthesis, or as a typological succession from the prefigurations
in the pagan pastoral through the higher types of Old Testament
pastoralism to the ultimate antitypes of the Christian pastoral
truth. From a third critical viewpoint the unity consists in the
coherent stages exhibited in the progressive education of "the
swain" as a poet, which, though complete in *Lycidas* itself, is
in turn taken to reflect Milton's own poetic maturation to the
point at which he is ready to undertake an epic poem.

In this respect also Stanley Fish's essay might seem an exception, for in it he derogates "the seekers of unity" who strive in
vain to domesticate the repeated disruptions that breach the
logic of the poem. Fish makes clear, however, that what he rejects are the efforts "to put the poem together" by reference
to a "unified consciousness" which is expressed by "an integrated
and consistent first person voice." He himself substitutes a critical hypothesis which he describes as a revival, "but with a difference," of John Crowe Ransom's argument that the poem's
discontinuities "reflect a tension between anonymity and personality." The application of this hypothesis results in an interpretation which in effect replaces the evolving consciousness of the
lyric speaker with an alternative principle of poetic unity: Fish
views the "plot" of the poem as an *agon*, a contest for "control
over the poem" between "the first person voice" and the many
other voices that break into its utterance. According to this
reading, *Lycidas* "begins in digression" ("the first person
voice," Fish explains, "is the digression"), proceeds through successive disjunctions which function "relentlessly" to deny "the
privilege of the speaking subject, of the unitary and separate

consciousness," and ends with "the great vision" in which, the personal voice having at last been totally silenced, the poem "is finally, and triumphantly, anonymous." The narrative coda, since it is spoken by "an unidentified third person voice," confirms the integrity of the overall plot by its function as "the perfect conclusion to a poem in which the personal has been systematically eliminated."

The boundaries of what I have called a "type" of *Lycidas* are sufficiently loose to make it a matter of individual judgment whether to classify Fish's essay, or any of the added essays, as an additional type or else as a variant on an existing type. No matter what type of critical hypothesis a reader may apply to the poem, however, he will find in each of the essays, with its expert application of an alternative perspective, valuable insights into the components and artistry of the poem. But with all the dazzling virtuosity of modern critical analytics, we need to keep in mind what Isabel MacCaffrey in her essay calls "the relevance, not only of the poem's form, but of its theme to ourselves." The calm accents and sublime assurance of the voice which, after facing up to the intervening horrors, recounts the concluding vision enforces our imaginative participation in the experience of that vision, whether or not we share its supporting creed that a bright reversion in the sky will make abundant recompense for the tears we shed in this earthly life.

Critics who propose a new reading of *Lycidas* still tend to justify their enterprise as a discovery of what *Lycidas* is really about. One thing its language is undeniably about is death, and how to cope in a world where the threat of death is constant, and may strike early and in stark violation of our human sense of merit and justice. Whatever the values of structure and intricate relations of detail one discovers in the poem, to overlook the enduring human relevance of the subject to which this artistry has been applied is to leave out what is essential to the power that has made *Lycidas* the lyric of lyrics, a standing challenge to critics and readers of English poetry.

Appendix
The Text of *Lycidas*

The sources for the text of *Lycidas* are four: (1) the manuscript of the poem, now at Trinity College, Cambridge, carrying the cancelled superscription "Novemb: 1637" (for the most significant corrections on this manuscript, see above, pp. 12–13); (2) the first published text, set in italic type, in the memorial volume *Justa Edovardo King*, 1638; (3) the second published text in *Poems of Mr. John Milton*, 1645; and (4) the third published text in *Poems upon Several Occasions*, 1673. In collation, the 1645 text emerged as the most reliable of the three versions. As can be seen from the following list, the earlier edition (1638) has by far the greatest number of variants, all of which were corrected by Milton in 1645, while the later edition (1673) is merely a reproduction of the 1645 text with a few misprints. The present edition, therefore, reproduces the 1645 text, though in six cases (ll. 63, 82, 94, 163, 178, and 183) obvious misprints and errors in punctuation have dictated the adoption of readings from the text either of 1638 or 1673 or both. I have additionally adopted the correction Milton himself made to l. 10 ("he well knew") on two copies of the 1638 volume now at Cambridge University and the British Library respectively.

In collating the three texts, the italic type of the 1638 edition was ignored. Variants in capitalization are not shown.

Headnote: not in the 1638 edition; the Trinity College manuscript contains only the first sentence; the present form dates from the 1645 edition.

1	1638	and once more,]	33	1638	oaten flute:]	
2	1638	never-sere,]	34	1638	Satyres]	
	1673	never sear,]		1638	cloven heel]	
3	1638	come]	36	1638	Dametas]	
4	1638	rude]		1673	Damætas]	
5	1638	yeare.]		1638	heare]	
6	1638	deare]	37	1638	oh]	
7	1638, 1673	Compells]		1638	gone,]	
8	1638, 1673	prime,]	38	1638	gone,]	
9	1638	(Young	39	1638	shepherds,]	
		Lycidas!)]	40	1638	wild]	
	1638	peere.]		1638	oregrown,]	
16	all eds.	he knew	42	1638	willows]	
		(amended by		1638	hasil-copses	
		Milton to "he			green]	
		well knew": see	43	1638	seen]	
		above)]	47	1638	flowers]	
12	1638	biere]		1638	wardrobe]	
13	1638	wind]	48	1638	white-thorn]	
14	1638	some]			blowes;]	
15	1638	well]	49	1638	losse]	
16	1638	spring;]		1638	eare.]	
17	1638, 1673	somewhat]	50	1638 *does not indent*		
	1638	string:]		1638	Nimphs,]	
18	1638	deniall]	51	1638	ore]	
	1638	excuse.]		1638	your lord	
19	1638, 1673	some]			Lycidas?]	
21	1638	passes, turn]	53	1638	the old Bards]	
22	1638	shroud.]		1638, 1673	*Druids,*]	
24	1673	flock;]		1638	lie,]	
	1638	rill;]	54	1638	shaggie]	
25	1638 *does not indent*		56	1638	Oh]	
26	1638	glimmering]	57	1638	been]	
27	1638	a-field]		1638	done?]	
30	1638	Oft till the ev'n-	59	1673	her self]	
		starre bright]		1638	sonne?]	
	1673	bright,]	60	1638	universall]	
31	1638	burnisht]	61	1638	rore]	
32	1638	rurall]	63	1645	*Letbian*]	
	1638	mute]	64	1638 *does not indent*		

65	1673	To end]
66	1638	stridly]
	1638	thanklesse]
	1673	thankless]
	1673	Muse?]
67	1638	done as others do,]
69	1638	Hid in]
	1638	Neera's]
70	1638	spurre]
	1638	raise,]
71	1638	infirmitie]
73	1638	guerdon where]
75	1638	Furie]
76	1638	thin-spun]
	1638	life;]
77	1638	Phebus]
	1638	eares.]
78	1638	growes]
	1638	mortall]
79	1638	glistring]
80	1638	lies;]
81	1638	lives, and spreads]
	1638	eyes]
82	1638	perfect witnesse]
	1645	all judging]
	1638	Jove:]
85	1638	*does not indent*
	1638	Oh]
86	1673	vocal]
	1638	reeds;]
87	1638	mood.]
90	1638	Neptunes plea.]
91	1638	felon]
93	1638	wings,]
94	1638	blowes]
	1638	Promontorie:]
	1645	Promontory,]
95	1638	storie;]

97	1638	stray'd;]
98	1638	aire]
	1673	Air]
	1638	brine]
99	1638	play'd:]
100	1673	fatal]
	1638	bark,]
103	1638	*does not indent*
	1638	Chamus (reverend sire)]
104	1638	hairie,]
106	1638	wo;]
107	1673	Ah;]
110	1638	massie]
	1638	metalls]
112	1638	mitred]
113	1638, 1673	thee, young swain,]
114	1638	Enough]
	1638	sake]
115	1638	intrude]
	1638	climbe]
116	1638	reckoning]
118	1673	guest;]
120	1638	sheephook,]
	1638	else]
123	1638	list]
	1638	flashie]
128	1638	grimme wolf]
129	1638	devoures]
	1638	little said,]
130	1638	doore,]
131	1638	smites no more.]
132	1638	Return,]
	1638	past]
133	1638	return,]
135	1638, 1673	Bells,]
	1638	flowrets]
136	1638	low,]
	1638	mild]

	1638	use]
137	1638	winds]
138	1638	starre]
139	1638	enammell'd]
140	1638	turf]
141	1638	vernall flowers.]
142	1638	primerose]
	1638	dies,]
145	1638	violet,]
146	1638	well-attir'd woodbine,]
147	1638, 1673	head,]
149	1673	*Amarantus*]
153	1638	surmise;]
154	1638	whil'st]
	1638	shores]
155	1638	farre]
	1638, 1673	hurl'd,]
156	1673	Hebrides]
157	1638	the humming tide]
159	1638	vowes deni'd,]
163	1645, 1673	ruth.]
164	1638	haplesse]
165	1638	wofull shepherds, weep no more;]
167	1638	floore:]
168	1638	day-starre]
170	1638	ore]
171	1638	skie:]

172	1638	high]
173	1638, 1673, and some copies of 1645 waves;]
175	1638	oazie locks]
176	1638	And heares]
	1673	nuptial]
	1638	song;]
177	*This entire line, present in the Trinity manuscript, is omitted in 1638; restored in 1645.*
178	*This line is indented one letter in 1645, 1673.*
	1645	*h*im]
	1638	above]
179	1638	troups,]
	1638	societies,]
182	1638	Now, Lycidas,]
183	1645	Hence forth]
	1638	shore]
185	1638	perillous]
	1638	floud.]
186	1638	oaks]
187	1638	gray;]
190	1638	sunne]
192	1638	blew,]
193	1638	woods]

Signature in 1638:   J. M.]

Bibliography

Abbreviations

AI	*American Imago*
AJP	*American Journal of Philology*
AN&Q	*American Notes and Queries*
Archiv	*Archiv für das Studium der neueren Sprachen und Literaturen*
CE	*College English*
DNB	*Dictionary of National Biography*
EA	*Etudes anglaises*
EIC	*Essays in Criticism*
ELH	*ELH: A Journal of English Literary History*
ELN	*English Language Notes*
ES	*English Studies*
Ex	*Explicator*
HLQ	*Huntington Library Quarterly*
JEGP	*Journal of English and Germanic Philology*
JHI	*Journal of the History of Ideas*
MLN	*Modern Language Notes*
MLR	*Modern Language Review*
MN	*Milton Newsletter*
MP	*Modern Philology*
MQ	*Milton Quarterly*
MS	*Milton Studies*
N&Q	*Notes and Queries*
PMLA	*Publications of the Modern Language Association*
PQ	*Philological Quarterly*
RES	*Review of English Studies*

RQ   *Renaissance Quarterly*
SEL   *Studies in English Literature*
SP   *Studies in Philology*
TLS   (London) *Times Literary Supplement*
TSLL   *Texas Studies in Literature and Language*
UTQ   *University of Toronto Quarterly*

For general bibliographies of Milton, see *The New Cambridge Bibliography of English Literature*, ed. George Watson (Cambridge, 1974), 1:1238–95, and the Goldentree bibliography of Milton compiled by James H. Hanford (New York, 1966, revised 1979). Detailed bibliographies of both primary and secondary sources are available in *The Age of Milton: Backgrounds to Seventeenth-Century Literature*, ed. C. A. Patrides and Raymond B. Waddington (Manchester and New York, 1980), 370–427, whose eleven chapters are as comprehensive as the overall title avers. Comprehensive in a different sense is *A Milton Encyclopedia*, gen. ed. William B. Hunter, Jr., 8 vols. (Lewisburg, Pa., 1978–80), which includes a lengthy essay on *Lycidas* by Balachandra Rajan (5:40–57).

On the Text of *Lycidas*

The manuscript of *Lycidas* as it was being revised by Milton has been reproduced in *Facsimile of the Manuscript of Milton's Minor Poems*, ed. William Aldis Wright (Cambridge, 1899), 28–32. The memorial volume in which *Lycidas* first appeared, *Justa Edovardo King* (Cambridge, 1638), is also available in facsimile, edited by Ernest C. Mossner (New York, 1939); but another facsimile, edited by Edward Le Comte (Norwood, Pa., 1978), additionally translates the poems in Latin. The poems in English within that volume are reproduced, again in facsimile, by Joseph A. Wittreich, Jr., *Visionary Poetics* (San Marino, Calif., 1979), App. B. The manuscript and the three published versions of *Lycidas* (1638, 1645, 1673) are jointly reproduced in facsimile in *John Milton's Complete Poetical Works*, ed. Harris F. Fletcher (Urbana, Ill., 1943), 1:52–56, 185–89, 347–52, and 434–43.

The text of the memorial volume and of *Lycidas* is discussed by John T. Shawcross, "Division of Labor in *Justa Edovardo King Naufrago (1638),*" *Library Chronicle* [University of Pennsylvania] 27 (1961):176–79, and "Establishment of a

Text of Milton's Poems through a Study of *Lycidas*," *Papers of the Bibliographical Society of America* 56 (1962):317–31. See also Hugh C. H. Candy, "Milton Autographs Established," *Library*, 4th ser. 13 (1932):192–200.

Lycidas has been edited and annotated on a number of occasions, among them in *The Poetical Works of John Milton*, ed. Henry J. Todd (London, 1801; 2d enl. ed., 1809), 6:3–62; *The Poetical Works of John Milton*, ed. David Masson (London, 1874; 2d ed., 1890), 1:187–201; *The Works of John Milton*, gen. ed. Frank A. Patterson (New York, 1931), 1:76–83, 459–74; *The Complete Poetical Works of John Milton*, ed. Harris F. Fletcher (Boston, 1941), 113–20; *The Poems of John Milton*, ed. James H. Hanford, 2d ed. (New York, 1953), 139–51; *The Major Poets*, ed. Charles M. Coffin (New York, 1954), 155–61; *The Poetical Works of John Milton*, ed. Helen Darbishire (Oxford, 1955), 2:165–70; *John Milton: Complete Poems and Major Prose*, ed. Merritt Y. Hughes (New York, 1957), 116–25; *The Poems of John Milton*, ed. John Carey and Alastair Fowler (London, 1968), 232–54; *The Minor Poems in English*, in The Macmillan Milton, gen. ed. C. A. Patrides (London, 1972), 279–95; and *Odes, Pastorals, Masques*, in The Cambridge Milton, gen. ed. J. B. Broadbent (Cambridge, 1975), 183–238. Among translations is one into French by Emile Saillens (Paris, 1971).

On the Tradition

The reader of *Lycidas* and *Epitaphium Damonis* might wish to study the original poems within the tradition, either through collections such as Harrison's and Kirkconnell's (see below) or through the translations of individual poets such as Sannazaro (trans. Ralph Nash [Detroit, 1966]). Studies of the tradition include:

Allen, Don Cameron. "The Translation of the Myth: The Epicedia and *Lycidas*." In his *The Harmonious Vision*, enl. ed., 41–70. Baltimore, 1970. See also his "Milton's Alpheus," *MLN* 71 (1956): 172–73.

Alpers, Paul J. "The Eclogue Tradition and the Nature of Pastoral." *CE* 34 (1972):352–71. See also his *The Singer of the Eclogues: A Study of Virgilian Pastoral* (Berkeley, 1979).

Austin, W. B. "Milton's *Lycidas* and Two Latin Elegies by Giles Fletcher, the Elder." *SP* 44 (1947):41–55.

Banks, Theodore H. "A Source for *Lycidas*, 154–58." *MLN* 62 (1947):39–40. On Shakespeare's *Pericles*, 3.1.57–65.

Chambers, Sir Edmund. "The English Pastoral." In his *Sir Thomas Wyatt and Some Collected Studies*, 146–80. London, 1933.

Cory, Herbert E. "The Golden Age of the Spenserian Pastoral." *PMLA* 25 (1910):241–67.

Evans, J. Martin. "Lycidas, Daphnis, and Gallus." In *English Renaissance Studies presented to Dame Helen Gardner*, 228–44. Oxford, 1980.

Godolphin, F. R. B. "Milton, *Lycidas*, and Propertius, *Elegies*, III, 7 [*On the Drowning of Paetus*]." *MLN* 49 (1934):162–66.

Grant, W. Leonard. *Neo-Latin Literature and the Pastoral*. Chapel Hill, N.C., 1965.

Greg, Walter W. *Pastoral Poetry and Pastoral Drama*. London, 1906. With some observations on *Lycidas* (131–35).

Guibbory, Achsah. "Natalis Comes and the Digression on Fame in Milton's *Lycidas*." *N&Q*, n.s. 18 (1971): 292.

Hall, H. M. *Idylls of Fishermen*. New York, 1914. On piscatory eclogues.

Hamilton, H. F. "The Sources of Milton's *Lycidas*." *Sewanee Review* 17 (1909):235–40.

Harrison, Thomas P., Jr. "The Latin Pastorals of Milton and Castiglione." *PMLA* 50 (1935):480–93. See also his "Spenser and the Earlier Pastoral Elegy," *Texas Studies in English* 13 (1933):36–53, and "Spenser, Ronsard, and Bion," *MLN* 49 (1934):139–45.

Harrison, Thomas P., Jr., ed. *The Pastoral Elegy*. English translations by Harry J. Leon. Austin, 1939. A convenient anthology containing all the poems discussed by Hanford (above, 31 ff.) as well as the best English pastoral elegies since *Lycidas* (Shelley's *Adonais*, Arnold's *Thyrsis*). See also under Elledge and Kirkconnell, below.

Heninger, S. K., Jr. "The Renaissance Perversion of Pastoral." *JHI* 22 (1961):254–61.

Hughes, Merritt Y. "Spenser and the Greek Pastoral Triad" [i.e., Theocritus, Bion, and Moschus]. *SP* 20 (1923):184–215.

———. "The Pastorals." Part 1 of his *Virgil and Spenser*. University of California Publications in English 2 (1929).

Jungman, Robert E. "Milton's Use of Catullus in *Lycidas*." *Classical Folia* 32 (1978):90–92.

Kane, Robert J. " 'Blind Mouths' in *Lycidas*" [l.119]. *MLN* 68 (1953):239–40. On classical antecedents.

Kelly, L. G. "*Contaminatio* in *Lycidas*: An Example of Vergilian Poetics." *Revue de l'Université d'Ottawa* 38 (1968):588–98.

Kirkconnell, Watson. *Awake the Courteous Echo: The Themes and Prosody of "Comus," "Lycidas," and "Paradise Regained" in World Literature with Translations of the Major Analogues*. Part 2. Toronto, 1973.

Knowlton, E. C. "The Allegorical Figure Genius." *Classical Philology* 15 (1920):380–84; "Genius as an Allegorical Figure." *MLN* 39 (1924):89–95. See also D. T. Starnes, "The Figure Genius in the Renaissance," *Studies in the Renaissance* 11 (1964):234–44. Cf. *Lycidas*, l. 123.

Lambert, Ellen Z. *Placing Sorrow: A Study of the Pastoral Elegy Convention from Theocritus to Milton*. Chapel Hill, N.C., 1976.

Lang, Andrew. *Theocritus, Bion and Moschus*. London, 1880.

Leach, Eleanor W. *Virgil's "Eclogues": Landscapes of Experience*. Ithaca, N.Y., 1974.

Low, Anthony. "Amaryllis, Neaera, and Fame in Milton's *Lycidas*." *Seventeenth-Century News*, Summer-Autumn 1971, 34–35.

———. "Some Notes on *Lycidas* [ll. 152–53] and the *Aeneid*." *ELN* 13 (1976):175–77.

McKenzie, Kenneth. "Echoes of Dante in Milton's *Lycidas*." *Italica* 20 (1943):121–26.

Major, John M. "Ovid's *Amores* III.ix: A Source for *Lycidas*." *MQ* 6 (1972):3, 1–3.

Mallette, Richard. *Spenser, Milton and Renaissance Pastoral*. Lewisburg, Pa., 1981. Especially note Ch. 4, "Spenser, Milton, and the Pastoral Elegy."

Montgomery, Walter A. "The *Epitaphium Damonis* in the Stream of the Classical Lament." In *Studies for William A. Read*, edited by N. M. Caffee and T. A. Kirby, 207–20. Baton Rouge, La., 1940.

Mulryan, John. "Milton's *Lycidas* and the Italian Mythographers." *MQ* 15 (1981):37–44.

Mustard, Wilfred P. "Later Echoes of the Greek Bucolic Poets." *AJP* 30 (1909):245–83. The author has also edited the eclogues of Mantuan, Sannazaro, et al. (Baltimore, 1911–31).

Norlin, George. "The Conventions of the Pastoral Elegy." *AJP* 32 (1911):294–312.

Poggioli, Renato. *The Oaten Flute: Essays on Pastoral Poetry and the Pastoral Ideal*. Cambridge, Mass., 1975. With an essay on *Lycidas* (83–104).

Putnam, Michael C. J. *Virgil's Pastoral Art: Studies in the "Eclogues."* Princeton, 1970.

Rand, E. K. *The Magical Art of Virgil*. Chap. 3–4. Cambridge, Mass., 1931. On the "Eclogues."

Riley, Joanne M. "Milton's *Lycidas*: New Light on the Title." *N&Q*, n.s. 24 (1977):545.

Rose, H. J. *The Eclogues of Vergil*. Berkeley, 1942.

Rosenmeyer, Thomas G. *The Green Cabinet: Theocritus and the European Pastoral Lyric*. Berkeley, 1969.

Sandys, Sir John. "The Literary Sources of Milton's *Lycidas*." *Transactions of the Royal Society of Literature*, 2d ser. 32 (1914): 233–64.

Shackforth, Martha H. "A Definition of the Pastoral Idyll." *PMLA* 19 (1904):583–92.

Sheidley, William E. "*Lycidas*: An Early Elizabethan Analogue by George Turberville." *MP* 69 (1972):228–30.

Smith, Hallett. *Elizabethan Poetry*. Chap. 1. Cambridge, Mass., 1952. On the "intellectual respectability" of pastoral poetry in Elizabethan England.

Starnes, DeWitt T., and E. W. Talbert. *Classical Myth and Legend in Renaissance Dictionaries*, 231, 257, 291–92, 319–20, 326–27, 384. Chapel Hill, N.C., 1955. Suggested sources—with references to other studies—for several of the poem's allusions.

Steadman, John M. "Eyelids of the Morn [*Lycidas*, l.26]: A Biblical Convention." *Harvard Theological Review* 56 (1963):159–67.

———. "St. Peter and Ecclesiastical Satire." *N&Q*, n.s. 5 (1958): 141–42.

Strathman, Ernest A. "*Lycidas* and the [Latin] Translation of Spenser's *May*." *MLN* 52 (1937):398–400.

Stroup, Thomas B. "*Lycidas* and the Marinell Story." In *SAMLA Studies in Milton*, edited by J. Max Patrick, 100–13. Gainesville, Fla., 1953.

Thompson, W. Lawrence. "The Source of the Flower Passage in *Lycidas*." *N&Q* 197 (1952):97–99.

Toynbee, Paget. *Dante in English Literature*, 1:123–24. New York, 1909. Relates *Lycidas*, ll. 108–31, to *Paradiso*, 27.19 ff.

Turlington, Bayly. "Milton's *Lycidas* and Horace's Odes, I.7." *Tennessee Philological Bulletin* 6 (1969), no. 1:2–12.

Weitzmann, Francis W. "Notes on the Elizabethan *Elegie*." *PMLA* 50 (1935):435–43.

Wilson, Elkin C. *Prince Henry and English Literature*. Part 3. Ithaca, N.Y., 1946. On the elegies written on the death of the young heir in 1612 and their probable influence on *Lycidas* (150–57).

On the Poem

Readers of *Epitaphium Damonis* might wish to consult the essays by Ralph W. Condee, "The Latin Poetry of John Milton," chap. 3 in *The Latin Poetry of English Poets*, edited by J. W. Binns (London, 1974) and "The Structure of Milton's *Epitaphium Damonis*," *SP* 62 (1965):577–94; John K. Hale, "Sion's Bacchanalia: An Inquiry into Milton's Latin in the *Epitaphium Damonis*," *MS* 16 (1982):115–29; William M. Jones, "Immortality in Two of Milton's Elegies," in *Myth and Symbol*, edited by Bernice Slote, 133–40 (Lincoln, Nebr., 1963); E. K. Rand, "Milton in Rustication," *SP* 19 (1922):109–35; John T. Shawcross, "Form and Content in Milton's Latin Elegies," *HLQ* 33 (1970):331–50. The fullest account of Charles Diodati, the poem's subject, is by Donald C. Dorian, *The English Diodatis*, chaps. 7–9 (New Brunswick, N.J., 1950). For a strictly conjectural "psychobiographical perspective," see John T. Shawcross, "Milton and Diodati: An Essay in Psychodynamic Meaning," *MS* 7 (1975):127–63, where the relationship of the two young men is presumed to be one of "latent homosexuality."

Readers of *Lycidas* will be surprised—and, hopefully, amused—by the obsession of scholars and critics with the "two-handed engine" (l. 130). The attempts to interpret the reference and to locate its source continue to proliferate, but, not surprisingly, they only serve to confirm its essential elusiveness. Parallels have been located in the writings of such diverse figures as St. Gregory the Great, Dante, John of Salisbury, Savonarola, du Bartas, John Knox, Phineas Fletcher, John Donne, Thomas Adams, Francis Quarles, Robert Burton, and others. The riddle itself has been variously interpreted as the two houses of Parliament, or liberty as wielded by them; the temporal and spiritual authority of the Court of High Commission; the destructive power of the imminent civil war; "Puritan zeal" in general; the combined forces of England and Scotland, or of France and Spain; the Catholic Church; the pastoral staff; the keys of Heaven and Hell given to St. Peter; the lock on St. Peter's door; St. Peter's sword (Matthew 26:51, John 18:10); the sword of Divine Justice (Ezekiel 21:9–17), particularly as wielded by Michael "with huge two-handed sway" (*Paradise Lost*, 6.251); the axe in general, or, specifically, the axe that was "laid unto the root of

the trees" (Matthew 3:10, Luke 3:9) ; the rod of Christ's anger;
the Word of God; the Son of God; the scythe of Time; Man "in
his dual capacity of labour and prayer" ; the sheephook; the iron
flail of Talus (*Faerie Queene*, 5.1.12; etc.) ; the temple of Janus;
and so on and so forth. Readers of *Lycidas* curious enough to
look further into the matter are referred to the conjectures of
the various editors of Milton's poetry as well as to the theses
advanced by the following writers, here invoked alphabetically:

E. C. Baldwin, *MLN* 33 (1918):211–15; R. H. Bowers, *N&Q*, n.s. 3
(1956):249–50; Lowell W. Coolidge, *PQ* 29 (1950):444–45; E. S. de
Beer, *RES*, n.s. 23 (1947):60–63; Donald C. Dorian, *PMLA* 45 (1930):
204–15; Ph. Dust, *Humanistica Lovaniensia* 22 (1973):320–24; Karl
E. Felsen, *MQ* 9 (1975):6–14, and 10 (1976):124–26; Robert F. Fleiss-
ner, *Anglia* 91 (1973):77–83; James F. Forrest, *MS* 16 (1982):131–40;
J. Milton French, *MLN* 68 (1953):229–31; E. S. Fussell, *N&Q* 193
(1948):338–39; A. W. Gibbs, *RES* 31 (1980): 178–83; William J.
Grace, *SP* 52 (1955):583–89; Leon Howard, *HLQ* 15 (1952):173–84;
R. E. Hughes, *N&Q*, n.s. 2 (1955):58–59; Maurice Hussey, *N&Q*
193 (1948):503; Maurice Kelley, *N&Q* 181 (1941):273; Thomas
Kranidas, *Ex* 38 (1979):129–30; Edward S. LeComte, *SP* 47 (1950):
589–606, and 49 (1952):548–50; George G. Loane, *N&Q* 181 (1941):
320; Kenneth McKenzie, *Italica* 20 (1943):121–26; Esmond L. Maril-
la, *Milton and Modern Man*, chap. 9 (University, Ala., 1968); Hein-
rich Mutschmann, *N&Q*, n.s. 2 (1955):515; Charles G. Osgood, *RES*
1 (1925):339–41; Byno R. Rhodes, *N&Q*, n.s. 13 (1966): 24; Harry
F. Robins, *RES*, n.s. 5 (1954):25–36; Philip Rollinson, *ELN*
9 (1971):28–35; R. J. Schoeck, *N&Q*, n.s. 2 (1955):235–37; William P.
Shaw, *Modern Language Studies* 7 (1977):1.39–42; Donald A. Stauffer,
MLR 31 (1936):57–60; John M. Steadman, *N&Q*, n.s. 3 (1956):249–50,
and 7 (1960):237; Daniel Stempel, *ELN* 3 (1966):259–63; Thomas B.
Stroup, *N&Q*, n.s. 6 (1959):366–67; Marian H. Studley, *English Jour-
nal*, coll. ed. 26 (1937):149–51; Kathleen M. Swaim, *MS* 2 (1970):
119–29; Claude A. Thompson, *SP* 59 (1962):184–200; E. M. W. Tillyard,
Milton, App. F (London, 1930); Michele C. Treip, *N&Q*, n.s. 6 (1959):
364–66; W. Arthur Turner, *JEGP* 49 (1950):562–65; Ernest Tuveson,
JHI 27 (1966):447–58; S. Viswanathan, *Archiv* 217 (1980):108–11;
George W. Whiting, *Milton and this Pendant World*, 29–58 (Austin,
1958); and numerous contributions in the *Athenaeum* and particularly
TLS. For an elaborate Continental effort, see Olivier Lutaud, *Arc de
Guerre our d'Alliance (l'engin énigmatique du poemè "Lycidas" de
Milton)*, vol. 2 in Travaux du Centre d'Histoire des Idées dans les
Iles Britanniques (Paris, 1982).

Studies much more relevant to the poem as a poem include the
following:

Abrams, M. H. "Five Ways of Reading *Lycidas*." In *Varieties of
Literary Experience*, edited by Stanley Burnshaw, 1–23. New
York, 1962. A reprint of the essay published above, pp. 216 ff.

Adams, Henry H. "The Development of the Flower Passage in *Lycidas*." *MLN* 65 (1950):468–72.

Adams, Robert M. "Bounding *Lycidas*." *Hudson Review* 23 (1970): 293–304.

Alpers, Paul. "*Lycidas* and Modern Criticism." *ELH* 49 (1982): 468–96.

Auffret, Jean. "Pagano-Christian Syncretism in *Lycidas*." *Anglia* 87 (1969):26–38.

Baker, Stewart A. "Milton's Uncouth Swain." *MS* 3 (1971):35–53.

Barker, Arthur. "The Pattern of Milton's *Nativity Ode*." *UTQ* 10 (1941):especially 171–72. Brief but influential comments on the three "movements" in *Lycidas*.

Battestin, Martin C. "John Crowe Ransom and *Lycidas*: A Reappraisal." *CE* 17 (1956):223–28.

Bell, Barbara C. "*Lycidas* and the Stages of Grief." *Literature and Psychology* 25 (1975):166–74.

Bell, Vereen M. "Johnson's Milton Criticism in Context." *ES* 49 (1968):127–32.

Berkeley, David S. *Inwrought with Figures Dim: A Reading of Milton's "Lycidas."* The Hague and Paris, 1974.

Berman, Ronald. "The Order of *Lycidas*." *Kenyon Alumni Bulletin* 21, no. 2 (1963):13–15. The poem's "cosmic milieu" is principally manifest in the movement "from dissonance to harmonic order both in form and content."

Beum, Robert. "The Pastoral Realism of *Lycidas*." *Western Humanities Review* 15 (1961):325–29.

Blondel, Jacques. "*Lycidas*: Panorama critique et interprétation." *EA* 25 (1972):104–15.

Blow, Suzanne. "The Angel and the Sheep in *Lycidas*." In *Milton Reconsidered*, edited by John K. Franson, 22–45. Salzburg, 1976.

Bouchard, Donald F. "The 'Dread Voice' and 'Dearest Pledge': Beyond Oppositions." Chap. 3 of his *Milton: A Structural Reading*. London and Montreal, 1974.

Brett, R. L. "Milton's *Lycidas*." In his *Reason and Imagination*, 21–50. London, 1960.

Brink, J. R. "Johnson and Milton." *SEL* 20 (1980):493–503. On the former's "personal esteem" for the latter, the strictures of *Lycidas* notwithstanding.

Brisman, Leslie. *Milton's Poetry of Choice and Its Romantic Heirs*. Ithaca, N.Y., 1973. Especially note 58–65, 76–85, 256–62.

Brooks, E. L. "*Lycidas* and Bible Pastoral" [Ezekiel 34]. *N&Q*, n.s. 3 (1956):67–68.

Burnett, Archie. *Milton's Style*. Chap. 3. London, 1981.

Cain, William E. "*Lycidas* and the Reader's Response." *Dalhousie Review* 58 (1978):272–84.

Carey, John. "Evading Death: *Lycidas*." Chap. 5 of his *Milton*. London, 1969.

Christopher, G. B. "A Note on the 'Blind mouths' of *Lycidas* [l. 119]." *N&Q*, n.s. 20 (1973):379–80.

Coffman, George R. "The Parable of the Good Shepherd, *De Contemptu Mundi*, and *Lycidas*: Excerpts from a Chapter on Literary History and Culture." *ELH* 3 (1939):101–13.

Condee, Ralph W. *Structure of Milton's Poetry*. Chap. 3. University Park, Pa., 1974.

Coolidge, John S. "Boethius and 'That Last Infirmity of Noble Mind.'" *PQ* 42 (1963):176–82. On the "articulate civilization" underlying *Lycidas*, notably l. 71.

Cornelius, David K., and Kathryn Thompson. "Milton's *Lycidas*, 119–27." *Ex* 31 (1972):25.

Cowper, William. *Correspondence*, edited by Thomas Wright, 1:164–65. London, 1904. The letter to the Rev. William Unwin, October 31, 1779, on Johnson's remarks on *Lycidas*; quoted partly above, xiv.

Creaser, John. "*Lycidas*: The Power of Art." *Essays and Studies*, n.s. 34 (1981):123–47.

Daniells, Roy. *Milton, Mannerism and Baroque*, 37–50. Toronto, 1963. On *Lycidas* as a mannerist poem.

Daniels, Edgar F. "Climactic Rhythms in *Lycidas*." *AN&Q* 6 (1968): 100–101.

————. "Milton's *Lycidas*, 29." *Ex* 21 (1963):43. *Batt'ning* means *enclosing*.

Darbishire, Helen. "Milton's Poetic Language." *Essays and Studies by Members of the English Association*, n.s. 10 (1957):35–40. On the "decorum" of the language in *Lycidas*.

Davies, Neville. "*Lycidas*: Poem and Pattern." *Cahiers elisabéthains* 14 (1978):23–37.

Diekhoff, John S. "Milton's Prosody in the Poems of the Trinity Manuscript." *PMLA* 54 (1939):177–83.

Dorfman, Ariel. "El *Lycidas* de Milton, poema barroco." *Anales de la Universidad de Chile* 123, no. 134 (1965):194–210.

Elledge, Scott, ed. *Milton's "Lycidas": Edited to Serve as an Introduction to Criticism*. New York, 1966. With several classical and Renaissance elegies, details on the lives of Edward King and Milton, and brief comments by critics from Thomas Warton (1785) to W. H. Auden (1962).

Elliott, Emory. "Milton's Uncouth Swain: The Speaker in *Lycidas*."

In *Milton Reconsidered*, edited by John K. Franson, 1–21. Salzburg, 1976.

Evans, J. Martin. "Lycidas and the Dolphins." *N&Q*, n.s. 25 (1978): 15–17. On the death of another poet, Hesiod, whose corpse was also borne by dolphins.

Fabian, David R. "The 'Blind mouths' Passage in *Lycidas*." *AN&Q* 6 (1968):136–37.

Finney, Gretchen L. "A Musical Background for *Lycidas*." *HLQ* 15 (1952):325–50. Reprinted as chap. 10 in her *Musical Backgrounds for English Literature*. New Brunswick, N.J., 1962.

Fixler, Michael. *Milton and the Kingdoms of God*, 56–64. London, 1964. On the apocalyptic aspects of *Lycidas*.

———. " 'Unexpressive Song': Form and Enigma Variations in *Lycidas*, A New Reading." *MS* 15 (1981): 213–55.

Fleischauer, Warren. "Johnson, *Lycidas*, and the Norms of Criticism." In *Johnsonian Studies*, edited by Magdi Wahba, 235–56. Cairo, 1962.

Forrest, James F. "The Significance of Milton's 'Mantle blue' [l. 192]." *MQ* 8 (1974):41–48.

Fowler, Alastair. " 'To Shepherd's Ear': The Form of Milton's *Lycidas*." In *Silent Poetry: Essays in Numerological Analysis*, edited by Fowler, 170–84. London, 1970.

Fox, Robert C. "Milton's *Lycidas*, 192–93." *Ex* 9 (1951):54. The blue in the shepherd's mantle is the traditional symbol of hope.

Fraser, G. S. "Approaches to *Lycidas*." In *The Living Milton*, edited by Frank Kermode, 32–54. London, 1960.

French, J. Milton. "The Digressions in Milton's *Lycidas*" [ll. 64–84 and 113–31]. *SP* 50 (1953):485–90.

French, Roberts W. "Voice and Structure in *Lycidas*." *TSLL* 12 (1970):15–25.

Friedland, Louis S. "Milton's *Lycidas* and Spenser's *Ruines of Time*." *MLN* 27 (1912):246–50.

Fujii, Haruhiko. "The Changing Landscape of *Lycidas*" and "Thomas Warton's Romantic Interpretation of *Lycidas*." In his *Time, Landscape and the Ideal Life*. Kyoto, 1974.

Glavin, John J. "*The Wreck of the Deutschland* and *Lycidas*: ubique naufragium est." *TSLL* 22 (1980):522–46. On parallels between Hopkins's poem and Milton's.

Grace, William J. "The Religious Vision of *Lycidas*." In his *Ideas in Milton*, 139–46. Notre Dame, Ind., 1968.

Graves, Robert. "The Ghost of Milton." In his *The Common Asphodel*. London, 1949. Especially note 321–25. Violently opposed to

Milton ("a monster and a renegade"), he concludes that *Lycidas* is "a poem strangled by art."

Grose, Christopher. "Lucky Words: Process of Speech in *Lycidas*." *JEGP* 70 (1971):383–403.

Hanford, James H. "The Youth of Milton: An Interpretation of his Early Development." Chap. 1 of his *John Milton: Poet and Humanist*. Cleveland, 1966.

Hardy, John Edward. "Reconsiderations: I. *Lycidas*." *Kenyon Review* 7 (1945):99–113. Reprinted as "Milton's *Lycidas*: The Sublime Pastoral." In his *The Curious Frame*, 22–44. Notre Dame, Ind., 1962. The "blueprint" for the essay printed above, 140 ff.

Hardy, J[ohn] P. "*Lycidas*." In his *Reinterpretations*, 28–49. London, 1971.

Hill, Archibald A. "Imagery and Meaning: A Passage from Milton [*Lycidas*, l.119–21], and from Blake." *TSLL* 11 (1969):1094–1105.

Hinnant, Charles H. "Freedom and Form in Milton's *Lycidas*." *Papers of the Michigan Academy and Science, Arts, and Letters* 53 (1968):321–28.

Hofmann, Klaus. "Das Evangelium in der Idylle: Miltons *Lycidas*." *Anglia* 88 (1970):461–87.

Hone, Ralph E. "The Pilot of the Galilean Lake." *SP* 56 (1959): 55–61. Is the reference in l. 109 to Christ?

Hunt, Clay. "*Lycidas*" and the Italian Critics. New Haven, 1979.

Huntley, Frank L. "A Background in Folklore for the 'Blind mouths' Passage in *Lycidas* (ll. 113–31)." *MN* 1 (1967):53–55.

Hyman, Lawrence W. "Belief and Disbelief in *Lycidas*." *CE* 33 (1972):532–42. See also "*Lycidas* and the Problem of Belief." Chap. 3 of his *The Quarrel Within: Art and Morality in Milton's Poetry*. Port Washington, N.Y., 1972.

Jones, Katherine. "A Note on Milton's *Lycidas*." *AI* 19 (1962):141–55. An extreme psychoanalytic approach, predictably including a reference to Milton's "repressed homosexuality."

Kellett, E. E. "Edward King and Milton." *Cambridge Review* 37 (1915):326–27.

Killeen, J. F. "Milton, *Lycidas*, 144." *N&Q*, n.s. 9 (1962):70, 73. *Freakt* means *adorned*.

King, Bruce. "*Lycidas* and *Oldham*." *EA* 19 (1966):60–63. On parallels between Milton's elegy and Dryden's.

Landy, Marcia. "Language and Mourning in *Lycidas*." *AI* 30 (1974): 294–312.

Latimer, Dan. *The Elegiac Mode in Milton and Rilke*. European University Papers, 18:10 Frankfurt and Bern, 1977

Lautermilch, Steven J. " 'That Fatal and Perfidious Bark': A Key to the Double Design and Unity of Milton's *Lycidas*." *RQ* 30 (1977):201–16.

Lawry, Jon S. " 'With Eager Thought Warbling his Doric Lay': Stance Achieved in *Lycidas*." Chap. 3 of his *The Shadow of Heaven*. Ithaca, N.Y., 1968. See also " 'The Faithful Herdman's Art' in *Lycidas*." *SEL* 13 (1973):111–25. Cf. above, 236 ff.

Leishman, J. B. "*Lycidas*." Chap. 9 of his *Milton's Minor Poems*, edited by Geoffrey Tillotson. London, 1969. A lengthy chapter (247–343) subdivided into "The Other Commemorations of Edward King," "*Lycidas* and the Pastoral Elegy," "The Two Digressions," "Revisions and Afterthoughts," and " 'Industrious and Select Reading.' "

Lieb, Michael. " 'Yet Once More': The Formulaic Opening of *Lycidas*." *MQ* 12 (1978):23–28.

Lloyd, Michael. "The Fatal Bark." *MLN* 75 (1960):103–8.

———. "*Justa Edovardo King*." *N&Q*, n.s. 5 (1958):432–34.

———. "The Two Worlds of *Lycidas*." *EIC* 11 (1961):390–402.

Low, Anthony. "Circular Rhymes in *Lycidas*?" With a response by Joseph A. Wittreich, Jr. *PMLA* 86 (1971):1032–35.

Mabbott, Thomas O. "Milton's *Lycidas*, ll. 164 and 183–85. *Ex* 5 (1947):26. The lines refer to Palaemon.

Madsen, William G. "The Voice of Michael in *Lycidas*." *SEL* 3 (1963):1–7. Incorporated into his *From Shadowy Types to Truth*, 6–16. New Haven, 1968.

Marshall, George O. "Milton's *Lycidas*, 15–22." *Ex* 17 (1959): 66. "Lucky" (l. 20) means "having an unstudied or unsought felicity."

Martz, Louis L. "Who is Lycidas?" *Yale French Studies* 47 (1972): 170–88. Revised as chap. 3 of his *Poet of Exile: A Study of Milton's Poetry*. New Haven, 1980.

More, Paul Elmer. "How to Read *Lycidas*." In his *On Being Human*, 184–202. Princeton, 1936. Also in the 1st edition of the present collection (1961), 82–95.

Morse, J. Mitchell. "A Pun in *Lycidas* [l. 103]." *N&Q*, n.s. 5 (1958): 211.

Nassar, Eugene Paul. "*Lycidas* as Pastiche." Chap. 2 of his *The Rape of Cinderella: Essays in Literary Continuity*. Bloomington, Ind., 1970.

Nelson, Lowry, Jr. *Baroque Lyric Poetry*, 64–76, 138–52. New Haven, 1961. On the poem's rhetorical and time structure.

Nemser, Ruby. "A Reinterpretation of 'the unexpressive nuptial song.' " *MN* 2 (1968):1–2. *Unexpressive* (1. 176) means *inappre-hensible*, not *inexpressible*.

Nicolson, Marjorie. *John Milton: A Reader's Guide to His Poetry*, 87–111. New York, 1963.

———. "Milton's 'Old Damoetas' [*Lycidas*, 1. 36]." *MLN* 41 (1926):293–300. Identifies him as Joseph Mede. For other suggestions see Fitzroy Pyle, *Hermathena* 71 (1948):83–92; E. S. de Beer, *N&Q*, n.s. 19 (1949):336–37; Harris F. Fletcher, *JEGP* 60 (1961):250–57; etc.

Nitchie, G. W. "*Lycidas*: A Footnote." *N&Q*, n.s. 13 (1966):377–78. The closing lines of St. Peter's speech (ll. 124–31) anticipate the final *ottava rima*.

Ogden, H. V. S. "The Principles of Variety and Contrast in Seventeenth Century Aesthetics, and Milton's Poetry." *JHI* 10 (1949):159–82.

Oman, Sir Charles. "Of Poor Mr. King, John Milton, and Certain Friends." *Cornhill Magazine* 156 (1937):577–87. On "the companions of *Lycidas*" in the memorial volume of 1638.

Oras, Ants. "Milton's Early Rhyme Schemes and the Structure of *Lycidas*." *MP* 52 (1954):12–22.

Otten, Charlotte F. "Garlanding the Dead: The Epicedial Garland in *Lycidas*." *MS* 16 (1982):141–51.

———. "Milton's 'Daffodillies' [*Lycidas*, 1. 150]." *ELN* 11 (1973): 48–49. The word is no more colloquial than *daffodils*.

———. "Milton's Myrtles [*Lycidas*, 1. 2]." *EIC* 24 (1974):105.

Owen, A. L. *The Famous Druids*, 52–58. Oxford, 1962. On the reference in *Lycidas* (1. 53) and Milton's interest in the subject.

Parker, William R. *Milton: A Biography*, 155–67. Oxford, 1968. On *Lycidas* as a record of "a crucial and complicated spiritual experience"; with a reminder of the poem's musical effects.

Pattison, Mark. *Milton*, 29. London, 1879. The definitive judgment on *Lycidas*, quoted above, xiv.

Pecheux, M. Christopher. "The Dread Voice in *Lycidas*." *MS* 9 (1976):221–41.

Pigman, G. W., III. "Versions of Imitation in the Renaissance." *RQ* 33 (1980):1–32.

Prince, F. T. "*Lycidas* and the Tradition of the Italian Eclogue." *English Miscellany* 2 (1951):95–105. The "blueprint" for the essay printed above, 157 ff.

Radzinowicz, Mary Ann. "Lycidas: The Autobiographical Swain and the Perfected Community." In her *Toward "Samson Agonistes": The Growth of Milton's Mind*, 119–29. Princeton, 1978.

Raleigh, J. H. *"Lycidas*: 'Yet Once More.' " *Prairie Schooner* 42 (1968):303–18.

Ramsey, Paul. *"Lycidas*: A Proper Poem." Chap. 4 of his *The Lively and the Just*. University, Ala., 1962.

Reesing, John. "Justice for Lycidas" and "The Decorum of St. Peter's Speech in *Lycidas.*" In his *Milton's Poetic Art*, 19–49. Cambridge, Mass., 1968.

Riggs, William G. "The Plant of Fame in *Lycidas.*" *MS* 4 (1972): 151–61.

Rinehart, Keith. "A Note on the First Fourteen Lines of Milton's *Lycidas.*" *N&Q* 198 (1953):103. On their approximation to the sonnet form.

Ruskin, John. *Sesame and Lilies*, 1:20–24. 1865. Reprint, 41–48. London, 1951. Observations on *Lycidas*, ll. 108–29, of which most famous is perhaps the comment on "blind mouths" (l. 119): "A 'Bishop' means 'a person who sees.' A 'Pastor' means 'a person who feeds.' The most unbishoply character a man can have is therefore to be blind. The most unpastoral, is instead of feeding, to want to be fed,—to be a Mouth." (For an exception to this interpretation, see John A. Himes, *MLN* 35 [1920]:441.)

Saintsbury, George. "Milton and the Grand Style." Chap. 3 of his *Collected Essays and Papers*, 175–96. London, 1923. Largely on *Lycidas*.

Saunders, J. W. "Milton, Diomede and Amaryllis." *ELH* 22 (1955): 254–86.

Schweitzer, Edward C. "Milton's *Lycidas*, 164." *Ex* 28 (1969):18. Cf. Mabbott, above.

Sendry, Joseph. *"In Memoriam* and *Lycidas.*" *PMLA* 82 (1967): 437–43.

Shawcross, John T. "Some Literary Uses of Numerology." *Hartford Studies in Literature* 1 (1969):50–62. Numerology in *Lycidas*; cf. Fowler, above.

Sigworth, Oliver F. "Johnson's *Lycidas*: The End of Renaissance Criticism." *Eighteenth-Century Studies* 1 (1967):159–68.

Sims, James H. "Perdita's 'Flowers o' th' Spring' [*The Winter's Tale*, 4.4. 118–27] and 'Vernal flowers' in *Lycidas* [ll. 142–51]." *Shakespeare Quarterly* 22 (1971): 87–90.

Smith, Eric. "Milton: *Lycidas.*" Chap. 2 of his *By Mourning Tongues: Studies in English Elegy*. Ipswich, 1977.

Stone, C. F., III. "Milton's Self-concerns and Manuscript Revisions in *Lycidas.*" *MLN* 83 (1968):867–81.

Sullivan, Edward E., Jr. "Romans 16:18 and St. Peter's Speech in *Lycidas.*" *N&Q*, n.s. 22 (1975):542–43.

―――. " 'Sweet Societies that Sing': The Voice of the Saints in *Lycidas*." *Essays in Literature* (Western Illinois University) 3 (1976):32–40.

Swaim, Kathleen M. "*Lycidas* and the Dolphins of Apollo." *JEGP* 72 (1973):340–49.

Sypher, Wylie. "The Metaphysical and the Baroque." *Partisan Review* 11 (1944):3–17. *Lycidas* in the mannerist tradition of Caravaggio, Rubens, Rembrandt, et al.

Taylor, George C. "Milton's English." *N&Q* 178 (1940):56–57. Milton demonstrates in *Lycidas* that his vocabulary is not unduly Latinate.

Thomas, W. K. "Mouths and Eyes in *Lycidas*." *MQ* 9 (1975):39–42. See also Wayne Shumaker. *MQ* 10 (1976):6–7.

Tillyard, E. M. W. *The Miltonic Setting*, 35–42. London, 1938. See also his *Poetry Direct and Oblique*, 81–84. Rev. ed. London, 1945. Further comments on *Lycidas*; cf. above, 62 ff.

Turner, Alberta T. "Milton and the Convention of the Academic Miscellanies." *Yearbook of English Studies* 5 (1975):86–93.

―――. "The Sound of Grief: A Reconsideration of the Nature and Function of the Unrhymed Lines in *Lycidas*." *MQ* 10 (1976): 67–73.

Tuveson, Ernest. "The Pilot of the Galilean Lake." *JHI* 27 (1966): 447–58. On "the unity and historical meaning of the Petrine speech" (ll. 108–31).

Wagenknecht, Edward. "Milton in *Lycidas*." *CE* 7 (1946):393–97.

Walker, D. P. "Orpheus the Theologian and Renaissance Platonists." *Journal of the Warburg and Courtauld Institutes* 16 (1953): 100–120. Useful in connection with the background sketched in Mayerson's essay (above, 116 ff.). See further John B. Friedman, *Orpheus in the Middle Ages* (Cambridge, Mass., 1970) and John Warden, ed., *Orpheus: The Metamorphoses of a Myth* (Toronto, 1982).

Wallerstein, Ruth. "Rhetoric in the English Renaissance: Elegies." *English Institute Essays 1948*, 153–78. New York, 1949. On *Lydicas* and Donne's elegy on Prince Henry. Greatly expanded in part 1 of her *Studies in Seventeenth-Century Poetic*. Madison, Wis., 1950.

Welch, Dennis M. "Theme and Form in *Comus* and *Lycidas*." *Cithara* 12.1 (1972):74–84.

Wentersdorf, Karl P. "The Thematic Significance of the Flower Catalogue in Milton's *Lycidas*." *ELH* 47 (1980):500–519.

West, Michael. "The *Consolatio* in Milton's Elegies." *HLQ* 34 (1971):233–49.

Whiting, George W. *Milton's Literary Milieu*, 101–7. Chapel Hill, N.C., 1939. On the geographical references in *Lycidas*.

Williamson, George. "The Obsequies for Edward King." Chap. 6 of his *Seventeenth Century Contexts*. London, 1960. On some of the contributors to the memorial volume of 1638.

Winter, Keith. "A Comprehensive Approach to *Lycidas*." *Research Studies* (Washington State University) 36 (1968):237–44.

Wittreich, Joseph A., Jr. "From Pastoral to Prophecy: The Genres of *Lycidas*." MS 13 (1970):59–80. Expands materials in his *Visionary Poetics*.

———. " 'Milton's Destined Urn': The Art of *Lycidas*." *PMLA* 84 (1969):60–70. Incorporated into his *Visionary Poetics*.

———. "Milton's *Lycidas*, 192." *Ex* 26 (1967):17. "Twitch't" means both "pulled tightly" and "moved the fingers across the strings of a musical instrument" (cf. l. 17).

———. *The Romantics on Milton*, 256–59, 336–37, 366–68. Cleveland, 1970. The views on *Lycidas* by the Romantics.

———. *Visionary Poetics: Milton's Tradition and His Legacy*. San Marino, Calif., 1979. Massively devoted to *Lycidas*: after an account of the prophetic impulse in relation to the Book of Revelation, the crucial argument—"A Fabric More Divine: *Lycidas* as a Prophetic Paradigm" (79–214)—subdivides into "*Lycidas* in Context," "The Genres of *Lycidas*." "*Lycidas* and the Book of Revelation," "The Art of *Lycidas*," and "Variations on the Paradigm in Milton's Last Poems."

Woodhouse, A. S. P. "Milton's Pastoral Monodies." In *Studies in Honour of Gilbert Norwood*, edited by M. E. White, 261–78. Toronto, 1952. Reprinted in his *The Heavenly Muse*, 83–98. Edited by Hugh MacCallum. Toronto, 1972.

Woodhouse, A. S. P., and Douglas Bush. *"Lycidas."* In *A Variorum Commentary on the Poems of John Milton*, 2.2.544–734. London and New York, 1972. Detailed and indispensable.

COPYRIGHT ACKNOWLEDGMENTS

Acknowledgment is gratefully made to the following publishers, agents, and individuals who have given permission to reprint the material used above:

Bobbs-Merrill Educational Publishing for permission to reprint the translation of the "Argument" to the *Epitaphium Damonis*, from *John Milton: Complete Poems and Major Prose*, ed. Merritt Y. Hughes (New York: The Odyssey Press, 1957), p. 132.

The University of California Press for permission to reprint Josephine Miles's remarks on *Lycidas* from her *The Primary Language of Poetry in the 1640's*, University of California Publications in English 19 (1948):86–90, as revised for the present volume by the author.

Case Western Reserve University for permission to reprint James H. Hanford's essay "The Pastoral Elegy and Milton's *Lycidas*," from his *John Milton: Poet and Humanist* (Cleveland: The Press of Western Reserve University, 1966), chap. 3, as revised for the present volume by the editor.

CBS College Publishing, of CBS Inc., for assigning, setting over, and transferring to the editor of the present volume the right, title, and interest in and to the first edition of *Milton's "Lycidas": The Tradition and the Poem* (New York: Holt, Rinehart and Winston, 1961).

Chatto and Windus, Ltd., for permission to reprint E. M.

W. Tillyard's remarks on *Lycidas*, from his *Milton* (London, 1930), 79–85.

Columbia University Press, and The English Institute, Inc., for permission to reprint Isabel G. MacCaffrey's essay *"Lycidas*: The Poet in a Landscape," from *The Lyric and Dramatic Milton: Selected Papers from the English Institute*, ed. Joseph H. Summers (New York: 1965), 65–92.

Constable and Co. Ltd., for permission to reprint Helen Waddell's translation of *Epitaphium Damonis*, privately printed in 1943 under the title *Lament for Damon*.

Cornell University Press and Andre Deutsch Ltd., as well as Mr. David Daiches, for permission to reprint his essay on *Lycidas* from *A Study of Literature* (Ithaca, N.Y., and London, 1948), as revised in his *Milton* (London, 1954), 73–92.

Duquesne University Press, as well as Mr. Edward W. Tayler, for permission to reprint his essay *"Lycidas* in Christian Time," from his *Milton's Poetry: Its Development in Time* (Pittsburgh, 1979), chap. 2 as condensed for the present volume by the author.

Harcourt Brace Jovanovich Inc., as well as Messrs. Cleanth Brooks and John Edward Hardy, for permission to reprint "Essays in Analysis: *Lycidas*," from their *Poems of Mr. John Milton* (New York, 1951), 169–86, copyright 1951 by Harcourt Brace Jovanovich Inc.; copyright 1979 by Cleanth Brooks; reprinted by permission of the publisher. Also the same publisher, as well as Mr. Northrop Frye, for permission to reprint his essay "Literature as Context: Milton's *Lycidas*," from his *Fables of Identity* (New York, 1963), 119–29, © 1959 by Harcourt Brace Jovanovich Inc.; reprinted by permission of the publisher.

Harvard University Press for permission to reprint Rosemond Tuve's essay "Theme, Pattern, and Imagery in *Lycidas*," from her *Images and Themes in Five Poems by Milton* (Cambridge, Mass., 1957), 73–111, copyright, 1957, by The President and Fellows of Harvard College.

David Higham Associates Ltd., as well as Routledge &

Kegan Paul Ltd., the University of Miami Press, and Mr. Balachandra Rajan, for permission to reprint his essay "*Lycidas*: The Shattering of the Leaves," from his *The Lofty Rhyme* (1970), chap. 4.

The Johns Hopkins University Press, as well as Mr. Stanley E. Fish, for permission to reprint his essay "*Lycidas*: A Poem Finally Anonymous," from *Glyph 8* (1981):1–18.

The Modern Language Association of America, as well as Richard P. Adams, James H. Hanford, Jon S. Lawry, Caroline W. Mayerson, and Wayne Shumaker, for permission to reprint five articles from the *Publications of the Modern Language Association*: Richard P. Adams's "The Archetypal Pattern of Death and Rebirth in Milton's *Lycidas*," 64 (1949):183–88, as condensed for the present volume by the author; James H. Hanford's "The Pastoral Elegy and Milton's *Lycidas*," 25 (1910): 403–47, as condensed for the present volume by the editor; Jon S. Lawry's " 'Eager Thought': Dialectic in *Lycidas*," 77 (1962):27–32, as revised for the present volume by the author; Caroline W. Mayerson's "The Orpheus Image in *Lycidas*," 69 (1949):189–207, as condensed for the present volume by the author; and Wayne Shumaker's "Flowerets and Sounding Seas: A Study in the Affective Structure of Milton's *Lycidas*," 66 (1951):485–94.

Oxford University Press for permission to reprint the text of Milton's *Epitaphium Damonis* as edited by W. H. Garrod in *The Poetical Works of John Milton*, ed. Helen Darbishire (Oxford, 1955), 2:278–83. Also the same publisher, as well as Mr. F. T. Prince, for permission to reprint his essay on *Lycidas* from his *The Italian Element in Milton's Verse* (Oxford, 1954), pp. 71–88.

University of Pittsburgh Press, as well as Mr. Donald M. Friedman, for permission to reprint his essay "*Lycidas*: The Swain's Paideia," from *Milton Studies*, ed. James D. Simmonds, 3 (1971):3–34, as condensed for the present volume by the author; published by the University of Pittsburgh Press; used by permission.

Charles Scribner's Sons for permission to reprint John